Back To Basics

HOME-TESTED RECIPES
FROM A TO Z

Favorite Recipes® Press

Credits

Great American Opportunities, Inc./Favorite Recipes® Press

President: Thomas F. McDow III

Editorial Manager: Mary Jane Blount
Editors: Georgia Brazil, Mary Cummings,
　　　　Jane Hinshaw, Linda Jones, Mary Wilson
Essayist: Laura Hill
Typography: Pam Newsome, Sara Anglin

Home Economics Editorial Advisory Board:
Favorite Recipes® Press wants to recognize the following persons who graciously serve on our Home Economics Advisory Board:

Carolyn L. Cotton, C.H.E.
Consumer, Homemaking Teacher
Bristow, Oklahoma

Karen A. Ogg, C.H.E.
Home Economics Teacher
Keene, New Hampshire

Brenda D. Long
Home Economics Teacher
Richlands, Virginia

Susan Rogers
Home Economics Teacher
Torrance, California

Emily Oates, State Supervisor
Home Economics Education
Little Rock, Arkansas

Sue Shackelford
Home Economics Teacher
Hackleburg, Alabama

Janice F. Stripes, C.H.E.
Home Economics Teacher
Spokane, Washington

This cookbook is a collection of our favorite recipes which are not necessarily original recipes.

Published by: Favorite Recipes® Press, a division of
　　　　　　Great American Opportunities, Inc.
　　　　　　P.O. Box 305142
　　　　　　Nashville, Tennessee 37230

Manufactured in the United States of America
First Printing: 1991, 25,000 copies
Second Printing: 1991, 25,000 copies

Recipe for Cover photograph is on page 27.

Contents

Back to Basics

Americans are returning to a simpler life and homier values. In a recent survey of 500 adults, 69% want to "slow down and live a more relaxed life." Over 89% said it was important to spend more time with their families.

Experts who forecast trends say that more and more families (due to finances, VCRs, stress, need of nurturing and other factors) are turning to the home as an "entertainment center." And as the home again becomes the family focus, often the kitchen becomes the family gathering place as it was generations ago.

Thomas F. McDow III
President

But the family cook is no longer just the mother. Almost every family member now helps out in food preparation. That's why the Home Economics Cookbooks from Favorite Recipes® Press with recipes tried and true are relevant and right up-to-date for every family member to enjoy using—good, solid, basic stuff for good nutrition, great taste and fun in the kitchen.

Home economics teachers and students for almost 30 years have been using their Favorite Recipes® Press cookbooks to earn profits—to date over $52,000,000 has been raised—for home economics activities all across America.

Home economics is the heart of education. Home economics teachers continue to meet the challenges and opportunities of today by preparing students to enter the work force in food service, clothing and textiles, and child development, just to name a few career areas; and by helping students to manage their lives and resources responsibly and establish solid, secure families as they mature into adulthood.

Thank you for supporting home economics education in your community.

The ABC's of Cooking

If the kitchen has traditionally been the heart of the American home, these days it's also serving as the living room, den and entertainment center. Americans are spending more time in more elaborately outfitted kitchens than ever before, and it seems as if cooking has become the new national pastime—for men and women alike. Sophisticated food magazines abound, cooking classes are mobbed, baffling new cuisines (with mysterious new ingredients) crop up weekly, and cooking equipment and techniques become ever more hi-tech.

Even for veteran cooks the variety of choices is a little daunting. But for the less experienced, all this sophisticated food mania may be traumatic. *Back to Basics* offers a way out of the *haute-cuisine* hassle, with a return to recipes and menus that utilize the ABC's of contemporary cooking. You don't need to have Julia Child's kitchen, or two days off from work, or a degree from the Cordon Bleu school to achieve the aim of all great cooks: delicious food, presented appealingly.

In the pages that follow, you'll find recipes suited to your busy lifestyle, ease of preparation, good nutrition and great taste that will please even the most discriminating palates. While most of the recipes call for familiar ingredients, we've also included what we think of as the new basics: fruits, vegetables, meats, seafood, herbs, spices that are fast becoming part of our daily menus alone and in interesting combinations.

We've arranged the recipes alphabetically, from almond bars to zucchini quiche, for easy browsing, and to help you take advantage of food that's in season or particularly plentiful. Along the way, you'll find ample opportunities to utilize these building blocks of today's culinary basics, from A to Z:

A for Apple. You know that one a day keeps the doctor away. In *Back to Basics* the apple 🍎 denotes recipes that pay special attention to our concerns about good nutrition and health. (Make that A for All right!)

B for Barbecue. Cooking out has become a mainstay of family dining and entertaining, because it's casual, quick, delicious and a type of cooking that everyone in the family can participate in. Today, the outdoor chef's repertoire has grown to include such health-wise treats as delicately grilled seafood and even vegetables. And with downdraft cooktops becoming more popular, we're even seeing outdoor cooking, indoors.

C for Charts. For those too-frequent days when you've got a maximum amount to do and a minimum amount of time, we've provided ten handy guides to fill you in quickly on everything from herbs and spices to the intricacies of pasta. Sound like a piece of cake? We've got that covered, too. See page 41.

D for Desserts. Even if you're watching your calories, cholesterol and other baddies, we've got the goodies for you. And if you've thrown caution completely to the winds, you'll be delighted with our tempting desserts. After all, what's life without an occasional chocolate downfall?

E for Eggs. One of the most versatile of all goods, eggs have suffered for years from their high-cholesterol label. But used in moderation (no more than three a week) alone or in recipes, they're a great, inexpensive source of protein, vitamins A, B, D and E, iron and minerals.

F for Fruit. A great American success story. No longer relegated to lunch pails or the occasional pie or cobbler, fruit turns up these days in entrées, soups and appetizers, as well as new, lighter desserts. For an updated take on the basics, try kiwis, ugli fruit, mangoes, papayas and star fruit, now as available as apples and bananas.

G for Greens. No longer limited to such familiar old friends as iceberg lettuce and spinach, today's greens include such new (to the U.S.) faces as arugula, rocket and mache, and such once-regional favorites as mustard, turnip and beet greens. Some greens, like radicchio, aren't even green any more. Just good—and chock full of vitamins and iron.

H for Herbs. Like cumin, coriander and chervil, which turn out to be no more exotic than parsley and paprika. Even the most basic cook can learn to handle these culinary mainstays, and with the help of our chart on page 159 you too can turn the ordinary into the exceptional.

I for International. Americans have broadened their taste for ethnic food in a big way in recent years. While international used to mean Italian (pizza) or Mexican (tacos), nowadays we're just as likely to be cooking up a batch of Greek Meatballs (page 101), Fettucini Alfredo (page 125) or African Honey Bread (page 98).

J for Jams and Jellies. They're not just for breakfast any more, either. You'll enjoy some nice new twists on these old favorites, like our kiwifruit jam or zucchini jelly, just as at home on the hors d'oeuvres tray as the breakfast tray.

K for Knead. Actually a clever way to introduce the subject of breads: versatile, nutritious, **the** most basic of basic foods, and one of the most delicious ways to incorporate fiber into your meals. If you don't have a couple of great yeast and quick bread recipes in your repertoire, by all means adopt a few here. It's not called the staff of life for nothing.

L for Low. We may be cooking more, but the emphasis is on less. Low-sodium, low-cholesterol, low-fat, low-calorie are watchwords for the way we cook now. But if you think healthy eating means boring eating, you're in for a surprise. Good for you, in today's cuisine, also means just plain good.

M for Microwave. Fifteen years ago you worried that those invisible rays might make you mysteriously ill. Now, can you really get through a whole day without one? Microwaves have become such a key element in today's kitchen, that we've devoted an entire section to microwaving.

N for Noodles. That's what your Mom called those wonder- ful little squiggly or stringy shapes we now refer to, elegantly, as Pasta. But whatever the name, the basic facts remain the same. Pasta is limitless in its possibilities, incredi- bly nutritious and unmatched in ease of preparation. All good reasons for its popularity with cooks—and their guests.

O for Oil. Cooking oils are all the same, right? Look again. A whole new bevy of oils has made its appearance on grocery shelves, offering a range of flavors and uses for this no-cholesterol staple. Keep an eye out for canola oil, the lowest in saturated fats, and the new, light olive oils that are finding popularity in the American market. If you've never tried it, sesame oil can open worlds of oriental-style possibilities.

P for Parties. While our emphasis here is on basics, every- one likes to cut loose and prepare a really special spread from time to time. We've taken dozens of wonderful dishes and combined them into festive menus for holidays, parties and special events you'll long remember. And our color pages will give you visual ideas on how to present these special meals.

Q for Quick. Long hours over a hot stove, mercifully, are a thing of the past for most of us. What little time we do have to spare between jobs, school, family and social commitments we don't want to spend in the kitchen. Most of our recipes let you spend more time enjoying and less time preparing meals.

R for Rice. One of the new staples of the American diet, rice is full of surprises, as a look at supermarket shelves attests. Oh sure, the old reliable instant rice is still there, in all its taste-free glory. But why not branch out and try something a bit different and exotic like brown rice, nutty-flavored basmati, or creamy arborio?

S for Seafood. With the advent of modern shipping methods, even those of us in landlocked cities enjoy seafood that was swimming just days earlier. And that's been a real boon to healthy cuisine. Seafood is lean, nutritious and a snap to prepare, just as delicious grilled or broiled as it is in more elaborate dishes.

T for Tomato. Cherry tomatoes, Italian plum tomatoes, big beefsteak slicers in the summer, sun-dried tomatoes in oil. A fruit? A vegetable? Who cares. It's just plain delicious, and you'll find it all over *Back to Basics* because it's so basic.

U for Unusual. One of the great things about basics is that they make such great backdrops for the extraordinary. Experiment a little with basic recipes, adding variety with a new ingredient, serving a hot dish cold or vice versa, or pairing a new side dish with a favorite entrée.

V for Vegetables. Fortunately we've lived through the cook-'em-to-death years and the baby vegetables era, and vegetables now have come into their simple, glorious own. As with fruit, now is the time to incorporate some of the less familiar veggies—exotic peppers, yellow potatoes, fennel, Vidalia onions, celery root, porcini and shiitake mushrooms, for example—into your classic recipes.

W for World. Cooks know, better than most people, about the tremendous impact our modern lifestyle has on the world's environment. That's why so many of us are paying close attention to ecological concerns when we cook. We're recycling, wasting less, eating lower on the food chain to save valuable land resources, and using energy thoughtfully.

X for the unknown. One of Webster's definitions of the letter X is "an unknown quantity or variable." One of the most basic aspects of cooking is that unknown variable, which usually makes its presence felt at the worst possible time. X is the bread that, for unknown reasons, decides not to rise (see chart on page 33). X is the extra guest for dinner. X is the Thanksgiving turkey that slides off the platter on its way into the dining room. X reminds us that a positive attitude can work wonders, even in the kitchen.

Y for Yogurt. Not just a diet lunch on the run, yogurt is a must for the health-conscious cook. Use it as a low-fat, low-calorie replacement for mayonnaise in a potato salad, or sour cream in a dressing, and only you and your waistline will know the difference.

Z for Zucchini. Overly-abundant in late-summer gardens, delicious in salads, soups, steamed or raw, this new American classic may be last in the alphabet, but it stands in the front ranks of versatile **Back to Basics** veggies.

GLOSSARY OF COOKING TECHNIQUES

Bake: To cook by dry heat in an oven, or under hot coals.

Bard: To cover lean meats with bacon or pork fat before cooking to prevent dryness.

Baste: To moisten, especially meats, with melted butter, pan drippings, sauce, etc. during cooking time.

Beat: To mix ingredients by vigorous stirring or with electric mixer.

Blanch: To immerse, usually vegetables or fruit, briefly into boiling water to inactivate enzymes, loosen skin, or soak away excess salt.

Blend: To combine 2 or more ingredients, at least 1 of which is liquid or soft, to produce a mixture that has a smooth uniform consistency quickly.

Boil: To heat liquid until bubbly; the boiling point for water is about 212 degrees, depending on the altitude and the atmospheric pressure.

Braise: To cook, especially meats, covered, in a small amount of liquid.

Brew: To prepare a beverage by allowing boiling water to extract flavor and/or color from certain substances.

Broil: To cook by direct exposure to intense heat such as a flame or an electric heating unit.

Caramelize: To melt sugar in a heavy pan over low heat until golden, stirring constantly.

Chill: To cool in the refrigerator or in cracked ice.

Clarify: To remove impurities from melted butter or margarine by allowing the sediment to settle, then pouring off clear yellow liquid. Other fats may be clarified by straining.

Cream: To blend shortening, butter or margarine, which usually has been softened, or sometimes oil, with a granulated or crushed ingredient until the mixture is soft and creamy. Usually described in method as light and fluffy.

Curdle: To congeal milk with rennet or heat until solid lumps or curds are formed.

Cut in: To disperse solid shortening into dry ingredients with a knife or pastry blender. Texture of the mixture should resemble coarse cracker meal. Described in method as crumbly.

Decant: To pour a liquid such as wine or melted butter carefully from 1 container into another leaving the sediment in the original container.

Deep-fry: To cook in a deep pan or skillet containing hot cooking oil. Deep-fried foods are generally completely immersed in the hot oil.

Deglaze: To heat stock, wine or other liquid in the pan in which meat has been cooked, mixing with pan juices and sediment to form a gravy or sauce base.

Degorger: To remove strong flavors or impurities before cooking, i.e. soaking ham in cold water or sprinkling vegetables with salt, then letting stand for a period of time and pressing out excess fluid.

Degrease: To remove accumulated fat from surface of hot liquids.

Dice: To cut into small cubes about 1/4-inch in size. Do not use dice unless ingredient can truly be cut into cubes.

Dissolve: To create a solution by thoroughly mixing a solid or granular substance with a liquid until no sediment remains.

Dredge: To coat completely with flour, bread crumbs, etc.

Filet: To remove bones from meat or fish. (Pieces of meat, fish or poultry from which bones have been removed are called filets.)

Flambé: To pour warmed Brandy or other spirits over food in a pan, then ignite and continue cooking briefly.

Fold in: To blend a delicate frothy mixture into a heavier one so that none of the lightness or volume is lost. Using a rubber spatula, turn under and bring up and over, rotating bowl 1/4 turn after each folding motion.

Fry: To cook in a pan or skillet containing hot cooking oil. The oil should not totally cover the food.

Garnish: To decorate food before serving.

Glaze: To cover or coat with sauce, syrup, egg white or a jellied substance. After applying, it becomes firm, adding color and flavor.

Grate: To rub food against a rough, perforated utensil to produce slivers, chunks, curls, etc.

Gratiné: To top a sauced dish with crumbs, cheese or butter, then brown under a broiler.

Grill: To broil, usually over hot coals or charcoal.

Grind: To cut, crush, or force through a chopper to produce small bits.

Infuse: To steep herbs or other flavorings in a liquid until liquid absorbs flavor.

Julienne: To cut vegetables, fruit, etc. into long thin strips.

Knead: To press, fold and stretch dough until smooth and elastic.

Lard: To insert strips of fat or bacon into lean meat to keep it moist and juicy during cooking. Larding is an internal basting technique.

Leaven: To cause batters and doughs to rise, usually by means of a chemical leavening agent. This process may occur before or during baking.

Marinate: To soak, usually in a highly seasoned oil-acid solution, to flavor and/or tenderize food.

Melt: To liquefy solid foods by the action of heat.

Mince: To cut or chop into very small pieces.

Mix: To combine ingredients to distribute uniformly.

Mold: To shape into a particular form.

Panbroil: To cook in a skillet or pan using a very small amount of fat to prevent sticking.

Panfry: To cook in a skillet or pan containing only a small amount of fat.

Parboil: To partially cook in boiling water. Most parboiled foods require additional cooking with or without other ingredients.

Parch: To dry or roast slightly through exposure to intense heat.

Pit: To remove the hard inedible seed from peaches, plums, etc.

Plank: To broil and serve on a board or wooden platter.

Plump: To soak fruits, usually dried, in liquid until puffy and softened.

Poach: To cook in a small amount of gently simmering liquid.

Preserve: To prevent food spoilage by pickling, salting, dehydrating, smoking, boiling in syrup, etc. Preserved foods have excellent keeping qualities when properly prepared and stored.

Purée: To reduce the pulp of cooked fruit and vegetables to a smooth and thick liquid by straining or blending.

Reduce: To boil stock, gravy or other liquid until volume is reduced, liquid is thickened and flavor is intensified.

Refresh: To place blanched drained vegetables or other food in cold water to halt cooking process.

Render: To cook meat or meat trimmings at low temperature until fat melts and can be drained and strained.

Roast: (1) To cook by dry heat either in an oven or over hot coals. (2) To dry or parch by intense heat.

Sauté: To cook in a skillet containing a small amount of hot cooking oil. Sautéed foods should never be immersed in the cooking oil and should be stirred frequently.

Scald: (1) To heat a liquid almost to the boiling point. (2) To soak, usually vegetables or fruit, in boiling water until the skins are loosened; see blanch, which is our preferred term.

Scallop: To bake with a sauce in a casserole. The food may either be mixed or layered with the sauce.

Score: To make shallow cuts diagonally in parallel lines, especially in meat.

Scramble: To cook and stir simultaneously, especially eggs.

Shirr: To crack eggs into individual buttered baking dishes, then bake or broil until whites are set. Chopped meats or vegetables, cheese, cream or bread crumbs may also be added.

Shred: To cut or shave food into slivers.

Shuck: To remove the husk from corn or the shell from oysters, clams, etc.

Sieve: To press a mixture through a closely meshed metal utensil to make it homogeneous.

Sift: To pass, usually dry ingredients, through a fine wire mesh in order to produce a uniform consistency.

Simmer: To cook in or with a liquid at or just below the boiling point.

Skewer: (1) To thread, usually meat and vegetables, onto a sharpened rod (as in shish kabob). (2) To fasten the opening of stuffed fowl closed with small pins.

Skim: To ladle or spoon off excess fat or scum from the surface of a liquid.

Smoke: To preserve or cook through continuous exposure to wood smoke for a long time.

Steam: To cook with water vapor in a closed container, usually in a steamer, on a rack, or in a double boiler.

Sterilize: To cleanse and purify through exposure to intense heat.

Stew: To simmer, usually meats and vegetables, for a long period of time. Also used to tenderize meats.

Stir-fry: To cook small pieces of vegetables and/or meat in a small amount of oil in a wok or skillet over high heat, stirring constantly, until tender-crisp.

Strain: To pass through a strainer, sieve, or cheesecloth in order to break down or remove solids or impurities.

Stuff: To fill or pack cavities especially those of meats, vegetables and poultry.

Toast: To brown and crisp, usually by means of direct heat or to bake until brown.

Toss: To mix lightly with lifting motion using 2 forks or spoons.

Truss: To bind poultry legs and wings close to the body before cooking.

Whip: To beat a mixture until air has been thoroughly incorporated and the mixture is light and fluffy, the volume is greatly increased, and the mixture holds its shape.

Wilt: To apply heat to cause dehydration, color change and a droopy appearance.

Almond

WHITE ALMOND BARS

4 eggs
2 c. sugar
1/4 tsp. salt
2 c. all-purpose flour

1 c. melted butter
2 tsp. almond flavoring
1/4 c. sugar
1 c. slivered almonds

Beat eggs, 2 cups sugar and salt in bowl until light. Add mixture of flour and butter. Add flavoring. Pour into greased and floured 9x13-inch baking pan. Sprinkle with 1/4 cup sugar and almonds. Bake at 325 degrees for 30 minutes. Yield: 3 dozen.

ALMOND STREUSEL COFFEE CAKE

2 c. milk
1/2 c. sugar
2 tsp. salt
3 pkg. dry yeast
2 eggs, at room
*   temperature*
1/2 c. oil

6 1/4 c. all-purpose flour
2   12-oz. cans almond
*   filling*
1 1/2 c. packed brown
*   sugar*
2 tsp. cinnamon
3/4 c. chopped walnuts

Heat milk to lukewarm in saucepan. Pour into medium bowl. Add sugar, salt and yeast; mix well. Add mixture of eggs and oil; mix well. Stir in flour. Knead gently on floured surface until dough forms soft ball. Place in greased bowl, turning to grease surface. Let rise until doubled in bulk. Divide into 4 portions. Roll each portion into 10x14-inch rectangle. Spread each with 1/2 can almond filling. Sprinkle with mixture of brown sugar, cinnamon and walnuts. Roll as for jelly roll. Brush with melted butter. Garnish with sugar crystals. Cut 4 or 5 slashes in top of each roll. Place on baking sheet. Let rise for 45 minutes. Bake at 325 degrees for 30 minutes. Yield: 32 servings.

ORIENTAL ALMONDS

2 c. whole almonds
1 tbsp. honey

1 tbsp. soy sauce
1 tsp. soybean oil

Spread almonds in single layer on ungreased baking sheet. Toast at 350 degrees for 15 minutes;

do not stir. Cool. Reduce oven temperature to 250 degrees. Mix honey and soy sauce in medium saucepan. Bring to a boil over low heat. Add almonds. Cook for 2 to 3 minutes, stirring constantly; remove from heat. Sprinkle with oil; toss to mix. Spread in single layer on baking sheet; separate almonds. Bake for 5 minutes; stir carefully. Bake for 5 minutes longer or to desired brown color; watch carefully during last 5 minutes of baking time to prevent overbrowning. Cool. Store in airtight containers. Yield: 2 cups.

ALMOND TARTS

1 egg, beaten
1/2 c. sugar
2 tbsp. butter, softened
1 c. ground almonds

1 tsp. almond extract
1 recipe 2-crust pie
*   pastry*
4 tsp. raspberry jam

Beat egg with sugar and butter in bowl. Add almonds and almond extract. Line muffin cups with pastry. Add 1/2 teaspoon jam to each. Fill cups 2/3 full with almond mixture. Bake at 425 degrees for 12 to 15 minutes or until set. Serve warm. Yield: 8 tarts.

ALMOND TEA

1 1/2 c. sugar
8 c. water
Rind of 1/2 lemon
Juice of 3 lemons

2 c. brewed tea
1 tsp. vanilla extract
3/4 tsp. almond extract

Combine sugar, water, lemon rind and juice of 1 lemon in saucepan. Bring to a boil. Boil for 5 minutes. Remove lemon rind. Add remaining lemon juice, tea and flavorings. Heat to serving temperature. Yield: 12 servings.

Ambrosia

APRICOT AMBROSIA

1 1/2 c. sugar
7 tbsp. cornstarch
1   46-oz. can apricot
*   nectar*
1   28-oz. can apricot
*   halves*

1 c. pecan pieces
1 angel food cake
1   8-oz. container extra
*   creamy whipped*
*   topping*

Combine sugar and cornstarch in 2-quart saucepan. Stir in apricot nectar gradually. Bring to a boil over medium heat, stirring constantly. Cook until mixture is thickened and clear, stirring constantly. Remove from heat. Drain apricots. Reserve 12 halves for decoration; chop remaining apricots.

Stir chopped apricots into cooked mixture. Add pecans. Tear angel food cake into bite-sized pieces. Add to cooked mixture. Pour into 9x13-inch dish. Refrigerate overnight. Top each serving with whipped topping. Place reserved apricot half cut side down on each. Yield: 12 servings.

HOLIDAY AMBROSIA

1 20-oz. can pineapple chunks, drained	*1 c. flaked coconut*
1 cup tangerine sections	*1 c. miniature marshmallows*
1¹/2 c. seedless grapes	*³/4 c. sour cream*
1/2 c. chopped pecans	*1 tbsp. sugar*

Combine pineapple, tangerine, grapes, pecans, coconut and marshmallows in bowl. mix sour cream and sugar in small bowl. Stir into fruit mixture. Chill until serving time. Yield: 6 servings.

SOUTHERN CITRUS AMBROSIA

2 lg. bananas	*1 tbsp. sugar*
4 med. oranges	*2 tsp. Fruit Fresh*
2 med. grapefruit	*1/2 c. chopped pecans*
1 c. red grapes	*1/2 c. coconut*
1/2 c. orange juice	

Slice bananas. Peel and section oranges and grapefruit. Cut grapes into halves and discard seed. combine fruits with orange juice and sugar in serving bowl. Sprinkle with Fruit Fresh; mix well. Top with pecans and coconut. Chill for 6 hours or longer. Yield: 12 servings.

Angel Cake

FOOLPROOF ANGEL FOOD CAKE

1¹/2 c. sifted cake flour	*1¹/2 tsp. cream of tartar*
2 c. sugar	*1¹/2 tsp. vanilla extract*
1/2 tsp. salt	*1 tsp. almond extract*
1¹/2 c. egg whites	

Sift flour and 1 cup sugar together 4 times. Sift 1 cup sugar 4 times. Beat salt with egg whites in mixer bowl until foamy. Add cream of tartar. Beat until stiff but not dry. Add sifted sugar 2 tablespoons at a time, beating at low speed. Stir in flavorings. Fold in flour mixture 2 tablespoons at a time. Spoon into ungreased 10-inch tube pan. Cut through batter with knife. Bake at 325 degrees for 65 minutes. Invert on funnel to cool. Loosen from side of pan with knife. Remove to serving plate. Yield: 16 servings.

LEMON ANGEL ROLL

1 pkg. 1-step angel food cake mix	*1/2 c. margarine, softened*
1 21-oz. can lemon pie filling	*4 c. confectioners' sugar*
1/2 c. confectioners' sugar	*1 tsp. vanilla extract*
8 oz. cream cheese, softened	*1 c. confectioners' sugar*
	1 to 2 tbsp. lemon juice

Combine cake mix and pie filling in mixer bowl. Beat until well blended. Spread in ungreased 10x15-inch cake pan. Bake at 350 degrees for 20 to 25 minutes or until cake tests done. Invert onto towel sprinkled with 1/2 cup confectioners' sugar. Roll up cake in towel. Cool. Beat cream cheese and margarine in mixer bowl until light and fluffy. Add 4 cups confectioners' sugar and vanilla; beat until smooth. Unroll cake. Spread with cream cheese mixture. Roll as for jelly roll. Place on serving plate. Mix 1 cup confectioners' sugar with enough lemon juice to make of glaze consistency. Drizzle over cake roll. Yield: 16 servings.

Apple

BAKED CHRISTMAS APPLES

1/2 pound cake, crumbled	*1/4 c. packed brown sugar*
8 Granny Smith apples, peeled, cored	*2 tbsp. seedless raisins*
1/4 c. melted butter	*Grated rind of 1 lemon*
1/2 10-oz. jar nesselrode	*Juice of 1 lemon*
	2 tbsp. butter

Bake crumbled cake on baking sheet at 275 degrees until dried. Coat apples with butter. Roll in crumbs. Fill with mixture of next 5 ingredients. Top with butter. Place in baking pan with a small amount of water. Bake at 375 degrees for 45 minutes or until tender. Spoon pan juices over hot apples. Cool. Serve at room temperature. Yield: 8 servings.

APPLE BURROS

1 can apple pie filling	*1 tbsp. sugar*
1/2 c. chopped pecans	*1 pkg. flour tortillas*
1/2 c. raisins	*Oil for deep frying*
1/2 c. sugar	

Combine pie filling and next 4 ingredients in bowl; mix well. Spoon 2 tablespoons into center of each tortilla. Fold in sides and roll to enclose filling. Deep-fry in 350-degree oil for 5 minutes or until golden. Drain on paper towels. Yield: 10 servings.

Apple Spice Cake...a spicy topping makes a moist old-fashioned cake.

APPLE SPICE CAKE

1 c. melted margarine	3 c. chopped cooking
1/2 c. oil	apples
3 eggs	1 c. chopped walnuts
2 tsp. vanilla extract	1/2 c. packed light
1/4 tsp. cinnamon	brown sugar
3 c. all-purpose flour	1/4 c. margarine
1 tsp. soda	3 tbsp. milk
2 tsp. salt	1 tbsp. cinnamon

Combine 1 cup melted margarine, oil and eggs in mixer bowl, mixing until thick and lemon-colored. Beat in vanilla, 1/4 teaspoon cinnamon and mixture of flour, soda and salt. Fold in apples and walnuts. Pour into greased and floured 10-inch tube pan. Bake at 325 degrees for 1 1/2 hours. Remove to wire rack to cool. Bring remaining ingredients to a boil in saucepan, mixing well. Cool. Pour over cake. Yield: 12 servings.

HOT FALL APPLES AND CRANBERRIES

6 c. sliced peeled apples	1/2 c. all-purpose flour
1 1/2 c. fresh cranberries	1/2 c. packed brown
1/2 c. sugar	sugar
1/2 tsp. cinnamon	1/4 c. butter
1/4 c. butter	

Combine apples, cranberries, sugar and cinnamon in bowl; mix well. Spoon into buttered 9x13-inch baking dish. Dot with 1/4 cup butter. Mix flour, brown sugar and remaining 1/4 cup butter in bowl until crumbly. Sprinkle over apples with additional cinnamon. Bake at 350 degrees for 1 hour. Yield: 8 servings.

RAISIN APPLE CRISP

8 c. sliced peeled apples	1 1/2 c. all-purpose flour
3/4 c. raisins	3/4 tsp. cinnamon
3/4 c. packed brown	1/2 tsp. nutmeg
sugar	3/4 c. butter, softened

Spread apple slices and raisins evenly in greased 9x13-inch baking dish. Combine brown sugar, flour, cinnamon and nutmeg in bowl. Blend in butter until crumbly. Sprinkle evenly over fruit; press lightly. Bake at 350 degrees for 45 minutes or until topping is crisp. Yield: 12 servings.

APPLE PANCAKES WITH CIDER SAUCE

2 c. buttermilk baking	2 tbsp. cornstarch
mix	1/4 tsp. cinnamon
1/2 tsp. cinnamon	1/4 tsp. nutmeg
1 egg	2 c. apple cider
1 1/3 c. milk	2 tbsp. lemon juice
3/4 c. grated apples	1/4 c. margarine
1 c. sugar	

Combine first 4 ingredients in bowl; mix well. Fold in apples. Bake 1/4 cup at a time on hot greased griddle until brown on both sides. Combine sugar, cornstarch, 1/4 teaspoon cinnamon and nutmeg in small saucepan; mix well. Stir in cider and lemon juice. Cook until thickened, stirring constantly. Cook for 1 minute longer, stirring constantly. Remove from heat; stir in butter. Serve warm over pancakes. Yield: 8 servings.

DEEP-DISH STREUSEL APPLE PIE
Photograph for this recipe is on page 17.

8 c. sliced peeled tart	2 c. flour
apples	1 c. packed brown
3/4 c. sugar	sugar
1/2 c. raisins	1/2 tsp. salt
1 tbsp. flour	1 tsp. apple pie spice
1 tsp. apple pie spice	1 c. butter or margarine

Combine first 5 ingredients in bowl; toss to mix. Spoon into 6x10-inch casserole. Combine 2 cups flour, brown sugar, salt and remaining 1 teaspoon apple pie spice in bowl. Cut in butter until crumbly. Sprinkle over apples. Bake at 375 degrees for 10 minutes. Reduce temperature to 350 degrees. Bake for 30 minutes longer. Yield: 8 to 10 servings.

Applesauce

APPLESAUCE CAKE

2 tsp. soda	1 tsp. cinnamon
2 c. unsweetened	1 tsp. allspice
applesauce	1 tsp. nutmeg
2 c. sugar	1 tsp. cloves
1 c. butter, softened	1 tsp. ginger
1 egg	1 1/2 to 2 c. black
4 c. all-purpose flour,	walnuts
sifted	
1 lb. raisins	

Grease tube pan. Line bottom with greased waxed paper. Stir soda into applesauce; set aside. Cream sugar and butter in mixer bowl until light and fluffy. Add egg. Beat well. Add applesauce; mix well. Sift flour over raisins in large bowl. Add spices and walnuts; mix well. Add applesauce mixture to raisin mixture; mix well. Pour into prepared pan. Bake at 325 degrees for 1 1/2 hours. Cool in pan. Invert onto cake plate. Yield: 20 servings.

APPLESAUCE MUFFINS

2 c. buttermilk baking	1 egg
mix	2 tbsp. oil
1/4 c. sugar	Melted butter
1 tsp. cinnamon	1/4 c. sugar
1/2 c. applesauce	1/4 tsp. cinnamon
1/4 c. milk	

Mix first 3 ingredients in bowl. Add applesauce, milk, egg and oil; mix well. Fill greased muffin cups 2/3 full. Bake at 400 degrees for 10 minutes. Dip warm muffin tops in melted butter, then into mixture of 1/4 cup sugar and 1/4 teaspoon cinnamon. Yield: 1 dozen.

SPICY HARVEST APPLESAUCE

1 lb. Winesap apples,	1/8 tsp. cinnamon
peeled	1 tbsp. sugar
1/3 c. water	2 tbsp. butter
3 whole cloves	1 tsp. lemon juice

Slice apples thinly. Combine first 5 ingredients in saucepan. Simmer until apples are tender, stirring frequently. Remove cloves. Stir in butter and lemon juice. Yield: 3 cups.

Apricot

APRICOT ALMOND ANTARCTICA

1 11-oz. pkg. vanilla	2 tbsp. almond extract
wafers, crushed	1 1/2 qt. vanilla ice
1 1/3 c. slivered almonds	cream, softened
1/2 c. melted butter	1 18-oz. jar apricot jam

Mix first 4 ingredients in bowl. Layer 1/3 of the crumbs and remaining ingredients 1/2 at a time in 9x13-inch dish, ending with crumbs. Freeze until firm. Yield: 12 servings.

APRICOT AND COCONUT BALLS

1 c. dried apricots	1 c. confectioners'
1/2 c. evaporated milk	sugar
3 c. flaked coconut	2 c. fine graham
2 tbsp. apricot Brandy	cracker crumbs

Chop apricots. Combine with evaporated milk, coconut, Brandy and sugar in bowl; mix well. Shape into 3/4-inch balls; roll in graham cracker crumbs. Store, wrapped, in refrigerator. Yield: 5 dozen.

APRICOT BREAD

1 1/2 c. boiling water	1/2 tsp. salt
1 c. chopped dried	1/2 tsp. baking powder
apricots	2 tsp. soda
1 1/2 c. sugar	1 c. chopped walnuts
1 egg, beaten	1 tbsp. melted
2 1/2 c. sifted	shortening
all-purpose flour	1 tsp. vanilla extract

Pour boiling water over apricots in bowl; let stand for 10 minutes. Beat sugar gradually into egg with spoon. Sift dry ingredients together into bowl. Stir in walnuts. Add dry ingredients alternately with sugar mixture to apricots, mixing well after each addition. Stir in shortening and vanilla. Pour into greased loaf pan. Bake at 350 degrees for 1 hour or until loaf tests done. Yield: 1 loaf.

APRICOT SALAD

2 3-oz. packages	1 14-oz. can
apricot gelatin	sweetened
2/3 c. water	condensed milk
2/3 c. sugar	8 oz. cream cheese,
2 4-oz. jars apricot	softened
baby food	1 20-oz. can crushed
1 c. chopped walnuts	pineapple

Bring gelatin, water and sugar to a boil in saucepan. Remove from heat. Stir in baby food. Add walnuts, condensed milk, cream cheese and pineapple; mix well. Spoon into large serving dish. Chill, covered, until set. Yield: 12 servings.

APRICOT NECTAR CAKE

1   2-layer pkg. yellow   2 tsp. lemon flavoring
    cake mix   1¹/₂ c. confectioners'
4 eggs   sugar
³/₄ c. oil   ¹/₃ c. lemon juice
³/₄ c. apricot nectar

Combine cake mix, eggs, oil, nectar and lemon flavoring in bowl; mix well. Pour into greased and floured 10-inch bundt pan. Bake at 350 degrees for 40 minutes. Cool in pan for 10 minutes. Mix confectioners' sugar and lemon juice in small bowl. Pour over cake. Let stand in pan until cool. Remove to serving plate. Yield: 16 servings.

APRICOT CRISP

¹/₂ c. margarine,   1¹/₂ c. small toasted
    softened   bread cubes
¹/₂ c. sugar   ¹/₂ tsp. vanilla extract
2 eggs   1   14-oz. can apricot
1 c. crushed Kellogg's   halves, drained
    cornflakes   2 tsp. lemon juice
¹/₂ tsp. nutmeg

Cream margarine and sugar in bowl until light and fluffy. Add eggs; beat until smooth. Stir in cornflakes, nutmeg, bread cubes, and vanilla. Spread half the mixture in buttered 6x10-inch baking dish. Arrange apricots over cereal mixture. Sprinkle with lemon juice. Top with remaining cornflake mixture. Bake at 375 degrees for 25 minutes or until light brown. Serve hot with ice cream. Yield: 5 servings.

APRICOT AND PINEAPPLE SALAD

2   3-oz. packages   2 tbsp. butter, melted
    orange gelatin   ¹/₂ c. sugar
2 c. boiling water   1 egg, slightly beaten
¹/₂ c. pineapple juice   1 c. apricot juice
¹/₂ c. apricot juice   1 c. pineapple juice
1   17-oz. can crushed   3 oz. cream cheese,
    pineapple, drained   softened
1   17-oz. can apricots,   1 c. whipped topping
    diced   8 oz. Cheddar cheese,
3 tbsp. all-purpose   shredded
    flour

Dissolve gelatin in boiling water in bowl. Add next 4 ingredients. Pour into 9x13-inch pan. Chill until firm. Blend flour and butter in saucepan. Add sugar, egg, 1 cup apricot juice and 1 cup pineapple juice. Cook until thickened, stirring constantly. Stir in cream cheese. Cool. Add whipped topping. Spread over gelatin. Sprinkle cheese on top. Yield: 15 servings.

Artichoke

ARTICHOKES AND GREEN BEANS

1   16-oz. can artichoke   ¹/₂ c. Italian bread
    hearts   crumbs
1   16-oz. can French-   ¹/₄ c. olive oil
    style green beans,   2 tsp. garlic powder
    drained   Bread crumbs
¹/₂ c. Parmesan cheese

Drain and chop artichoke hearts. Mix with green beans, cheese, ¹/₂ cup crumbs, olive oil and garlic powder in bowl. Place in greased 1-quart casserole. Top with additional bread crumbs. Bake at 350 degrees for 30 minutes. Yield: 6 to 8 servings.

ARTICHOKE CASSEROLE

1 clove of garlic,   Oil
    minced   2 cans artichokes, cut
1 med. onion, chopped   into halves
2   4-oz. cans   Romano cheese
    mushrooms, drained   1¹/₂ c. seasoned bread
1 tbsp. oregano   crumbs
Butter   Wine to taste

Sauté garlic, onion, mushrooms and oregano in a small amount of butter and oil in skillet. Spread in 2-quart baking dish. Layer artichokes, cheese and bread crumbs over sautéed vegetables. Drizzle with additional oil. Pour wine over layers. Bake at 350 degrees for 30 minutes. Yield: 8 servings.

ARTICHOKE DIP

1   14-oz. can mild   ¹/₂ c. mayonnaise
    green chilies   ¹/₂ c. Parmesan cheese
1   14-oz. can artichokes

Drain and chop green chilies and artichokes. Place in 9-inch pie plate. Mix mayonnaise and cheese in bowl. Spread over artichokes and chilies. Bake at 350 degrees for 10 to 15 minutes or just until top shows slight sign of browning. Serve with ridged potato chips, corn chips or thick crackers. Yield: 6 to 8 servings.

⇨

Recipes for this photograph are on pages 14, 38 and 117.

Fireside Company Dinner

Brie with Brandy and Pecans

page 46

Fresh Cauliflower and Broccoli Salad

page 45

Roast Pork with Orange Glaze

page 136

Baked Acorn Squash

page 163

Deep-Dish Streusel Apple Pie or

page 14

Winter Strawberry Chiffon Pie

page 165

Buttermilk Meringue Pie or Nutmeg Custard Pie

pages 38 and 117

Southern Coffee Comfort

page 68

*Invite friends over on a cold, frosty
day, and warm their spirits with a
festive dinner. Good company, classic dishes
and an old-fashioned pie board make a cold day cozy.*

ARTICHOKE RICE

1 pkg. Far East rice pilaf	4 green onions, finely chopped
2 6-oz. jars marinated artichoke hearts	12 stuffed olives, sliced
1/3 c. mayonnaise	1/2 green bell pepper, finely chopped
1/4 tsp. curry powder	

Cook pilaf using package directions. Cool. Drain artichokes, reserving 2 tablespoons marinade. Blend reserved marinade with mayonnaise and curry powder in small bowl. Combine pilaf, artichokes and remaining ingredients in salad bowl. Add mayonnaise mixture; toss lightly. Serve at room temperature. Yield: 6 servings.

ARTICHOKE HEART SALAD

2 10-oz. packages frozen broccoli	1 med. cucumber, peeled, chopped
1 9-oz. package French-style beans	1 sm. onion, chopped
2 6-oz. jars marinated artichoke hearts	1 env. buttermilk ranch salad dressing mix, prepared

Cook chopped broccoli and green beans using package directions for half the time; drain. Cut artichoke hearts into bite-sized pieces. Combine all vegetables and dressing in bowl; mix well. Chill overnight. Yield: 10 to 12 servings.

ARTICHOKE-BLUE CHEESE SALAD

1/3 c. olive oil	1 lg. head lettuce, torn
2 tbsp. red wine vinegar	1 16 oz. can artichoke hearts
4 tsp. lemon juice	
1 tsp. sugar	1/4 c. crumbled blue cheese
1/4 tsp. pepper	

Combine first 5 ingredients in bowl; mix well. Add lettuce. Drain artichoke hearts; cut into halves. Add with blue cheese to lettuce. Yield: 8 servings.

Asparagus

CHEESY ASPARAGUS CASSEROLE

1 16-oz. can asparagus spears, drained	1 can cream of mushroom soup
4 hard-boiled eggs, sliced	1/4 c. broken cashews
8 oz. Velveeta cheese, sliced	1 1/2 c. bread crumbs
	1/4 c. melted butter

Layer asparagus, eggs and cheese 1/2 at a time in well greased casserole. Top with mushroom soup and cashews. Toss crumbs with butter; sprinkle over top. Bake at 350 degrees for 45 minutes. Yield: 6 servings.

LINGUINE WITH FRESH ASPARAGUS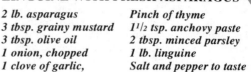

2 lb. asparagus	Pinch of thyme
3 tbsp. grainy mustard	1 1/2 tsp. anchovy paste
3 tbsp. olive oil	2 tbsp. minced parsley
1 onion, chopped	1 lb. linguine
1 clove of garlic, minced	Salt and pepper to taste

Cook asparagus in a small amount of water in saucepan for 3 minutes. Drain; rinse under cold water. Combine mustard, olive oil, onion, garlic, thyme, anchovy paste and parsley in bowl; mix well. Cook linguine using package directions for 7 to 10 minutes; drain well. Combine linguine with dressing and asparagus in serving bowl. Season with salt and pepper. Serve warm or at room temperature. Yield: 4 servings.

SPRING ASPARAGUS CASSEROLE

1 1/2 c. sour cream	1/2 tsp. pepper
1 onion, chopped	3 lbs. fresh aparagus, cooked
1/4 tsp. dry mustard	
1 clove of garlic, finely chopped	1 c. bread crumbs
	3 tbsp. butter, melted
3/4 tsp. salt	

Combine sour cream, onion, dry mustard, garlic, salt and pepper in bowl; mix well. Place asparagus in 1 1/2-quart casserole. Pour sour cream mixture over asparagus. Mix bread crumbs with melted butter; sprinkle over top. Bake at 350 degrees for 30 minutes. Yield: 8 servings.

ASPARAGUS ROLL-UPS

8 oz. cream cheese, softened	1 lg. loaf sandwich bread
3 oz. blue cheese, softened	1 16-oz. can asparagus spears
1 egg	1 c. melted butter

Blend cream cheese, blue cheese and egg in bowl. Trim crust from bread. Flatten with rolling pin. Spread with cheese mixture. Place asparagus spear on end of bread; roll up. Dip in melted butter. Freeze until firm. Cut in thirds. Store in freezer bags. Thaw before baking. Place on baking sheet. Bake at 375 degrees for 20 minutes. Broil until light brown. Yield: 24 servings.

SESAME GARDEN ASPARAGUS

8 oz. fresh asparagus   *1 tbsp. lemon juice*
2 tbsp. unsalted butter   *1 tbsp. sesame seed*
1 tsp. oil   *Salt and pepper to taste*

Trim asparagus. Cook in a small amount of water in skillet for 3 to 4 minutes or until tender-crisp; drain. Cover with ice water; drain. Melt butter in skillet. Add oil, lemon juice, sesame seed and seasonings; mix well. Add asparagus. Heat to serving temperature, shaking skillet constantly. Arrange on serving plate. Yield: 2 servings.

Aspic

RUBY RED ASPIC

1 12-oz. can V-8 juice   *2 tbsp. vinegar*
1/2 c. water   *1/4 tsp. allspice*
2 3-oz. packages   *1 16-oz. can whole*
* orange gelatin*   * cranberry sauce*

Bring V-8 juice and water to a boil in saucepan. Pour over gelatin in bowl; stir until gelatin is dissolved. Add vinegar, allspice and cranberry sauce. Pour into 5-cup mold. Chill until firm. Unmold onto salad green-lined serving plate. Serve with sour cream. Yield: 6 servings.

TOMATO ASPIC SALAD

1 20-oz. can whole   *1 sm. bottle of stuffed*
* tomatoes*   * olives, finely chopped*
1 tbsp. vinegar   *1 sm. bottle of cocktail*
1/4 c. water   * onions*
2 tsp. sugar   *1 3-oz. package*
1/2 c. chopped celery   * lemon gelatin*

Combine tomatoes, vinegar, water and sugar in saucepan. Bring to a boil; remove from heat. Add remaining ingredients; stir until gelatin dissolves. Pour into mold. Chill until firm. Unmold onto serving plate. Yield: 6 servings.

Avocado

GUACAMOLE DIP

2 ripe avocados   *Lemon juice to taste*
1 sm. tomato, chopped   *Salt and pepper to taste*
Dash of garlic powder   *2 canned green chilies,*
1 tbsp. chopped onion   * seeded, chopped*

Mash avocado in bowl. Add tomato, garlic powder, onion, lemon juice, salt, pepper and chilies; mix well. Spoon into serving bowl. Store covered, chilled. Yield: 2 cups.

AVOCADO DIP FOR VEGETABLES

1 lg. avocado, mashed   *3 tbsp. sour cream*
4 slices crisp-fried   *1/2 tsp. onion juice*
* bacon, crumbled*   *2 tsp. lemon juice*
8 oz. cream cheese,   *1 tsp. grated lemon*
* softened*   * rind*
1/2 tsp. salt

Combine avocado, bacon, cream cheese, salt, sour cream, onion juice, lemon juice and lemon rind in bowl; mix well. Chill, covered, for 1 hour. Spoon into serving dish. Serve with carrot, celery and cucumber sticks. Yield: 24 servings.

AVOCADO BREAD

2 2/3 c. sifted   *1 3/4 c. plus 2 tbsp.*
* all-purpose flour*   * sugar*
3/4 tsp. cinnamon   *3/4 c. buttermilk*
3/4 tsp. allspice   *1 1/2 c. mashed avocados*
3/4 tsp. salt   *3/4 c. chopped pecans*
1 1/2 tsp. soda   *1/2 c. raisins*
1 tsp. baking powder   *1/3 c. sugar*
1/2 c. butter, softened   *1 tsp. cinnamon*
3 eggs

Sift first 6 dry ingredients together. Combine butter, eggs and 1 3/4 cup plus 2 tablespoons sugar in mixer bowl. Beat for 2 minutes. Add buttermilk and avocados; mix well. Add dry ingredients. Beat for 2 minutes. Stir in pecans and raisins. Pour into 2 greased loaf pans. Sprinkle with mixture of 1/3 cup sugar and 1 teaspoon cinnamon. Bake at 350 degrees for 1 hour or until loaves test done. Yield: 2 loaves.

SPICY SUMMER AVOCADO SALAD

3 lg. ripe avocados   *Freshly ground pepper*
3 lg. firm tomatoes   * to taste*
2 med. onions   *Garlic powder to taste*
2 tbsp. lemon juice

Chop ripe avocados, tomatoes and onions into bite-sized pieces. Combine in serving bowl. Sprinkle with lemon juice and seasonings; mix gently. Chill in refrigerator until serving time. Yield: 12 servings.

Bacon

ZESTY BACON DIP

1 c. low-fat cottage cheese	1 tbsp. horseradish
8 oz. cream cheese, softened	1 tbsp. chopped scallions
4 slices bacon, crisp-fried, crumbled	1 tbsp. chopped parsley
	1 tbsp. chopped pimento

Mix cottage cheese and cream cheese in bowl. Stir in bacon, horseradish, scallions, parsley and pimento. Chill for 1 hour. Serve with vegetable-flavored crackers. Yield: 2 cups.

BACON AND CHEESE TOAST BARS

1 egg, beaten	Pepper to taste
1/3 c. mayonnaise	5 or 6 drops of hot sauce
1 c. shredded sharp Cheddar cheese	8 slices bacon, crisp fried, crumbled
1/2 tsp. Worcestershire sauce	8 slices bread
1/8 tsp. dry mustard	Paprika to taste

Combine egg, mayonnaise, cheese, Worcestershire sauce, dry mustard, pepper, and hot sauce in bowl; mix well. Stir in bacon. Trim crusts from bread; toast lightly on both sides. Spread toast evenly with cheese mixture. Cut each slice into 3 strips. Sprinkle with paprika. Place on baking sheet. Bake at 350 degrees for 12 to 15 minutes or until light brown. Yield: 24 bars.

PARMESAN AND BACON STICKS

5 slices bacon, cut into halves	1/2 c. Parmesan cheese
	10 thin bread sticks

Coat 1 side of each bacon strip in cheese. Roll 1 strip bacon diagonally around each bread stick. Place on baking sheet. Bake at 350 degrees for 10 minutes or until bacon is crisp. Roll in cheese. Yield: 10 sticks.

WATER CHESTNUT-BACON ROLL-UPS

2 8-oz. cans whole water chestnuts	1 c. sugar
	1 c. catsup
1 lb. bacon	

Drain water chestnuts and cut into halves. Cut bacon slices into thirds. Wrap bacon around water chestnuts; secure with toothpicks. Place in 9x13-inch baking dish. Bake at 400 degrees for 20 minutes or until bacon is crisp; drain. Pour mixture of sugar and catsup over top. Bake for 10 minutes longer. Yield: 48 servings.

FETTUCINI CARBONARA

4 oz. bacon	1 c. Parmesan cheese
1 16-oz. package fettucini	1/2 tsp. salt
	1 tsp. pepper
4 eggs	1/2 c. margarine
1/2 c. cream	

Fry bacon in skillet until crisp. Drain and crumble bacon. Cook fettucini *al dente* according to package directions; drain. Beat eggs in large bowl. Add cream, Parmesan cheese, salt and pepper; mix well. Heat margarine in large skillet. Add egg mixture. Cook over low heat just until thickened; do not overcook. Spoon mixture over warm fettucini in serving bowl. Stir in crumbled bacon.
Yield: 5 servings.

Baked Alaska

INDIVIDUAL BAKED ALASKAS

2 egg whites	2 chocolate-coated peppermint ice cream patties
1/8 tsp. cream of tartar	
1/4 tsp. vanilla extract	
1/8 tsp. salt	2 tbsp. crushed peppermint stick
1/4 c. sugar	
2 individual sponge cake cups	

Combine egg whites, cream of tartar, vanilla and salt in mixer bowl. Beat until soft peaks form. Add sugar gradually, beating constantly until stiff peaks form. Place sponge cake cups on foil-lined wooden cutting board. Place 1 ice cream patty in each cup. Cover each with meringue, sealing meringue to bottom of sponge cups. Sprinkle with crushed peppermint candy. Bake at 500 degrees for 2 to 3 minutes or until light brown. Serve immediately. Yield: 2 servings.

ALASKA MELBA PIE

1 10-oz. package	1 baked 9-in. pie shell
frozen raspberries,	4 egg whites
thawed	1 tsp. cream of tartar
2/3 c. sugar	1/2 c. sugar
1 tsp. cream of tartar	1 tsp. vanilla extract
1 qt. vanilla ice cream	

Purée raspberries in blender; press through sieve to remove seed. Bring purée, 2/3 cup sugar and 1 teaspoon cream of tartar to a boil in saucepan, stirring constantly. Cook for 3 minutes. Chill. Layer raspberry sauce and ice cream in pie shell, mounding top. Freeze overnight. Beat egg whites and 1 teaspoon cream of tartar in mixer bowl until doubled in volume. Add 1/2 cup sugar 1 tablespoon at a time, beating constantly until stiff peaks form. Stir in vanilla. Spread over pie, sealing to edge. Bake at 425 degrees for 5 minutes or until golden brown. Serve immediately. Yield: 6 servings.

Banana

BANANA FRUIT PUNCH

5 c. sugar	1 12-oz. can frozen
4 c. water	lemonade concentrate
1 12-oz. can frozen	2 46-oz. cans
orange juice	unsweetened
concentrate	pineapple juice
5 bananas	3 to 4 l. 7-Up

Bring sugar and water to a boil in medium saucepan, stirring until sugar dissolves. Cool. Combine orange juice concentrate, bananas, lemonade concentrate, and pineapple juice in blender; process until smooth. Add to sugar syrup; mix well. Pour into freezer containers. Store in freezer. Thaw for 1 hour before serving. Spoon into punch bowl. Add 7-Up just before serving. Ladle into punch cups. Yield: 25 servings.

ALOHA BANANA BREAD

2 c. all-purpose flour	1 c. mashed banana
1 c. sugar	1 tbsp. grated orange
1 tsp. soda	rind
1/2 tsp. salt	1 tsp. vanilla extract
1/2 c. margarine,	1/2 tsp. almond extract
softened	1 c. flaked coconut
2 eggs	1/2 c. chopped walnuts
1/4 c. milk	1/2 c. crushed pineapple

Combine first 4 dry ingredients, margarine, eggs, milk, banana, orange rind and flavorings in mixer bowl. Beat at low speed until moistened. Beat at medium speed for 3 minutes. Stir in coconut, walnuts and pineapple. Pour into 5x9-inch loaf pan greased on bottom only. Bake at 350 degrees for 60 to 70 minutes or until toothpick inserted in center comes out clean. Remove to wire rack to cool. Yield: 1 loaf.

WHOLE WHEAT BANANA BREAD

1 c. sugar	1 c. all-purpose flour
1/2 c. melted margarine	1 c. whole wheat flour
1 c. mashed banana	1 tsp. soda
1/3 c. water	1/2 tsp. salt
2 eggs, slightly beaten	1/2 c. chopped pecans

Blend sugar and margarine in large mixer bowl. Add banana, water and eggs; mix well. Add sifted mixture of flours, soda and salt gradually, mixing well after each addition. Fold in pecans. Pour into 5x9-inch loaf pan greased on bottom only. Bake at 350 degrees for 55 to 65 minutes or until toothpick inserted in center comes out clean. Cool in pan for 10 minutes. Remove to wire rack to cool completely. Store, tightly wrapped, in refrigerator. Yield: 1 loaf.

BANANA RIPPLE CAKE

1/2 c. semisweet	1 c. sugar
chocolate chips	2 egg yolks
1/4 c. water	1 c. mashed banana
2 c. all-purpose flour	1/3 c. sour cream
3/4 tsp. soda	1 tsp. vanilla extract
1/2 tsp. salt	1/3 c. chopped
1/4 tsp. baking powder	maraschino cherries
1/2 c. margarine,	2 egg whites
softened	1/2 c. sugar

Grease and flour bottom of 9-inch tube pan. Melt chocolate chips in water in saucepan over low heat, stirring constantly. Cool. Combine flour, soda, salt and baking powder. Cream margarine in large mixer bowl. Add 1 cup sugar gradually, beating at high speed until light and fluffy. Add egg yolks; beat well. Combine banana, sour cream and vanilla in bowl. Add to egg mixture alternately with dry ingredients, beginning and ending with dry in-gredients and beating at low speed until well blended after each addition. Stir in cherries. Beat egg whites in bowl until soft peaks form. Add 1/2 cup sugar gradually, beating until stiff. Fold into batter. Place 1/3 of the batter in prepared pan; drizzle with half the chocolate mixture. Repeat layers, ending with batter. Bake at 350 degrees for 50 to 60 minutes or until cake springs back when lightly touched. Cool. Invert onto serving plate. Yield: 12 servings.

BANANAS FOSTER

1/2 c. margarine
*1/3 c. packed light
brown sugar*
1 tsp. cinnamon

6 bananas, sliced
1/4 c. rum
*6 to 8 scoops vanilla
ice cream*

Melt margarine in saucepan. Add brown sugar and cinnamon. Bring to a boil; reduce heat. Add bananas. Simmer over low heat for 5 minutes, stirring occasionally. Heat rum in small saucepan. Pour over bananas; ignite carefully. Allow flames to subside. Place ice cream in serving dishes. Spoon banana mixture over ice cream.
Yield: 6 to 8 servings.

BANANA SPLIT DESSERT

*2 c. graham cracker
crumbs*
1/2 c. melted margarine
*2 c. confectioners'
sugar*
*1 c. margarine,
softened*

2 eggs
1 tsp. vanilla extract
*7 bananas, cut into
halves lengthwise*
*2 env. whipped topping
mix, prepared*

Mix crumbs with melted margarine in 9x13-inch dish. Cream confectioners' sugar and softened margarine in mixer bowl until light and fluffy. Blend in eggs and vanilla. Beat for 20 minutes. Spread over crumb layer. Layer bananas, pineapple and whipped topping over creamed mixture. Garnish with chopped nuts and maraschino cherries. Chill for several hours. Yield: 20 servings.

FLUFFY BANANA TARTS

*1 sm. package
pistachio instant
pudding mix*
1 c. cold milk
4 oz. whipped topping

*4 oz. German's sweet
chocolate*
2 tbsp. margarine
2 bananas, sliced
Cookie Tart Shells

Prepare pudding mix according to package directions, using 1 cup milk. Fold in whipped topping. Chill in refrigerator. Melt chocolate and margarine in double boiler over hot water, stirring constantly. Dip 8 banana slices in chocolate, coating halfway. Chill until firm. Place remaining banana slices in Cookie Tart Shells. Drizzle with remaining chocolate. Spoon pudding mixture into shells. Garnish with chocolate-dipped banana slices. Serve immediately. Yield: 8 servings.

Cookie Tart Shells

1/4 c. butter, softened
1/3 c. sugar
2 egg whites

1/3 c. all-purpose flour
1/4 c. ground almonds
1/8 tsp. almond extract

Grease bottoms of 8 inverted 2 1/2-inch diameter glasses. Cream butter and sugar in mixer bowl until light and fluffy. Add egg whites 1 at a time, mixing well after each addition. Add flour, almonds and almond extract; mix well. Drop by 2 tablespoonfuls onto greased cookie sheet. Spread into 8-inch rounds. Bake at 350 degrees for 7 to 8 minutes or just until edges are light brown. Place cookies immediately on bottoms of glasses; press toward glass to form fluted cups. Cool on glasses. Yield: 8 tart shells.

Barley

BARLEY CASSEROLE

1 onion, chopped
1 c. fine pearl barley
1/4 c. margarine
1/2 c. slivered almonds
1 env. onion soup mix

2 c. chicken broth
3/4 c. fresh mushrooms
*1 5-oz. can sliced
water chestnuts,
drained*

Sauté onion and barley in butter in skillet until lightly browned. Add slivered almonds, soup mix, chicken broth, mushrooms and water chestnuts; mix well. Spoon into 1 1/2-quart casserole. Bake at 350 degrees for 1 hour. Yield: 8 servings.

BARLEY SOUP

1/2 c. barley
1/2 c. split peas
1/2 c. lentils

1/2 c. chopped onion
4 c. water
Salt and pepper to taste

Combine barley, peas, lentils, onion and water in stockpot. Season with salt and pepper to taste. Simmer for 45 minutes or until peas and lentils are tender. Yield: 4 servings.

Beans

GREEN BEAN CASSEROLE

*2 16-oz. cans cut
green beans, drained*
2/3 c. milk
Pepper to taste

*1 can cream of
mushroom soup*
*1 3-oz. can French-
fried onions*

Combine beans, milk, pepper, soup and 1/2 can onions in bowl; mix well. Spoon into 1 1/2-quart baking dish. Bake at 350 degrees for 30 minutes. Top with remaining onions. Bake for 5 minutes longer. Yield: 6 servings.

HOT BEAN DIP

8 oz. cream cheese	2 tbsp. chopped parsley
1 c. sour cream	1/4 c. chopped green
1 lg. can bean dip	onions
1/2 env. taco seasoning	2 c. shredded Cheddar
mix	cheese
5 drops of Tabasco	2 c. shredded Monterey
sauce	Jack cheese

Mix cream cheese with sour cream in bowl. Add bean dip, seasonings, parsley, green onions and half the Cheddar and Monterey Jack cheeses. Spoon into baking dish. Top with remaining cheeses. Bake at 350 degrees for 20 minutes or until heated through. Serve with taco chips. Yield: 7 cups.

BUNDLE BEANS

2 16-oz. cans whole	1 16-oz. bottle of
green beans, drained	Catalina salad
8 slices bacon	dressing

Divide beans into 16 small bundles. Cut bacon slices into halves. Wrap each bundle with 1/2 slice bacon; secure with toothpick. Place in 9x13-inch baking dish. Drizzle with salad dressing. Marinate in refrigerator overnight. Bake at 350 degrees for 45 minutes. Yield: 8 servings.

SAVORY BAKED BEANS

2 29-oz. cans pork	2 tsp. Worcestershire
and beans	sauce
1 lb. bacon, chopped	1 c. catsup
2 green bell peppers,	1 c. packed brown
chopped	sugar
2 onions, chopped	

Combine beans, bacon, green peppers, onions, Worcestershire sauce, catsup and brown sugar in bowl; mix well. Spoon into baking dish. Bake, covered, at 325 degrees for 2 1/2 hours, stirring occasionally. Bake, uncovered, for 30 minutes longer. Yield: 20 servings.

BAKED SWISS GREEN BEANS

2 tbsp. margarine	1 c. shredded Swiss
2 tbsp. all-purpose	cheese
flour	1 16-oz. can green
1 tsp. grated onion	beans, drained
1 tsp. sugar	1 c. shredded Swiss
1/4 tsp. salt	cheese
1/2 tsp. pepper	1/2 tsp. paprika
1 c. sour cream	

Melt margarine in saucepan. Blend in flour. Add onion, sugar, salt and pepper; mix well. Stir in sour cream. Cook until smooth and well blended. Stir in 1 cup cheese until melted. Place beans in 1-quart baking dish. Pour sauce over beans. Sprinkle with remaining 1 cup cheese and paprika. Bake at 350 degrees for 20 minutes. Yield: 5 servings.

CROCK•POT BEAN SUPREME

1 15-oz. can pinto	1 onion, chopped
beans, drained	1 green bell pepper,
1 15-oz. can black-	chopped
eyed peas, drained	2 c. catsup
1 15-oz. can lima	1 c. dry red wine
beans, drained	1/2 c. packed light
1 15-oz. can kidney	brown sugar
beans, drained	1 tbsp. dry mustard
1 31-oz. can pork and	1 tbsp. Worcestershire
beans	sauce
2 lb. ground beef	

Combine drained beans and undrained pork and beans in Crock•Pot. Brown ground beef with onion and green pepper in skillet, stirring until crumbly; drain. Stir into bean mixture. Add catsup and remaining ingredients; mix well. Cook on Low for 8 hours. Yield: 12 servings.

FRESH GREEN BEANS WITH TOMATO

1 1/2 lb. fresh tender	1 tsp. oregano
green beans	1 lg. tomato, peeled,
1 onion, minced	seeded, chopped
1 clove of garlic,	1 8-oz. can chopped
minced	green chili peppers
2 tbsp. olive oil	Salt to taste

Trim green beans; cut into 2-inch lengths. Combine with a small amount of water in saucepan. Cook over medium heat just until tender-crisp. Rinse with cold water; drain. Sauté onion and garlic in oil in skillet over medium heat for 5 minutes. Add oregano, green beans, tomato and green chilies; mix well. Cook over medium heat for 10 minutes, stirring occasionally. Add salt to taste. Serve hot or at room temperature. Yield: 4 to 6 servings.

LIMA BEAN-BROCCOLI CASSEROLE

1 12-oz. package	1 c. sour cream
frozen lima beans	1 can cream of
1 10-oz. package	mushroom soup
frozen chopped	1 env. dry onion soup
broccoli	mix
1 8-oz. can sliced	1 c. crisp rice cereal
water chestnuts	1/4 c. margarine

Cook lima beans and broccoli separately, using directions on each package; drain. Combine cooked vegetables, water chestnuts, sour cream, soup and dry soup mix in bowl; mix gently. Spoon into 8x11-inch baking dish. Top with cereal. Dot with margarine. Bake at 325 degrees for 20 to 30 minutes or until bubbly. Yield: 8 to 10 servings.

LIMA BEAN SUPREME

2 10-oz. packages
frozen baby lima beans
1 can cream of
mushroom soup
1 onion, chopped
8 slices bacon,
crisp-fried, crumbled

1 to 2 tbsp. bacon
drippings
8 oz. Velveeta cheese,
shredded
1/2 c. bread crumbs
2 tbsp. melted
margarine

Cook lima beans using package directions; drain. Add soup, onion, bacon, bacon drippings and cheese; mix well. Spoon into buttered baking dish. Sprinkle with mixture of crumbs and melted margarine. Bake at 350 degrees for 30 minutes. Yield: 6 servings.

CHEESY BEAN AND GRITS BAKE

3 c. water
1 tsp. salt
3/4 c. yellow grits
4 oz. bacon, crisp-
fried, crumbled
8 oz. pepper cheese,
cubed
2 tbsp. margarine
2 eggs, beaten
1/2 c. milk
1 c. shredded Cheddar
cheese
1 15-oz. can garbanzo
beans

1 15-oz. can kidney
beans
1 c. chopped celery
3/4 c. chopped green
bell pepper
3/4 c. tomato juice
1/4 c. corn oil
1/4 c. vinegar
1 env. chili seasoning
mix
1 c. cherry tomato
halves

Bring water and salt to a boil in saucepan. Stir in grits. Bring to a boil; reduce heat. Cook for 5 minutes, stirring frequently. Remove from heat. Stir in bacon, pepper cheese and margarine. Combine eggs and milk in bowl. Stir a small amount of hot grits into eggs; stir eggs into grits. Spoon into buttered 7x12-inch baking dish. Bake at 350 degrees for 35 minutes, or until knife inserted in center comes out clean. Sprinkle with Cheddar cheese. Bake for 3 minutes longer. Let stand for 5 minutes. Drain and rinse garbanzo and kidney beans. Combine with celery, bell pepper, tomato juice, oil, vinegar and chili seasoning mix in saucepan. Cook until heated through, stirring frequently. Stir in cherry tomatoes. Spoon around edge of casserole. Serve remaining bean mixture with casserole. Yield: 12 servings.

RED BEANS AND RICE

1 lb. dried red kidney
beans
1 ham bone
2 c. chopped onions
2 or 3 cloves of garlic,
chopped
2 c. chopped celery
with leaves

2 tsp. salt
1/2 tsp. pepper
Cayenne pepper to taste
2 qt. water
1 lb. smoked sausage,
sliced
6 c. hot cooked rice

Soak kidney beans in water to cover in large bowl overnight. Drain. Combine with ham bone, onions, garlic, celery, salt, pepper, cayenne pepper and 2 quarts water in large saucepan. Bring to a boil; reduce heat. Simmer, covered, for several hours or until beans are tender and liquid is thickened. Sauté sausage in skillet; drain. Add to beans. Simmer for 30 minutes longer. Adjust seasonings. Serve over hot cooked rice. Yield: 6 servings.

MEXICAN BEAN SALAD

1 16-oz. can kidney
beans, drained
1 16-oz. can garbanzo
beans, drained
1 16-oz. can whole
kernel corn, drained
1 2-oz. jar chopped
pimento, drained

1 green bell pepper,
chopped
1 onion, chopped
1 tomato, chopped
1 9-oz. can sliced
black olives
French salad dressing

Combine beans, corn, pimento, green pepper, onion, tomato and black olives in large bowl. Add desired amount of French salad dressing; toss gently to coat. Marinate in refrigerator for 2 hours or longer. Serve on lettuce-lined plate. Yield: 8 to 10 servings.

SMOKEY BEAN SOUP

1 lb. sausage
1 16-oz. can kidney
beans
1 16-oz. can butter
beans
2 16-oz. cans pork
and beans
1 c. chopped onion

8 oz. bacon, crisp-
fried, crumbled
1 c. catsup
3 tbsp. vinegar
1/4 c. packed brown
sugar
1 tbsp. liquid smoke
1/2 tsp. garlic salt

Brown sausage in skillet, stirring until crumbly; drain. Combine with undrained beans, chopped onion and crumbled bacon in Crock•Pot. Add catsup, brown sugar, liquid smoke and garlic salt; mix well. Cook on Low for 4 to 6 hours. Ladle into soup bowls. Serve with corn bread. Yield: 10 servings.

LIMA BEAN SOUP

1¹/2 c. dried baby lima
  beans
6 c. water
1 16-oz. can tomatoes,
  chopped
1 8-oz. can tomato
  sauce
1 c. chopped onion

1 c. chopped celery
2 vegetable bouillon
  cubes
¹/4 tsp. Worcestershire
  sauce
¹/2 tsp. chili powder
1 tsp. salt

Combine lima beans and water in large saucepan. Bring to a boil; reduce heat. Simmer for 2 minutes. Remove from heat; let stand for 1 hour. Add tomatoes, tomato sauce, onion, celery, bouillon, Worcestershire sauce, chili powder and salt; mix well. Bring to a boil; reduce heat. Simmer, covered, for 1¹/2 to 2 hours or until beans are tender. Mash beans slightly if desired. Ladle into soup bowls. Yield: 6 to 8 servings.

Beef

BEEFY BRUNCH CASSEROLE

1 6-oz. jar dried beef,
  chopped
¹/2 c. margarine
¹/2 c. all-purpose flour
3 c. milk
1¹/2 c. shredded
  cheddar cheese

8 hard-cooked eggs,
  sliced
1 c. bread crumbs
2 tbsp. melted
  margarine

Sauté dried beef in ¹/2 cup margarine in skillet for several seconds. Sprinkle with flour; mix well. Stir in milk. Cook until thickened, stirring constantly. Stir in cheese until melted. Add eggs; mix gently. Spoon into greased 1¹/2-quart baking dish. Top with mixture of bread crumbs and melted margarine. Bake at 350 degrees until brown. Yield: 6 servings.

CORNED BEEF DIP

1 12-oz. can corned
  beef
2 tbsp. chopped onion
2 tbsp. chopped parsley
1¹/2 c. sour cream
1¹/2 c. mayonnaise

2 tsp. Beau Monde
  seasoning
1 tsp. chives
1 tsp. dillweed
1 tsp. garlic powder
1 round loaf rye bread

Shred corned beef into bowl with fork. Add onion, parsley, sour cream, mayonnaise and seasonings; mix well. Scoop out center of loaf to form shell; cut scooped-out bread into bite-sized pieces. Spoon corned beef mixture into bread shell. Serve with bread pieces. Yield: 4¹/2 cups.

CORNED BEEF SALAD

1 3-oz. package lemon
  gelatin
³/4 c. boiling water
³/4 c. half and half
1 c. mayonnaise
1 10-oz. can corned
  beef, shredded

1 tbsp. lemon juice
2 c. chopped celery
¹/4 c. minced onion
¹/2 c. chopped stuffed
  olives
3 hard-cooked eggs,
  chopped

Dissolve gelatin in boiling water in large bowl. Mix half and half and mayonnaise in small bowl. Add to gelatin mixture; mix well. Let stand until cool. Stir in remaining ingredients. Spoon into 8x12-inch dish. Chill for several hours or until set. Cut into squares. Serve on lettuce-lined plates. Yield: 10 servings.

TENDERLOIN DELUXE

1 3-lb. beef tenderloin
2 tbsp. margarine,
  softened
¹/4 c. chopped scallions
2 tbsp. margarine

2 tbsp. soy sauce
1 tsp. Dijon mustard
Pepper to taste
³/4 c. dry Sherry

Let tenderloin stand at room temperature for 2 hours or longer. Spread with softened margarine. Place on rack in shallow roaster. Bake, uncovered, at 400 degrees for 20 minutes. Sauté scallions in 2 tablespoons margarine in skillet. Add soy sauce, mustard and pepper. Stir in Sherry. Bring to a boil. Pour over tenderloin. Bake for 20 to 25 minutes longer for medium-rare. Yield: 8 servings.

Artichoke Pot Roast Dinner...replace potatoes with artichokes for a different flavor.

FALL ARTICHOKE POT ROAST DINNER

1 3 to 4-lb. beef pot roast	8 sm. onions
Salt and pepper to taste	4 carrots, cut into 1-in. pieces
1 8-oz. bottle of Catalina salad dressing	6 artichokes, trimmed
	1/2 c. water
1/2 c. water	1/4 c. all-purpose flour

Season roast with salt and pepper. Brown in 1/4 cup salad dressing in heavy saucepan over low heat. Add remaining salad dressing and 1/2 cup water. Simmer, covered, for 2 hours. Add onions, carrots and artichokes. Simmer, covered, for 1 hour or until roast and vegetables are tender. Remove roast and vegetables to platter. Blend 1/2 cup water and flour in small bowl. Stir into pan juices gradually. Cook until thickened, stirring constantly. Simmer for 3 minutes, stirring constantly. Serve with roast and vegetables. Yield: 6 servings.

BEEF GOULASH

Photograph for this recipe is on the cover.

1/4 c. butter	3 lb. round steak cubes
1/4 c. flour	1 8-oz. can tomatoes, drained, chopped
2 c. beef broth	4 tsp. paprika
1/2 tsp. Tabasco sauce	1 bay leaf
4 c. sliced onions	1/2 tsp. marjoram
2 cloves of garlic, minced	1/2 tsp. salt
1/4 c. butter	

Melt 1/4 cup butter in heavy saucepan. Cook until golden brown, stirring constantly. Blend in flour. Cook over low heat until golden brown, stirring constantly. Stir in broth gradually. Add Tabasco sauce. Cook until thickened, stirring constantly; set aside. Sauté onions and garlic in 1/4 cup butter in large saucepan. Add beef cubes. Cook until brown on all sides. Stir in reserved sauce, tomatoes and seasonings. Simmer, covered, for 1 1/2 to 2 hours or until beef is tender. Remove bay leaf. Serve over spaetzle. Yield: 6 to 8 servings.

GRILLED FLANK STEAK 🍎

1 2-lb. flank steak	1/2 c. corn oil
Garlic powder and seasoned pepper to taste	Several dashes of Worcestershire sauce
1 c. picante sauce	Several dashes of A-1 sauce
1/4 c. lemon juice	

Sprinkle steak with seasonings. Place in plastic bag. Mix picante sauce, lemon juice, oil, Worcestershire sauce and A-1 sauce in bowl. Add to steak; seal tightly. Marinate in refrigerator for 24 hours. Drain, reserving marinade. Grill over hot coals for 7 minutes on each side or to desired degree of doneness, basting with reserved marinade. Slice diagonally across the grain. May serve on warm flour tortillas with guacamole, shredded cheese, onions, tomatoes, sour cream, olives and salsa. Yield: 8 to 10 servings.

STEAK ROULADES

1 recipe Mushroom Stuffing	1/4 c. margarine
12 3x5x1/4-inch thick pieces round steak	2/3 c. chopped celery
	1/2 c. sliced mushrooms
Salt and pepper to taste	2 c. beef broth
1 c. all-purpose flour	1 c. sour cream

Prepare Mushroom Stuffing. Pound round steak very thin with meat mallet. Sprinkle with salt and pepper. Place 2 tablespoons stuffing on each piece. Roll as for jelly roll; tie with butcher's string. Coat with flour. Brown several at a time on all sides in margarine in Dutch oven for 5 to 7 minutes. Drain on paper towel. Add celery and mushrooms to Dutch oven. Stir-fry for 2 minutes. Add steak rolls and broth; cover tightly. Simmer or bake at 350 degrees for 1 1/2 hours. Place roulades on heated serving plate; remove string. Stir sour cream into pan juices. Heat to serving temperature; do not boil. Spoon gravy over roulades. Serve with remaining gravy. Yield: 12 servings.

Mushroom Stuffing

1 c. chopped onion	1/2 c. water
2 tbsp. margarine	1 egg, beaten
1/2 c. chopped mushrooms	1/2 tsp. salt
	1/8 tsp. pepper
2 c. soft bread crumbs	2 tbsp. chopped parsley

Sauté onion in margarine in skillet until golden. Add mushrooms. Sauté for 1 minute. Remove from heat. Add remaining ingredients; mix well. Yield: stuffing for 12 roulades.

TERIYAKI STEAK

1/4 c. soy sauce	1 clove of garlic, crushed
3/4 c. oil	
3 tbsp. honey	1 scallion, chopped
2 tbsp. red wine vinegar	1 2-lb. flank steak
1 1/2 tsp. ground ginger	

Combine first 7 ingredients in bowl; mix well. Pour over steak in shallow dish. Marinate for 5 hours or longer. Drain, reserving marinade. Grill over hot coals for 5 to 7 minutes on each side. Warm and skim reserved marinade. Serve over steak. Yield: 8 servings.

STIR-FRY BEEF AND BROCCOLI 🍎

2 tbsp. cornstarch	2 tbsp. oil
2 tbsp. soy sauce	3 tbsp. water
1 tsp. ginger	1 tbsp. oil
2 tbsp. oil	2 c. beef broth
1 1-lb. round steak	2 tbsp. cornstarch
4 c. chopped fresh	2 tbsp. soy sauce
broccoli	

Blend 2 tablespoons cornstarch, 2 tablespoons soy sauce, ginger and 2 tablespoons oil in bowl. Slice steak diagonally 1/4 inch thick. Place in soy sauce mixture, coating well. Marinate for 15 minutes. Stir-fry broccoli in 2 tablespoons hot oil in wok for 3 minutes or until bright green. Add water; cover. Steam for 1 minute; drain wok. Add 1 tablespoon oil to wok. Stir-fry steak for 4 minutes. Remove steak. Add broth to wok. Bring to a boil. Blend in 2 tablespoons cornstarch and 2 tablespoons soy sauce. Add broccoli and steak. Cook, covered, for 4 minutes. Serve over hot rice. Yield: 4 servings.

BEEF AND FRESH BROCCOLI SOUP 🍎

Photograph for this recipe is on page 35.

2 lb. boneless beef	2 c. water
round, cut into	1 lb. fresh mushrooms,
1/2-in. cubes	sliced
2 lg. leeks, sliced	2 lb. broccoli, cut into
3 cans beef broth	flowerets
3 bay leaves	2 yellow summer
2 tsp. thyme	squash, sliced
1/2 tsp. pepper	1/4 c. Parmesan cheese

Combine first 6 ingredients in saucepan. Bring to a boil; reduce heat. Simmer, covered, for 1 hour or until beef is tender. Remove bay leaves. Add water and mushrooms. Simmer for 5 minutes. Add broccoli. Simmer for 4 minutes. Add squash. Simmer for 3 minutes. Serve with Parmesan cheese. Yield: 6 to 8 servings.

OVEN STROGANOFF

1 c. red wine	1 can cream of
1 env. dry onion soup	mushroom soup
mix	1 tsp. salt
2 8-oz. jars sliced	1/2 tsp. pepper
mushrooms	1 3-lb. round steak,
1 can cream of chicken	cut into cubes
soup	2 c. sour cream
1 can cream of celery	1 lb. wide noodles,
soup	cooked

Combine first 8 ingredients in roaster; mix well. Add beef. Bake at 300 degrees for 3 to 4 hours. Stir in sour cream just before serving. Serve over noodles. Yield: 10 servings.

FAJITAS PRONTO

1 c. picante sauce	1/2 tsp. salt
2 green onions with	1 15-oz. can pinto
tops, sliced	beans, drained
1/4 c. chopped fresh	2 tomatoes, seeded,
cilantro	chopped
1/4 c. corn oil	1 avocado, chopped
1 tsp. lemon juice	1 lb. lean sirloin steak
1 clove of garlic,	Salt and pepper to taste
minced	4 c. shredded lettuce

Combine picante sauce, green onions, cilantro, oil, lemon juice, garlic and salt in bowl; mix well. Combine 1/4 cup sauce with beans in bowl. Combine 1/4 cup sauce with tomatoes and avocado in bowl. Chill bean mixture and tomato mixture in refrigerator for 1 hour. Sprinkle steak with salt and pepper. Place on rack in broiler pan. Broil to desired degree of doneness. Slice thinly across the grain. Combine with 1/4 cup sauce in bowl. Combine lettuce with remaining sauce in large serving bowl; toss lightly. Layer beans, tomato mixture and steak over lettuce. Serve with warm tortillas and additional picante sauce if desired. Yield: 12 servings.

MEXICAN STIR-FRY

2 tbsp. corn oil	1 green bell pepper,
1 lb. sirloin steak, cut	cut into thin strips
into thin strips	2/3 c. picante salsa
1 onion, cut into	8 flour tortillas,
wedges	warmed
1 clove of garlic,	Avocado slices
minced	Sour cream

Heat corn oil in wok or large skillet. Add steak, onion, garlic and green pepper. Stir-fry for 3 to 4 minutes or until vegetables are tender-crisp. Add picante salsa. Stir-fry for 1 minute or until sauce is heated. Spoon 1/2 cup mixture onto each tortilla. Top with avocado slices, sour cream and additional salsa. Yield: 4 servings.

GRILLED BEEF WITH RED BUTTER SAUCE

1 2-lb. boneless	Salt and pepper to taste
sirloin steak, 11/2	6 tbsp. chopped shallots
inches thick	11/2 c. red Burgundy
2 tbsp. peanut oil	3/4 c. butter

Rub steak on both sides with oil; sprinkle with salt and pepper. Place on rack in broiler pan. Broil 4 to 5 inches from heat source for 3 to 5 minutes; turn. Broil for 3 to 5 minutes longer or to desired degree of doneness. Place on heated platter; cover loosely with foil. Let stand for 5 minutes. Slice steak diagonally across the grain. Boil shallots in wine in saucepan until liquid is reduced to 1/3 cup. Add butter. Season to taste. Cook just until butter melts. Serve with steak. Yield: 4 servings.

Beets

BEET CAKE

1 c. vegetable oil	*1 c. canned Harvard*
2 c. sugar	*beets*
2¹/2 c. all-purpose flour	*1 c. drained crushed*
2 tsp. cinnamon	*pineapple*
2 tsp. soda	*1 c. cottage cheese*
1 tsp. salt	*1 c. chopped walnuts*
2 tsp. vanilla extract	

Combine oil, sugar, flour, cinnamon, soda and salt in large bowl. Beat with spoon until smooth. Beat in vanilla. Combine beets, pineapple, cottage cheese and walnuts in blender or food processor. Process until smooth. Add to flour mixture; mix well. Pour into greased and floured bundt pan. Bake at 370 degrees for 45 minutes or until cake tests done. Remove to wire rack to cool. Garnish with confectioners' sugar or confectioners' sugar glaze. Yield: 16 servings.

CRANBERRY BEETS

1 16-oz. can small	*1 tbsp. grated orange*
whole beets	*rind*
1 8-oz. can whole	*1 tbsp. cornstarch*
cranberry sauce	*1 tbsp. cold water*

Combine undrained beets and cranberry sauce in saucepan. Heat until cranberry sauce is melted. Stir in orange rind and mixture of cornstarch and cold water. Cook over low heat until thickened, stirring constantly. Yield: 4 servings.

FRESH BEETS WITH PINEAPPLE

2 tbsp. brown sugar	*1 tbsp. margarine*
1 tbsp. cornstarch	*1 tbsp. lemon juice*
1/4 tsp. salt	*2 c. sliced cooked beets*
1 c. pineapple tidbits	

Mix brown sugar, cornstarch and salt in saucepan. Add undrained pineapple; mix well. Cook until thickened, stirring constantly. Add margarine, lemon juice and beets. Cook over medium heat for 5 minutes or until heated through. Yield: 4 servings.

Biscuits

BUTTERMILK BISCUITS WITH CHILIES

1 tbsp. sesame seed	*1 tsp. salt*
1 pkg. dry yeast	*2 tbsp. margarine*
1/4 tsp. sugar	*3/4 c. buttermilk*
2 tbsp. 110-degree	*1 4-oz. can chopped*
water	*green chili peppers,*
1¹/2 c. unbleached flour	*drained*
1/2 c. white cornmeal	*1 tbsp. melted*
1¹/2 tsp. baking powder	*margarine*
1/2 tsp. soda	*1 tsp. sesame seed*

Sprinkle buttered 10-inch baking pan with 1 tablespoon sesame seed. Dissolve yeast and sugar in warm water in cup. Let stand for several minutes or until bubbly. Combine flour, cornmeal, baking powder, soda and salt in bowl. Cut in 2 tablespoons margarine with pastry cutter until crumbly. Add buttermilk, green chilies and yeast mixture; mix well. Knead dough on floured surface for 2 minutes. Pat 3/4 inch thick; cut with floured biscuit cutter. Place in prepared pan. Drizzle with melted margarine. Sprinkle with 1 tablespoon sesame seed. Bake at 425 degrees for 18 to 20 minutes or until golden brown. Serve hot. Yield: 16 biscuits.

CINNAMON AND RAISIN BISCUITS

2 c. all-purpose flour	*1/4 c. plumped golden*
1 tbsp. sugar	*raisins*
1/2 tsp. soda	*3/4 c. (about) buttermilk*
1/2 tsp. cinnamon	*Cinnamon*
6 tbsp. margarine	*Vanilla Glaze*

Combine flour, sugar, soda and 1/2 teaspoon cinnamon in bowl. Cut in 6 tablespoons margarine until crumbly. Mix in raisins. Add buttermilk, mixing to form soft dough. Knead lightly on floured surface. Pat into rectangle. Sprinkle generously with additional cinnamon. Knead lightly. Pat to 1/2 to 3/4-inch thickness. Cut into biscuits. Place on baking sheet. Bake at 425 degrees for 12 to 15 minutes or until light brown. Spread hot biscuits with Vanilla Glaze. Yield: 1 dozen.

Vanilla Glaze

2 tbsp. margarine,	*1/4 tsp. vanilla extract*
softened	*1 to 1¹/4 c.*
2 tbsp. (about) milk	*confectioners' sugar*

Blend softened margarine, milk, vanilla and confectioners' sugar in bowl. Spread over hot biscuits. Serve warm.

EASY BISCUITS

4 tsp. sugar
1/3 c. sour cream
1/3 c. club soda
1 1/2 c. buttermilk
baking mix

Mix sugar, sour cream and club soda with whisk in 2-quart bowl. Stir in baking mix. Knead in bowl 12 times or until smooth. Shape into 6 biscuits. Arrange in greased 8-inch baking pan. Brush tops with melted margarine. Bake at 450 degrees for 16 to 18 minutes or until light brown. Yield: 6 biscuits.

SAVORY BISCUITS

1 10-oz. package
refrigerator biscuits
1/3 c. melted margarine
3 tbsp. blue cheese

Cut biscuits into quarters. Arrange in 11x17-inch baking pan. Combine margarine and cheese in bowl; mix well. Pour over biscuits. Bake at 400 degrees for 15 minutes. Yield: 40 biscuits.

Blackberry

OLD FASHIONED BLACKBERRY-BANANA CAKE

1/2 15-oz. package
raisins
2 c. chopped pecans
1 c. sifted all-purpose
flour
1 c. butter, softened
2 c. sugar
4 eggs
2 1/2 c. all-purpose flour
2 tsp. soda
2 tsp. nutmeg
2 1/2 tsp. cinnamon
1 tsp. cloves
2 c. blackberry jam
3/4 c. strawberry
preserves
2 bananas, sliced

Toss raisins and pecans with 1 cup flour in bowl; set aside. Cream butter and sugar in mixer bowl until light and fluffy. Mix in eggs by hand. Sift 2 1/4 cups flour with soda and spices. Add to creamed mixture; mix well. Stir in raisin mixture, jam, preserves and bananas. Pour into tube pan lined with greased baking parchment. Bake at 275 degrees for 3 hours or until cake tests done. Remove to wire rack to cool. Yield: 16 servings.

COOL BLACKBERRY CHEESECAKE

1 pkg. cheesecake mix
1 sm. package
blueberry gelatin
1 c. sugar
1/4 c. cornstarch
1 3/4 c. water
1 1/2 c. fresh or drained
frozen blackberries

Prepare cheesecake according to package directions. Chill in refrigerator. Mix gelatin, sugar and cornstarch in saucepan. Add water; mix well. Cook over medium heat for 3 to 7 minutes or until thickened and clear, stirring constantly. Cool. Stir in blackberries. Spoon over cheesecake. Store in refrigerator. Yield: 8 servings.

FRESH BLACKBERRY SPICE CAKE

3 eggs
2 c. sugar
1 c. margarine,
softened
2 c. blackberries
2 c. all-purpose flour
2 tsp. soda
1/2 tsp. salt
1 tsp. cinnamon
1 tsp. cloves
1 tsp. allspice
1 tsp. nutmeg

Combine eggs, sugar and margarine in bowl; mix until smooth. Add blackberries; mix well. Sift in flour, soda, salt and spices; beat until smooth. Pour into 2 greased and floured 9-inch cake pans. Bake at 375 degrees until cake tests done. Frost with favorite frosting or serve plain with ice cream. Yield: 12 servings.

Blueberry

SUMMER BLUEBERRY TEA BREAD

3 c. all-purpose flour
2 tsp. baking powder
1 tsp. soda
1/2 tsp. salt
2/3 c. shortening
1 1/3 c. sugar
4 eggs
1/2 c. milk
1 1/2 tsp. lemon juice
1 c. drained crushed
pineapple
2 c. blueberries
1 c. chopped pecans
1/2 c. coconut

Sift flour with baking powder, soda and salt. Cream shortening in mixer bowl until light. Add sugar gradually, beating until fluffy. Beat in eggs 1 at a time. Stir in milk, lemon juice and pineapple. Add dry ingredients gradually, mixing well after each addition. Fold in blueberries, pecans and coconut. Spoon into 3 greased 3x6-inch loaf pans. Bake at 350 degrees for 40 minutes or until loaves test done. Cool in pans for 10 minutes. Remove to wire rack to cool completely. Yield: 3 small loaves.

BLUEBERRY TOPPING

4 c. fresh blueberries
1/2 c. sugar
2/3 c. brown sugar
2 1/2 tbsp. all-purpose
flour
1 tbsp. margarine
1 tbsp. lemon juice
1/2 tsp. cinnamon
1/8 tsp. nutmeg
1/4 tsp. salt

Combine 2 cups blueberries, sugar, brown sugar, flour, margarine, lemon juice, spices and salt in medium saucepan. Bring to a boil over low heat, stirring constantly. Simmer for 10 minutes or until thickened. Cool. Stir in 2 cups blueberries. Chill in refrigerator. Serve over ice cream. May pour into baked pie shell and top with ice cream.
Yield: 8 servings.

BLUEBERRY CRUNCH

1/4 c. shortening	*1/4 tsp. cloves*
3/4 c. sugar	*1 1/2 c. fresh blueberries*
2 eggs	*1/2 c. sugar*
1/2 c. milk	*1/3 c. all-purpose flour*
1 1/2 c. all-purpose flour	*1/4. c. margarine,*
2 tsp. baking powder	*softened*
1/2 tsp. salt	*1/2 tsp. cinnamon*
1/2 tsp. nutmeg	

Cream shortening and 3/4 cup sugar in mixer bowl until light and fluffy. Blend in eggs and milk. Add 1 1/2 cups flour, baking powder, salt, nutmeg and cloves; mix well. Fold in blueberries. Spoon into greased 9x9-inch baking pan. Combine remaining ingredients in bowl; mix until crumbly. Sprinkle over blueberry mixture. Bake at 375 degrees for 45 to 50 minutes or until top springs back when lightly touched. Cut into squares. Serve warm with whipped cream, ice cream or lemon sauce.
Yield: 9 servings.

PATRIOTIC BLUEBERRY SALAD

1 3-oz. package	*8 oz. cream cheese,*
raspberry gelatin	*softened*
2 c. boiling water	*1/2 c. chopped pecans*
1 env. unflavored	*1 3-oz. package*
gelatin	*raspberry gelatin*
1/2 c. cold water	*1 c. boiling water*
1 c. half and half	*1 21-oz. can blueberry*
1 c. sugar	*pie filling*
1 tsp. vanilla extract	

Dissolve 1 package raspberry gelatin in 2 cups boiling water in deep glass dish. Chill until firm. Soften unflavored gelatin in 1/2 cup cold water in saucepan. Add half and half, sugar and vanilla. Heat until gelatin is dissolved, stirring constantly; do not boil. Remove from heat. Stir in cream cheese until melted. Add pecans. Cool. Pour over congealed layer. Chill until firm. Dissolve remaining package raspberry gelatin in 1 cup boiling water in bowl. Stir in blueberry pie filling. Pour over cream cheese layer. Chill until firm.
Yield: 10 servings.

Bran

BRAN BROWN BREAD

2 pkg. yeast	*1/2 c. all-Bran cereal*
2 tsp. sugar	*2/3 c. molasses*
1 c. lukewarm water	*1 tbsp. salt*
1/4 c. shortening	*2 eggs, beaten*
1 c. water	*7 c. all-purpose flour*

Dissolve yeast and sugar in 1 cup lukewarm water in large bowl. Combine shortening and 1 cup water in saucepan. Heat until shortening is melted. Cool to lukewarm. Add to yeast mixture. Add cereal, molasses, salt, eggs and flour, mixing well after each addition. Knead on floured surface until smooth and elastic. Place in greased bowl, turning to grease surface. Let rise until doubled in bulk. Punch dough down. Let rise again until doubled in bulk. Shape into 3 loaves. Place in greased 5x9-inch loaf pans. Let rise until doubled in bulk. Bake at 350 degrees for 25 to 30 minutes or until loaves test done. Remove to wire rack to cool.
Yield: 3 loaves.

HIGH FIBER BRAN MUFFINS

1 c. stone-ground	*1/2 c. raisins*
whole wheat flour	*1 egg, slightly beaten*
1 1/2 c. whole bran	*1/2 c. honey*
cereal	*3/4 c. skim milk*
1 tsp. soda	*2 tbsp. safflower oil*
1/8 tsp. salt	

Mix whole wheat flour, bran cereal, soda, salt and raisins in bowl. Add egg, honey, milk and oil; mix just until moistened. Fill greased or paper-lined muffin cups 2/3 full. Bake at 400 degrees for 15 to 20 minutes or until brown. Yield: 1 dozen.

BRAN ROLLS

2 pkg. dry yeast	*1 tbsp. salt*
2 c. 110-degree water	*2 c. boiling water*
2 c. shortening	*4 eggs, beaten*
1 1/2 c. sugar	*12 c. all-purpose flour*
1/2 c. All-Bran cereal	

Dissolve yeast in 2 cups 110-degree water in bowl. Combine shortening, sugar, cereal, salt and boiling water in large bowl. Stir until shortening is melted. Cool to lukewarm. Add yeast mixture and eggs. Add enough flour to form a soft dough, beating at low speed. Place in lightly greased bowl; cover. Chill in refrigerator. Shape into balls half the size of greased muffin cups. Let rise for 2 hours. Bake at 425 degrees for 15 minutes. Yield: 8 dozen.

BRAN AND OATMEAL
REFRIGERATOR MUFFINS 🍎

2 c. 100% bran cereal	*4 eggs, beaten*
2 c. boiling water	*1 qt. buttermilk*
1 c. shortening	*5 c. all-purpose flour*
1 1/2 c. packed light	*1 tsp. salt*
brown sugar	*5 tsp. soda*
1 1/2 c. sugar	*4 c. oats*

Mix bran cereal and boiling water in bowl. Set aside. Cream shortening, brown sugar and sugar in large mixer bowl until fluffy. Add eggs, buttermilk, flour, salt and soda in order listed, mixing well after each addition. Add bran mixture and oats; mix well. Cover tightly. Store in refrigerator for up to 3 months. Fill greased muffin cups 3/4 full. Bake at 375 degrees for 20 minutes or until muffins test done. May add raisins, chopped nuts or chopped dates to batter just before baking. Yield: 5 dozen.

Bread

BROWN BREAD 🍎

1 c. sifted all-purpose	*3 tbsp. melted*
flour	*shortening*
2 tsp. soda	*3 tbsp. molasses*
1 tsp. salt	*2 c. buttermilk*
1/4 c. sugar	*3/4 c. raisins*
2 c. whole wheat flour	

Sift flour, soda, salt and sugar into bowl. Stir in whole wheat flour. Add mixture of shortening, molasses, buttermilk and raisins; mix well. Pour into 2 greased 4x7-inch loaf pans. Bake at 350 degrees for 45 minutes. Remove to wire rack to cool. Yield: 2 loaves.

NO-KNEAD LIGHT BREAD

1 tbsp. yeast	*1/2 c. margarine,*
1/4 c. sugar	*softened*
1/2 c. warm water	*6 to 8 eggs, beaten*
1 tbsp. salt	*4 c. all-purpose flour*

Combine yeast, sugar and water in large mixer bowl. Let stand until bubbly. Add salt, margarine and eggs; mix well. Beat in flour with large spoon. Let rise, covered, for 30 minutes. Stir dough down. Pour into 2 greased 5x9-inch loaf pans. Bake at 350 degrees for 30 minutes. Remove to wire rack to cool. Yield: 2 loaves.

BREAD STICKS

1 pkg. dry yeast	*2 tbsp. unprocessed*
1/4 c. 115-degree water	*bran*
1 tbsp. molasses	*2 tbsp. sesame seed*
1/2 c. buttermilk	*1 tsp. baking powder*
1/4 c. cottage cheese	*3/4 tsp. salt*
2 tbsp. oil	*1 to 1 1/4 c. all-purpose*
1 egg	*flour*
1 c. whole wheat flour	*1 egg*
1/2 c. rye flour	*1 tbsp. water*
1/2 c. salted sunflower	*2 tbsp. Parmesan*
seed	*cheese*
2 tbsp. wheat germ	

Dissolve yeast in mixture of warm water and molasses in large mixer bowl. Add buttermilk, cottage cheese, oil and 1 egg; mix for 2 minutes. Add whole wheat flour, rye flour, sunflower seed, wheat germ, bran, sesame seed, baking powder and salt; mix well. Add enough all-purpose flour to form a soft dough; mix for 3 minutes. Knead on lightly floured surface or with dough hook for 10 minutes. Place in greased bowl, turning to grease surface. Let rise, covered, in warm place until doubled in bulk. Punch dough down. Divide into 2 portions. Divide each portion into 12 balls. Roll each ball into 10 to 12-inch rope on floured surface. Place 1 1/2 inches apart on greased baking sheets. Let rise, covered, in warm place until doubled in bulk. Brush with 1 egg beaten with 1 tablespoon water. Sprinkle with cheese. Bake at 350 degrees for 20 minutes or until golden brown. Yield: 24 bread sticks.

HOLIDAY BREAD

1 c. oats	*2 1/2 tsp. salt*
2 c. boiling water	*1/2 c. molasses*
2 pkg. dry yeast	*2 tbsp. butter, softened*
1/3 c. 110 to 115-	*6 c. all-purpose flour*
degree warm water	

Combine oats and boiling water in bowl; mix well. Let stand for 30 minutes. Dissolve yeast in warm water. Add salt, molasses and butter to oats; mix well. Stir in yeast. Add flour 2 cups at a time; mixing well after each addition. Knead on floured surface for 5 to 10 minutes or until smooth and elastic. Place in greased bowl, turning to grease surface. Let rise, covered, for 2 hours or until doubled in bulk. Punch dough down. Shape into 2 loaves. Place in greased 5x9-inch loaf pans. Let rise, covered, for 1 hour or until doubled in bulk. Preheat oven to 325 degrees. Place loaf pans on rack 4 inches from bottom of oven. Bake for 50 minutes. Remove from pan onto wire rack. Note: Add 2 teaspoons sage, 1/2 teaspoon caraway seed and 1 teaspoon marjoram for herb bread. Yield: 2 loaves.

BREAD BAKING CHART

The pleasure of baking homemade bread is matched
only by eating it, except when something goes
wrong. Most problems can be determined
and easily avoided the next time.

PROBLEM	POSSIBLE CAUSE
Bread or biscuits are dry	Too much flour; too slow baking; over-handling of dough
Bread has too open or uneven texture	Too much liquid; over-handling in the kneading
Strong yeast smell from baked bread	Too much yeast; over-rising
Tiny white spots on crusts	Too rapid rising; dough not covered properly while rising
Crust has bad color	Too much flour used in shaping
Small flat loaves	Old yeast; not enough rising or rising too long; oven temperature too hot
Heavy compact texture	Too much flour worked into bread when kneading; insufficient rising time; oven temperature too hot
Coarse texture	Too little kneading
Crumbly bread	Too much flour; undermixing; oven temperature too cool
Yeasty sour flavor	Too little yeast; rising time too long
Fallen center	Rising time too long
Irregular shape	Poor technique in shaping
Surface browns too quickly	Oven temperature too hot
Bread rises too long during baking and is porous in the center and the upper portion of loaf	Oven temperature too cool

Broccoli

HOT BROCCOLI AND CHEESE DIP

3 stalks celery, thinly
  sliced
1 onion, chopped
1 4-oz. can sliced
  mushrooms, drained
1/4 c. margarine
3 tbsp. all-purpose
  flour

1 5-oz. roll garlic
  cheese, slice
1 10-oz. package
  frozen chopped
  broccoli, thawed
2 cans cream of
  celery soup

Sauté celery, onion and mushrooms in margarine in skillet. Stir in flour, Pour into lightly greased Crock•Pot. Add cheese, broccoli and celery soup. Cook on High until cheese is melted, stirring occasionally. Cook on Low for 2 hours or until serving time. Serve with assorted crackers or bite-sized vegetables such as broccoli, cauliflower and green bell pepper. Yield: 4 cups.

BROCCOLI WITH CHOWDER SAUCE

2 10-oz. packages
  frozen broccoli spears
1 10-oz. can New
  England clam
  chowder

1/2 c. sour cream
1/2 tsp. salt
4 slices American
  cheese, chopped

Cook broccoli spears according to package directions; drain. Arrange in 8x8-inch baking dish. Combine clam chowder, sour cream and salt in saucepan. Cook over low heat until heated through, stirring constantly. Spoon over broccoli. Bake at 325 degrees for 20 minutes. Sprinkle with chopped cheese. Bake just until cheese is melted. Yield: 6 servings.

PARTY BROCCOLI

2 tbsp. minced onion
2 tbsp. margarine
1 1/2 c. sour cream
2 tsp. sugar
1 tsp. cider vinegar
1/2 tsp. poppy seed
1/2 tsp. paprika

1/4 tsp. salt
2 10-oz. packages
  frozen chopped
  broccoli
Cashews
Cayenne pepper to taste

Sauté onion in margarine in saucepan until light brown; remove from heat. Stir in sour cream, sugar, vinegar, poppy seed, paprika and salt. Cook broccoli according to package directions; drain. Place in serving bowl. Spoon sour cream sauce over top. Sprinkle with cashews and cayenne pepper. Yield: 6 to 8 servings.

COZY BROCCOLI CASSEROLE

1 1/2 lb. fresh broccoli
2 eggs, slightly beaten
3/4 c. cottage cheese
1/2 c. shredded
  Cheddar cheese
2 tbsp. finely chopped
  onion

1/8 tsp. pepper
1 tsp. Worcestershire
  sauce
1/4 c. fine dry bread
  crumbs
1 tbsp. melted
  margarine

Trim broccoli and cut into spears. Cook in a small amount of water in saucepan for 10 minutes; drain. Place in 1 1/2-quart baking dish. Combine eggs, cottage cheese, Cheddar cheese, onion, pepper and Worcestershire sauce in bowl; mix well. Spoon over broccoli spears. Toss bread crumbs with melted margarine in small bowl. Sprinkle over casserole. Bake at 350 degrees for 15 to 20 minutes or until bubbly. Yield: 4 servings.

BROCCOLI-WILD RICE CASSEROLE

1 6-oz. package long
  grain and wild rice
  mix
20 fresh mushrooms
1 c. chopped red onion

1 tbsp. margarine
1 bunch fresh broccoli
1 lb. Monterey Jack
  cheese, shredded
Paprika

Cook rice mix according to package directions. Sauté mushrooms and onion in margarine in saucepan. Add rice; mix well. Spread in 9x13-inch baking dish. Trim broccoli and cut into spears. Cook in a small amount of water in saucepan until tender-crisp; drain. Arrange over rice. Top with cheese and paprika. Bake at 375 degrees for 15 minutes or until bubbly. Yield: 8 servings.

BROCCOLI AND CORN CASSEROLE

1 10-oz. package
  frozen broccoli
1 16-oz. can cream-
  style corn
1 egg, beaten
1/2 c. cracker crumbs
1 tbsp. onion flakes

2 tbsp. melted
  margarine
1/2 tsp. salt
Dash of pepper
1/2 c. cracker crumbs
1 tbsp. melted
  margarine

Cook chopped broccoli according to package directions; drain. Combine with corn, egg, 1/2 cup cracker crumbs, onion flakes, 2 tablespoons margarine, salt and pepper in bowl; mix well. Pour into 1-quart baking dish. Mix 1/2 cup cracker crumbs and 1 tablespoon margarine in small bowl. Sprinkle over casserole. Bake at 350 degrees for 35 minutes or until bubbly. Yield: 6 servings.

⇨
Recipe for this photograph is on
page 28.

Cozy Soup Supper

Peppy Popcorn

page 135

Winter Oranges and Red Onions

page 121

Beef and Fresh Broccoli Soup

page 28

Jalapeño Corn Bread

page 70

Fresh Fall Fruit Betty

page 86

Almond Tea

page 12

Nothing fills the house with more promising aromas or is as satisfying on cold winter days as hearty soup. Gather round the supper table on chilly days and warm up.

BROCCOLI QUICHE

1 10-oz. package	*1/4 tsp. pepper*
chopped broccoli,	*1 unbaked 9-in. pie*
thawed	*shell*
1 1/2 c. shredded cheese	*2 eggs, beaten*
1/2 c. chopped onion	*1 c. milk*
1/2 tsp. basil	*1 tbsp. cornstarch*
1/2 tsp. salt	

Drain broccoli well. Combine with cheese, onion, basil, salt and pepper in bowl; mix well. Spoon into pie shell. Beat eggs with milk and cornstarch in bowl. Pour over broccoli. Bake at 375 degrees for 40 to 45 minutes or until knife inserted in center comes out clean. Yield: 6 servings.

BROCCOLI SALAD

Flowerets of 1 bunch	*1 red onion, sliced into*
broccoli	*rings*
1 c. sunflower seed	*1 c. mayonnaise*
1/2 c. raisins	*1/2 c. sugar*
6 slices bacon, crisp-	*2 tbsp. vinegar*
fried, crumbled	

Combine broccoli, sunflower seed, raisins, bacon and onion in bowl. Mix mayonnaise, sugar and vinegar in small bowl. Add to broccoli mixture; mix well. Chill until serving time.
Yield: 6 servings.

BROCCOLI AND CHEDDAR SOUP

4 cans Cheddar cheese	*2 10-oz. packages*
soup	*frozen chopped*
6 c. milk	*broccoli, thawed*
2 c. frozen hashed	*1 c. chopped onion*
brown potatoes	

Combine soup and milk in saucepan; mix well. Heat oven medium heat until smooth, stirring frequently. Add potatoes, broccoli and onion. Cook until bubbly, stirring frequently; reduce heat. Simmer, covered, for 30 minutes. Ladle into soup bowls. Yield: 12 servings.

Brownies

CARAMEL BROWNIES

50 caramels	*1 2-layer package*
1/3 c. evaporated milk	*chocolate cake mix*
3/4 c. margarine	*1 c. chopped pecans*
1/3 c. evaporated milk	*1 c. chocolate chips*

Melt caramels with 1/3 cup evaporated milk in large saucepan; set aside. Melt margarine with 1/3 cup evaporated milk in saucepan. Combine with cake mix and pecans in large bowl. Pat half the mixture into greased 9x13-inch baking pan. Bake at 350 degrees for 6 minutes. Sprinkle with chocolate chips; spread melted caramel mixture over chips. Pat remaining cake mix over top. Bake for 15 minutes longer. Cool. Cut into squares.
Yield: 2 1/2 dozen.

DOUBLE CHOCOLATE BROWNIES

2 c. all-purpose flour	*1 tsp. salt*
2 c. sugar	*4 eggs*
1/4 c. (heaping)	*1 c. oil*
unsweetened baking	*2 tsp. vanilla extract*
cocoa	*2 c. chocolate chips*
1 tsp. baking powder	*1 c. chopped walnuts*

Mix dry ingredients in bowl. Combine eggs, oil and vanilla in small bowl; whisk until smooth. Add to dry ingredients; mix well. Fold in chocolate chips and walnuts. Spoon into greased 9x13-inch baking pan. Bake at 350 degrees for 30 minutes. Cool. Cut into squares. Yield: 3 dozen.

HEAVENLY HASH BROWNIES

4 eggs	*1 c. melted margarine*
2 c. sugar	*1 1/2 c. chopped pecans*
1 1/2 c. all-purpose flour	*1 7-oz. jar*
1 tsp. vanilla extract	*marshmallow creme*
1/3 c. unsweetened	*Heavenly Frosting*
baking cocoa	

Combine eggs, sugar, flour and vanilla extract in bowl; mix well. Mix cocoa and margarine in small bowl. Add to egg mixture; beat until smooth. Mix in pecans. Pour into greased 9x13-inch baking pan. Bake at 350 degrees for 25 minutes. Spread with marshmallow creme. Cool. Spread Heavenly Frosting over top. Cut into squares. Yield: 2 dozen.

Heavenly Frosting

1/2 c. melted margarine	*1 tsp. vanilla extract*
3 tbsp. unsweetened	*4 c. confectioners'*
baking cocoa	*sugar*
1/3 c. milk	

Blend margarine, cocoa and milk in bowl. Add vanilla and confectioners' sugar. Mix until smooth and creamy.

HONEY AND CAROB BROWNIES

1/2 c. melted margarine	1 tsp. baking powder
1/2 c. carob powder	1/4 tsp. salt
1 c. honey	1 tsp. vanilla extract
2 eggs, beaten	1/2 c. chopped walnuts
1 c. whole wheat flour	

Combine first 4 ingredients in bowl; mix well. Sift in flour, baking powder and salt; mix well. Stir in vanilla and walnuts. Pour into greased 8x8-inch baking pan. Bake at 350 degrees for 40 minutes. Cool. Cut into squares. Yield: 1 1/2 dozen.

MINT BROWNIE PETIT FOURS

1 c. sugar	2 1/2 c. confectioners' sugar
1/2 c. margarine, softened	1/2 c. margarine, softened
4 eggs	1 tsp. peppermint extract
1 tsp. vanilla extract	Green food coloring
1 c. all-purpose flour	1 1/2 c. chocolate chips
1/2 tsp. salt	6 tbsp. margarine
1 16-oz. can chocolate syrup	

Cream sugar and 1/2 cup softened margarine in mixer bowl until light and fluffy. Blend in eggs. Add vanilla extract, flour, salt and chocolate syrup; mix with spoon. Spoon into greased and lightly floured 9x13-inch baking pan. Bake at 350 degrees for 30 minutes. Cool. Blend confectioners' sugar, 1/2 cup softened margarine, peppermint extract and food coloring in bowl. Spread over cooled brownies. Melt chocolate chips with 6 tablespoons margarine in small saucepan over low heat. Pour over frosting; shake pan to distribute chocolate evenly to edges of pan. Chill. Cut into small squares. Serve at room temperature. Yield: 3 dozen.

BROWNIE PIES

2 c. chocolate chips	1/2 tsp. vanilla extract
1 c. margarine	1/2 c. milk
3/4 c. all-purpose flour	2 c. chopped pecans
2 c. sugar	2 unbaked 9-in.
4 eggs	deep-dish pie shells

Melt chocolate chips and margarine in saucepan over low heat. Combine flour and sugar in bowl. Beat eggs, vanilla and milk in bowl. Add flour mixture and chocolate mixture; mix well. Add pecans; mix well. Pour into pie shells. Bake at 350 degrees for 45 minutes. Yield: 2 pies.

Brussels Sprouts

FIRESIDE BRUSSELS SPROUTS

2 lb. Brussels sprouts	1 tbsp. sugar
4 slices bacon, chopped	3/4 tsp. salt
1/2 c. minced onion	1/4 tsp. dry mustard
2 tbsp. cider vinegar	1/8 tsp. pepper

Wash Brussels sprouts; pat dry. Remove outer leaves; trim stems. Make crisscross cut in stem ends with sharp knife. Brown bacon in saucepan, stirring frequently. Remove bacon with slotted spoon. Add Brussels sprouts, onion, vinegar, sugar and seasonings. Cook for 10 minutes or until Brussels sprouts are tender-crisp. Stir in bacon. Spoon into heated serving dish. Yield: 8 servings.

BRUSSELS SPROUTS CASSEROLE

1 lb. bacon	1 c. shredded Gruyère cheese
3 10-oz. packages frozen Brussels sprouts	1 c. heavy cream
1 c. fresh bread crumbs	1/4 tsp. pepper

Cut bacon into 1/2-inch pieces. Fry in skillet until crisp. Drain, reserving 1/4 cup drippings. Cut Brussels sprouts into halves. Reserve 3 tablespoons bread crumbs. Combine remaining bread crumbs, bacon, thawed Brussels sprouts, cheese, cream and pepper in reserved bacon drippings in skillet; mix well. Spoon into 9x13-inch baking dish. Top with reserved crumbs. Bake at 375 degrees until bubbly and brown. Yield: 10 servings.

Buttermilk

BUTTERMILK MERINGUE PIE
Photograph for this recipe is on page 17.

1/4 c. butter, softened	1/8 tsp. allspice
2/3 c. sugar	1/4 tsp. salt
1 tsp. vanilla extract	2 c. buttermilk
3 eggs, separated	Sesame Seed Pastry Shell
1/4 c. flour	
1/2 tsp. grated lemon rind	1/4 tsp. cream of tartar
1/2 tsp. nutmeg	Dash of salt
	1/3 c. sugar

Cream butter and 2/3 cup sugar in mixer bowl until light and fluffy. Add vanilla and egg yolks 1 at a time, beating well after each addition. Stir in flour, lemon rind, spices and 1/4 teaspoon salt; blend well. Pour in buttermilk. Turn into Sesame Seed Pastry Shell. Bake in preheated 425-degree oven for 8 minutes. Reduce temperature to 325 degrees. Bake for 40 minutes or until set. Cool for 30 minutes. Beat egg whites with cream of tartar and dash of salt until soft peaks form. Add remaining 1/3 cup sugar gradually, beating until stiff peaks form. Spread over filling, sealing to edges. Bake in preheated 375-degree oven for 6 minutes or until meringue is golden. Cool. Chill until serving time. Yield: 8 servings.

Sesame Seed Pastry Shell

1 c. flour
1/3 c. yellow cornmeal
3 tbsp. sesame seed, toasted
1/2 c. shortening
1/4 c. shredded sharp Cheddar cheese
1 tbsp. sugar
1/2 tsp. salt
2 tbsp. cold water

Combine flour, cornmeal and sesame seed in bowl. Cut in shortening until crumbly. Stir in cheese. Combine sugar, salt and water in bowl; mix well. Pour over flour mixture; mix well. Roll between 2 sheets of lightly floured waxed paper. Fit into 9-inch pie plate; flute edges. Yield: 1 pie shell.

BUTTERMILK PIE

3 eggs
1 1/2 c. sugar
1/2 c. melted margarine
3 tbsp. all-purpose flour
1 c. buttermilk
1 tsp. vanilla extract
1 unbaked 9-in. pie shell

Combine first 6 ingredients in bowl; mix well. Pour into pie shell. Bake at 350 degrees for 50 minutes or until golden brown. Cool completely before serving. Yield: 6 servings.

Butterscotch

BUTTERSCOTCH SALAD

1 3 1/2-oz. package butterscotch instant pudding mix
1 c. chopped walnuts
1 8-oz. can crushed pineapple
1 c. miniature marshmallows
3 c. chopped unpeeled apples
1 8-oz. container whipped topping

Combine all ingredients in bowl; mix well. Chill until serving time. Yield: 6 servings.

BUTTERSCOTCH SQUARES

1/2 c. margarine
1 c. peanut butter
12 oz. butterscotch chips
1 10-oz. package miniature marshmallows
1 c. coconut

Combine margarine, peanut butter and butterscotch chips in saucepan. Heat until melted, stirring frequently. Cool to lukewarm. Fold in marshmallows. Sprinkle coconut in 9x13-inch dish. Spread butterscotch mixture over coconut. Let stand until firm. Cut into squares. Yield: 24 squares.

OLD-FASHIONED BUTTERSCOTCH PIE

3 egg yolks
1 c. packed brown sugar
1/2 c. all-purpose flour
1 1/2 c. milk
1/4 c. margarine
1 baked 9-in. pie shell
3 egg whites
Sugar to taste

Combine egg yolks, brown sugar, flour, milk and margarine in double boiler. Cook until thickened, stirring constantly. Pour into pie shell. Beat egg whites in mixer bowl until stiff peaks form, adding sugar to taste. Spread over pie. Bake at 350 degrees until light brown. Yield: 6 servings.

BUTTERSCOTCH PECAN TORTE

6 egg yolks
1 1/2 c. sugar
1 tsp. baking powder
2 tsp. vanilla extract
1 tsp. almond extract
6 egg whites
1 c. chopped pecans
2 c. graham cracker crumbs
3 c. whipping cream
4 1/2 tbsp. confectioners' sugar
Butterscotch Sauce

Beat egg yolks in bowl. Add sugar gradually, beating constantly. Mix in baking powder and flavorings. Beat egg whites in bowl until stiff peaks form. Fold into egg yolk mixture. Fold in pecans and crumbs. Pour into two 9-inch cake pans lined with waxed paper. Bake at 325 degrees for 30 to 35 minutes or until cake tests done. Cool. Whip cream in mixer bowl until soft peaks form. Beat in confectioners' sugar. Spread between layers and over top of torte. Pour Butterscotch Sauce over torte, allowing sauce to run down side. Yield: 16 servings.

Butterscotch Sauce

1/2 c. water
1 c. packed brown sugar
1 tbsp. all-purpose flour
1/2 c. melted margarine
1 egg, beaten
1/4 c. orange juice
1/2 tsp. vanilla extract

Blend first 4 ingredients in small saucepan. Add egg, orange juice and vanilla; mix well. Bring to a boil, stirring constantly; reduce heat. Cook until thickened, stirring constantly. Cool completely.

Cabbage

CABBAGE AU GRATIN

1 med. head cabbage,
sliced
1 sm. onion, thinly
sliced

1 c. shredded Cheddar
cheese
1 can mushroom soup
1 c. soft bread crumbs

Cook cabbage and onion in a small amount of boiling salted water in saucepan for 10 minutes or until wilted; drain well. Layer cabbage mixture, cheese and soup 1/2 at a time in casserole. Top with crumbs. Bake at 400 degrees for 15 minutes. Yield: 8 servings.

CABBAGE CASSEROLE

1 c. (or more) shredded
cabbage
1 1/2 c. crushed
cornflakes
1/2 melted margarine
1/4 tsp. salt

1/2 c. mayonnaise
1 c. milk
1 can cream of celery
soup
1 c. shredded cheese
1 c. crushed cornflakes

Combine cabbage with cold water to cover in bowl. Let stand for 30 minutes. Mix 1 1/2 cups cornflake crumbs and melted margarine in 9x13-inch baking dish, spreading mixture evenly. Drain cabbage well. Layer over cornflake mixture. Sprinkle with salt. Combine mayonnaise, milk and soup in saucepan. Heat until bubbly. Pour over cabbage. Top with cheese and 1 cup cornflake crumbs. Bake at 325 degrees for 35 minutes. Yield: 8 to 10 servings.

CABBAGE SOUP

1 lb. ground beef
6 c. water
2 c. chopped peeled
potatoes
1 c. chopped celery
1 c. whole kernel corn

2 onions, chopped
2 c. shredded cabbage
4 c. stewed tomatoes
1/4 c. uncooked rice
1 1/2 tsp. salt

Brown ground beef in saucepan, stirring until crumbly; drain. Add water. Bring to a boil. Stir in vegetables. Bring to a boil. Add rice and salt. Simmer for 1 1/2 hours. Yield: 8 servings.

SPRING GERMAN SLAW

8 c. shredded cabbage
2 green bell peppers,
finely chopped
1 red bell pepper,
finely chopped
4 med. onions, finely
chopped

1 1/3 c. cider vinegar
2 1/2 c. sugar
1 tsp. celery seed
1 1/2 tsp. mustard seed
1 1/2 tsp. salt
1/2 tsp. turmeric

Mix cabbage, peppers and onions in glass bowl. Combine vinegar and remaining ingredients in saucepan. Bring to a boil. Pour over cabbage mixture. Chill in refrigerator for 24 hours or longer before using. Yield: 12 cups.

FRUIT AND NUT TROPICAL SLAW

2 tbsp. pineapple juice
2 tbsp. mandarin
orange juice
1 tbsp. lemon juice
1 med. banana, sliced
1 c. thinly sliced celery
3 c. shredded cabbage
1/2 c. chopped walnuts
1/4 c. raisins

1 8-oz. can pineapple
slices, drained,
chopped
1 11-oz. can mandarin
oranges, drained,
chopped
1 8 oz. carton orange
yogurt
1/2 tsp. salt

Mix pineapple juice, mandarin orange juice and lemon juice in small bowl. Pour over banana in large bowl. Add celery, cabbage, walnuts, raisins and fruit. Add yogurt and salt; toss to mix. Chill until serving time. Yield: 8 servings.

Caesar Salad

CAESAR SALAD

1/2 c. olive oil
3 tbsp. wine vinegar
1 tbsp. lemon juice
1 tbsp. Dijon-style
mustard
3 tbsp. Romano cheese
1 egg

1 clove of garlic,
finely chopped
Pepper to taste
1 bunch romaine
lettuce
1 c. croutons

Combine olive oil, vinegar, lemon juice, mustard, cheese, egg, garlic and pepper in small bowl; mix well. Combine lettuce and croutons in salad bowl. Add dressing; toss lightly. Yield: 4 servings.

CAKE BAKING GUIDE

PROBLEM	POSSIBLE CAUSE	
	Butter-Type Cakes	**Sponge-Type Cakes**
Cake falls	Too much sugar, liquid, leavening or shortening; too little flour; temperature too low; insufficient baking.	Too much sugar; over-beating egg whites; underbeaten egg yolks; use of greased pans; insufficient baking
Cake cracks or humps	Too much flour or too little liquid; overmixing; batter not spread evenly in pan; oven temperature too high	Too much flour or sugar; temperature too high
Cake has one side higher	Batter not spread evenly; uneven pan; pan too close to side of oven; oven rack or range not even; uneven oven heat	Uneven pan; oven rack or range not level
Cake has hard top crust	Temperature too high; overbaking	Temperature too high; overbaking
Cake has sticky top crust	Too much sugar or shortening; insufficient baking	Too much sugar; insufficient baking
Cake has soggy layer at bottom	Too much liquid; underbeaten eggs; undermixing; insufficient baking	Too many eggs or egg yolks; underbeaten egg yolks; undermixing
Cake crumbles or falls apart	Too much sugar, leavening or shortening; undermixing; improper pan treatment; improper cooling	
Cake has heavy compact quality	Too much liquid or shortening; too many eggs; too little leavening or flour; temperature too high; overmixing	Egg yolks insufficiently beaten; overbeaten egg whites; overmixing
Cake falls out of pan before completely cooled		Too much sugar; use of greased pans; insufficient baking

CANDY CHART

PRODUCT	TEST IN COLD WATER*	DEGREES F ON CANDY THERMOMETER			
		SEA LEVEL	2000 FEET	5000 FEET	7500 FEET
FUDGE, PENUCHE AND FONDANT	SOFT BALL (can be picked up but flattens)	234° to 240°	230° to 236°	224° to 230°	219° to 225°
CARAMELS	FIRM BALL (holds shape unless pressed)	242° to 248°	238° to 244°	232° to 238°	227° to 233°
DIVINITY, TAFFY AND CARAMEL CORN	HARD BALL (holds shape though pliable)	250° to 268°	246° to 264°	240° to 258°	235° to 253°
BUTTERSCOTCH AND ENGLISH TOFFEE	SOFT CRACK (separates into hard threads but not brittle)	270° to 290°	266° to 286°	260° to 280°	255° to 275°
BRITTLES	HARD CRACK (separates into hard and brittle threads)	300° to 310°	296° to 306°	290° to 300°	285° to 295°

* Drop about 1/2 teaspoon of boiling syrup into one cup water, and test firmness of mass with fingers.

Cantaloupe

FRESH FRUIT SALAD

*1 cantaloupe, cut into
    bite-sized pieces
10 strawberries, sliced
1/2 c. blueberries*

*3/4 c. bing cherry halves
1/4 watermelon, diced,
    seeded
2 bananas, sliced*

Combine cantaloupe, strawberries, blueberries, cherry halves and watermelon in large bowl; toss gently. Refrigerate for 3 to 4 hours. Add bananas; toss gently. Serve immediately. Yield: 8 servings.

SUMMER CANTALOUPE SALAD

*1 med. cantaloupe
1/2 honeydew melon
1 papaya
1 lb. seedless grapes
1/2 c. plain low-fat
    yogurt*

*2 tbsp. apricot
    preserves
2 tbsp. fresh orange
    juice*

Peel and seed cantaloupe and honeydew; cut into bite-sized pieces. Peel papaya and cut into bite-sized pieces. Combine melon pieces, papaya pieces and grapes in large bowl. Chill until serving time. Combine yogurt, preserves and orange juice in small bowl; blend well. Add to salad; mix well. Yield: 8 servings.

Caramel

MAGIC COOKIE BARS

*1/2 c. margarine
1 1/2 c. graham cracker
    crumbs
1 14-oz. can
    sweetened condensed
    milk*

*1 c. semisweet
    chocolate chips
1 1/3 c. flaked coconut
1 c. coarsely chopped
    pecans*

Melt margarine in 9x13-inch baking pan in oven. Sprinkle crumbs evenly over margarine. Drizzle with condensed milk. Layer with remaining ingredients in order listed. Press down gently. Bake at 350 degrees for 25 minutes. Cool. Cut into bars. Store, loosely covered, at room temperature. Yield: 24 bars.

CARAMEL BUTTERFLIES

1 lb. caramels	12 oz. semisweet
3 tbsp. whipping cream	chocolate
1 tbsp. margarine	2 tbsp. shortening
3 c. Jordan almonds	Candy sprinkles

Combine caramels, whipping cream and margarine in double boiler. Cook over hot water until caramels melt and are smooth and creamy, stirring constantly. Shape 1 teaspoon caramel mixture into ball. Insert 4 almonds into caramel ball to resemble butterfly wings. Flatten slightly on foil-covered surface. Repeat process until all caramel is used. Cool. Melt chocolate with shortening in double boiler over hot water, stirring constantly. Cool slightly. Spread chocolate over caramel, leaving almond wings uncovered. Decorate with candy sprinkles. Cool. Store in airtight container. Yield: 4 dozen.

GRANDMA'S CARAMEL PIE

1/2 c. butter, softened	1 c. cream
2 c. sugar	5 egg whites
5 egg yolks, beaten	1 tsp. vanilla extract
1 c. damson plum	1 9-in. pie shell
preserves	

Cream butter and sugar in mixer bowl until light. Add egg yolks; mix well. Stir in preserves and cream. Beat egg whites in mixer bowl until stiff peaks form. Fold into preserve mixture with vanilla. Pour into pie shell. Bake at 450 degrees for 10 minutes. Reduce temperature to 325 degrees. Bake for 25 minutes longer or until knife inserted in center comes out clean. Serve warm or cold. Yield: 6 servings.

CARAMEL ICE CREAM PIE

1 c. flour	1 12-oz. jar caramel
1/2 c. melted margarine	ice cream topping
1/4 c. packed brown	1 qt. vanilla ice cream,
sugar	softened
1/2 c. chopped pecans	

Press mixture of flour, melted margarine, brown sugar and pecans to 1/4-inch thickness on baking sheet. Bake at 350 degrees for 10 minutes or until light brown. Crumble into bowl. Reserve 1/4 cup crumbs. Press remaining crumbs into greased pie plate. Drizzle with 3/4 cup caramel topping. Chill in freezer until firm. Spread softened ice cream into frozen crust. Sprinkle with reserved crumbs. Drizzle with remaining caramel topping. Freeze, tightly covered, until serving time. Yield: 6 servings.

Carrot

CARROT BREAD

2 eggs, well beaten	1 1/2 c. sifted flour
1 c. sugar	1 tsp. baking powder
1/2 c. oil	1 tsp. soda
1 c. grated carrot	1/2 tsp. salt
1/2 c. raisins	1 tsp. cinnamon

Beat eggs with sugar and oil in bowl. Stir in carrot and raisins. Add sifted dry ingredients; mix lightly. Pour into greased 4x8-inch loaf pan; smooth top. Bake in 325-degree oven for 1 hour. Cool in pan for 5 minutes. Remove to wire rack to cool completely. Yield: 12 slices.

CARROT CAKE

4 eggs	3 c. finely grated
2 c. sugar	carrots
2 1/2 c. all-purpose flour	1/2 c. margarine,
2 tsp. soda	softened
1/2 tsp. salt	8 oz. cream cheese,
2 tsp. baking powder	softened
2 tsp. cinnamon	2 tsp. vanilla extract
1 1/2 c. oil	1 lb. confectioners'
1 c. chopped pecans	sugar

Beat eggs into sugar 1 at a time in mixer bowl. Add next 5 sifted dry ingredients; mix well. Stir in oil gradually. Beat for 2 minutes. Mix in pecans and carrots. Pour into 3 greased and floured 9-inch cake pans. Bake at 350 degrees for 25 to 30 minutes or until cake tests done. Cool. Blend margarine and cream cheese in bowl. Add vanilla and confectioners' sugar; beat until smooth and creamy. Spread frosting between layers and over top and side of cake. Yield: 16 servings.

GERMAN WINTER CARROT SALAD

8 med. carrots, peeled	8 oz. bacon, chopped
3/4 c. mayonnaise	1 lg. onion, chopped
1 tbsp. parsley flakes	1/2 c. sugar
1/2 tsp. salt	1/2 c. vinegar
1/2 tsp. pepper	

Cook carrots in water to cover in saucepan until tender; drain. Slice carrots. Combine with mayonnaise, parsley, salt and pepper in serving bowl; mix well. Fry bacon in skillet until crisp; drain on paper towel. Sauté onion in bacon drippings in skillet. Stir in sugar and vinegar. Add to carrot mixture; mix well. Sprinkle with bacon. Serve warm. Yield: 4 to 6 servings.

CHEESY CARROT CASSEROLE

2 lbs. carrots, peeled,
  sliced
1 c. shredded Velveeta
  cheese

1/4 c. melted butter
1 1/2 c. buttered
  croutons

Cook carrots in a small amount of water until tender; drain. Place in 2-quart casserole. Cover with cheese and butter. Bake, covered, at 350 degrees for 20 minutes. Stir in croutons. Bake for 10 minutes longer. Yield: 6 to 8 servings.

ORANGE-BUTTERED CARROTS

1 1/2 lbs. sliced
  steamed carrots
1/4 c. melted butter

1/2 6-oz. can frozen
  orange juice
  concentrate

Combine carrots, butter and orange juice concentrate in saucepan. Cook over low heat until carrots are glazed, stirring frequently. Season with salt and pepper to taste. Yield: 4 servings.

FIRESIDE CARROT RING

1 c. margarine,
  softened
1 c. packed light
  brown sugar
2 eggs
2 1/2 c. sifted cake flour
2 tsp. baking powder
1 tsp. soda

3 c. finely grated
  carrots
2 tsp. lemon juice
2 tsp. water
1 16-oz. package
  frozen peas
1 tbsp. melted
  margarine

Cream 1 cup margarine and brown sugar in mixer bowl until light and fluffy. Add eggs 1 at a time, beating well after each addition. Add sifted cake flour, baking powder and soda to creamed mixture; mix well. Stir in carrots, lemon juice and water. Spoon into lightly greased ring mold. Bake at 350 degrees for 50 minutes or until set. Cook peas in a small amount of water in saucepan until tender; drain. Add margarine. Unmold carrot ring onto serving plate. Fill center with peas.
Yield: 8 servings.

ZESTY WINTER CARROTS

6 carrots
2 tbsp. horseradish
2 tbsp. grated onion
1/2 c. mayonnaise
1 tsp. salt

1/4 tsp. pepper
1/4 c. water
1/4 c. bread crumbs
1 tbsp. melted
  margarine

Scrape carrots and cut into thin strips. Cook in water to cover in saucepan until tender; drain. Place in 6x10-inch baking dish. Combine horseradish, onion, mayonnaise, salt, pepper and 1/4 cup water in bowl; mix well. Pour over carrots. Sprinkle with mixture of bread crumbs and margarine. Bake at 375 degrees for 15 minutes. Yield: 4 servings.

Cashew

CASHEW BUTTER

2 tbsp. corn oil
2 c. salted cashews

1 to 3 tbsp. corn oil

Combine 2 tbsp. corn oil and cashews in food processor container. Pulse 15 times. Add 1 to 3 tablespoons corn oil, processing for several pulses or to desired consistency. Spoon into small jars. Store in refrigerator. Mix well before serving. Yield: 1 cup.

CASHEW NUT COOKIES

1 c. margarine,
  softened
1/2 c. confectioners'
  sugar
1/4 tsp. almond extract

2 c. cake flour
1 c. finely ground
  cashews
1 c. sugar

Cream margarine and confectioners' sugar in mixer bowl until light and fluffy. Add almond extract, flour and cashews; mix well. Chill for several hours. Shape into balls. Place on cookie sheet. Flatten with hand. Bake at 325 degrees for 10 minutes; do not brown. Roll hot cookies in sugar. Yield: 4 dozen.

Catfish

DEEP-FRIED CATFISH

8 4-oz. catfish fillets
1/2 c. Dijon mustard
1/4 c. buttermilk
Seafood seasoning
Juice of 2 lemons
1 c. mayonnaise
3 tbsp. Dijon mustard

1 tsp. thyme
1 tsp. chopped garlic
1 tsp. oregano
1 tsp. minced dillweed
Juice of 1 lemon
1/2 c. yellow cornmeal
Peanut oil for frying

Marinate catfish in mixture of next 4 ingredients overnight. Blend mayonnaise and next 6 ingredients in bowl. Chill until serving time. Pat fillets dry. Roll in cornmeal. Brown in hot oil in skillet. Drain on paper towel. Serve with sauce. Yield: 4 servings.

CATFISH STEW

8 oz. salt pork	*Red pepper and*
5 lg. onions	*Tabasco sauce*
1 can cream of	*to taste*
tomato soup	*3 lb. catfish fillets,*
1 soup can water	*skinned*
1/4 c. butter	

Slice salt pork 1/4 inch thick. Rinse to remove excess salt. Fry in heavy saucepan over low heat until crisp. Remove to paper towel. Drain saucepan, reserving 1/4 cup drippings. Cut each onion into 8 wedges. Sauté in drippings in saucepan. Stir in fried salt pork, tomato soup, water and butter. Add red pepper and Tabasco sauce to taste. Season with salt and pepper to taste. Bring to a boil; reduce temperature. Simmer for 10 minutes. Cut fish into serving pieces. Add to stew. Bring to a boil over low heat. Simmer, covered, for 20 minutes, stirring occasionally.
Yield: 6 servings.

Cauliflower

HARVEST CAULIFLOWER SCALLOP

1 med. head cauliflower	*4 hard-boiled eggs,*
3 tbsp. margarine	*sliced*
1/4 c. all-purpose flour	*1 c. shredded*
1 c. warm milk	*American cheese*
1/2 tsp. salt	

Cut cauliflower into flowerets. Cook in a small amount of water in saucepan until tender-crisp; drain. Place in lightly greased 9x13-inch baking dish. Melt margarine in saucepan. Blend in flour. Add milk gradually. Cook until thickened, stirring constantly. Stir in salt. Simmer for 5 minutes. Spoon half the white sauce over cauliflower. Sprinkle with half the cheese. Arrange egg slices over top. Layer remaining white sauce and cheese over eggs. Bake at 350 degrees for 30 minutes.
Yield: 6 servings.

APPLE AND CAULIFLOWER SALAD

1 egg	*1 tsp. poppy seed*
1/2 c. sugar	*1 tsp. sesame seed*
1 tsp. Dijon mustard	*4 lg. unpeeled red*
1 tsp. salt	*Delicious apples*
1/3 c. cider vinegar	*2 c. sliced cauliflower*
1 tbsp. minced onion	*Lemon juice to taste*
1 c. oil	

Combine egg, sugar, mustard, salt, vinegar, and onion in food processor container fitted with steel blade. Process on Low until blended. Add oil gradually, processing constantly until thick. Fold in poppy seed and sesame seed. Core and quarter apples. Slice in food processor container. Combine with cauliflower, desired amount of poppy seed dressing and lemon juice in bowl; toss until coated. Serve in lettuce cups. Good served with roast pork or spareribs, turkey or ham, or with baked beans and dark bread. Yield: 8 servings.

FRESH CAULIFLOWER AND BROCCOLI SALAD

1 head cauliflower	*2 c. mayonnaise-type*
1 head broccoli	*salad dressing*
1 sm. onion, sliced	*1/2 c. sugar*
8 oz. bacon, crisp-	*3 tbsp. vinegar*
fried, crumbled	*8 oz. Cheddar cheese,*
1 1/2 pkg. dry Italian	*shredded*
salad dressing mix	

Wash and drain vegetables; cut into small pieces. Mix vegetables, bacon and salad dressing mix in bowl. Mix salad dressing, sugar, vinegar and cheese in bowl. Pour over vegetable mixture; mix gently. Refrigerate overnight. Yield: 6 cups.

MOCK FALL POTATO SALAD

1 head cauliflower	*Salt and pepper to taste*
3 stalks celery, chopped	*2 tablespoons pickle*
1/2 green bell pepper,	*relish*
chopped	*1/2 c. mayonnaise*

Cook whole cauliflower as desired until tender. Chill. Break cauliflower into pieces; place in large bowl. Add chopped celery, green pepper and remaining ingredients; mix well. Chill until serving time. Yield: 6 servings.

Celery

ORIENTAL CELERY 🍎

1/2 c. chicken broth	*2 tbsp. minced onion*
1 tbsp. cornstarch	*2 tbsp. margarine*
1/4 tsp. ginger	*6 c. 1/2-inch diagonal*
2 tbsp. soy sauce	*celery slices*

Blend chicken broth, cornstarch, ginger and soy sauce in bowl; set aside. Stir-fry onion in margarine in skillet for 1 minute. Add celery. Stir-fry for 6 to 8 minutes or until tender-crisp. Add broth mixture. Cook over low heat until thickened. May add water chestnuts, mushrooms, nuts or leftover chopped cooked chicken or meat. Yield: 6 servings.

CELERY CASSEROLE

3 c. chopped celery	1 c. chicken broth
1/4 c. slivered almonds	3/4 c. half and half
1 8-oz. can water chestnuts, drained, chopped	1/2 c. sliced canned mushrooms, drained
3 tbsp. margarine, melted	1/2 c. Parmesan cheese
	1/2 c. bread crumbs
3 tbsp. all-purpose flour	2 tbsp. margarine

Parboil celery in saucepan for 5 minutes; drain. Combine celery, almonds and water chestnuts in 9x13-inch baking dish. Blend 3 tablespoons margarine and flour in saucepan. Stir in chicken broth and half and half gradually. Cook over low heat for 5 minutes or until thickened, stirring constantly. Stir in mushrooms. Pour over celery mixture. Sprinkle with Parmesan cheese and bread crumbs. Dot with 2 tablespoons margarine. Bake at 350 degrees until hot and bubbly. Yield: 6 servings.

Charlotte

HOLIDAY ORANGE CHARLOTTE

6 egg yolks	1 tbsp. unflavored gelatin
1 c. sugar	1/2 c. cold water
Juice and grated rind of 1 orange	6 egg whites
Juice and grated rind of 1 lemon	

Beat egg yolks and sugar in double boiler until light and lemon-colored. Add juices and grated rinds; mix well. Cook until thickened, stirring constantly. Cool. Soften gelatin in cold water in double boiler for 5 minutes. Heat over hot water until dissolved. Add to egg yolk mixture; mix well. Beat egg whites in mixer bowl until stiff peaks form. Fold gently into egg mixture. Line 2-quart mold with ladyfingers. Spoon in orange mixture. Chill until set. Unmold onto serving plate. Garnish with whipped cream. Yield: 8 servings.

COUNTRY CHARLOTTE WITH BERRY SAUCE

3 envelopes unflavored gelatin	2 10-oz. packages frozen strawberries
3 c. milk	1 tbsp. orange juice
12 egg yolks	1 c. whipping cream, whipped
1 1/2 c. sugar	
1 tbsp. vanilla extract	1 5 1/2-oz. package chocolate-laced pirouettes
1 1/2 c. whipping cream	
1 1/2 c. sour cream	

Soften gelatin in milk in saucepan for 5 minutes. Heat over low heat until gelatin dissolves, stirring constantly. Beat egg yolks and sugar in bowl. Add hot milk mixture gradually, beating constantly. Pour into saucepan. Cook over low heat just until mixture coats silver spoon, stirring constantly. Stir in vanilla. Cover surface of custard with plastic wrap. Chill until completely thickened. Beat 1 1/2 cups whipping cream and sour cream in mixer bowl until soft peaks form. Fold into custard with sour cream. Pour into lightly oiled 8-inch springform pan. Chill for 6 hours to overnight. Purée thawed strawberries with 1 tablespoon orange juice in blender. Chill until serving time. Loosen custard from side of pan with sharp knife. Remove side of pan. Place on serving plate. Spread very thin layer of whipped cream around side of custard. Press pirouettes into whipped cream about 1/2 inch apart. Pipe remaining whipped cream between pirouettes. Pipe rosettes around top edge of custard. Spoon a small amount of strawberry sauce into center. Serve with remaining strawberry sauce. Use 2 envelopes gelatin if serving Charlotte in crystal bowl. Yield: 12 to 14 servings.

Cheese

BRIE WITH BRANDY AND PECANS

1/4 c. packed light brown sugar	1/4 c. chopped pecans
2 tbsp. Brandy	1 8 to 12-oz. wheel Brie

Combine first 3 ingredients in saucepan. Cook over low heat until blended, stirring frequently. Place Brie in baking dish. Pour Brandy mixture over Brie. Bake at 400 degrees for 10 minutes or until softened. Serve with apple slices or crackers. Yield: 12 servings.

SOUTHWESTERN CHEESE BALL

16 oz. cream cheese, softened	1 c. shredded Cheddar cheese
1 c. chopped black olives	2 tbsp. grated onion
	Garlic salt and pepper to taste
1 c. chopped ham	
3 jalapeño peppers	Chopped pecans

Combine cream cheese, black olives, ham, jalapeño peppers, Cheddar cheese, onion and seasonings in bowl; mix well. Shape into ball. Roll in chopped pecans. Refrigerate until firm. Yield: 1 cheese ball.

CHEESE CHART

CHEESE	GOES WITH	USE FOR	FLAVOR, TEXTURE
Blue (France)	Fresh fruit Bland crackers	Dessert Dips, Salads	Marbled, blue-veined, semisoft, piquant
Brie (France)	Fresh fruit	Dessert Snack	Soft, edible crust, creamy
Brick (U.S.)	Crackers Bread	Sandwiches Snack	Semisoft, mild, cream-colored to orange
Camembert (France)	Apples	Dessert Snack	Mild to pungent, edible crust, yellow
Cheddar (England)	Fresh fruit Crackers	Dessert Cooking, Snack	Mild to sharp, cream-colored to orange
Cottage (U.S.)	Canned or Fresh fruit	Fruit salads Cooking	Soft, moist, mild, white
Cream (U.S.)	Crackers and Jelly	Dessert, Cooking Sandwiches	Soft, smooth, mild, white
Edam (Holland)	Fresh fruit	Dessert Snack	Firm, mild, red wax coating
Feta (Greece)	Greek salad	Salad Cooking	Salty, crumbly, white
Gouda (Holland)	Fresh fruit Crackers	Dessert Snack	Softer than Edam, mild, nutty
Gruyére (Switzerland)	Fresh fruit	Dessert Fondue	Nutty, bland, firm, tiny holes
Mozzarella (Italy)	Italian foods	Cooking Pizza	Semisoft, delicate, mild, white
Muenster (Germany)	Crackers Bread	Sandwiches Snack	Semisoft, mild to mellow
Parmesan (Italy)	Italian foods	Cooking	Hard, brittle, sharp, light yellow
Port Salut (France)	Fresh fruit Crackers	Dessert Snack	Buttery, semisoft
Provolone (Italy)	Italian foods	Cooking Dessert	Salty, smoky, mild to sharp, hard
Ricotta (Italy)	Italian foods	Cooking Fillings	Soft, creamy, bland, white
Roquefort (France)	Bland crackers Fresh fruit	Dips, Salads Dessert	Semisoft, sharp blue-veined, crumbly
Swiss (Switzerland)	Fresh fruit French bread	Cooking, Snack Sandwiches	Sweetish, nutty, holes, pale yellow

SPICY CHEESE MOLD

1 lb. Velveeta cheese, chopped	1 lb. mild Cheddar cheese, shredded
1 lb. sharp Cheddar cheese, shredded	1 lb. hot sausage

Melt cheeses in top of double boiler. Cook sausage in skillet until brown and crumbly; drain. Mix cheeses and sausage together. Pour into well-greased bundt or ring mold. Chill until firm. Unmold onto serving platter. Yield: 1 cheese mold.

MOZZARELLA CARROZZA

8 thin slices bread, trimmed	All-purpose flour
2 tbsp. melted butter	2 eggs, beaten
3/4 lb. mozzarella cheese, thinly sliced	Salt and pepper to taste
	1/2 c. butter

Brush bread with melted butter. Place cheese between buttered bread. Dip in flour, then in beaten egg. Season with salt and pepper. Fry in 1/2 cup butter in skillet until golden. Yield: 4 servings.

CHEESE ROLLS

1 36-count pkg. Parker House rolls	1/2 c. margarine, softened
1 c. mayonnaise	1 c. Parmesan cheese

Separate rolls. Blend mayonnaise, margarine and cheese in bowl. Coat rolls on all sides with margarine mixture; place on lightly greased baking sheet. Bake at 350 degrees for 15 minutes or until hot and bubbly. Yield: 3 dozen rolls.

GARDEN ZUCCHINI-CHEDDAR BREAD

1 c. chopped onion	1/4 c. milk
1/4 c. margarine	3 eggs
2 1/2 c. buttermilk baking mix	1 1/2 c. shredded zucchini
1 tbsp. minced parsley	1 c. shredded Cheddar cheese
1/2 tsp. dried basil leaves	3/4 c. toasted chopped almonds
1/2 tsp. dried thyme leaves	

Sauté onion in margarine in skillet until tender. Cool slightly. Combine with baking mix and next 5 ingredients in bowl. Beat vigorously for 1 minute. Stir in zucchini, Cheddar cheese and almonds. Spread in greased and floured 9-inch round baking pan. Bake at 400 degrees for 40 minutes or until toothpick inserted in center comes out clean. Cool slightly before removing from pan. Yield: 12 slices.

THREE-CHEESE CASSEROLE

1/2 c. butter, softened	Paprika to taste
20 slices bread, crusts trimmed	4 eggs
2 c. shredded Cheddar cheese	2 c. milk
	1 tsp. salt
2 c. sliced Swiss cheese	1/4 c. Sherry
12 oz. whipped cream cheese	1/8 tsp. pepper
	1 tsp. dried onion
	1 tsp. dry mustard

Grease bottom and sides of 9x13-inch glass baking dish. Spread butter on each side of bread. Alternate layers of bread, shredded cheese, bread, Swiss cheese and whipped cream cheese in prepared baking dish. Combine paprika, eggs, milk, salt, Sherry, pepper, onion and mustard in bowl; mix well. Pour over layers. Cover with foil. Chill overnight. Bake at 350 degrees for 1 hour. Yield: 8 servings.

CHEESE SOUFFLÉ

3 tbsp. butter	1/2 c. Parmesan cheese
3 tbsp. all-purpose flour	1/2 c. shredded Cheddar cheese
1 c. milk	2 tbsp. Parmesan cheese
3 eggs, separated	

Melt butter in small saucepan. Add flour. Cook over low heat for 2 minutes, stirring constantly. Stir in milk gradually. Cook until smooth and thick, stirring constantly. Cool for 2 minutes. Stir in lightly beaten egg yolks, 1/2 cup Parmesan cheese and Cheddar cheese. Beat egg whites in bowl until stiff peaks form. Stir a small amount of egg whites into cheese mixture. Fold in remaining egg whites gently. Butter side and bottom of straight-sided 7 1/2-inch souffle dish. Sprinkle with 2 tablespoons Parmesan cheese. Add souffle mixture. Bake at 350 degrees for 25 to 30 minutes or until puffed and browned. Yield: 3 servings.

EASY CHEESE SOUFFLÉ

4 slices bread	2 c. milk
1 tsp. dry mustard	1/8 to 1/4 tsp. garlic powder
3 eggs	1/2 tsp. salt
1 5-oz. jar Old English cheese spread	1/4 tsp. cayenne pepper
	Paprika to taste

Trim bread and tear into pieces. Place in greased baking dish. Sprinkle with dry mustard. Combine next 6 ingredients in blender container; process until smooth. Pour over bread. Sprinkle with paprika. Chill overnight. Let stand at room temperature for 1 hour before baking. Bake at 300 degrees for 45 to 60 minutes or until set and brown. Yield: 4 servings.

CHEDDAR CHEESE PIE

3 c. shredded sharp Cheddar cheese	*1/2 tsp. salt*
1 tsp. instant minced onion	*3 eggs*
1/2 tsp. Worcestershire sauce	*1 partially baked 9-in. pie shell*
1/2 tsp. dry mustard	*6 med. tomatoes, peeled, sliced*

Combine cheese, onion, Worcestershire sauce, dry mustard and salt in saucepan. Heat over low heat until cheese is melted, stirring constantly. Remove from heat. Beat eggs in large bowl until frothy. Add cheese mixture; mix well. Pour into pie shell. Bake at 325 degrees for 25 minutes or just until filling is set. Arrange tomatoes in overlapping ring around edge of pie. Bake for 15 minutes longer. Garnish center with green bell pepper if desired. Yield: 6 servings.

Cheesecake

NEW YORK CHEESECAKE

2 1/4 c. graham cracker crumbs	*40 oz. cream cheese, softened*
4 1/2 tbsp. sugar	*6 eggs, at room temperature*
3/4 c. melted butter	*1 1/2 tsp. vanilla extract*
1 1/2 c. sugar	

Combine graham cracker crumbs, 4 1/2 tablespoons sugar and melted butter in bowl; mix well. Press over bottom and side of greased 9-inch springform pan. Bake at 350 degrees for 10 minutes. Beat 1 1/2 cups sugar and cream cheese in mixer bowl. Add eggs 1 at a time, beating well after each addition. Beat in vanilla. Bake at 350 degrees for 45 minutes. Reduce temperature to 250 degrees. Bake for 45 minutes. Turn off oven. Let stand in oven with door ajar until cool. Chill in refrigerator. Place on serving plate; remove side of pan. Yield: 16 servings.

REFRIGERATOR CHEESECAKE

1 sm. package lemon gelatin	*1 c. sugar*
1 c. boiling water	*1 tsp. vanilla extract*
2 pkg. whipped topping mix	*1 graham cracker pie shell*
8 oz. cream cheese, softened	*Graham cracker crumbs*

Dissolve gelatin in boiling water in bowl. Chill until slightly thickened. Prepare topping mix according to package directions. Beat cream cheese in mixer bowl until light. Add sugar and vanilla; beat until fluffy. Add gelatin; mix well. Fold in whipped topping. Spoon into pie shell. Garnish with graham cracker crumbs. Chill for 2 hours or longer. Yield: 6 to 8 servings.

SOUR CREAM CHEESECAKE

1 1/2 c. graham cracker crumbs	*6 egg yolks*
3 tbsp. sugar	*2 c. sour cream*
1/4 c. melted butter	*1/3 c. all-purpose flour*
1/2 tsp. cinnamon	*Grated rind of 1 lemon*
24 oz. cream cheese, softened	*Juice of 1/2 lemon*
1 1/4 c. sugar	*2 tsp. vanilla extract*
	6 egg whites

Combine cracker crumbs, 3 tablespoons sugar, butter and cinnamon in bowl; mix well. Press over bottom and side of greased 9-inch springform pan. Chill in refrigerator. Beat cream cheese in mixer bowl until light. Add 1 1/4 cups sugar gradually, beating until fluffy. Beat in egg yolks 1 at a time. Add sour cream, flour, lemon rind, lemon juice and vanilla; mix well. Beat egg whites in bowl until stiff peaks form. Fold gently into creamed mixture. Spoon into crust. Bake at 350 degrees for 1 hour and 15 minutes. Turn off oven. Let cheesecake stand in closed oven for 1 hour. Cool in pan on wire rack for 4 hours or longer. Chill overnight. Place on serving plate; remove side of pan. Yield: 10 servings.

TEXAS CHEESECAKE

8 eggs	*2 tbsp. cinnamon*
2 c. sugar	*3 tbsp. sugar*
3 lb. cream cheese, softened	*3 tbsp. melted butter*
16 graham crackers, crushed	*1 pt. sour cream*
	2 tbsp. sugar
	1 tsp. vanilla extract

Combine eggs, 2 cups sugar and cream cheese in mixer bowl. Beat for 20 minutes. Mix graham cracker crumbs, cinnamon, 3 tablespoons sugar and 3 tablespoons melted butter in bowl. Press into large springform pan. Pour cream cheese mixture into prepared pan. Bake at 325 for 45 minutes. Mix sour cream with 2 tablespoons sugar and vanilla. Remove from oven. Let stand for 10 minutes. Pour sour cream mixture over top. Bake for 10 minutes longer. Turn off oven. Let stand in closed oven until cool enough to handle. Cool to room temperature. Chill for 8 hours or longer. Increase baking time to 1 hour when using gas oven. Yield: 24 servings.

Cherry

CHERRY MASH BALLS

1 16-oz. package
   confectioners' sugar
1/4 c. melted margarine
1 11-oz. package
   cherry frosting mix
1/2 14-oz. can
   sweetened condensed
   milk

2 tsp. vanilla extract
1 4-oz. jar maraschino
   cherries, drained,
   chopped
1 12-oz. package milk
   chocolate chips
1 oz. paraffin, chopped
8 oz. peanuts, ground

Combine confectioners' sugar, margarine, frosting mix, condensed milk and vanilla in bowl; mix until smooth and creamy. Add chopped cherries to frosting mixture. Chill until firm enough to handle. Shape into small balls. Place in single layer on foil-covered tray. Freeze until firm. Combine chocolate chips and paraffin in double boiler. Heat over hot water until melted, stirring constantly. Stir in peanuts. Dip candy balls into chocolate mixture to coat; place on foil-lined tray. Cool. Store, covered, in refrigerator. Yield: 3 pounds.

CHERRY DELIGHTS

4 egg whites
1 c. sugar
1/2 tsp. baking powder
1 c. chopped walnuts
40 Ritz crackers, finely
   crushed
8 oz. cream cheese,
   softened

1 c. confectioners'
   sugar
1 tsp. sugar
1 8-oz. container
   whipped topping
1 21-oz. can cherry pie
   filling

Beat egg whites in mixer bowl until soft peaks form. Add sugar gradually, beating until stiff. Fold in baking powder, walnuts and crumbs. Press about 1/2 inch thick into bottoms of well-greased muffin cups. Bake at 350 degrees for 10 to 12 minutes. Cool. Loosen from side of cup. Cool on wire rack. Beat cream cheese with next 3 ingredients until smooth. Drop by spoonfuls onto cups. Top with cherry pie filling. Chill until serving time. Yield: 2 dozen.

CHERRY-BERRY ON A CLOUD

6 egg whites, at
   room temperature
1/2 tsp. cream of tartar
1 1/2 c. sugar
2 c. whipping cream
1 c. sugar
2 c. miniature
   marshmallows

6 oz. cream cheese,
   softened
1 20-oz. can cherry
   pie filling
2 c. sliced strawberries
1 tsp. lemon juice

Beat egg whites in bowl until foamy. Add cream of tartar. Beat until soft peaks form. Add 1 1/2 cups sugar gradually, beating until very stiff peaks form. Spread in greased 9x13-inch baking pan. Bake at 275 for 1 hour. Turn off oven. Let stand in closed oven for 12 hours. Do not open oven during standing time. Whip cream in bowl until soft peaks form. Fold in 1 cup sugar, marshmallows and cream cheese gently. Spread over meringue. Chill for 12 hours. Combine remaining ingredients in bowl; mix well. Spoon over cream layer. Chill until serving time. Yield: 12 to 15 servings.

CHERRY CHOCOLATE SUPREME

1/2 c. all-purpose flour
1/4 c. confectioners'
   sugar
1/4 c. margarine,
   softened
1 egg yolk
1 c. chocolate chips
2 tbsp. milk
1 egg yolk

1 3-oz. package
   vanilla instant
   pudding mix
1 1/2 c. milk
1 20-oz. can cherry
   pie filling
2 c. whipped topping
Chocolate curls

Combine flour and confectioners' sugar in bowl. Cut in margarine until crumbly. Stir in 1 egg yolk. Pat into greased 9x9-inch baking pan. Bake at 375 degrees for 8 minutes. Cool. Melt chocolate chips in 2 tablespoons milk in double boiler. Cool slightly. Blend in remaining egg yolk. Spread over cooled crust. Combine pudding mix and 1 1/2 cups milk in bowl. Beat until thickened. Spread over chocolate layer. Spoon 1 1/2 cups pie filling and whipped topping over pudding. Chill, covered, for several hours. Top with remaining pie filling and chocolate curls. Yield: 12 servings.

CHERRY SPLIT DESSERT

3 c. graham cracker
   crumbs
3/4 c. melted margarine
2 20-oz. cans cherry
   pie filling
1/2 gal. vanilla ice
   cream, sliced
1 c. chopped walnuts

2 c. chocolate chips
1/2 c. margarine
2 c. confectioners'
   sugar
1 1/2 c. milk
1 tsp. vanilla extract
2 c. whipping cream,
   whipped

Mix cracker crumbs with 3/4 cup margarine in bowl. Layer 2 cups crumb mixture, pie filling and ice cream in 9x13-inch pan. Sprinkle with walnuts. Freeze for 1 to 2 1/2 hours. Melt chocolate chips and 1/2 cup margarine in saucepan over low heat, stirring constantly. Add confectioners' sugar and milk. Bring to a boil, stirring constantly. Cook until thickened. Add vanilla. Cool. Spread over frozen mixture. Freeze for 1 to 2 1/2 hours. Top with whipped cream and remaining crumb mixture.

Freeze for 12 hours or longer. Let stand at room temperature for 5 to 10 minutes before serving. Yield: 15 servings.

WHOLE-GRAIN CHERRY CRISP

1 21-oz. can cherry   2 tbsp. toasted wheat
  pie filling   germ
1/2 c. whole wheat flour 1/2 c. sugar
1/2 c. old-fashioned oats 1/3 c. margarine
2 tbsp. bran (opt.)

Pour pie filling into 9-inch round baking pan. Combine remaining ingredients in food processor container or bowl; mix until crumbly. Pat evenly over pie filling. Bake at 350 degrees for 35 to 40 minutes. Serve warm or cold with ice cream or whipped topping. Yield: 6 servings.

CHERRY SALAD

1 21-oz. can cherry   1 c. miniature
  pie filling   marshmallows
1 16-oz. can crushed 1/2 c. chopped pecans
  pineapple, drained 1 12-oz. carton frozen
1 14-oz. can   whipped topping,
  sweetened   thawed
  condensed milk

Combine pie filling, pineapple, condensed milk, marshmallows and pecans in bowl; mix well. Fold in whipped topping. Chill until serving time. Yield: 6 servings.

CHERRY COLA SALAD

1 21-oz. can cherry   1 7-oz. can juice-
  pie filling   pack crushed
1/2 c. water   pineapple
1 6-oz. package   1 8-oz. container
  cherry gelatin   whipped topping
1 10-oz. bottle of cola 3 oz. cream cheese
1/2 c. chopped pecans

Mix pie filling and water in saucepan. Bring to a boil. Add gelatin; stir until dissolved. Remove from heat. Add cola, pecans and pineapple. Pour into 8-inch square pan. Chill until firm. Beat whipped topping and cream cheese in bowl until smooth. Spread over gelatin. Yield: 8 servings.

REGAL CHERRY SALAD

1 17-oz. can pitted   1 tsp. lemon juice
  very sweet cherries 1 banana, sliced
1 3-oz. package   1 c. sour cream
  black cherry gelatin 1/3 c. chopped pecans
11/2 c. boiling water

Drain cherries, reserving syrup. Dissolve gelatin in water in bowl. Add reserved syrup. Pour into 8x8-inch dish. Chill until set. Sprinkle lemon juice over banana in bowl. Add cherries. Pour over congealed layer. Chill until firm. Spread sour cream over fruit layer. Sprinkle with pecans. Serve on lettuce-lined plates. Yield: 9 servings.

FROSTY CHERRY SOUP

1 lb. dark sweet   1 stick cinnamon
  cherries, pitted   3 tbsp. sugar
1 c. dry red wine   2 tbsp. cornstarch
1 lemon, sliced,   2 tbsp. lemon juice
  seeded

Combine cherries, wine, lemon and cinnamon stick in 21/2-quart saucepan. Bring to a boil on medium-high heat. Cook for 10 minutes or until thickened, stirring constantly. Cool slightly. Pour half the mixture into blender or food processor container. Blend until smooth. Transfer to bowl. Repeat with remaining cherry mixture. Mix sugar and cornstarch. Stir into cherry mixture. Add lemon juice. Pour into saucepan. Bring to a boil over medium-high heat, stirring constantly. Cool to room temperature. Chill in refrigerator. Garnish each serving with lemon slice and dollop of sour cream. Yield: 6 servings.

CHERRY PIE

3/4 c. cherry juice   1 c. whole wheat
2 tbsp. cornstarch   pastry flour
1/3 c. honey   1/2 tsp. salt
3 c. sour cherries,   2 tbsp. nonfat dry milk
  drained   powder
1 tbsp. margarine   3/4 c. shortening
1/8 tsp. almond extract 1/3 c. low-fat (1%) milk
1 c. unbleached flour

Blend cherry juice with cornstarch in saucepan. Stir in honey. Cook until thickened and clear; remove from heat. Add cherries, margarine and almond extract. Mix unbleached flour, whole wheat flour, salt and dry milk powder in large bowl. Cut in shortening with pastry blender until crumbly. Stir in milk with fork to form dough. Divide into 2 slightly unequal portions. Roll larger portion on floured surface. Fit into 9-inch pie plate. Fill with cherry mixture. Roll remaining pastry. Cut into strips. Weave strips into lattice on top of pie. Trim and flute pastry. Place 3-inch wide strip of foil over rim of pastry. Bake at 350 degrees for 45 minutes or until golden brown. Yield: 6 servings.

Chess

CHESS BARS

1 2-layer pkg. yellow cake mix	8 oz. cream cheese, softened
1/2 c. margarine, softened	1 16-oz. package confectioners' sugar
3 eggs	1 tsp. lemon extract

Mix cake mix, margarine and 1 egg in mixer bowl. Press into greased 9x13-inch baking pan. Combine remaining ingredients in mixer bowl; mix well. Pour over cake mix layer. Bake at 325 degrees for 55 minutes or until brown. Center will fall as mixture cools. Cut into bars. Yield: 24 bars.

CHOCOLATE CHESS PIE

6 tbsp. (scant) melted butter	3 tbsp. baking unsweetened cocoa
3 tbsp. all-purpose flour	1/2 c. milk
1 1/2 c. sugar	1/2 tsp. vanilla extract
2 eggs	1 unbaked 9-inch deep-dish pie shell

Combine butter, flour and sugar in mixer bowl; mix well. Blend in eggs. Mix cocoa with enough water to make a paste. Stir in milk and vanilla. Add to sugar mixture, mixing well. Pour into 9-inch deep-dish pie shell. Bake at 375 degrees for 45 minutes. Yield: 8 servings.

Chestnut

CHESTNUT STUFFING

1 lb. chestnuts	1 1/2 tsp. salt
1 c. melted margarine	3/4 tsp. pepper
1 c. minced onion	1/3 c. chopped parsley
1 tsp. thyme	3/4 c. chopped celery
1 tsp. sage	8 c. soft bread crumbs

Slash flat side of chestnuts. Place in saucepan. Add enough water to cover. Bring to a boil. Cook for 1 minute. Remove outer shells and inner skins. Cook in boiling water to cover for 35 minutes or until tender. Drain and chop. Combine chestnuts with margarine, onion, seasonings, parsley, celery and bread crumbs in large bowl; mix lightly. Yield: Stuffing for one 12-pound goose.

BEEF AND CHESTNUTS

3 lbs. lean beef	1/4 tsp. pepper
1 1/2 lbs. mushrooms	1 tsp. instant beef bouillon
1 lb. carrots	1 1/4 c. water
1 lb. small white onions	1 16-oz. can chestnuts, drained
1 bunch celery	
6 slices bacon	2 tbsp. all-purpose flour
2 tbsp. corn oil	
1 c. dry red wine	1/4 c. water
2 tsp. sugar	1 tbsp. minced parsley
1 tsp. salt	

Cut beef into 1 1/2-inch cubes. Cut mushrooms into halves. Peel and chop carrots. Peel onions. Chop celery and bacon. Brown beef 1/2 at a time in oil in 5-quart saucepan over medium-high heat. Remove beef with slotted spoon. Sauté mushrooms in pan drippings, adding a small amount of additional oil if necessary. Remove with slotted spoon. Add carrots, onions, celery and bacon. Sauté until vegetables are browned. Add wine, sugar, salt, pepper, bouillon and 1 1/4 cups water. Bring to a boil; reduce heat. Simmer, covered, over low heat for 1 1/2 hours or until beef is tender, stirring occasionally. Add mushrooms and chestnuts. Cook for 15 minutes. Skim fat. Blend flour and 1/4 cup water in small bowl. Stir into beef mixture. Cook over medium heat until thickened, stirring constantly. Pour into serving dish. Sprinkle with parsley. Yield: 12 servings.

Chicken

CHICKEN BREAST APPETIZERS 🍎

4 chicken breast filets	1 med. yellow bell pepper, cut into strips
2 tbsp. soy sauce	
2 c. shredded bok choy	2 c. chopped celery
2 c. shredded spinach	1 to 2 tbsp. chopped cilantro
1 med. red bell pepper, cut into strips	1/2 c. picante sauce

Place chicken in saucepan with 2 tablespoons soy sauce and water to cover. Simmer over medium heat for 10 minutes. Keep warm. Combine bok choy, spinach, red and yellow peppers and celery on large platter. Cut chicken breasts lengthwise 1 at a time into thin slices, retaining filet shape. Place on vegetables. Sprinkle with cilantro. Serve with picante sauce. Yield: 12 servings.

➡
Recipes for this photograph are on pages 58, 141 and 144.

Menu
Menu
Menu
Menu
Menu
Menu
Menu
Menu
Menu
Menu
Menu
Menu
Menu
Menu
Menu
Menu
Menu
Menu
Menu
Menu
Menu

Country Spring Picnic

Spring Strawberry Soup
page 163

Golden Garden Rice Salad
page 144

Roasted Chicken
page 58

Sweet Pepper Chutney
page 58

Marinated Olives
page 119

Raisin and Apple Cake
page 141

Lemon and Coconut Cooler
page 102

*Take advantage of Spring's invitation to go
outdoors with a refreshing picnic feast. With all the
food prepared ahead, you can make any
outdoor gathering an occasion for celebration.*

CHICKEN FINGERS

12 chicken breast filets	*1 tsp. pepper*
2 tbsp. lemon juice	*4 c. soft bread crumbs*
1¹/2 c. buttermilk	*¹/2 c. sesame seed*
2 tsp. soy sauce	*¹/4 c. melted margarine*
2 tsp. Worcestershire	*¹/4 c. melted shortening*
* sauce*	*1¹/2 c. red plum jam*
2 cloves of garlic,	*1¹/4 tbsp. mustard*
* minced*	*1¹/2 tbsp. horseradish*
1 tsp. paprika	*1¹/2 tsp. lemon juice*
1 tsp. salt	

Cut chicken into ¹/2-inch strips. Combine 2 tablespoons lemon juice with next 7 ingredients in bowl; mix well. Add chicken. Marinate in refrigerator overnight. Drain well. Combine bread crumbs and sesame seed in bowl. Add chicken a little at a time, coating well. Place in 2 greased 9x13-inch baking dishes. Brush with mixture of margarine and shortening. Bake at 350 degrees for 35 to 40 minutes or until brown. Heat jam, mustard, horseradish and 1¹/2 teaspoons lemon juice to serving temperature in saucepan. Pour into serving bowl. Serve with chicken fingers.
Yield: 12 to 14 servings.

CHICKEN WING APPETIZERS

5 lb. (about 36)	*¹/2 tsp. soy sauce*
* chicken wings*	*1 tsp. ginger*
1 c. spiced peach juice	*1 tsp. salt*
2 tsp. lemon juice	

Cut wings into 3 pieces, discarding wing tip pieces. Place remaining chicken pieces in foil-lined 15x18-inch baking pan. Combine remaining ingredients in bowl. Brush over chicken. Bake at 350 degrees for 1¹/2 hours, turning chicken and basting with sauce frequently. Yield: 12 servings.

CHICKEN MOUSSE SUPREME

3 env. unflavored	*1¹/2 c. finely diced*
* gelatin*	* celery*
¹/2 c. cold water	*1 tsp. Worcestershire*
1 10-oz. can cream of	* sauce*
* chicken soup*	*1¹/2 tbsp. grated onion*
2¹/2 c. chicken broth	*2 tbsp. lemon juice*
2 tsp. salt	*2 tbsp. chopped parsley*
¹/4 tsp. pepper	*1 c. whipping cream,*
1 c. mayonnaise	* whipped*
5 c. chopped cooked	*1 8-oz. bottle of*
* chicken*	* French dressing*

Soften gelatin in cold water. Combine soup, broth, salt and pepper in saucepan. Cook until hot and blended, stirring frequently. Add gelatin; stir until dissolved. Cool. Blend in mayonnaise. Add chicken and next 5 ingredients. Fold in whipped cream.

Spoon into 3-quart ring mold rinsed with cold water. Chill for 4 hours or until set. Unmold onto lettuce-lined serving plate. Serve with French dressing. Yield: 16 servings.

CHICKEN AND RICE SUMMER SALAD

1 pkg. long grain and	*¹/3 c. milk*
* wild rice mix*	*¹/3 c. lemon juice*
4 chicken breasts,	*1 c. crushed almonds*
* cooked, chopped*	*2 c. white grape*
1 sm. onion, grated	* quarters*
²/3 c. mayonnaise	

Cook rice mix according to package directions. Combine hot rice with chicken and onion in bowl. Mix in mayonnaise, milk and lemon juice. Cool. Stir in almonds and grapes gently. Chill until serving time. Yield: 8 servings.

FLYING FARMER'S CHICKEN SALAD

5 c. chopped cooked	*1¹/2 c. mayonnaise*
* chicken*	*1¹/2 c. chopped celery*
2 tbsp. orange juice	*¹/2 c. small green*
2 tbsp. corn oil	* grapes*
2 tbsp. vinegar	*1 13-oz. can pineapple*
1 tsp. salt	* chunks*
3 c. cooled cooked rice	*1 c. toasted sliced*
1 11-oz. can mandarin	* almonds*
* oranges*	

Marinate chicken in mixture of orange juice, oil, vinegar and salt in bowl for several minutes. Combine rice and remaining ingredients in salad bowl. Add chicken; toss gently. Chill until serving time. Yield: 6 to 8 servings.

MANDARIN CHICKEN SALAD

2 c. chopped cooked	*1 c. chopped mandarin*
* chicken*	* oranges*
1 tbsp. minced onion	*1 c. cooked macaroni*
¹/2 tsp. salt	* rings*
1 c. seedless green	*1 c. mayonnaise-type*
* grape halves*	* salad dressing*
1 c. chopped celery	*1 c. whipping cream,*
¹/3 c. slivered almonds	* whipped*

Combine chicken, onion and salt in bowl. Chill for 1 hour. Add grapes, celery, almonds, oranges and macaroni. Add salad dressing; mix well. Chill until serving time. Fold in whipped cream just before serving. Serve on lettuce-lined plates. Yield: 8 servings.

LAYERED CHICKEN SALAD

1 sm. head lettuce, torn
1 10-oz. package
  frozen peas, thawed
3 5-oz. cans chunky
  chicken
1 c. sour cream
1 1/2 c. mayonnaise
1/3 c. minced fresh
  parsley
2 1/2 tsp. dried dillweed
1 1/2 tsp. Beau Monde
  seasoning
1/4 tsp. garlic powder
1 1/2 c. shredded carrots
4 hard-cooked eggs,
  sliced
1 1/2 c. thinly sliced
  celery
1 sm. red onion, thinly
  sliced
1/4 c. Parmesan cheese
8 slices crisp-fried
  bacon, crumbled

Layer lettuce and peas in large salad bowl. Drain chicken, reserving broth. Mix reserved broth, sour cream and next 5 ingredients in small bowl. Spread half the mixture evenly over peas. Add layers of carrots, chicken, eggs, celery and onion. Spread remaining sour cream mixture over top, sealing to edge of bowl. Sprinkle with Parmesan cheese. Chill, covered, overnight. Sprinkle bacon on top just before serving. Yield: 10 to 12 servings.

BAKED CHICKEN REUBEN

8 chicken breast filets
1/4 tsp. salt
1/8 tsp. pepper
1 16-oz. can
  sauerkraut
4 slices Swiss cheese
1 1/4 c. Thousand
  Island salad dressing
1 tbsp. chopped fresh
  parsley

Arrange chicken in greased baking pan. Sprinkle with salt and pepper. Drain sauerkraut; squeeze dry. Spread over chicken; top with Swiss cheese. Pour salad dressing evenly over cheese. Cover with foil. Bake at 325 degrees for about 1 1/2 hours. Sprinkle with parsley. Yield: 4 servings.

BARBECUED CHICKEN

1/4 c. vinegar
1/2 c. water
1/2 tsp. salt
1/4 tsp. cayenne pepper
1 clove of garlic,
  minced
Juice of 1 lemon
1 large onion, sliced
2 tbsp. light brown
  sugar
1 tbsp. prepared
  mustard
1/2 tsp. pepper
1/4 c. margarine
1/2 c. catsup
2 tbsp. Worcestershire
  sauce
1 1/2 tsp. liquid smoke
6 to 8 chicken pieces

Combine first 11 ingredients in saucepan. Cook for 20 minutes. Add catsup and next 2 ingredients; mix well. Place chicken in roasting pan. Pour half the sauce over chicken. Bake at 325 degrees for 1 1/2 hours, turning and basting frequently. Yield: 4 servings.

CHICKEN ALBERGHETTI

6 chicken breast filets
Salt and pepper to taste
2 eggs, slightly beaten
3/4 c. dry bread crumbs
1/2 c. butter
8 oz. prepared
  spaghetti sauce
1 c. half and half
6 slices mozzarella
  cheese
6 slices Swiss cheese
Butter
Parmesan cheese

Season chicken with salt and pepper. Dip in egg, roll in crumbs. Sauté in 1/2 cup butter until browned. Dilute spaghetti sauce with half and half. Reserve 2 tablespoons. Pour sauce in baking dish. Add chicken. Top each chicken breast with 1 slice of mozzarella and Swiss cheese. Spoon reserved sauce on top. Dot with butter, sprinkle with Parmesan cheese. Bake, covered, at 350 degrees for 45 to 50 minutes. Yield: 6 servings.

CHICKEN AND RICE

1 c. long grain rice
1 fryer, cut up
1 env. dry onion
  soup mix
4 c. boiling water
2 tsp. chicken bouillon

Sprinkle rice evenly in bottom of greased 12x16-inch baking pan; arrange chicken over rice. Sprinkle onion mix on top. Pour mixture of boiling water and bouillon over chicken and rice. Bake at 375 degrees for 1 hour. Yield: 4 to 6 servings.

CHICKEN BREASTS FLORENTINE

2 10-oz. packages
  frozen spinach
6 large chicken breast
  filets
1 stalk celery, chopped
1/2 med. onion, chopped
1/2 tsp. salt
1 c. water
1/4 c. melted butter
1/4 c. all-purpose flour
Dash of pepper
1 c. light cream
Dash of nutmeg
1/2 c. Parmesan cheese

Cook chopped spinach using package directions; drain well. Combine chicken, celery, onion, salt and 1 cup water in saucepan. Bring to a boil; reduce heat. Simmer for 20 minutes or until tender. Drain, reserving 1 cup broth; discard vegetables. Blend butter, flour and pepper in saucepan. Stir in reserved broth and cream. Cook until thickened and bubbly, stirring constantly; remove from heat. Stir 1/2 cup sauce, nutmeg and half the cheese into drained spinach. Spread in 6x10-inch baking dish. Arrange chicken over top. Pour remaining sauce over top. Sprinkle with remaining cheese and additional nutmeg if desired. Cover with plastic wrap. Chill until ready to bake. Bake, uncovered, at 375 degrees for 30 to 35 minutes or until light brown. Yield: 6 servings.

CHICKEN BREASTS NEPTUNE

1¹/2 to 2 lb. chicken	*3 tbsp. butter*
breast filets	*2 shallots, minced*
¹/2 tsp. salt	*¹/2 c. chopped green*
¹/4 tsp. pepper	*bell pepper*
1 6-oz. package	*1 tbsp. all-purpose flour*
king crab meat	*¹/2 c. white wine*
1 tbsp. lemon juice	*¹/2 c. whipping cream*
¹/4 c. cornstarch	*Chopped parsley*

Pound chicken to ¹/4-inch thickness between plastic wrap. Sprinkle with salt and pepper. Place crab meat at end of each; sprinkle with lemon juice. Roll to enclose filling. Coat generously with cornstarch. Brown evenly in butter in skillet over medium heat. Remove and keep warm. Sauté shallots and green pepper in pan drippings for 1 minute. Mix in flour. Add wine, stirring to deglaze skillet. Stir in cream. Cook until thickened, stirring constantly. Add chicken. Simmer for 5 minutes. Garnish with parsley. Yield: 4 servings.

CHICKEN BREASTS IN ORANGE SAUCE

6 chicken breast filets	*¹/2 c. chicken broth*
¹/2 c. all-purpose flour	*¹/2 c. orange juice*
¹/2 tsp. salt	*¹/2 c. dry white wine*
¹/2 tsp. paprika	*¹/4 tsp. nutmeg or mace*
Dash of pepper	*2 tsp. light brown sugar*
Dash of garlic powder	*4 to 8 oz. fresh*
6 tbsp. corn oil	*mushrooms, sliced*
1 10-oz. can cream	*2 c. sliced carrots*
of mushroom soup	

Coat chicken with mixture of flour, salt, paprika, pepper and garlic powder. Brown chicken in oil in electric skillet; drain. Blend mushroom soup, chicken broth, orange juice, wine, nutmeg and brown sugar in bowl. Pour over chicken. Add mushrooms and carrots. Cook, covered, at 225 degrees for 1 hour or until chicken is tender. Yield: 6 servings.

CHICKEN BREASTS ORIENTAL

1 4-oz. jar sweet	*1 16-oz. can whole*
and sour sauce	*cranberry sauce*
1 env. dry onion	*8 chicken breast filets*
soup mix	

Mix sweet and sour sauce, onion soup mix and cranberry sauce in bowl. Pour over chicken breasts in 7x11-inch baking dish. Bake, covered, at 325 degrees for 30 minutes. Bake, uncovered, for 30 minutes longer. Serve over hot cooked rice. Yield: 8 servings.

CHICKEN DIJON

4 chicken breast filets	*1 c. half and half*
3 tbsp. butter	*2 tbsp. Dijon-style*
3 tbsp. all-purpose flour	*mustard*
1 c. chicken broth	*Hot cooked rice*

Cut chicken into strips. Cook in butter in large skillet over medium heat for 20 minutes. Remove to warm serving platter. Blend flour into drippings. Stir in chicken broth and half and half gradually. Cook until thickened, stirring constantly. Stir in mustard; add chicken. Cook, covered, for 10 minutes. Spoon rice into ring around outer edge of platter. Spoon chicken pieces into center. Serve remaining sauce in gravy boat. Yield: 4 servings.

CHICKEN ENCHILADAS

1 c. chopped onion	*¹/3 c. all-purpose flour*
¹/2 c. chopped green	*1 tsp. coriander*
bell pepper	*³/4 tsp. salt*
2 tbsp. margarine	*3 c. chicken broth*
2 c. chopped cooked	*1 c. sour cream*
chicken	*¹/2 c. shredded*
1 4-oz. can chopped	*Monterey Jack cheese*
green chilies	*12 6-in. corn tortillas*
3 tbsp. melted	*1 c. shredded Monterey*
margarine	*Jack cheese*

Sauté onion and green pepper in 2 tablespoons margarine in skillet until tender. Mix with chicken and green chilies in bowl. Blend 3 tablespoons melted margarine, flour, coriander and salt in saucepan. Stir in broth gradually. Cook until thickened, stirring constantly. Cook for 2 minutes longer. Add sour cream and ¹/2 cup cheese; stir until cheese melts. Add about ¹/2 c. sauce to chicken mixture; mix well. Dip tortillas 1 at a time into sauce. Place ¹/4 cup chicken mixture on tortilla; roll to enclose filling. Place seam side down in 9x13-inch baking pan. Spoon remaining sauce over top. Sprinkle with 1 cup remaining cheese. Bake at 350 degrees for 25 minutes. Yield: 6 servings.

SUMMER CHICKEN JUBILEE

2 broiler-fryers, cut up	*2 c. dark sweet*
1 tsp. salt	*cherries, drained*
¹/4 tsp. pepper	*¹/2 c. chili sauce*
¹/4 c. melted margarine	*1 8-oz. bottle of sweet*
2 c. peach slices	*and sour sauce*
1 med. onion, sliced	

Place chicken skin side up in baking pan. Sprinkle with salt and pepper. Drizzle with margarine. Broil until brown. Combine remaining ingredients in bowl. Spoon over chicken. Bake at 325 degrees for 1 hour. Thicken sauce if desired. Serve over hot cooked rice. Yield: 6 servings.

SOUTH SEAS CHICKEN

1/2 c. all-purpose flour	*1/2 c. chopped carrots*
1 1/2 tsp. salt	*1 c. sliced celery*
1/4 tsp. pepper	*1 tbsp. light brown*
1 tbsp. paprika	*sugar*
1 2 1/2 to 3-lb. chicken,	*1/4 tsp. ginger*
cut up	*1/2 6-oz. can frozen*
1/4 c. corn oil	*orange juice*
1 8-oz. can whole	*concentrate*
onions, drained	*3/4 c. water*

Combine flour, salt, pepper and paprika in paper bag. Add chicken; shake to coat. Reserve 2 tablespoons flour mixture for gravy. Brown chicken in oil in skillet. Place chicken in 9x13-inch baking dish. Add onions, carrots and celery. Blend reserved flour mixture, brown sugar and ginger into pan drippings; stir to make smooth paste. Add orange juice concentrate and 3/4 cup water. Cook and stir until bubbly. Pour over chicken. Bake, covered, at 350 degrees, for 1 1/2 hours.
Yield: 4 servings.

CHICKEN KIEV

8 chicken breast filets	*1/4 c. Parmesan cheese*
1 7-oz. can chopped	*1 tbsp. chili powder*
green chilies	*1/2 tsp. salt*
4 oz. Monterey Jack	*1/4 tsp. cumin*
cheese, cut into strips	*1/4 tsp. pepper*
3/4 c. melted butter	*1 8-oz. jar of salsa*
1/2 c. bread crumbs	

Pound chicken to 1/4-inch thickness. Place 2 tablespoons green chilies and 1 strip of Monterey Jack cheese in center of each piece; roll up and tuck ends under. Dip into melted butter; coat with mixture of crumbs and next 5 ingredients. Place in baking dish. Drizzle with any remaining butter. Chill, covered, for 4 hours or longer. Bake at 400 degrees for 25 minutes or until tender. Serve with salsa. Yield: 8 servings.

ROASTED CHICKEN
Photograph for this recipe is on page 53.

2 broiler-fryers, cut up	*1/2 c. olive oil*
4 cloves of garlic,	*Salt and pepper to taste*
crushed	*Sweet Pepper Chutney*

Marinate chicken in mixture of garlic, 1/2 cup olive oil, salt and pepper in bowl for 15 minutes. Drain, reserving marinade. Arrange on rack in shallow baking dish. Bake at 450 degrees for 10 minutes, turning once. Reduce temperature to 350 degrees. Bake for 30 minutes or until tender, basting several times with reserved marinade. Serve chicken warm or chilled with Sweet Pepper Chutney.
Yield: 6 to 8 servings.

South Seas Chicken...brings a touch of the tropics to your table.

Sweet Pepper Chutney

1 yellow onion, sliced	*2 tbsp. olive oil*
1 red bell pepper, cut	*1 c. raisins*
into chunks	*1 14-oz. can whole*
1 1/2 tsp. chopped	*tomatoes, drained*
jalapeño pepper	*1/4 c. packed brown*
1/2 to 1 tsp. red pepper	*sugar*
flakes	*1/4 c. lemon juice*
1/4 tsp. cloves	*Grated rind of 1 lemon*

Sauté onion, peppers, red pepper flakes and cloves in 2 tablespoons olive oil in saucepan until onion is transparent. Add raisins, tomatoes, brown sugar, lemon juice and lemon rind. Simmer for 10 minutes. Cool. May store in refrigerator for up to 2 weeks. Serve at room temperature.
Yield: 3 1/2 cups.

TERIYAKI CHICKEN

2 c. soy sauce	*Cornstarch*
1 1/2 c. unsweetened	*1 4-oz. bottle of*
pineapple juice	*maraschino cherries,*
1 c. pancake syrup	*drained*
3/4 tsp. ground ginger	*1 16-oz. can pineapple*
1 clove of garlic,	*chunks, drained*
chopped	*1 11-oz. can mandarin*
1 chicken, skinned,	*oranges, drained*
cut up	

Combine soy sauce, pineapple juice, syrup, ginger and garlic in bowl. Add chicken. Marinate for 2 hours or longer. Place chicken and sauce in baking pan. Bake at 350 degrees for 1 hour. Drain, reserving marinade. Thicken marinade with cornstarch in saucepan. Add maraschino cherries, pineapple and mandarin oranges. Serve over rice with sauce.
Yield: 6 servings.

Chili

CINCINNATI CHILI

2 lb. ground beef
2 dashes of
  Worcestershire
  sauce
3 bay leaves
2 med. onions, chopped
2 red bell peppers,
  chopped
1 6-oz. can tomato
  paste
1/2 tsp. cinnamon
1 1/2 tsp. vinegar
1/2 tsp. cumin
2 tbsp. chili powder
1 tbsp. salt
1/2 tbsp. pepper
1/2 tsp. red pepper
1/2 tsp. oregano
1/2 tbsp. allspice
5 c. water

Brown ground beef in stockpot; drain. Add Worcestershire sauce, bay leaves, onions, red bell peppers, tomato paste, cinnamon, vinegar, cumin, chili powder, salt, pepper, red pepper, oregano, allspice and water. Simmer for 2 to 3 hours. Remove bay leaves before serving. Yield: 8 servings.

CROCK•POT CHILI

1 lb. ground beef
2 lg. onions, chopped
1 lg. green bell pepper,
  chopped
2 tbsp. chili powder
2 tsp. salt
1/8 tsp. paprika
1/8 tsp. crushed red
  pepper
1 28-oz. can tomatoes
1 20-oz. can kidney
  beans, drained
1 lg. bay leaf

Brown ground beef in skillet for 10 minutes; drain. Add onions, green pepper, chili powder, salt, paprika and red pepper. Simmer for 10 minutes. Add tomatoes, beans and bay leaf. Pour into Crock•Pot and cook on Medium for 6 to 8 hours. Add a small amount of water if necessary. Remove bay leaf before serving. Yield: 4 servings.

PRIZE-WINNER CHILI

1 lb. pinto beans
1 lb. coarsely ground
  beef
1 lb. ground venison
2 1/2 c. chopped yellow
  onion
3 12-oz. cans beer
3 tbsp. ground cumin
1/4 c. chili powder
7 c. mixed vegetable
  juice cocktail
1 c. instant mashed
  potato flakes

Soak beans in water to cover overnight; drain. Brown ground beef and venison in skillet, stirring until crumbly; drain. Add onion. Cook until transparent. Add beans and remaining ingredients. Simmer for 5 hours. Yield: 8 to 10 servings.

WHITE CHILI

2 lbs. large white beans
12 c. chicken broth
4 cloves of garlic,
  minced
4 med. onions, chopped
2 tbsp. corn oil
4 4-oz. cans chopped
  green chilies
4 tsp. ground cumin
1 tbsp. oregano
1/2 tsp. cloves
1/2 tsp. cayenne pepper
8 c. chopped cooked
  chicken breasts
6 c. shredded Monterey
  Jack cheese

Soak beans in water to cover in stockpot overnight. Drain. Add chicken broth, garlic and half the onion. Bring to a boil; reduce heat. Simmer for 3 hours or until beans are very soft. Add additional broth if necessary. Sauté remaining onion in oil in skillet until tender. Add chilies and seasonings; mix well. Add to bean mixture with chicken. Simmer for 1 hour. Serve topped with shredded cheese. Yield: 16 to 20 servings.

Chili Peppers

CHILIES RELLENOS CASSEROLE

2 7-oz. cans whole
  green chilies, rinsed,
  seeded
8 oz. sharp Cheddar
  cheese, cut into sticks
4 eggs, slightly beaten
1 c. unsweetened
  evaporated milk
2 tbsp. all-purpose
  flour
1/2 tsp. dry mustard
1/4 tsp. pepper
Dash of Worcestershire
  sauce
1 lb. Monterey Jack
  cheese, shredded

Stuff each chili with Cheddar cheese stick. Arrange in single layer in greased 7x11-inch casserole. Combine remaining ingredients in bowl; mix well. Pour over chilies. Bake at 350 degrees for 30 minutes or until set and golden. Cool for 5 minutes before serving. Yield: 6 to 8 servings.

GREEN CHILI AND RICE CASSEROLE

4 c. cooked rice
1 c. cottage cheese
2 c. sour cream
1 c. chopped onion
1/4 c. margarine
1 bay leaf, crumbled
1/2 tsp. salt
1/4 tsp. pepper
3 10-oz. cans peeled
  whole green chilies,
  drained
2 c. shredded Cheddar
  cheese

Mix rice with cottage cheese, sour cream, onion, margarine, bay leaf, salt and pepper in bowl. Spread half the mixture in bottom of greased casserole. Cover with half the chilies; sprinkle with half the cheese. Repeat layers. Bake at 375 degrees for 25 to 30 minutes. Yield: 8 servings.

GREEN CHILI QUICHE

2 c. all-purpose flour	1/2 tsp. salt
2 tsp. sugar	1/4 tsp. pepper
1 tsp. salt	1/4 tsp. garlic powder
3/4 c. shortening	1/4 tsp. cilantro
1 egg	3/4 c. chopped mild
1/4 c. cold water	green chilies
3/4 tsp. apple cider	3/4 c. medium-hot
vinegar	thick salsa
4 eggs	1 1/2 c. shredded mild
3/4 c. evaporated milk	Cheddar cheese

Combine flour, sugar and salt in bowl. Cut in shortening until crumbly. Add mixture of egg, water and vinegar; mix well. Roll on floured surface into 14-inch circle. Fit into pie plate; flute edges. Combine 4 eggs and evaporated milk in bowl. Stir in remaining ingredients. Pour into pie shell. Bake at 375 degrees for 30 minutes. Cover edges with foil. Increase temperature to 400 degrees. Bake for 15 minutes longer or until knife inserted near center comes out clean. Let stand for 10 minutes before serving. Yield: 10 servings.

Chocolate

CHOCOLATE MAYONNAISE CAKE

2 c. all-purpose flour	1 c. mayonnaise
1 c. sugar	1 tsp. vanilla extract
2 tsp. soda	Confectioners' sugar
4 tsp. unsweetened	1/4 c. shortening
baking cocoa	Water
1 c. cold water	1 tsp. almond flavoring

Mix first 4 dry ingredients in bowl. Add water, mayonnaise and vanilla; beat until well mixed. Pour into 2 greased and floured 8 or 9-inch cake pans. Bake at 350 degrees for 45 minutes. Cool. Combine remaining ingredients in bowl; mix well. Spread between layers and over cooled cake. Yield: 12 servings.

CHOCOLATE MOUSSE CAKE

8 oz. unsweetened	5 egg whites
baking chocolate	1 tbsp. baking cocoa
1 c. butter, chopped	1 tsp. confectioners'
8 egg yolks	sugar
1 1/4 c. sugar	

Melt chocolate and butter in double boiler over hot water; blend well. Beat egg yolks and sugar in mixer bowl until thick and lemon-colored. Add chocolate; mix well. Beat egg whites in bowl until stiff but not dry. Fold gently into chocolate mixture.

Spoon 3/4 of the mixture into greased 8-inch springform pan. Bake at 250 degrees for 1 hour and 15 minutes. Cool in pan on wire rack for 10 minutes. Remove side of pan. Cool completely. Spread reserved chocolate mixture over top and side of mousse. Sift cocoa over top. Sift confectioners' sugar over cocoa. Store in refrigerator. Yield: 8 servings.

WHITE CHOCOLATE MOUSSE CAKE

4 c. chocolate cookie	1 c. butter, softened
crumbs	4 c. whipping cream,
1 tsp. cinnamon	whipped
1/2 c. clarified butter	12 oz. white chocolate
18 oz. white chocolate	chips
16 egg yolks	Grated rind of 1 orange

Mix cookie crumbs, cinnamon and clarified butter in bowl. Press over bottom and 1 1/2 inches up side of 12-inch springform pan. Bake at 350 degrees for 5 to 7 minutes or until firm. Cool. Melt chocolate in double boiler over hot water. Cool to lukewarm. Add egg yolks. Beat until light and fluffy. Beat in butter. Fold in whipped cream, chocolate chips and orange rind. Pour into prepared pan. Chill for 4 hours. Garnish with bittersweet chocolate curls. Yield: 16 servings.

MILKY WAY CAKE

6 Milky Way candy bars	2 1/2 c. sifted
1 c. butter, softened	all-purpose flour
2 c. sugar	1 1/4 c. buttermilk
4 eggs	1 tsp. vanilla extract
1/2 tsp. soda	1 c. chopped pecans

Melt candy bars and 1/2 cup butter in saucepan over low heat. Cream remaining 1/2 cup butter and sugar in mixer bowl until fluffy. Add eggs 1 at a time, beating well after each addition. Add soda and sifted flour alternately with buttermilk, beginning and ending with flour mixture and beating well after each addition. Stir in melted candy, vanilla and pecans. Pour into greased and floured 10-inch tube pan. Bake at 350 degrees for 1 hour and 20 minutes. Cool. Invert onto serving plate. Yield: 12 to 24 servings.

CHOCOLATE SYRUP SWIRL CAKE

Photograph for this recipe is on page 71.

1 c. butter, softened	1/2 tsp. soda
1 3/4 c. sugar	1/2 tsp. salt
3 eggs	1 1/4 c. milk
2 3/4 c. all-purpose	1 tsp. vanilla extract
flour	1/4 tsp. soda
1 1/2 tsp. baking powder	3/4 c. chocolate syrup

Cream butter and sugar in large mixer bowl until light and fluffy. Add eggs 1 at a time, beating well after each addition. Combine flour, baking powder, 1/2 teaspoon soda and salt. Add to creamed mixture alternately with milk and vanilla, beating well after each addition. Reserve 1 3/4 cups batter. Spoon remaining batter into greased and floured 10-inch tube pan. Stir mixture of remaining 1/4 teaspoon soda and chocolate syrup into reserved batter. Spoon over vanilla batter; swirl. Bake at 350 degrees for 60 minutes or until cake tests done. Cool in pan for 15 minutes. Remove to wire rack to cool completely. Yield: 12 to 14 servings.

TEXAS SHEET CAKE

2 c. all-purpose flour	1 tsp. vanilla extract
2 c. sugar	1/2 tsp. salt
1/2 c. margarine	2 eggs
1/2 c. shortening	1/2 c. buttermilk
1 c. water	1 tsp. soda
1/4 c. unsweetened baking cocoa	Texas Sheet Cake Frosting

Mix flour and sugar in large bowl. Combine next 4 ingredients in saucepan. Heat until blended. Add to flour mixture; mix well. Add vanilla, salt, eggs and buttermilk; mix by hand with large spoon. Pour into greased 15x17-inch sheet cake pan. Bake at 400 degrees for 20 minutes. Frost with Texas Sheet Cake Frosting. Yield: 24 servings.

Texas Sheet Cake Frosting

1/3 c. evaporated milk	1 lb. confectioners' sugar
1/2 c. margarine	1 tbsp. vanilla extract
1/4 c. unsweetened baking cocoa	1 c. chopped pecans
1/8 tsp. salt	

Bring milk, margarine and cocoa to a boil in saucepan. Beat in next 3 ingredients until creamy. Spread frosting on hot cake. Sprinkle with pecans.

CHOCOLATE FRANGOS

1 c. butter, softened	2 tsp. vanilla extract
2 c. confectioners' sugar	1 c. crushed vanilla wafers
4 sq. baking chocolate, melted	1 c. whipping cream, whipped
4 eggs	18 small maraschino cherries
3/4 tsp. peppermint extract	

Beat butter and confectioners' sugar in mixer bowl until light and fluffy. Add melted chocolate; beat well. Add eggs 1 at a time, beating well after each addition. Beat until fluffy. Beat in peppermint and vanilla. Sprinkle half the vanilla wafer crumbs into paper-lined muffin cups. Fill half full with chocolate mixture. Top with remaining crumbs. Freeze until serving time. Top with whipped cream and cherries. Yield: 18 servings.

CHOCOLATE LOVER'S CHEESECAKE

2 c. chocolate wafer crumbs	1 tbsp. rum
1/2 c. melted butter	1 1/2 tsp. vanilla extract
1/4 c. sugar	1/8 tsp. salt
32 oz. cream cheese, softened	4 eggs
1 1/4 c. sugar	1/4 c. chocolate chips
3 1/2 oz. sweet chocolate, melted	2 c. sour cream
	1/4 c. sugar
	1 tsp. almond extract

Mix cookie crumbs, butter and 1/4 cup sugar in bowl. Press over bottom and side of 10-inch springform pan. Beat cream cheese and 1 1/4 cups sugar in mixer bowl for 2 minutes. Add melted chocolate, rum, vanilla and salt; mix well. Add eggs 1 at a time, beating just until mixed after each addition. Stir in chocolate chips. Pour into crust. Bake at 350 degrees for 40 minutes. Let stand for 10 minutes. Combine remaining ingredients in bowl. Spread over cheesecake. Bake for 10 minutes longer. Place in refrigerator immediately to cool. Place cooled cheesecake on serving plate; remove side of pan. Yield: 12 servings.

GERMAN CHOCOLATE CHEESECAKE

1 1/4 c. chocolate wafer crumbs (about 18)	3 eggs
2 tbsp. sugar	2 tbsp. butter
3 tbsp. butter, melted	1/3 c. cream
19 oz. cream cheese, softened	2 tbsp. light brown sugar
1 c. sugar	1 egg
1/4 c. unsweetened baking cocoa	1/2 tsp. vanilla extract
2 tsp. vanilla extract	1/2 c. chopped pecans
	1/2 c. flaked coconut

Mix crumbs and 2 tablespoons sugar in bowl; mix in melted butter. Press evenly over bottom of ungreased springform pan. Bake at 350 degrees for 10 minutes. Cool. Reduce temperature to 300 degrees. Beat cream cheese in large mixer bowl. Add 1 cup sugar and cocoa gradually, beating until fluffy. Add 2 teaspoons vanilla. Beat in eggs 1 at a time. Pour into prepared pan. Bake for 1 hour or until firm in center. Cool. Combine 2 tablespoons butter, cream, brown sugar and 1 egg in saucepan. Cook over low heat until thickened, stirring constantly. Remove from heat. Stir in vanilla, pecans and coconut. Cool. Spoon over cooled cheesecake. Yield: 12 servings.

CHOCOLATE FUDGE

5 c. sugar	2 7-oz. jars
1 c. margarine	marshmallow creme
1 12-oz. can	2 tsp. vanilla extract
evaporated milk	2 c. pecans
18 oz. semisweet	
chocolate chips	

Bring first 3 ingredients to a boil in saucepan. Cook for 6 minutes. Remove from heat. Add chocolate chips. Stir until melted. Add marshmallow creme, vanilla and pecans; mix well. Pour into greased dish. Cool. Cut into squares.
Yield: 5 pounds.

OLD-FASHIONED CHOCOLATE CHIP COOKIES

2/3 c. shortening	2 tsp. vanilla extract
2/3 c. margarine,	2 c. chocolate chips
softened	1 c. chopped pecans
1 c. sugar	3 1/4 c. all-purpose flour
1 c. packed dark	1 tsp. soda
brown sugar	1 tsp. salt
2 eggs	

Cream shortening and margarine in mixer bowl until light. Add sugar, brown sugar, eggs and vanilla; mix until fluffy. Stir in chocolate chips and pecans. Stir in mixture of dry ingredients with wooden spoon. Drop by teaspoonfuls onto ungreased cookie sheet. Bake at 375 degrees for 8 to 10 minutes or until light brown. Cool on wire rack. Yield: 48 cookies.

SWISS CHOCOLATE SQUARES

1 c. water	1/2 tsp. salt
1/2 c. margarine	1/2 c. margarine
1 1/2 sq. unsweetened	6 tbsp. milk
baking chocolate	1 1/2 sq. unsweetened
2 c. all-purpose flour	baking chocolate
2 c. sugar	4 1/2 c. confectioners'
2 eggs	sugar
1/2 c. sour cream	1 tsp. vanilla extract
1 tsp. soda	1/2 c. chopped almonds

Combine first 3 ingredients in saucepan. Bring to a boil; remove from heat. Stir in mixture of flour and sugar. Add eggs, sour cream, soda and salt; mix well. Pour into greased 10x15-inch baking pan. Bake at 375 degrees for 20 to 25 minutes. Combine next 3 ingredients in saucepan. Bring to a boil. Cook for 1 minute. Stir in confectioners' sugar and vanilla. Spread on baked layer. Sprinkle with almonds. Cut into squares. Yield: 2 dozen.

CHOCOLATE ÉCLAIR DESSERT

1 16-oz. package	2 pkg. liquid baking
graham crackers	chocolate
2 sm. packages French	2 tsp. white corn syrup
vanilla instant	3 tbsp. milk
pudding mix	1 1/2 c. confectioners'
3 c. milk	sugar
1 8-oz. container	2 tsp. vanilla extract
whipped topping	

Arrange 1 layer of graham crackers in bottom of 9x13-inch dish. Combine next 3 ingredients in bowl; mix well. Spread half the mixture over crackers. Add a second layer of crackers and remaining pudding mixture. Top with third layer of crackers. Combine remaining ingredients in bowl; mix well. Spread over dessert. Chill for 6 hours or longer. Yield: 12 servings.

EASY HEAVENLY DESSERT

1 1/2 c. self-rising flour	1 c. whipped topping
2 tbsp. (heaping) sugar	1 7-oz. package
3/4 c. melted margarine	chocolate instant
1 c. crushed pecans	pudding mix
2 c. confectioners'	1 7-oz. package vanilla
sugar	instant pudding mix
8 oz. cream cheese,	4 c. cold milk
softened	2 c. whipped topping

Combine flour, sugar, melted margarine and pecans in bowl; mix well. Press over bottom of 9x13-inch baking dish. Bake at 350 degrees for 20 minutes. Cool. Cream confectioners' sugar and cream cheese in mixer bowl until light. Mix in 1 cup whipped topping. Spread over baked layer. Combine chocolate pudding mix and vanilla pudding mix with cold milk in large bowl; mix until smooth. Spread over cream cheese layer. Top with remaining 2 cups whipped topping. Chill overnight. Yield: 15 servings.

FUDGY ICE CREAM

5 oz. unsweetened	4 egg yolks
baking chocolate,	2 c. half and half
melted	1 c. chopped pecans
1 14-oz. can	2 c. whipping cream,
sweetened condensed	whipped
milk	

Combine chocolate, condensed milk, egg yolks and half and half in bowl; mix well. Add pecans. Fold in whipped cream. Pour into 5x9-inch loaf pan. Cover with foil. Freeze for 6 hours.
Yield: 8 cups.

FROZEN CHOCOLATE MOUSSE

Oreo Cookies	*2 eggs, separated*
1/3 c. melted margarine	*1/4 c. sugar*
8 oz. cream cheese,	*1 c. whipping cream,*
softened	*whipped*
1/4 c. sugar	*3/4 c. chopped pecans*
1 tsp. vanilla extract	*Heavenly Hot Fudge*
1 c. semisweet	*Sauce*
chocolate chips, melted	

Separate Oreos; discard creamy filling. Crush enough to yield 1/2 cup fine crumbs. Mix with melted margarine in bowl. Press into bottom of 9-inch springform pan. Bake at 350 degrees for 10 minutes. Combine cream cheese, 1/4 cup sugar and vanilla in mixer bowl; beat until blended. Blend in chocolate and well-beaten egg yolks. Beat egg whites in mixer bowl until stiff peaks form. Beat in 1/4 cup sugar gradually. Fold in chocolate mixture, whipped cream and pecans. Pour into prepared springform pan. Freeze until firm. Serve with Heavenly Hot Fudge Sauce.
Yield: 10 servings.

Heavenly Hot Fudge Sauce

4 1-oz. squares	*Dash of salt*
unsweetened baking	*3 c. sugar*
chocolate	*1 2/3 c. evaporated milk*
1/2 c. margarine	*1 tsp. vanilla extract*

Melt chocolate and margarine in double boiler. Add salt. Stir in sugar gradually. Add evaporated milk very gradually, stirring constantly. Remove from heat. Add vanilla. Serve hot sauce over frozen mousse. Yield: 4 cups.

CHOCOLATE PIE

1 12-oz. package	*1 c. semisweet*
chocolate wafers,	*chocolate chips,*
crushed	*melted*
1/3 c. melted butter	*1 tsp. vanilla extract*
8 oz. cream cheese,	*2 egg whites*
softened	*2 c. whipping cream*
2 egg yolks, beaten	*1/2 c. sugar*
1/2 c. sugar	*1/2 c. chopped pecans*

Mix cookie crumbs with butter in bowl. Press into pie plate. Combine cream cheese, egg yolks, 1/2 cup sugar, melted chocolate and vanilla in mixer bowl; mix well. Beat egg whites in mixer bowl until stiff peaks form. Fold into chocolate mixture. Pour into prepared 9-inch pie plate. Bake at 325 degrees for 10 minutes. Cool. Whip cream in mixer bowl until soft peaks form. Fold in 1/2 cup sugar. Spread over pie. Sprinkle with pecans. Store pie in refrigerator. Yield: 6 servings.

CHOCOLATE CHEESE PIE

6 oz. cream cheese,	*1/4 c. chopped pecans*
softened	*1 graham cracker pie*
1 c. sugar	*shell*
1/4 to 1/2 c. milk	*1 16-oz. container*
1 1/3 c. semisweet	*whipped topping*
chocolate chips,	*1 2-oz. milk chocolate*
melted	*candy bar, shaved*

Beat cream cheese, sugar and milk in bowl. Stir in chocolate and pecans. Spoon into pie shell. Freeze until firm. Thaw for 15 minutes. Garnish with whipped topping and shaved chocolate. Yield: 6 to 9 servings.

BLENDER CHOCOLATE MOUSSE

1 12-oz. package	*3 eggs*
semisweet chocolate	*1 c. hot milk*
chips	*2 to 4 tbsp. Brandy*
1/2 c. sugar	*Whipped cream*

Combine chocolate, sugar and eggs in blender container. Add hot milk and Brandy. Process on medium speed until smooth. Pour into dessert dishes. Chill for 1 hour. Garnish with whipped cream. Yield: 6 servings.

CHOCOLATE CHIP PIE

2 eggs, beaten	*1 c. melted butter*
1/2 c. all-purpose flour	*1 c. chocolate chips*
1/2 c. packed light	*1 unbaked 9-inch pie*
brown sugar	*shell*
1/2 c. sugar	

Beat first 4 ingredients in bowl until well blended. Blend in butter; stir in chocolate chips. Pour into pie shell. Bake at 325 degrees for 1 hour. Serve with ice cream or whipped cream.
Yield: 8 servings.

CHOCOLATE SILK PIE

1/2 c. butter, softened	*1 tsp. vanilla extract*
3/4 c. sugar	*2 eggs*
2 1-oz. squares semi-	*1 baked 9-in. pie shell*
sweet chocolate	*Whipped cream*

Cream butter and sugar in mixer bowl until light and fluffy. Stir in melted chocolate and vanilla. Add eggs 1 at a time, beating for 5 minutes after each addition. Do not underbeat. Pour into pie shell. Chill for 2 hours or longer. Garnish with whipped cream. Yield: 6 servings.

PIE MARCHAND

1 qt. mint chocolate chip ice cream, softened	*2 1-oz. squares unsweetened baking chocolate*
1 9-in. chocolate wafer pie shell	*8 oz. whipping cream*
1/2 c. sugar	*2 tbsp. sugar*
2/3 c. evaporated milk	*8 maraschino cherries*
1 tbsp. butter	*Crushed salted peanuts*

Spread softened ice cream in pie shell. Freeze until firm. Combine 1/2 cup sugar, evaporated milk, butter and chocolate in saucepan. Cook over medium heat until thickened, stirring constantly. Cool, uncovered, in refrigerator. Spread chocolate mixture over ice cream. Whip cream in mixer bowl until thick. Add 2 tablespoons sugar gradually, beating until soft peaks form. Spread whipped cream in 2-inch ring around edge of pie. Place cherries evenly over whipped cream. Sprinkle crushed peanuts over pie. Yield: 8 servings.

Chowder

NEW ENGLAND-STYLE CLAM CHOWDER

2 cans chopped clams and juice	*1/2 c. all-purpose flour*
2 med. potatoes	*4 c. half and half*
2 tbsp. chopped onion	*1/2 tsp. salt*
1/2 c. margarine	*1/4 tsp. pepper*

Cook clams and vegetables in saucepan until tender. Melt margarine in large saucepan. Add flour; mix well. Add half and half. Cook until thickened, stirring constantly. Add salt and pepper. Combine with clam mixture. Cook until heated through. Yield: 8 servings.

SUMMER CORN CHOWDER

4 slices bacon, chopped	*1 tsp. sugar*
1 onion, sliced	*1/4 c. butter*
4 c. cubed potatoes	*2 c. milk*
1 c. water	*Salt and white pepper to taste*
4 c. corn	
1 c. heavy cream	

Sauté bacon until brown. Add onion, potatoes and 1 cup water in skillet; cover. Bring to a boil. Simmer until potatoes are tender but not mushy. Combine corn, cream, sugar and butter in saucepan. Simmer, covered, for 10 minutes. Add bacon mixture, milk and salt and pepper. Cook until heated through. Yield: 4 servings.

FISH CHOWDER

1 lb. white fish	*4 or 5 potatoes, peeled, chopped*
1 sm. piece salt pork	
2 or 3 med. onions, chopped	*2 12-oz. cans evaporated milk*

Cook fish in water in 3-quart saucepan until fish flakes easily. Brown salt pork in skillet; remove from skillet. Sauté onions in drippings until golden. Add onions and salt pork to saucepan. Add potatoes and water to cover. Cook until potatoes are tender. Add evaporated milk. Heat to serving temperature. Yield: 6 servings.

Fish Chowder...rich with potatoes and onions, will warm a winter evening.

Chutney

CRANBERRY CHUTNEY

1 lb. fresh cranberries	*1 firm pear, chopped*
2 c. sugar	*1 apple, chopped*
1 c. water	*1 tbsp. grated orange rind*
1 env. unflavored gelatin	
1/4 c. water	*2 1/2 tsp. ginger*
1 c. orange juice	*1 c. golden raisins*
1 c. chopped celery	*1 c. chopped pecans*

Combine cranberries, sugar and 1 cup water in saucepan. Bring to a boil over medium heat. Cook until sugar is dissolved, stirring constantly. Simmer for 15 minutes, stirring occasionally. Remove from heat. Soften gelatin in 1/4 cup water. Stir into cranberry mixture until dissolved. Add orange juice, celery, pear, apple, orange rind, ginger and raisins; mix well. Chill, covered, for 3 hours. Stir in pecans. Spoon into serving dish. Yield: 8 servings.

HARVEST APPLE CHUTNEY

8 c. apples, peeled,
  chopped
2 c. seedless white
  raisins
2 oranges, peeled,
  chopped
1 c. coarsely chopped
  pecans
3 c. sugar
1/2 c. vinegar
1/3 tsp. ground cloves

Combine fruit and pecans in glass container. Add mixture of next 3 ingredients. Store in refrigerator. Yield: 12 cups.

ZUCCHINI CHUTNEY

6 c. grated unpeeled
  zucchini
2 green bell peppers,
  coarsely ground
2 c. grated unpeeled
  tart apples
1 onion, finely ground
1 c. honey
3/4 lb. raisins, ground
1 tbsp. celery seed
Juice and grated rind
  of 1 lemon
1 1/3 c. vinegar
1/3 c. frozen orange
  juice concentrate

Combine all ingredients in stockpot. Simmer until of desired consistency. Ladle into hot sterilized jars, leaving 1/2-inch headspace; seal with 2-piece lids. Process in boiling water bath for 10 minutes. Let stand for 1 to 2 weeks before serving to allow flavors to mellow. Yield: Five 1/2-pint jars.

Cinnamon

CINNAMON CRISPAS

1 pkg. light and crispy
  flour tacos for salad
  shells
1 tbsp. cinnamon
1/2 c. sugar

Place flour tacos on baking sheet. Cut each into 6 wedges. Bake wedges according to package directions until light brown. Coat wedges with mixture of cinnamon and sugar while hot. Yield: 2 dozen.

CINNAMON PIE

2 egg yolks
3/4 c. sugar
2 tbsp. all-purpose
  flour
1 tbsp. cinnamon
1 1/2 c. milk
2 egg whites, beaten
1 unbaked 9-in. pie
  shell

Combine first 5 ingredients in saucepan. Heat to 110 degrees, stirring constantly. Beat egg whites until stiff peaks form. Fold into warm mixture. Pour into pie shell. Bake at 350 degrees for 35 minutes or until set. Yield: 6 servings.

Clam

CLAM CANAPÉS

2 cloves of garlic,
  minced
1 tbsp. minced onion
1/2 tsp. parsley
1/2 tsp. oregano
1/4 c. bread crumbs
2 tbsp. corn oil
1 8-oz. can minced
  clams
1/8 tsp. salt
1/4 c. bread crumbs
Parmesan cheese
Saltine crackers

Sauté garlic, onion, parsley, oregano and 1/4 cup bread crumbs in oil in skillet for 2 minutes. Remove from heat when garlic and onion start to brown. Mix in undrained clams and salt. Pour into 3-cup ovenproof dish; sprinkle lightly with remaining 1/4 cup bread crumbs and Parmesan cheese. Bake at 350 degrees for 25 to 30 minutes or until crusty. Serve on saltines. Yield: 2 to 3 dozen.

MANHATTAN CLAM CHOWDER

3 slices bacon, chopped
1 c. chopped onion
1 c. chopped celery
4 c. clam juice
4 c. chopped clams
3 16-oz. cans stewed
  tomatoes
1 10-oz. package
  frozen mixed
  vegetables
Salt and pepper to taste
1 tsp. oregano
1 tsp. sweet basil
2 tbsp. parsley

Brown bacon with onion and celery in skillet; drain. Add next 4 ingredients in order listed; mix well. Stir in seasonings. Cook until clams are tender. Yield: 3 1/2 quarts.

PASTA WITH WHITE CLAM SAUCE

2 or 3 cloves of garlic
2 tbsp. butter
1 4-oz. can mushroom
  stems and pieces
2 6 1/2-oz. cans minced
  clams
Pepper to taste
2 tbsp. all-purpose
  flour
1/4 c. Parmesan cheese
4 oz. spaghetti, cooked

Peel garlic cloves. Place between 4 thicknesses of waxed paper. Crush with mallet. Sauté garlic in butter in skillet; do not brown. Drain mushrooms and clams, reserving liquids. Add mushrooms to skillet. Cook for 3 minutes. Add clams and pepper. Blend reserved liquids with flour in small bowl. Stir into clam mixture. Cook until heated through, stirring constantly; do not boil. Serve with cheese over hot spaghetti. Yield: 2 servings.

Coconut

COCONUT-PECAN RING

1 24-ct. package frozen rolls, thawed	1/2 c. chopped pecans
1/4 c. milk	1/2 c. sifted confectioners' sugar
2/3 c. sugar	1 tbsp. milk
1/2 tsp. cinnamon	1/4 tsp. vanilla extract
1/2 c. coconut	2 tbsp. chopped pecans

Dip rolls in 1/4 cup milk, then roll in mixture of sugar and cinnamon, coating well. Arrange half the rolls in overlapping layer in greased tube pan. Sprinkle with 1/4 cup coconut and 1/4 cup pecans. Repeat layers. Bake at 375 degrees for 25 to 30 minutes or until golden brown. Invert onto serving plate. Mix confectioners' sugar, 1 tablespoon milk and vanilla in small bowl. Drizzle over ring. Sprinkle with 2 tablespoons pecans. Yield: 8 servings.

COCONUT CREAM CAKE

1 15-oz. package white cake mix with pudding	1 c. cream of coconut
3 eggs	1 14-oz. can sweetened condensed milk
1/3 c. vegetable oil	
1 c. water	1 c. whipping cream
1/2 tsp. coconut flavoring	1 tbsp. sugar
	1 c. flaked coconut

Combine first 5 ingredients in mixer bowl. Beat at medium speed for 2 minutes. Pour into greased 9x13-inch cake pan. Bake at 350 degrees for 30 minutes. Poke holes in warm cake with 2-prong serving fork. Pour mixture of cream of coconut and condensed milk into holes. Chill overnight. Whip cream in bowl until soft peaks form. Sprinkle with sugar. Beat until smooth and mixture holds shape. Frost cake; sprinkle with coconut. Chill until serving time. Yield: 12 servings.

MACAROON CAKE

1/3 c. butter, softened	1/2 c. milk
1/2 c. sugar	1/2 tsp. almond extract
4 egg yolks	4 egg whites
1 c. sifted all-purpose flour	1 c. sugar
	1/2 tsp. almond extract
1 1/2 tsp. baking powder	1 c. flaked coconut

Combine first 7 ingredients in bowl; mix well. Pour into greased 9x13-inch cake pan. Beat egg whites until very stiff peaks form. Add 1 cup sugar and 1/2 teaspoon almond extract gradually, beating constantly. Fold in coconut. Spread over batter.

Bake at 325 degrees for 30 minutes or until cake tests done. Yield: 15 servings.

COCONUT POUND CAKE

1 c. margarine, softened	3 c. all-purpose flour
	1 tsp. baking powder
2/3 c. shortening	1 c. milk
3 c. sugar	1 tsp. coconut flavoring
5 eggs	1 4-oz. can coconut

Cream margarine, shortening and sugar in mixer bowl until light and fluffy. Blend in eggs. Add remaining ingredients in order listed, mixing well after each addition. Pour into greased 10-inch tube or bundt pan. Bake at 325 degrees for 1 1/2 hours. Yield: 16 servings.

COCONUT CHEESE BARS

1 2-layer pkg. yellow cake mix	2 eggs
	8 oz. cream cheese, softened
1/2 c. margarine	
1 egg	1 16-oz. package confectioners' sugar
1 c. chopped pecans	
1 c. coconut	

Combine cake mix, margarine and egg in bowl; mix well. Pat into 10x15-inch baking pan. Sprinkle nuts and coconut over dough. Cream eggs, cream cheese and confectioners' sugar in bowl until light and fluffy. Pour evenly over pecans and coconut. Bake at 350 degrees for 40 minutes. Cool in pan. Cut into small bars. Sprinkle with additional confectioners' sugar. Yield: 3 dozen.

EASY MACAROONS

2 8-oz. packages shredded coconut	1 15-oz. can sweetened condensed milk
2 tsp. vanilla extract	

Combine all ingredients in bowl; mix well. Drop by teaspoonfuls onto greased cookie sheet. Bake at 350 degrees for 10 to 12 minutes. Yield: 4 dozen cookies.

FRENCH COCONUT PIE

1/2 c. margarine	1 tbsp. vinegar
1 1/2 c. sugar	1 1/2 c. coconut
1 tsp. vanilla extract	1 unbaked 9-in. pie shell
3 eggs	

Combine first 5 ingredients in mixer bowl; beat until blended. Stir in coconut. Pour into pie shell. Bake at 350 degrees for 45 to 60 minutes. Yield: 6 servings.

OLD-FASHIONED COCONUT PIE

3 eggs	*1/8 tsp. salt*
1 c. sugar	*1 tsp. all-purpose flour*
1/2 c. milk	*1 c. coconut*
6 tbsp. melted	*2 tsp. vanilla extract*
margarine	*1 9-in. pie shell*

Combine eggs, sugar, milk, melted margarine, salt, flour, coconut and vanilla in large bowl; beat well with wire whisk. Pour into 9-inch pie shell. Bake at 350 degrees for 45 minutes or until set. Yield: 8 servings.

Coffee

CAFÉ AU LAIT

1 6-oz. jar instant	*1/4 c. instant coffee*
nondairy creamer	*powder*
1/4 c. packed light	*Dash of salt*
brown sugar	

Combine creamer, brown sugar, coffee powder and salt in bowl; mix well. Store in airtight container. Combine 1/4 cup mix and 2/3 cup boiling water in cup for each serving or 2 cups mix and 5 1/3 cups boiling water in coffeepot for 8 servings. Yield: 2 cups mix or 8 servings.

COFFEE AND CREAM CHEESECAKE

1 1/2 c. fine graham	*1 c. sour cream*
cracker crumbs	*6 eggs*
5 tbsp. melted butter	*6 tbsp. all-purpose*
3 tbsp. sugar	*flour*
1 tsp. cinnamon	*3 tbsp. instant coffee*
24 oz. cream cheese,	*powder*
softened	*1/4 c. coffee-flavored*
1/2 c. sugar	*liqueur*

Mix graham cracker crumbs, butter, 3 tablespoons sugar and cinnamon in bowl. Press evenly over bottom and about 1 inch up side of 11-inch springform pan. Bake at 350 degrees for 15 minutes. Cool. Reduce temperature to 300 degrees. Beat cream cheese and 1/2 cup sugar in mixer bowl at high speed until blended. Beat in sour cream, eggs and flour. Dissolve coffee powder in coffee liqueur; stir into cream cheese mixture. Pour into cooled crust. Bake for 1 hour or until cheesecake is firm, except for 4-inch area in center, when shaken gently. Cool for 4 hours or longer. Garnish individual servings with drizzle of additional liqueur. Yield: 10 to 12 servings.

COFFEE MOCHA PUNCH

2 sq. unsweetened	*1 1-liter bottle of club*
chocolate, melted	*soda, chilled*
1 gal. strong hot coffee	*4 c. half and half*
1 c. sugar	*1 8-oz. container*
Dash of salt	*whipped topping*
1 tsp. vanilla extract	*Chocolate syrup*
1/2 gal. vanilla ice	
cream	

Combine melted chocolate, coffee, sugar, salt and vanilla in large container. Chill for several hours. Slice ice cream into cubes. Pour coffee mixture into punch bowl. Add club soda, half and half and ice cream; mix gently. Ladle into serving cups. Top with dollops of whipped topping. Drizzle chocolate syrup over whipped topping. Yield: 64 cups.

COFFEE MERINGUE TORTE

6 egg whites, at room	*1 tsp. almond extract*
temperature	*1/4 tsp. allspice*
1/4 tsp. cream of tartar	*1/4 tsp. ground mace*
1 c. sugar	*Coffee Butter Cream*

Beat egg whites in bowl until foamy. Add cream of tartar. Beat until stiff peaks form. Add sugar gradually, beating well after each addition. Add flavorings. Beat for 2 minutes longer. Cut four 8-inch circles from parchment. Pipe meringue into 4 equal circles; spread evenly with spatula. Place on baking sheets. Bake at 250 degrees for 1 hour and 15 minutes. Cool. Remove parchment. Spread Coffee Butter Cream between layers. Garnish top and side with whipped cream and dusting of cocoa over top. Serve within 2 hours. Yield: 16 servings.

Coffee Butter Cream

2 3/4 c. sugar	*4 egg yolks, at room*
1 1/4 c. water	*temperature*
2 1/2 tsp. cream of tartar	*4 c. unsalted butter*
5 eggs, at room	*1 1/2 tsp. instant coffee*
temperature	*3/4 tsp. water*

Combine sugar, water and cream of tartar in heavy saucepan; mix well. Cover. Bring to a boil over high heat. Cook for about 5 minutes. Uncover. Wash down side of pan. Cook to 240 to 248 degrees on candy thermometer, firm-ball stage, stirring constantly. Beat eggs and egg yolks in bowl until doubled in volume and very light. Stir a small amount of hot syrup into beaten eggs; stir eggs into hot syrup. Beat over ice water bath until cool. Beat in sliced butter gradually. Blend in mixture of coffee and water.

COFFEE CUSTARD

6 egg yolks, slightly beaten	*1 tbsp. all-purpose flour*
1/2 c. sugar	*1 c. margarine,*
1/2 c. coffee	*softened*

Mix egg yolks, sugar, coffee and flour together in double boiler. Cook until thickened, stirring constantly. Cool. Add margarine, 1 tablespoon at a time, beating well after each addition. Pour into dessert dishes. Yield: 4 servings.

SOUTHERN COFFEE COMFORT

2 qt. strong cold coffee	*1/2 c. sugar*
2 c. cold milk	*1 qt. vanilla ice cream*
2 tsp vanilla extract	*Nutmeg to taste*

Combine coffee, milk, vanilla and sugar in punch bowl; stir until sugar is dissolved. Add small scoops of ice cream. Sprinkle lightly with nutmeg. Yield: 20 servings.

Coffee Cake

BASIC COFFEE CAKE

1 c. milk, scalded	*2 eggs, beaten*
1/2 c. margarine	*1/4 c. margarine,*
1/2 c. sugar	*softened*
2 tbsp. cardamom	*3/4 c. packed brown*
1 tsp. salt	*sugar*
2 pkg. dry yeast	*3/4 c. chopped toasted*
1/4 c. warm water	*almonds*
5 c. sifted all-purpose flour	*1 egg*
	1 tsp. water

Combine warm milk, 1/2 cup margarine, sugar, cardamom and salt in bowl. Cool to lukewarm. Dissolve yeast in 1/4 cup warm water. Add to milk mixture. Stir in enough flour to make thick batter. Add 2 eggs; mix well. Stir in enough remaining flour to make soft dough. Knead on floured surface until smooth and elastic. Place in greased bowl, turning to grease surface. Let rise in warm place until doubled in bulk. Punch dough down. Let rise for 45 minutes. Roll into rectangle on floured surface. Spread with 1/4 cup margarine. Sprinkle with brown sugar and almonds. Roll as for jelly roll. Cut into slices. Shape as desired on baking sheet. Brush with mixture of 1 egg and 1 teaspoon water. Bake at 375 degrees for 20 to 30 minutes or until brown. Yield: 18 servings.

OVERNIGHT COFFEE CAKE

1 c. packed light brown sugar	*1 tsp. salt*
1/2 c. coconut	*2 4-oz. packages vanilla instant pudding mix*
1/2 c. pecans	
1 tsp. cinnamon	*1 c. water*
2 c. all-purpose flour	*3/4 c. corn oil*
1 c. sugar	*1 tsp. vanilla extract*
2 tsp. baking powder	*4 eggs*

Mix brown sugar, coconut, pecans and cinnamon in bowl; set aside. Combine flour and remaining ingredients in mixer bowl. Beat at low speed for 30 seconds. Beat at medium speed for 2 minutes. Layer batter and coconut mixture 1/2 at a time in greased and floured 9x13-inch baking pan. Refrigerate overnight if desired. Bake at 325 degrees for 40 to 60 minutes or until coffee cake tests done. Yield: 12 to 15 servings.

SOUR CREAM COFFEE CAKE

1 c. margarine, softened	*1 tbsp. baking powder*
2 c. sugar	*1/4 tsp. salt*
2 eggs, beaten	*3/4 c. packed brown sugar*
2 c. sour cream	*2 c. chopped pecans*
1 tbsp. vanilla extract	*1 tbsp. cinnamon*
2 c. unbleached flour	

Cream margarine and sugar in mixer bowl until light and fluffy. Blend in eggs, sour cream and vanilla. Sift flour, baking powder and salt together. Fold into creamed mixture, mixing just until moistened. Combine brown sugar, pecans and cinnamon in small bowl. Layer batter and pecan mixture 1/2 at a time in greased and floured 10-inch bundt pan. Bake at 350 degrees on middle rack of oven for 1 hour or until toothpick inserted in center comes out clean. Remove to wire rack to cool. Yield: 10 servings.

TWIN MOUNTAIN COFFEE CAKE

2 c. all-purpose flour	*2 eggs, beaten*
1 tbsp. baking powder	*1 c. milk*
1/4 tsp. salt	*1 1/2 c. blueberries*
1 c. sugar	*1 1/3 c. flaked coconut*
1/2 c. shortening	

Sift dry ingredients into bowl. Cut in shortening until crumbly. Beat eggs with milk. Stir into dry ingredients. Fold in blueberries. Pour into 2 greased 8-inch round cake pans. Sprinkle flaked coconut over top. Bake at 375 degrees for 25 minutes. Yield: 16 servings.

Corn

CHEESY CORN CASSEROLE

1/2 c. chopped onion
1/2 c. chopped celery
*1/4 c. chopped green
   bell pepper*
*1/2 c. shredded sharp
   Cheddar cheese*
*1 16-oz. can French-
   style green beans,
   drained*

*1 16-oz. can Shoe
   Peg corn*
*1 can cream of
   celery soup*
1 c. sour cream
Salt and pepper to taste
1/2 c. melted margarine
*1 stack butter crackers,
   crushed*

Combine onion, celery, green pepper, cheese, green beans and corn in large bowl. Add soup, sour cream and salt and pepper to taste. Spoon into 9x13-inch baking dish. Top with mixture of margarine and cracker crumbs. Bake at 350 degrees for 45 minutes. Yield: 10 to 12 servings.

GULLIVER'S CORN CASSEROLE

*2 10-oz. packages
   frozen corn*
1 c. milk
1 c. whipping cream
1 tsp. salt
1 tsp. MSG
7 tsp. sugar

Pinch of white pepper
*2 tbsp. melted
   margarine*
*2 tbsp. all-purpose
   flour*
Parmesan cheese

Combine corn, milk, whipping cream, salt, MSG, sugar and white pepper in saucepan; mix well. Bring to a simmer, stirring frequently. Blend margarine and flour in small bowl. Stir into corn mixture; mix well. Pour into 1 1/2-quart casserole. Sprinkle with Parmesan cheese. Broil until brown and bubbly. Yield: 6 to 8 servings.

MEXICAN CORN SCRAMBLE

1 c. chopped onion
1/4 c. margarine
10 eggs, beaten
1 12-oz. can Mexicorn
*1 2 1/2-oz. can sliced
   black olives, drained*

*1 c. shredded Monterey
   Jack cheese*
4 oz. dry salami, sliced
Tortilla chips
Taco sauce

Sauté onion in margarine in large skillet over medium heat until tender-crisp. Add eggs, corn and olives; stir gently until eggs begin to set. Stir in cheese and salami. Cook until eggs are set and cheese is melted, stirring frequently. Stand tortilla chips around edge of skillet; top with taco sauce. Yield: 10 to 12 servings.

MEXI-CORN

*2 16-oz. cans cream-
   style corn*
2 c. soft bread crumbs
*1/2 c. chopped green
   onions*
*1/2 c. chopped green
   bell pepper*

1/2 c. chopped pimento
*2 12-oz. cans whole
   kernel corn*
2 tsp. salt
1/2 tsp. pepper
2 eggs, beaten

Combine cream-style corn, bread crumbs, onions, green pepper, pimento, whole kernel corn, salt, pepper and eggs in bowl; mix well. Pour into greased 9x13-inch baking dish. Bake at 350 degrees for 45 to 60 minutes or until set. Yield: 25 servings.

CORN SLAW

1/4 c. sour cream
1/4 c. mayonnaise
1 tsp. prepared mustard
2 tbsp. white vinegar
1 tbsp. sugar
1/2 tsp. salt
1/4 tsp. pepper

*1 17-oz. can whole
   kernel corn, drained*
2 carrots, grated
*1 green bell pepper,
   finely chopped*
*1/2 c. finely chopped
   onion*

Combine sour cream, mayonnaise, mustard, vinegar, sugar, salt and pepper in large bowl; mix well. Add corn, carrots, green pepper and onion; mix well. Refrigerate until serving time. Yield: 4 to 6 servings.

AMERICAN CORN SOUFFLÉ

Parmesan cheese
1/4 c. melted butter
1/4 c. all-purpose flour
1/4 tsp. salt
1/8 tsp. pepper
1 c. milk
*1 c. shredded Colby
   cheese*

4 eggs, separated
*1 10-oz. package
   frozen whole kernel
   corn, cooked, drained*
*6 slices bacon, crisp-
   fried, crumbled*
1/4 tsp. cream of tartar

Sprinkle Parmesan cheese to coat bottom and side of well-buttered 1 1/2 quart soufflé dish. Blend butter, flour, salt and pepper in medium saucepan over medium heat. Whisk in milk gradually. Cook until mixture thickens, stirring constantly. Cook for 1 minute longer; remove from heat. Stir in Colby cheese until melted. Whisk half the hot mixture into beaten egg yolks; whisk egg yolk mixture into hot mixture. Stir in corn and bacon. Beat egg whites with cream of tartar until stiff peaks form. Fold in corn mixture gently. Pour into prepared soufflé dish. Bake at 350 degrees for 45 to 50 minutes or until puffed and brown. Serve immediately. Yield: 6 servings.

CORN AND POTATO SOUP

2 stalks celery, chopped
2 lg. potatoes, peeled,
  chopped
1 med. onion, chopped
1 16-oz. can whole
  kernel corn
2 soup cans milk

1 2-oz. jar pimento
  strips
1 10-oz. can cream
  of mushroom soup
1 10-oz. can cream
  of chicken soup

Cook celery, potatoes and onion in water to cover in large saucepan until tender. Add remaining ingredients; mix well. Heat to serving temperature, stirring frequently; do not boil. Yield: 10 servings.

Corn Bread

BEST CORN BREAD

3/4 c. sugar
2 c. buttermilk baking
  mix
3/4 c. yellow cornmeal
1/2 tsp. baking powder

1 c. milk
2 eggs, slightly beaten
1 tsp. vanilla extract
3/4 c. melted margarine

Combine all ingredients in bowl in order listed, mixing well after each addition. Pour into greased and floured 8x8-inch baking pan. Bake at 350 degrees for 35 to 40 minutes or until golden brown. Serve warm with butter and honey.
Yield: 9 servings.

BROCCOLI CORN BREAD

1 10-oz. package
  frozen chopped
  broccoli
1 8-oz. package corn
  bread mix

1 med. onion, chopped
4 eggs, beaten
1/2 c. melted margarine
3/4 c. cottage cheese
Tabasco sauce to taste

Cook broccoli according to package directions; drain. Combine next 5 ingredients in bowl; mix well. Stir in cooked broccoli and Tabasco sauce. Pour into greased 9x13-inch baking pan. Bake at 400 degrees for 25 to 30 minutes or until brown. Yield: 24 small squares.

JALAPEÑO CORN BREAD

3 c. corn bread mix
2 lg. onions, grated
1 c. cream-style corn
1 1/2 c. shredded
  longhorn cheese
2 tbsp. sugar
Garlic to taste

3 eggs, beaten
1/2 c. corn oil
2 c. milk
1 lb. bacon, crisp-fried,
  crumbled
1 c. chopped jalapeño
  peppers

Combine first 9 ingredients in bowl; mix well. Stir in bacon and jalapeño peppers. Pour into well-greased 9x13-inch baking pan. Bake at 350 degrees for 35 to 40 minutes or until golden brown. Yield: 12 to 15 servings.

ZUCCHINI CORN BREAD

6 eggs
1/4 c. sugar
1 1/2 c. margarine
1/2 c. self-rising flour

2 1/2 c. self-rising
  cornmeal
1 1/2 c. cottage cheese
4 c. shredded zucchini

Combine first 5 ingredients in bowl, mixing well. Stir in cottage cheese and zucchini. Pour into greased 9x13-inch baking pan. Bake at 400 degrees for 30 minutes or until brown. Yield: 12 servings.

CORNMEAL CRISPS

2 c. yellow cornmeal
1/4 tsp. salt
1/8 tsp. seasoned salt
Pepper to taste

Dash of cayenne
  pepper
2 1/2 c. boiling water
3 to 4 tsp. margarine

Mix cornmeal and seasonings in bowl. Add boiling water; stir until smooth. Melt margarine in large heavy iron skillet. Pour into batter; mix well. Drop by tablespoonfuls into 2 1/2 to 3-inch circles in hot skillet; circles may touch. Bake at 375 degrees for 45 minutes. Turn crisps over. Decrease temperature to 250 degrees. Bake for 15 minutes longer. Turn off oven. Let stand in warm oven for 15 minutes. Yield: 20 crisps.

CORN BREAD SALAD

2 pkg. jalapeño corn
  bread mix
1 green onion, chopped
1 green bell pepper,
  chopped
2 tomatoes, chopped
1 16-oz. can corn
1 1/2 c. mayonnaise

1 c. shredded Cheddar
  cheese
8 slices bacon, crisp-
  fried, crumbled
1/2 c. sour cream
1/2 tsp. chili powder
Pepper to taste
Avocado slices

Prepare corn bread according to package directions. Cool and crumble into bowl. Add vegetables, mayonnaise, cheese, bacon, sour cream and seasonings; mix well. Chill overnight. Garnish with avocado. Yield: 10 to 12 servings.

⇨
Recipe for this photograph is on
page 60.

Family Easter Dinner

Strawberry and Cheese Ring

page 163

Cold Spring Cucumber Soup

page 76

Fresh Spinach Salad

page 162

Roast Leg of Lamb or

page 101

Glazed Cornish Game Hens

page 73

Sesame Garden Asparagus

page 20

New Spring Potatoes

page 138

Chocolate Syrup Swirl Cake

page 60

The first celebration of Spring, Easter is the perfect time to gather family to enjoy the tender new vegetables and fruits of the season and to look forward to the promise of golden days ahead.

Cornish Hen

BARBECUED HERB-MUSTARD CORNISH HEN 🍎

1/2 c. dry white wine	2 cloves of garlic,
2/3 c. oil	minced
6 tbsp. wine vinegar	1/2 tsp. pepper
2 tbsp. finely chopped	1/4 c. spicy brown
onion	mustard
1/2 tsp. salt	3 Cornish hens, cut
1 tsp. Italian seasoning	into halves

Combine wine, oil, vinegar, onion, salt, seasoning, garlic, pepper and mustard in bowl; mix well. Pour over hens in dish, coating all pieces, cover. Chill for 4 hours or overnight, stirring frequently. Drain, reserving marinade. Cook over low coals for 30 to 45 minutes or until tender, turning and basting frequently with reserved marinade.
Yield: 6 servings.

CORNISH HENS FOR TWO

1/2 envelope dry onion	2 oven-ready Cornish
soup mix	game hens
6 tbsp. water	1 tbsp. melted
1 c. unseasoned	margarine
stuffing mix cubes	1/2 c. water
1/4 c. chopped peanuts	1 1-serving env.
3 tbsp. raisins	instant cream of
Pinch of ginger	chicken soup mix

Combine onion soup mix and 6 tablespoons water in bowl. Add next 4 ingredients. Spoon stuffing into game hens. Place in shallow baking dish. Brush with margarine. Bake at 375 degrees for 45 minutes or until tender. Place on heated serving plate. Combine 3 tablespoons pan drippings, 1/2 cup water and chicken soup mix in saucepan. Heat to serving temperature. Serve with game hens.
Yield: 2 servings.

GLAZED CORNISH GAME HENS

6 1-lb. Cornish	1 tbsp. all-purpose flour
game hens	1 tbsp. sugar
1/2 tsp. salt	2 tsp. curry powder
1/4 tsp. pepper	2 tsp. instant chicken
1/4 tsp. thyme	bouillon
1/2 c. melted butter	1/2 tsp. salt
4 slices bacon, chopped	1 c. apricot nectar
1 med. onion, finely	1 tbsp. lemon juice
chopped	

Remove giblets from hens. Wash hens and pat dry. Combine 1/2 teaspoon salt, pepper and thyme.

Sprinkle mixture in cavities of hens; truss with string. Place breast side up in large roasting pan. Brush with melted butter. Roast at 375 degrees for 1 hour, basting with melted butter and pan drippings. Sauté bacon in skillet until almost crisp. Add onion. Sauté until transparent. Stir in flour, sugar, curry powder, chicken bouillon and 1/2 teaspoon salt. Cook until bubbly. Stir in apricot nectar and lemon juice. Simmer for 5 minutes or until thickened, stirring constantly. Cut away string from hens. Drain pan drippings. Spoon half the apricot glaze over hens in roasting pan. Roast for 10 minutes. Spoon remaining glaze over top.
Yield: 6 servings.

Crab

CORN AND CRAB MEAT BISQUE

1/2 c. melted butter	1/2 tsp. Worcestershire
2 tbsp. all-purpose	sauce
flour	1/2 tsp. Tabasco sauce
1/2 c. chopped onion	1/4 c. shredded cheese
1 lb. white crab meat	1/4 c. chopped parsley
1 16-oz. can cream-	1/4 c. chopped shallots
style corn	1 tbsp. Konriko
1 10-oz. can cream	seasoning
of potato soup	

Blend butter and flour in 5-quart soup pot. Add onion. Cook over low heat for 10 minutes, stirring frequently. Add crab meat and next 4 ingredients. Cook over low heat for 15 to 20 minutes. Stir in cheese, parsley, shallots and seasoning just before serving. Yield: 15 to 20 servings.

WILD CRAB CASSEROLE

1 1/2 c. chopped celery	1/4 c. butter
1 c. chopped onion	1/2 c. all-purpose flour
1 c. chopped	4 c. light cream
mushrooms	2 egg yolks, beaten
3 shallots, chopped	1 c. Parmesan cheese
2 cloves of garlic,	1 c. wild rice, cooked
minced	1 1/2 lb. crab meat
1 tsp. thyme	

Sauté celery, onion, mushrooms, shallots, garlic, thyme and salt and pepper to taste in 1/4 cup butter in skillet until tender. Sprinkle with flour. Stir in cream. Cook until thickened, stirring constantly. Stir 1 cup cream mixture into egg yolks; stir egg yolks into hot mixture. Bring to a boil, stirring constantly. Stir in cheese. Mix in rice and crab meat. Spoon into 9x13-inch baking pan. Bake at 425 degrees for 15 minutes. Yield: 8 servings.

CRAB TARTS

1 7¹/₂-oz. can king crab meat	¹/₂ tsp. Worcestershire sauce
1 tbsp. lemon juice	3 drops of Tabasco sauce
¹/₄ c. chopped celery	
¹/₄ c. minced scallions	¹/₄ tsp. seasoned salt
¹/₂ c. shredded Cheddar cheese	24 unbaked Miniature Pastry Shells

Drain crab meat; slice larger pieces. Toss with lemon juice in bowl. Mix in celery, scallions, Cheddar cheese and seasonings. Spoon into unbaked Miniature Pastry Shells. Bake at 350 degrees for 30 minutes or until pastry is delicately golden. Cool for 2 minutes. Lift from muffin cups with tip of small, sharp knife. Serve at once. Yield: 24 tarts.

Miniature Pastry Shells

3 oz. cream cheese, softened	¹/₂ c. butter, softened
	1 c. all-purpose flour

Blend cream cheese and butter in bowl with wooden spoon. Work in flour gradually. Press dough flat in bowl. Refrigerate for 30 minutes. Mark dough into 24 equal portions with knife or spatula. Shape each portion into ball; press over bottom and up side of ³/₄-inch diameter muffin cup. Yield: 24 shells.

CRAB AND ASPARAGUS BELMONT

2 tbsp. melted butter	¹/₂ tsp. salt
2 tbsp. all-purpose flour	¹/₂ tsp. dry mustard
1¹/₂ c. milk	¹/₈ tsp. cayenne pepper
1 c. shredded Cheddar cheese	¹/₈ tsp. paprika
	1 lb. asparagus, cooked
	1 lb. back-fin crab meat

Blend butter and flour in saucepan. Stir in milk. Cook until thickened, stirring constantly; reduce heat. Add cheese and seasonings. Cook until cheese melts, stirring constantly. Arrange asparagus in ramekins. Sprinkle with crab meat. Pour sauce over crab meat. Broil until bubbly. Yield: 4 servings.

CRAB PUFFS

¹/₂ c. margarine, softened	1¹/₂ tsp. garlic salt
1 5-oz. jar Old English cheese spread	2 tbsp. mayonnaise
	1 7-oz. can crab meat, drained
	12 bagels, split

Combine margarine, cheese spread, garlic salt, mayonnaise and crab meat in bowl. Spread on bagels. Cut into quarters. Place on baking sheet. Freeze until firm. Broil crab puffs for 5 minutes. Yield: 8 dozen.

CREAMY CRAB SANDWICH

8 oz. cream cheese, softened	2 dashes hot sauce
¹/₄ tsp. margarine	8 oz. crab meat
1 tsp. Worcestershire sauce	4 English muffins, split
1 tbsp. chopped onion	8 tomato slices
1 tsp. prepared mustard	8 slices white American cheese
1 tbsp. lemon juice	16 half-slices crisp-fried bacon

Combine first 7 ingredients in bowl. Beat until light and fluffy. Fold in crab meat. Spread on English muffin halves. Top each with tomato, cheese and bacon. Place on baking sheet. Bake at 350 degrees for 8 to 10 minutes or until cheese melts. Yield: 8 servings.

Cranberry

HOLIDAY CRANBERRY CAKE

4¹/₂ tbsp. margarine, softened	3³/₄ c. whole fresh cranberries
1¹/₂ c. sugar	³/₄ c. margarine
3 c. flour	1¹/₂ c. sugar
1 tbsp. baking powder	1 c. plus 2 tbsp. whipping cream
¹/₈ tsp. salt	
1¹/₂ c. milk	

Cream margarine and sugar in mixer bowl until light and fluffy. Add mixture of flour, baking powder and salt alternately with milk, mixing well after each addition. Fold in cranberries. Pour into greased and floured 11x13-inch cake pan. Bake at 350 degrees for 45 minutes or until cake tests done. Cook remaining ingredients in saucepan for 10 minutes, stirring constantly. Serve hot sauce over cake. Yield: 15 servings.

FALL CRANBERRY MUFFINS

¹/₂ c. oil	1 c. all-purpose flour
2 eggs	1 tbsp. baking powder
²/₃ c. milk	1 tsp. soda
1¹/₂ c. cranberries, chopped	¹/₄ c. sugar
1 c. whole wheat flour	1 tsp. cinnamon
	1 c. chopped pecans

Combine oil, eggs, milk and cranberries in mixer bowl; mix well. Add flours, baking powder, soda, sugar, cinnamon and pecans; mix just until moistened. Fill oiled muffin cups ¹/₂ full. Bake at 350 degrees for 15 to 20 minutes or until golden brown. Yield: 12 servings.

ALL-SEASON SALAD

1 16-oz. can whole
  cranberry sauce
1 tbsp. lemon juice
1 c. whipped topping
1/2 c. chopped pecans

1/4 c. confectioners'
  sugar
1 c. drained crushed
  pineapple

Combine cranberry sauce and lemon juice in bowl; mix well. Spoon into lightly oiled 6-cup mold. Freeze until firm. Mix whipped topping, pecans, confectioners' sugar and pineapple in bowl. Spoon over frozen layer. Freeze until firm. Serve on lettuce-lined plates. Yield: 8 servings.

CRANBERRY SUNDAES JUBILEE

1 10-oz. package
  frozen cranberry-
  orange relish
4 sugar cubes

Orange extract
4 scoops vanilla ice
  cream

Heat relish in saucepan over low heat, stirring occasionally. Soak sugar cubes in orange extract for 5 to 10 minutes. Spoon hot relish over ice cream in dessert dishes. Top each with sugar cube; ignite. Serve immediately. May substitute one 8-ounce can whole cranberry sauce for relish. Yield: 4 servings.

CRANBERRY CHILL

1 lb. cranberries
2 c. boiling water
1 tsp. unflavored
  gelatin

1/4 c. cold water
2 c. sugar
2 c. ginger ale

Cook cranberries in 2 cups boiling water in saucepan until berries pop. Press through sieve. Dissolve gelatin in cold water. Stir gelatin and sugar into hot mixture until dissolved. Add ginger ale. Place in freezer container. Freeze until firm, stirring several times. Yield: 6 servings.

Crêpes

COMPANY CHICKEN CRÊPES

3 chicken breasts
1 chicken bouillon cube
1 cup water
1 cup finely chopped
  celery
1/2 c. diced onion

6 tbsp. butter
1/3 c. all-purpose flour
1 tsp. salt
1 c. half and half
16 Crêpes
1/4 c. slivered almonds

Place chicken, bouillon cube and water in medium saucepan. Simmer, covered, for 40 minutes, or until chicken is tender. Remove chicken; bone and chop. Add enough water to broth to measure 1 1/2 cups. Add celery and onion. Simmer for 10 minutes. Melt butter in saucepan. Stir in flour and salt. Add broth mixture and half and half. Cook until sauce thickens, stirring constantly. Stir in chicken. Spoon chicken mixture onto crêpes; roll to enclose filling. Place seam side down in 9x13-inch baking pan. Spoon any remaining chicken mixture over top. Sprinkle with almonds. Bake at 350 degrees for 20 minutes. Yield: 8 servings.

Crêpes

1 c. milk
3 eggs, well beaten
1 tbsp. sugar

3/4 c. sifted all-purpose
  flour
1/4 tsp. salt

Blend milk and eggs in mixer bowl; sift in sugar, flour and salt. Beat until smooth. Preheat lightly greased 8-inch skillet over medium heat. Pour in 3 to 4 tablespoons batter, rotating pan to spread batter evenly. Bake until light golden brown on both sides. Repeat with remaining batter. Stack between layers of waxed paper.

SPRING CRÊPES CHANTILLY

1 1/2 c. all-purpose flour
1 tbsp. sugar
1/2 tsp. baking powder
1/2 tsp. salt
2 c. milk
2 eggs

2 tbsp. melted butter
1/2 tsp. vanilla extract
Chantilly Cream
15 slices fresh
  strawberries

Sift flour, sugar, baking powder and salt into mixer bowl. Add milk, eggs and butter; beat until smooth. Add vanilla. Beat for 15 seconds; batter will be thin. Pour 1/4 cup into lightly oiled crêpe pan, tilting to coat evenly. Cook until light brown on both sides, turning once. Repeat with remaining batter, stacking crêpes between waxed paper. Spoon Chantilly Cream onto crêpes; roll to enclose filling. Place on serving plates. Top with remaining Chantilly Cream and strawberry slice. Yield: 15 crêpes.

Chantilly Cream

3/4 c. whipping cream
1/4 c. sifted
  confectioners' sugar

3/4 c. sliced fresh
  strawberries

Beat chilled whipping cream and confectioners' sugar in mixer bowl until soft peaks form. Fold strawberries gently into whipped cream.

Cucumber

CUCUMBER SALAD WITH YOGURT

2 lg. cucumbers, thinly sliced	*1/4 c. chopped fresh cilantro*
1 tbsp. coarse salt	*1/2 tsp. salt*
2 c. low-fat yogurt	*2 med. tomatoes, seeded, chopped*
1/2 c. low-fat sour cream	*Curly leaf lettuce*
1 tsp. ground cumin	

Sprinkle cucumbers with coarse salt; cover. Let stand, covered, for 30 minutes. Rinse several times in cold water; drain well. Squeeze dry with paper towels. Set aside. Mix yogurt, sour cream, cumin, cilantro and 1/2 teaspoon salt in small bowl. Chill, covered, until serving time. Combine cucumber, yogurt mixture and tomatoes in large bowl; toss gently to mix well. Spoon into lettuce-lined salad bowl. Yield: 8 servings.

COLD SPRING CUCUMBER SOUP

3 tbsp. margarine, melted	*2 tbsp. all-purpose flour*
2 leeks, finely chopped	*3 c. chicken broth*
3 cucumbers, thinly sliced	*1 tsp. salt*
2 bay leaves	*2 c. half and half*
	Chopped fresh dill
	1/3 c. sour cream

Combine margarine, leeks, cucumbers and bay leaves in 2-quart saucepan. Simmer for 20 minutes; discard bay leaves. Mix in flour. Stir in broth gradually. Add salt. Bring to a boil, stirring constantly. Simmer for 30 minutes. Process in blender container; strain through ricer or large strainer. Chill in refrigerator. Stir in half and half. Chill until serving time. Garnish with fresh dill and sour cream. Serve with crackers. Yield: 6 servings.

Curry

CURRIED CHICKEN SALAD

3 c. chopped cooked chicken	*1/2 c. chopped celery*
1/2 c. sliced water chestnuts	*1 c. mayonnaise*
	2 tbsp. curry powder
1/2 c. seedless grape halves	*1 tbsp. soy sauce*
	1 tbsp. lemon juice

Combine chicken, water chestnuts, grapes and celery in bowl. Mix mayonnaise and remaining ingredients in small bowl. Add to chicken; toss to mix well. Chill until serving time. Serve on a bed of lettuce. Garnish with toasted sliced almonds. Yield: 4 servings.

AFRICAN TURKEY CURRY

3 c. coarsely chopped cooked turkey	*2 bananas, mashed*
	1 apple, chopped
1/2 c. all-purpose flour	*1 c. chopped orange*
2 lg. onions, cut into quarters	*1 c. pineapple chunks*
	1/2 c. raisins
2 tbsp. (or more) curry powder	*1 tsp. cardamom*
	1 tsp. nutmeg
1/2 c. butter	*2 bananas, sliced*
1 c. milk	

Coat turkey with flour; set aside. Sauté onions and curry powder in butter in large skillet. Add turkey. Cook over low heat for 5 minutes. Add milk and mashed bananas; mix well. Stir in apple, orange, pineapple, raisins and spices. Simmer for 20 minutes. Add sliced bananas. Simmer for 10 minutes longer. Serve with rice, chutney and shredded coconut. Yield: 8 servings.

Dates

ORANGE AND DATE BREAD

1 c. boiling water	*1 c. sugar*
Juice and grated rind of 1 orange	*1 tsp. vanilla extract*
	1 egg, beaten
1 c. dates	*2 c. all-purpose flour*
1 tsp. soda	*1 tsp. baking powder*
2 tbsp. margarine, softened	*1/4 tsp. salt*
	1/2 c. chopped walnuts

Add enough boiling water to orange juice to measure 1 cup. Process orange rind in food processor container until grated. Add dates; process until smooth. Place date mixture in bowl; add orange juice. Stir in soda, margarine, sugar and vanilla. Add egg, flour, baking powder and salt; beat well. Fold in walnuts. Pour into greased loaf pan. Bake at 350 degrees for 50 minutes. Cool on rack. Yield: 1 loaf.

BACON-WRAPPED DATES

50 whole almonds
1 16-oz. package
pitted dates
1 16-oz. package
thinly sliced bacon

Place 1 almond in each date. Cut each bacon slice into 3 pieces. Wrap 1 piece around each date; secure with toothpick. Place on baking sheet. Bake for 20 to 30 minutes or until bacon is crisp. Yield: 50 appetizers.

DATE NUT BREAD

8 oz. dates, pitted
2 tsp. soda
2 c. boiling water
4 c. all-purpose flour
2 eggs
2 tbsp. margarine
2 tsp. vanilla extract
1/2 c. chopped pecans
2 c. sugar
1 tsp. salt

Combine first 3 ingredients in bowl. Let stand until cool. Mix in flour, eggs, margarine, vanilla, pecans, sugar and salt. Pour into 5 greased 16-ounce cans. Bake at 350 degrees for 1 hour or until bread tests done. Cool in cans for 5 minutes. Remove to wire rack to cool completely. Yield: 5 loaves.

DATE AND PEANUT BUTTER BALLS

1 c. chopped dates
1 c. finely chopped
peanuts
1 1/2 c. peanut butter
1 c. confectioners'
sugar
1 egg
1 tsp. vanilla extract
1/2 tsp. cinnamon
1/4 stick paraffin
1 8-oz. bar milk
chocolate candy

Mix first 4 ingredients in bowl. Add egg, vanilla and cinnamon; mix well. Shape into balls. Chill for 1 to 2 hours. Melt paraffin and candy bar in double boiler. Dip balls into chocolate mixture; place on waxed paper. Yield: 24 balls.

DATE PINWHEEL COOKIES

8 oz. dates, chopped
1/3 c. sugar
1/3 c. water
1/2 c. chopped pecans
1/2 tsp. vanilla extract
1/2 c. shortening
1 c. packed brown
sugar
2 eggs
1/2 tsp. vanilla extract
2 1/3 c. all-purpose flour
1/2 tsp. baking powder
1/4 tsp. soda
1/4 tsp. salt
1/4 tsp. cinnamon

Combine dates, sugar and water in saucepan. Bring to a boil. Cook over low heat until thickened, stirring constantly. Remove from heat. Stir in pecans and 1/2 teaspoon vanilla. Chill. Cream shortening and brown sugar in mixer bowl until light and fluffy. Blend in eggs and 1/2 teaspoon vanilla. Add sifted dry ingredients. Roll to 10x18-inch rectangle on floured surface. Spread with date mixture. Roll from long side as for jelly roll; seal edges. Cut into halves crosswise. Chill, wrapped in waxed paper. Slice rolls 1/4 inch thick. Place cut side down on greased cookie sheet. Bake at 350 degrees for 8 minutes. Cool. Yield: 6 dozen.

DATE PUDDING

2 c. packed brown
sugar
2 c. water
1 c. dates
1/4 c. hot water
1 c. chopped pecans
1 1/2 c. all-purpose flour
1 c. sugar
2 tsp. baking powder
1 c. milk

Mix brown sugar and 2 cups water in 9x13-inch dish. Mix dates and 1/4 cup hot water in small bowl. Add date mixture and pecans to brown sugar mixture. Combine remaining ingredients in bowl; mix well. Pour into prepared dish. Bake at 350 degrees for 35 to 40 minutes. Yield: 12 servings.

DATE AND PECAN TORTE

1 c. boiling water
3/4 c. chopped dates
1 tsp. soda
1 tsp. margarine,
softened
1 c. sugar
1 egg
1 1/2 c. all-purpose flour
1 tsp. baking powder
1/2 c. chopped pecans
2 c. whipping cream
1/4 c. sugar

Pour boiling water over dates and soda in bowl. Let stand for several minutes. Beat margarine, 1 cup sugar and egg in mixer bowl until light. Stir in date mixture. Add flour, baking powder and pecans; mix well. Spoon into greased cake pans. Bake at 375 degrees for 45 to 60 minutes. Remove to wire rack to cool. Beat whipping cream in mixer bowl until soft peaks form. Mix in 1/4 cup sugar. Spread between layers and over top and side of cake. Store in refrigerator. Yield: 12 servings.

Dill

DILLY CHEESE BREAD

3 c. buttermilk
baking mix
1 1/2 c. shredded sharp
Cheddar cheese
1 tbsp. sugar
1/2 tsp. dillweed
1/2 tsp. dry mustard
1 1/4 c. milk
1 egg, beaten
1 tbsp. oil

Combine first 5 ingredients in large bowl; mix well. Add milk, egg and oil; stir until moistened. Spoon into greased loaf pan. Bake at 350 degrees for 50 minutes or until golden brown. Yield: 1 loaf.

DILLY BREAD

3 c. all-purpose flour
l tbsp. baking powder
1/2 tsp. soda
1 tsp. salt
1 tbsp. sugar
1/4 c. Parmesan cheese
1/2 tsp. dry mustard
1 egg, beaten
1/4 c. oil
1 1/4 c. buttermilk
1/4 c. sour cream
1/2 tsp. dried dillweed

Sift first 7 dry ingredients into bowl. Beat egg with oil, buttermilk, sour cream and dillweed. Mix into flour mixture; do not beat. Pour into large well-greased loaf pan. Bake at 350 degrees for 45 minutes or until loaf tests done. Yield: 12 slices.

Divinity

PINWHEEL DIVINITY

2 1/2 c. sugar
1/2 c. light corn syrup
1/2 c. water
1/4 tsp. salt
2 egg whites
1/2 tsp. almond extract
Confectioners' sugar
1 c. finely chopped toasted almonds
1 c. finely chopped mixed red and green candied cherries

Combine sugar, corn syrup, water and salt in 2-quart saucepan. Bring to a boil over low heat; stir until sugar dissolves. Cook, covered, over high heat for 2 minutes or until steam dissolves sugar crystals from side of pan. Cook over medium heat to 260 degrees on candy thermometer, hard-ball stage; do not stir. Beat egg whites in large mixer bowl until stiff peaks form. Add hot syrup in fine stream; beat constantly at high speed. Add almond flavoring. Beat for 4 minutes or until very stiff. Place on tea towel dusted generously with confectioners' sugar. Roll as thin as possible. Cut into strips about 4 inches wide. Sprinkle with mixture of almonds and candied cherries; press in lightly. Roll each strip tightly as for jelly roll from long side. Rolls should not be more than l inch in diameter. Wrap individually in foil. Store in refrigerator. Cut into thin slices. Yield: 2 pounds.

DIVINITY CANDY

3 c. sugar
1 c. light corn syrup
1/2 c. water
3 egg whites, stiffly beaten
1/2 c. coarsely chopped pecans
1/2 tsp. almond or vanilla extract

Bring sugar, corn syrup and water to a boil in saucepan over medium heat, stirring until sugar is completely dissolved. Cook over high heat to 250 to 268 degrees on candy thermometer, hard-ball stage, stirring occasionally. Pour in very thin stream over egg whites in bowl, beating constantly until mixture is very stiff and loses its luster. Stir in pecans and flavoring. Drop by spoonfuls onto waxed paper or pour 3/4 inch thick in greased dish. Let stand until firm. Yield: 30 ounces.

Doughnuts

CAKE DOUGHNUTS

2 1/2 c. sugar
6 eggs
1 c. cold unseasoned mashed potatoes
12 tbsp. shortening
8 tsp. baking powder
7 1/2 c. all-purpose flour
1 tsp. salt
1 tbsp. vanilla extract
1 1/4 c. milk
Oil for deep frying

Beat sugar and eggs in mixer bowl until thick and foamy. Add potatoes and shortening; beat until smooth. Sift dry ingredients together. Add vanilla to milk. Add dry ingredients to egg mixture alternately with milk mixture, mixing well after each addition. Batter will be very stiff. Chill for 2 hours to overnight. Roll about 1/2 inch thick on lightly floured surface; cut with doughnut cutter. Deep-fry at 365 to 370 degrees. Drain on paper towels. Roll in additional sugar. Yield: 4 1/2 dozen.

FRENCH DOUGHNUTS

5 tbsp. margarine, softened
1/2 c. sugar
1 egg, beaten
1 1/2 c. all-purpose flour
2 1/4 tsp. baking powder
1/4 tsp. salt
1/2 c. milk
Cinnamon-sugar

Cream margarine and sugar in bowl until light and fluffy. Add egg; mix well. Sift flour, baking powder and salt together. Add to creamed mixture alternately with milk, beating well after each addition. Fill greased muffin cups 1/2 full. Top with cinnamon-sugar. Bake at 350 degrees for 20 to 25 minutes. Serve warm. Yield: 6 to 8 doughnuts.

MILO DOUGHNUTS

2 cakes compressed yeast
1/4 c. warm water
1 1/2 c. milk
1/4 c. shortening
1/2 c. sugar
2 tsp. salt
2 eggs
4 to 5 c. all-purpose flour
2 c. milo flour
Oil for deep frying
1 lb. confectioners' sugar
1/4 c. (about) milk

Dissolve yeast in warm water in large bowl. Heat 1½ cups milk to scalding in saucepan. Stir in shortening, sugar and salt. Cool to lukewarm. Add milk mixture and beaten eggs to yeast. Add 2½ cups all-purpose flour; beat until smooth. Stir in milo flour and enough remaining all-purpose flour to make soft dough. Let rise, covered, in warm place for 10 minutes. Knead on floured surface until smooth and elastic, kneading in up to ½ cup flour. Place in greased bowl; brush with melted shortening. Let rise, covered, for 1 hour. Punch dough down. Let rise, covered, in warm place for 45 minutes. Roll on lightly floured surface. Cut with floured doughnut cutter. Let stand for 20 to 30 minutes. Deep-fry in 365 degree oil until golden. Drain on paper towel. Mix confectioners' sugar with ¼ cup milk. Dip hot doughnuts into glaze. Drain on wire rack. Note: Make milo flour by processing milo in blender container until finely ground. Sift to remove unprocessed particles. Yield: 36 doughnuts.

Duck

ROAST BREAST OF DUCK

4 to 8 duck breasts, skinned
1 med. apple, quartered
Leaves of 5 or 6 celery stalks
1 6-oz. jar plum jelly
1 pkg. instant brown gravy mix
1 6-oz. can frozen orange juice concentrate

Place duck, apple and celery in medium oven-cooking bag, according to manufacturer's instructions. Place in 9x13 baking dish. Purée remaining ingredients in blender container. Spoon orange juice mixture over duck in bag; fasten bag securely. Bake at 375 degrees for 1 hour or until tender. Remove duck to warm serving platter. Serve with orange sauce. Yield: 4 to 8 servings.

DUCKLING WITH KUMQUAT SAUCE

1 duckling
1½ tsp. salt
1 tsp. pepper
2 tsp. paprika
2 tsp. poultry seasoning
½ c. puréed preserved kumquats
½ c. Burgundy
1 tsp. lemon juice
1 tbsp. butter
¼ c. sugar
¼ tsp. salt
1 tsp. instant chicken bouillon
½ c. hot water
Pinch each of nutmeg, cloves, thyme and allspice
2 tsp. cornstarch
1 tbsp. green peppercorns

Cut duckling into quarters. Rinse and pat dry. Rub with 1½ teaspoons salt, pepper, paprika and poultry seasoning. Place skin side down in skillet. Cook over medium heat for 1 hour, turning every 20 minutes. Do not drain during cooking. Combine kumquat purée, wine, lemon juice, butter, sugar and ¼ teaspoon salt in saucepan. Stir in bouillon dissolved in hot water and spices. Cook until mixture is reduced by half. Add mixture of cornstarch and a small amount of water. Cook until thickened, stirring constantly. Rinse and drain peppercorns. Stir into sauce. Place duckling on serving plate. Spoon hot sauce over top. Yield: 4 servings.

Dumplings

DUMPLINGS

2 c. water
½ c. margarine
4 c. all-purpose flour
1 tsp. salt
6 c. chicken broth

Bring 2 cups water to a boil in saucepan. Stir in margarine until melted; remove from heat. Add flour and salt; mix well. Knead lightly on floured surface. Roll ¼ at a time to ⅛-inch thickness on lightly floured surface. Cut into 1-inch squares. Bring broth to a boil in large saucepan. Drop dumplings into boiling broth. Simmer for 20 minutes or until dumplings are tender. Yield: 8 servings.

POTATO DUMPLINGS

1½ tsp. salt
1 c. sifted all-purpose flour
½ tsp. nutmeg
2 tsp. baking powder
2 eggs, slightly beaten
2 lb. potatoes, cooked, mashed
2 qt. boiling water
Melted butter
Minced parsley

Mix 1½ teaspoons salt, all-purpose flour, nutmeg and baking powder in bowl. Add slightly beaten eggs and flour mixture to cooled mashed potatoes; mix well. Drop mixture by spoonfuls into rapidly boiling salted water in saucepan. Cook until dumplings rise to surface. Simmer, covered, for 5 minutes or until centers are cooked through; drain. Place in serving bowl. Pour melted butter over dumplings to prevent sticking. Sprinkle dumplings with minced parsley. Serve immediately. Yield: 2 dozen.

PERFECT DUMPLINGS

2 c. all-purpose flour   *¹/₂ c. milk*
2 tsp. baking powder   *2 slices bread, toasted*
2 eggs, slightly beaten

Sift flour and baking powder into bowl. Add eggs and milk; mix lightly. Cut toast into cubes. Add to dough; mix lightly. Let stand for 30 minutes. Shape into 2 loaves on floured surface. Bring enough water to cover dumplings to a boil in saucepan. Add dumplings. Cook, covered, for 10 minutes. Turn dumplings over. Cook, covered, for 10 minutes longer. Yield: 6 servings.

Eclairs

DEEP-FRIED ÉCLAIRS

3 frozen pastry shells,   *1¹/₂ c. milk*
   thawed but still cold   *¹/₄ c. sour cream*
Oil for deep frying   *2 tbsp. Brandy*
1 3-oz. package   *Confectioners' sugar*
   vanilla pudding mix

Roll pastry shells into 5 x 8 rectangles on floured surface; trim edges evenly with sharp knife. Cut each rectangle in half; each piece should be about 2¹/₂ x 8 inches. Heat 3 inches oil in wok to 375 degrees. Drop 2 or 3 cold pastry strips into hot oil. Fry until puffed and golden on both sides; drain on paper towels. Slit into halves horizontally. Place in single layer in shallow paper towel-lined dish; cover with paper towels. Let stand in dry place until ready to assemble. Combine pudding mix and milk in large saucepan. Bring to a boil over low heat, stirring constantly. Cool to lukewarm. Stir in sour cream and Brandy. Cover with plastic wrap. Chill for 2 to 3 hours or until very thick. Spoon chilled filling on bottom half of each pastry; cover with top. Dust with confectioners' sugar. Chill for up to 2 hours before serving. Yield: 6 servings.

EGGNOG FILLING FOR ÉCLAIRS

2 c. commercial eggnog   *¹/₂ tsp. nutmeg*
3¹/₂ tbsp. cornstarch   *2 tbsp. confectioners'*
2 egg yolks, beaten   *sugar*
1 tbsp. rum extract   *12 baked éclairs*

Combine eggnog and cornstarch in saucepan; mix well. Cook over medium heat until thickened, stirring constantly. Stir a small amount of hot mixture into egg yolks; stir egg yolks into hot mixture. Cook over medium heat for 1 minute longer, stirring constantly; remove from heat. Add rum, nutmeg and confectioners' sugar. Cool to room temperature, stirring occasionally. Chill in refrigerator. Fill éclairs. Yield: 12 éclairs.

ÉCLAIR RING

¹/₂ c. margarine   *1 tsp. vanilla extract*
1 c. water   *2 1-oz. squares*
1 c. all-purpose flour   *semisweet baking*
4 eggs   *chocolate, melted*
2 sm. packages French   *2 tbsp. margarine*
   vanilla instant   *2 tbsp. milk*
   pudding mix   *1 c. confectioners'*
2¹/₂ c. milk   *sugar*
9 oz. whipped topping   *1 tsp. vanilla extract*

Bring ¹/₂ cup margarine and water to a boil in saucepan; reduce heat. Stir in flour all at once. Beat until mixture forms ball. Cool for 10 minutes. Beat in eggs 1 at a time. Spoon into ring on baking sheet. Bake at 400 degrees for 45 to 50 minutes or until light brown. Cool completely in draft-free place. Combine pudding mix and 2¹/₂ cups milk in mixer bowl; mix until smooth. Beat in whipped topping and 1 teaspoon vanilla. Split ring horizontally. Spoon pudding mixture into ring; replace top. Combine remaining ingredients in bowl; mix well. Drizzle over ring. Chill until serving time. Yield: 12 servings.

Egg

GOURMET STUFFED EGGS

6 hard-boiled eggs   *3 tbsp. crumbled crisp-*
¹/₂ tsp. prepared   *fried bacon*
   mustard   *1 tsp. chopped*
2 tbsp. shredded   *green olives*
   Cheddar cheese   *¹/₂ tsp. salt*
1 tbsp. melted   *Pepper to taste*
   margarine   *Paprika to taste*
2 tsp. lemon juice   *12 strips pimento*

Cut eggs into halves lengthwise. Remove yolks, reserving whites. Combine yolks with next 8 ingredients in bowl; mix well. Fill reserved egg whites with yolk mixture. Sprinkle with paprika. Garnish egg halves with pimento. Yield: 6 servings.

DEVILED EGG CASSEROLE

12 hard-boiled eggs	Dash of hot sauce
3 tbsp. mayonnaise	1/8 tsp. Worcestershire
2 tbsp. prepared	sauce
mustard	1 4-oz. jar mushroom
2 tsp. vinegar	caps, drained
Salt and pepper to taste	8 to 12 oz. cooked
1/4 c. all-purpose flour	shrimp (opt.)
1/4 c. melted margarine	1 c. (or more) shredded
2 c. milk	sharp cheese

Cut eggs into halves lengthwise; remove yolks. Mash yolks with mayonnaise, mustard, vinegar, salt and pepper in bowl. Spoon into egg whites. Place in 9x13-inch baking dish. Blend flour with melted margarine in saucepan. Add milk. Cook until mixture thickens, stirring constantly. Stir in hot sauce, Worcestershire sauce, mushrooms and shrimp. Pour over eggs. Sprinkle with cheese. Bake at 350 degrees for 30 minutes.
Yield: 8 to 12 servings.

EGG AND CHEESE BAKE

8 eggs	1/3 c. all-purpose flour
1 env. Italian salad	1 tsp. baking powder
dressing mix	1/3 c. melted margarine
12-oz. cottage cheese	3 c. shredded Monterey
1/2 c. chopped green	Jack cheese
bell pepper	

Beat eggs and dry salad dressing mix in bowl until smooth. Stir in cottage cheese and green pepper; mix well. Add mixture of flour and baking powder. Stir in margarine and cheese. Pour into greased 8x8-inch baking pan. Bake at 375 degrees for 35 minutes or until golden. Yield: 8 servings.

SUMMER VEGETABLE FRITTATA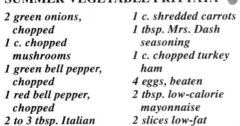

2 green onions,	1 c. shredded carrots
chopped	1 tbsp. Mrs. Dash
1 c. chopped	seasoning
mushrooms	1 c. chopped turkey
1 green bell pepper,	ham
chopped	4 eggs, beaten
1 red bell pepper,	2 tbsp. low-calorie
chopped	mayonnaise
2 to 3 tbsp. Italian	2 slices low-fat
seasoning	mozzarella cheese

Spray skillet with butter-flavored nonstick cooking spray. Sauté vegetables and seasonings in skillet for 2 minutes. Add turkey ham. Sauté for 1 minute. Combine eggs and mayonnaise in bowl; mix well. Stir into vegetables. Spoon into 9-inch pie plate sprayed with cooking spray. Bake at 350 degrees for 25 minutes. Top with cheese. Bake until cheese is melted. Yield: 4 to 6 servings.

HUEVOS RANCHEROS

1/4 c. oil	2 16-oz. cans tomatoes
6 corn tortillas	1/2 tsp. cumin
1 1/4 c. chopped onion	1/2 tsp. chili powder
3/4 c. chopped green	1/8 tsp. pepper
bell pepper	6 eggs
1 clove of garlic,	8 black olives, sliced
minced	3/4 c. shredded sharp
3 tbsp. oil	Cheddar cheese
1 tbsp. all-purpose	
flour	

Heat 1/4 cup oil in skillet. Fry tortillas 1 at a time for 4 seconds on each side or just until softened. Arrange over bottom and 1/2 inch up sides of 8x12-inch baking dish. Sauté onion, green pepper and garlic in 3 tbsp. oil in skillet for 5 minutes. Sprinkle with flour. Cook for 5 minutes. Drain tomatoes, reserving 1/4 cup juice. Chop tomatoes. Add tomatoes, reserved juice and seasonings to sautéed vegetables; mix well. Pour over tortillas. Make 6 indentations in mixture. Break eggs into indentations. Bake, covered, at 350 degrees for 25 minutes. Top with olives and cheese. Bake, uncovered, for 5 minutes longer. Yield: 6 servings.

FESTIVE SCRAMBLED EGGS

1 med. zucchini, sliced	8 eggs, beaten
4 c. fresh mushrooms	1/4 c. milk
2 med. red bell	2 tbsp. melted
peppers, sliced	margarine
2 lg. onions, sliced	1/2 c. shredded
1/4 c. melted margarine	Cheddar cheese
1/2 tsp. salt	

Cut zucchini slices and mushrooms in half. Sauté peppers and onions in 1/4 cup margarine in skillet for 5 minutes. Add zucchini, mushrooms and salt. Cook until tender, stirring occasionally. Remove vegetables; keep warm. Beat eggs and milk in bowl. Add 2 tablespoons margarine to skillet. Add eggs. Cook until eggs are almost set, stirring frequently. Stir in cheese. Spoon eggs and vegetables onto serving platter. Yield: 8 servings.

MEXICAN STRATA

4 c. cheese-flavored	4 oz. green chilies,
tortilla chips	chopped
2 c. shredded Monterey	1 c. chopped onion
Jack cheese	3 tbsp. catsup
6 eggs, beaten	1/2 tsp. salt
2 1/2 c. milk	1/4 tsp. Tabasco sauce

Layer tortilla chips, cheese and mixture of remaining ingredients in greased 7x12-inch baking pan. Refrigerate overnight. Bake at 325 degrees for 50 minutes or until set. Yield: 4 servings.

Eggnog

EGGNOG BREAD

3/4 c. sugar
2 eggs
1/4 c. melted margarine
2 1/4 c. all-purpose flour
2 tsp. baking powder
1 tsp. salt
1/8 tsp. nutmeg

1 c. eggnog
1/2 c. raisins
1/2 c. coarsely
  chopped pecans
1/2 c. chopped candied
  cherries

Combine sugar, eggs and margarine in mixer bowl. Beat until light. Mix flour, baking powder, salt and nutmeg. Add to sugar mixture alternately with eggnog, mixing well after each addition. Fold in raisins, pecans and cherries. Pour into well-greased and floured 5x9-inch loaf pan. Bake at 350 degrees for 1 hour and 10 minutes. Cool in pan for 10 minutes. Remove to wire rack to cool completely. Wrap in plastic wrap. Yield: 1 loaf.

CHRISTMAS CITRUS EGGNOG

3 eggs
2 tbsp. sugar
1/4 tsp. cinnamon
1/8 tsp. ground cloves
1 pt. vanilla ice cream

3 c. orange juice
2 tbsp. lemon juice
2 c. ginger ale, chilled
1/4 tsp. nutmeg

Combine eggs, sugar, cinnamon and cloves in mixer bowl. Beat at medium speed until very light. Add vanilla ice cream, orange juice and lemon juice. Beat at low speed until blended. Chill, covered, until serving time. Stir in ginger ale gradually. Pour into glasses. Sprinkle with nutmeg. Yield: 10 cups.

PERFECT EGGNOG

6 eggs
1/2 c. corn syrup
1/4 tsp. ground ginger
1/4 tsp. ground cloves
1/4 tsp. ground
  cinnamon
1/4 tsp. ground nutmeg

2 qt. orange juice,
  chilled
1/2 c. lemon juice,
  chilled
1 qt. vanilla ice cream
1 qt. ginger ale, chilled
Nutmeg to taste

Beat eggs in large bowl. Mix in syrup, ginger, cloves, cinnamon and nutmeg. Stir in orange juice and lemon juice. Scoop ice cream into egg-sized chunks. Place in large punch bowl. Pour ginger ale over ice cream. Stir in egg mixture. Sprinkle with nutmeg. Yield: 24 cups.

HOLIDAY EGGNOG

6 eggs, at room
  temperature,
  separated
3/4 c. sugar
1 c. Brandy
1/2 c. rum
4 c. cold milk
3 c. cold whipping
  cream

2 tsp. vanilla extract
1/8 tsp. cream of tartar
1 c. whipping cream,
  whipped
1/2 c. confectioners'
  sugar
Freshly grated nutmeg
  to taste

Beat egg yolks in large mixer bowl until light. Add sugar gradually, beating until thick and lemon-colored. Stir in Brandy, rum, milk, 3 cups whipping cream and vanilla. Beat egg whites with cream of tartar in mixer bowl until stiff peaks form. Fold into egg yolk mixture. Pour into punch bowl. Sweeten whipped cream with confectioners' sugar. Ladle eggnog into punch cups; top with whipped cream and sprinkle of nutmeg. Yield: 24 servings.

Eggplant

SUMMER EGGPLANT CASSEROLE

1 med. eggplant
1/2 c. chopped onion
1/4 c. chopped green
  bell pepper
2 tbsp. margarine
1 c. sliced black olives
1/4 tsp. salt

1/8 tsp. pepper
1 c. shredded
  American cheese
1/2 c. bread crumbs
2 tbsp. melted
  margarine

Peel and slice eggplant. Cook in water to cover in saucepan until tender-crisp; drain. Sauté onion and green pepper in margarine in skillet. Add eggplant, olives, salt, pepper and cheese. Spoon into greased 1-quart baking dish. Sprinkle with mixture of bread crumbs and margarine. Bake at 350 degrees for 30 minutes. Yield: 4 servings.

ITALIAN EGGPLANT

1 med. eggplant,
  peeled, sliced 1/2
  inch thick
1/2 c. melted margarine
3/4 c. fine dry bread
  crumbs

1/4 tsp. salt
1 8-oz. can spaghetti
  sauce with mushrooms
1 tbsp. dried oregano
4 oz. mozzarella
  cheese, shredded

Dip eggplant into margarine; coat with mixture of bread crumbs and salt. Place on greased baking sheet. Spoon sauce over each slice; sprinkle with oregano and cheese. Bake at 450 degrees for 10 to 15 minutes or until tender. Yield: 4 servings.

RATATOUILLE

1 lg. eggplant	*1/2 tsp. oregano*
2 or 3 zucchini	*2 cloves of garlic,*
2 lg. onions	*crushed*
2 med. green bell	*1/2 tsp. fennel seed*
peppers, sliced	*1 tbsp. salt*
1 16-oz. can Italian	*1/4 tsp. pepper*
plum tomatoes	*1/4 c. olive oil*
1 tsp. basil	

Chop unpeeled eggplant. Slice zucchini; chop. Combine remaining ingredients in large heavy saucepan. Add vegetables; mix well. Cook over low heat for 1 1/2 hours, stirring occasionally. Let stand for several hours. Serve hot as a vegetable or cold as an appetizer. Yield: 10 servings.

EGGPLANT PARMESAN

1 20-oz. can solid-	*1/4 tsp. pepper*
pack tomatoes	*1 1 1/2-lb. eggplant*
1/2 c. finely chopped	*1/2 c. all-purpose flour*
onion	*1/4 c. olive oil*
2 tbsp. olive oil	*8 oz. mozzarella*
6 tbsp. tomato sauce	*cheese, thinly sliced*
1 tsp. basil	*1/2 c. Parmesan cheese*
1 tsp. sugar	*2 tsp. basil*
1/2 tsp. salt	

Drain tomatoes, reserving juice; chop tomatoes. Sauté onion in 2 tablespoons olive oil in saucepan. Add chopped tomatoes, reserved juice, tomato sauce, 1 teaspoon basil, sugar, salt and pepper; mix well. Simmer for 40 minutes. Peel eggplant; cut into 1/2-inch thick slices. Arrange in single layer on platter. Season with salt to taste. Let stand for 30 minutes. Pat dry with paper towel. Coat slices with flour, shaking off excess. Brown slices a few at a time in 1/4 cup olive oil in skillet; drain on paper towel. Spread 1/2 cup tomato sauce in greased 2-quart baking dish. Arrange layers of eggplant and mozzarella cheese over sauce. Sprinkle with a small amount of Parmesan cheese and basil. Repeat layers until all ingredients are used, ending with tomato sauce. Bake at 350 degrees for 30 minutes. Yield: 6 servings.

EGGPLANT-TOMATOES AU GRATIN

4 lg. tomatoes	*Salt and pepper to taste*
2 sm. eggplant, peeled	*1 1/4 c. freshly grated*
Salt to taste	*Parmesan cheese*
1 c. olive oil	*2 tbsp. margarine,*
2 onions, chopped	*softened*

Parboil tomatoes for 10 seconds. Peel and slice. Cut eggplant into 1/4-inch slices. Place on cutting board. Sprinkle with salt. Let stand for 20 minutes. Brown in 1/2 inch oil in skillet, adding oil as

necessary. Drain well. Sauté onions in skillet until brown. Sprinkle in casserole. Layer eggplant, salt and pepper and Parmesan cheese over onions. Top with layer of tomato and margarine. Repeat layers with remaining ingredients, ending with cheese and margarine. Bake at 350 degrees for 1 hour. Serve warm with angel hair pasta or at room temperature with crackers. Yield: 8 servings.

Filbert

CREAM-FILLED FILBERT CAKE

1/2 c. margarine	*3 egg whites, stiffly*
2/3 c. sugar	*beaten*
3 egg yolks	*1 1/2 c. whipping cream*
1/4 c. all-purpose flour	*1/4 c. sugar*
1/2 tsp. baking powder	*1/2 c. finely ground*
1/4 tsp. cinnamon	*filberts*
1/2 c. ground filberts	

Cream margarine in mixer bowl at medium speed for 30 seconds. Add 2/3 cup sugar; beat until fluffy. Beat in egg yolks. Add mixture of flour, baking powder and cinnamon; beat well. Stir in 1/2 cup filberts. Fold in stiffly beaten egg whites. Pour into greased 8-inch round cake pan. Bake at 350 degrees for 30 to 35 minutes or until cake tests done. Split into 2 layers. Whip cream with 1/4 cup sugar until stiff peaks form. Add 1/2 cup filberts. Spread whipped cream between layers and over top of cake. Yield: 12 to 16 servings.

FILBERT SHORTBREAD

1/3 c. chopped filberts	*1/2 c. sugar*
1 1/4 c. margarine,	*2 c. all-purpose flour*
softened	*1 c. cornstarch*

Process filberts in food processor container until finely ground. Cream margarine and sugar in mixer bowl until light and fluffy. Add mixture of flour, cornstarch and filberts; mix well. Divide into 6 portions. Roll each portion into 6-inch circle on ungreased cookie sheet. Smooth edges with fingers. Score each circle into 8 wedges. Press edges with fork. Bake at 325 degrees for 35 minutes. Cool on wire rack. Break into wedges. Store in tightly covered container. Yield: 4 dozen.

FILBERT TORTE

6 egg yolks
1½ c. sugar
3 tbsp. all-purpose
  flour
1 tsp. salt
1 tsp. baking powder
2 tbsp. rum
3 c. ground filberts
6 egg whites

1 c. whipping cream,
  whipped
2 tbsp. confectioners'
  sugar
1 tsp. rum
1 c. milk chocolate
  chips, melted
½ c. sour cream

Beat egg yolks until thick and light. Beat in 1 cup sugar gradually. Add flour, salt, baking powder and 2 tablespoons rum. Fold in filberts. Beat egg whites until stiff peaks form. Beat in remaining ½ cup sugar until mixture is glossy and holds soft peaks. Fold into egg yolk mixture. Line cake pans with greased waxed paper. Spoon batter into pans. Bake at 350 degrees for 25 minutes or until tops are shiny and layers test done. Remove from pans. Cool thoroughly. Spread mixture of whipped cream, confectioners' sugar and 1 teaspoon rum between layers. Frost with mixture of melted chocolate and sour cream. Yield: 12 servings.

Flan

FLAN

1 c. sugar
3 c. milk, scalded
1 cinnamon stick
9 tbsp. sugar

9 eggs, beaten
⅛ tsp. salt
2 tsp. vanilla extract

Melt 1 cup sugar in skillet over low heat until golden, stirring constantly. Pour into ovenproof bowl, tilting to coat surface. Let stand until hardened. Scald milk with cinnamon in saucepan. Remove cinnamon. Stir in 9 tablespoons sugar. Pour hot mixture into eggs, beating constantly. Add salt and vanilla. Pour into prepared bowl. Place in baking pan half-filled with hot water. Bake at 325 degrees for 50 minutes. Cool. Chill in refrigerator. Invert onto serving dish. Yield: 8 servings.

OLD-FASHIONED FLAN

¼ c. sugar
1 15-oz. can
  evaporated milk
1 14-oz. can
  sweetened
  condensed milk

1 tsp. salt
1 tbsp. sugar
2 tbsp. vanilla extract
1 c. milk
4 eggs, beaten

Caramelize ¼ cup sugar in bottom of 1½-quart metal mold; tilt to coat all sides. Mix remaining ingredients except eggs in bowl. Strain beaten eggs into milk mixture. Pour into mold; cover with aluminum foil and secure with rubber band. Place in pressure cooker. Add water to ½ the depth of mold. Cover tightly. Cook at 10 pounds pressure for 10 minutes. Remove from pressure cooker. Cool. Invert onto serving plate. Yield: 10 servings.

Flounder

ASPARAGUS-STUFFED FLOUNDER

1 med. onion, chopped
1 tsp. margarine
6 3-oz. flounder fillets
18 asparagus spears
2 tsp. melted margarine
2 tsp. flour
1 c. milk

½ c. shredded sharp
  Cheddar cheese
Salt and pepper to taste
Pinch of cayenne
  pepper
Dash of nutmeg

Sauté onion in 1 teaspoon margarine in skillet. Sprinkle on fillets. Place 3 asparagus spears crosswise on each fillet; roll up. Secure with toothpicks. Place in greased pan. Blend melted margarine and flour in saucepan. Cook for 1 minute, stirring constantly. Add milk. Cook until thickened, stirring constantly. Stir in cheese and seasonings. Pour over fillets. Sprinkle with nutmeg. Bake at 350 degrees for 20 minutes. Yield: 6 servings.

FLOUNDER BAKED IN SOUR CREAM

1 lb. flounder
All-purpose flour
Pepper to taste
¼ c. margarine
1 to 2 tsp. paprika

¼ c. Parmesan cheese
1 c. sour cream
Bread crumbs
Lemon slices

Coat flounder with mixture of flour and pepper. Sauté in margarine in skillet until brown. Place in baking dish. Sprinkle with paprika. Spoon mixture of cheese and sour cream on fish. Sprinkle with bread crumbs. Bake at 400 degrees for 10 minutes. Garnish with lemon slices. Yield: 2 servings.

POOR MAN'S LOBSTER

1 tbsp. vinegar
1 tsp. seafood
  seasoning

½ tsp. salt
2 c. water
1 lb. flounder fillets

Combine vinegar, seafood seasoning and salt with water in saucepan. Bring to a boil. Add flounder. Simmer for 15 minutes or until fish flakes easily. Place on rack in broiler pan. Broil until brown. Serve with drawn butter. Yield: 2 servings.

STEGT RODSPAETTE

4 8-oz. flounder fillets	*2 tbsp. water*
Salt to taste	*2 tbsp. vegetable oil*
All-purpose flour	*1/4 c. margarine*
1/2 c. dried bread crumbs	*8 oz. cooked shrimp*
2 eggs	*1/4 c. margarine*
	Lemon wedges

Rinse fish with cold water. Pat dry. Season with salt; coat with flour. Shake off excess. Spread bread crumbs on waxed paper. Beat eggs with water in bowl. Dip each fillet into egg; coat with bread crumbs. Let stand for 10 minutes. Heat 2 tablespoons oil and 2 tablespoons margarine in heavy skillet over moderate heat until foam subsides. Sauté fillets for 3 to 4 minutes on each side. Place on warm platter. Melt 2 tablespoons margarine in saucepan over moderate heat. Add shrimp. Stir-fry for 2 to 3 minutes or until well coated. Arrange shrimp down each fillet. Heat remaining 1/4 cup margarine in saucepan over low heat until nutty brown; pour over fillets. Garnish with lemon wedges. Yield: 4 servings.

Fondue

MILK CHOCOLATE FONDUE

1 16-oz. pound cake	*2 lb. milk chocolate, grated*
1 8-oz. angel food cake	*2 tbsp. instant coffee powder*
2 c. apple slices	*1/4 c. hot water*
2 c. pear slices	*2 tsp. vanilla extract*
2 pt. fresh strawberries	*1/4 tsp. cinnamon*
2 c. fresh pineapple cubes	
1 c. whipping cream	

Cut pound cake and angel food cake into 1 1/2-inch cubes. Arrange fruit and cake cubes on serving tray. Combine cream and chocolate in fondue pot. Cook over very low heat until chocolate melts, stirring constantly. Dissolve coffee in hot water. Add to chocolate mixture with vanilla and cinnamon; mix well. Keep warm over fondue flame. Serve with cake and fruit. Yield: 16 servings.

ORANGE CUSTARD FONDUE

1 3 oz. package no-bake custard mix	*1 4 1/2-oz. container whipped topping*
1 3/4 c. milk	*1 tbsp. grated orange rind*
2 tbsp. orange liqueur	

Prepare custard mix according to package directions, using 1 3/4 cups milk and omitting egg yolk. Spoon into bowl. Chill in refrigerator. Fold in liqueur and whipped topping. Sprinkle with orange rind. Serve with bite-sized fresh fruits and cubes of angel food cake. Yield: 4 to 6 servings.

PIZZA FONDUE

1/2 lb. ground beef	*1/4 tsp. garlic powder*
1 onion, chopped	*2 1/2 c. shredded Cheddar cheese*
2 tbsp. margarine	*1 c. shredded mozzarella cheese*
2 10 1/2-oz. cans pizza sauce	*1 loaf French bread, cubed*
1 tbsp. cornstarch	
1 1/2 tsp. fennel seed	
1 1/2 tsp. oregano	

Cook ground beef in skillet until brown and crumbly; drain. Sauté onion in margarine in fondue pot on High until brown. Add ground beef; reduce heat to Medium. Blend pizza sauce, cornstarch and seasonings in bowl. Stir into ground beef mixture. Cook until bubbly, stirring constantly. Add cheeses gradually, stirring constantly. Serve with bread cubes for dipping. Yield: 25 to 30 servings.

Frankfurters

FANCY FRANKS

2 tbsp. finely chopped onion	*1 c. packed brown sugar*
1 tbsp. margarine	*3/4 c. Bourbon*
1 c. catsup or chili sauce	*1 lb. frankfurters*

Sauté onion in margarine in skillet. Add catsup, brown sugar and Bourbon; mix well. Cut franks into 1-inch pieces. Add to sauce. Simmer for 25 minutes or until sauce begins to glaze, stirring occasionally. Serve hot. Yield: 8 servings.

FRANKS AND BEANS WESTERN STYLE

1 sm. can pork and beans	*1/4 c. water*
1 or 2 tbsp. bacon drippings	*2 or 3 tbsp. brown sugar*
1 tsp. prepared yellow mustard	*1 med. onion, chopped*
3 or 4 tbsp. catsup	*2 frankfurters, cut into bite-sized pieces*

Combine all ingredients in casserole. Bake at 450 degrees for 30 minutes. Yield: 2 servings.

Fruit

SUMMER FRUIT CUP
Photograph for this recipe is on page 105.

1 pt. strawberries	1/2 pt. blueberries
1 pt. orange and	
cream sorbet and	
cream	

Slice strawberries. Line 4 parfait glasses with sliced strawberries. Add 2 scoops of sorbet. Garnish with blueberries. Yield: 4 servings.

SORBET AND CREAM FRUIT SALAD
Photograph for this recipe is on page 105.

1 cantaloupe	2 peaches, sliced
1 honeydew melon	12 lg. strawberries
1 Crenshaw melon	1 pt. lime and cream
1 kiwifruit	sorbet and cream
1 head Bibb lettuce	1 pt. orange and cream
1 c. blueberries	sorbet and cream

Slice melons and kiwifruit. Arrange on lettuce-lined plates. Add blueberries and peaches. Slice strawberries as for blossoms. Fill with small scoops of lime-cream sorbet. Place on lettuce. Add large scoop orange-cream sorbet.
Yield: 4 servings.

FRESH FALL FRUIT BETTY

1 1/3 c. graham cracker	1 lg. apple, peeled,
crumbs	sliced
1/4 c. melted butter	1 lg. pear, peeled, sliced
1/4 c. sugar	2/3 c. chopped pecans
1/2 tsp. cinnamon	1 1/4 c. orange juice
1/4 tsp. nutmeg	2 tbsp. lemon juice
1 banana, sliced	

Preheat oven to 350 degrees. Mix crumbs, butter, sugar and spices in bowl. Mix fruit and pecans in bowl. Layer fruit and crumb mixtures 1/2 at a time in 2-quart casserole. Pour juices over top. Bake for 1 hour. Serve warm. Yield: 8 servings.

PATRIOTIC PARFAIT
Photograph for this recipe is on page 105.

2 c. strawberries	1 1/2 c. blueberries
2 bananas	
1 pt. blueberry and	
cream sorbet and	
cream	

Reserve 4 whole strawberries. Slice bananas and strawberries into bowl. Combine 1 cup sliced strawberries and 1/2 cup banana in blender container; purée until smooth. Spoon 1 tablespoon purée into parfait glass. Top with 1 scoop sorbet. Layer half the blueberries, sliced bananas, sliced strawberries and purée on top. Top with 1 scoop sorbet. Repeat layers ending with sorbet. Garnish with whole strawberries. Yield: 4 servings.

Fudge

TRIPLE CHOCOLATE FUDGE

4 c. chopped pecans	1/2 c. margarine
4 4-oz. bars German's	1 tsp. salt
sweet chocolate	2 c. semisweet
9 oz. milk chocolate	chocolate chips
4 1/2 c. sugar	1 1/2 7-oz. jars
1 13-oz. can	marshmallow creme
evaporated milk	2 tsp. vanilla extract

Spread pecans in baking pan. Bake at 350 degrees for 8 to 10 minutes or until toasted. Cool. Break German's chocolate and milk chocolate into 1-inch pieces. Bring sugar, evaporated milk, margarine and salt to a simmer in saucepan over medium heat, stirring constantly. Simmer for 8 minutes. Remove from heat. Add pecans, broken chocolate, chocolate chips, marshmallow creme and vanilla; stir until chocolate is melted. Pour into two 9x13-inch greased baking dishes. Chill, covered with foil, until firm. Let stand until room temperature. Cut into squares. Store in refrigerator or freezer. Yield: 80 servings.

PEANUT BUTTER-APPLE FUDGE

6 oz. semisweet	1/2 c. creamy peanut
chocolate chips	butter
5 oz. marshmallow	2 c. sugar
creme	2/3 c. apple juice
1 tsp. vanilla extract	

Combine chocolate chips, marshmallow creme, vanilla and peanut butter in large bowl. Combine sugar and apple juice in saucepan. Cook over medium heat until sugar dissolves and mixture comes to a boil, stirring constantly. Cook to 140 degrees on candy thermometer, soft-ball stage, stirring constantly. Pour over chocolate chip mixture. Stir until ingredients are blended. Pour into greased 9x9-inch dish. Let stand until cool. Cut into squares. Yield: 2 pounds.

PINTO BEAN FUDGE

1 c. cooked pinto beans	*6 tbsp. margarine*
1/2 c. milk	*1 tsp. vanilla extract*
6 oz. unsweetened baking chocolate	*2 lb. confectioners' sugar*

Mash beans with milk in bowl to consistency of mashed potatoes. Heat chocolate and margarine in double boiler until melted. Stir into bean mixture until slightly thickened. Add vanilla and confectioners' sugar. Beat until blended. Spread into greased dish. Chill in refrigerator. Cut into squares. Yield: 56 ounces.

VELVEETA FUDGE

1 lb. Velveeta cheese, softened	*1 c. unsweetened baking cocoa*
2 c. margarine, softened	*1 18-oz. jar peanut butter*
4 16-oz. packages confectioners' sugar, sifted	*3 c. chopped pecans*
	4 tbsp. vanilla extract

Combine Velveeta cheese, margarine, confectioners' sugar and cocoa in large bowl. Knead until well mixed. Add peanut butter, pecans and vanilla. Knead until smooth. Press into greased baking dish. Chill in refrigerator. Cut into small squares. Store in airtight containers in refrigerator or freezer. Yield: 10 pounds.

Game

RABBIT DIVAN

1 16-oz. package frozen broccoli cuts	*1/2 c. mayonnaise*
4 c. chopped cooked rabbit	*1/4 c. milk*
	1 tsp. lemon juice
1 can cream of mushroom soup	*1/2 c. shredded Cheddar cheese*

Cook broccoli partially according to package directions; drain. Layer broccoli and rabbit in 9x13-inch baking dish. Combine mushroom soup, mayonnaise, milk and lemon juice in bowl; mix well. Pour over layers. Sprinkle with cheese. Bake at 350 degrees for 30 minutes. Yield: 4 servings.

VENISON STEW

4 carrots, sliced	*1 tsp. salt*
3 potatoes, chopped	*1 tsp. onion flakes*
2 lb. 1-inch venison cubes	*1 stalk celery, chopped*
1 c. beef consomme	*1 4-oz. can sliced mushrooms, drained*

Combine carrots, potatoes, venison, consommé, salt, onion flakes, celery and mushrooms in Crock•Pot; mix well. Cook on Low for 10 to 12 hours. Yield: 4 servings.

VENISON STRIPS

1 1/2 lb. venison round steak	*1 onion, thinly sliced*
1 green bell pepper	*1 tbsp. Wagner's game seasoning*
2 tbsp. margarine	

Trim all fat from venison. Partially freeze steak for easy slicing. Cut into paper-thin slices. Seed green pepper; slice into thin rounds. Heat margarine in heavy skillet over medium heat. Add green pepper and onion. Cook for 5 minutes or until onion is transparent, stirring frequently. Remove to heated plate with slotted spoon. Heat additional butter in skillet if necessary. Add venison strips in single layer. Sprinkle with seasoning. Cook over medium-high heat for 1 minute; turn strips over. Cook for 2 minutes longer. Add green pepper and onion. Cook for several minutes longer, stirring constantly; do not overcook. Serve immediately. Yield: 4 to 6 servings.

Game Birds

PHEASANT DELUXE

1 lg. pheasant	*4 c. broth*
1 onion, chopped	*3 eggs, beaten*
1 1/2 c. chopped celery	*1 1/2 c. shredded American cheese*
4 c. crushed Ritz crackers	*1/2 tsp. pepper*
1 can cream of mushroom soup	*1/2 tsp. salt*

Combine pheasant with salted water to cover in saucepan. Simmer until tender. Chop pheasant into bite-sized pieces, discarding skin and bones. Combine with onion, celery, cracker crumbs, soup, broth, eggs, cheese and seasonings in bowl; mix well. Spoon into shallow baking dish. Bake at 350 degrees for 1 hour. Yield: 8 servings.

QUAIL WITH GREEN PEPPERCORNS

8 quail
1 tbsp. green
  peppercorns
Salt to taste
1/4 c. margarine
1 c. chicken stock

1 tbsp. green
  peppercorns
1 tbsp. Sherry
1/4 c. margarine
6 tbsp. chopped parsley

Rinse quail and pat dry. Crush 1 tablespoon peppercorns. Rub into quail. Season with salt to taste. Sauté in 1/4 cup margarine in skillet until brown on all sides; drain. Place in roaster. Add chicken stock, 1 tablespoon peppercorns and Sherry. Bake at 375 degrees for 15 minutes or until tender. Pour pan juices into small saucepan. Cook until reduced by 1/2. Remove from heat. Whisk in 1/4 cup margarine. Place quail on heated serving dish. Spoon sauce over top. Sprinkle with parsley. Yield: 8 servings.

Gazpacho

SPANISH GAZPACHO

1 green bell pepper
1 cucumber
1 onion
4 cloves of garlic
1/2 c. olive oil
1/2 c. wine vinegar
1 lg. can vegetable
  juice cocktail
1/2 c. water

4 slices bread
1 tbsp. Worcestershire
  sauce
Dash of Tabasco sauce
Salt and pepper to taste
1 green bell pepper
1 onion
2 tomatoes
1 cucumber

Combine 1 green pepper, 1 cucumber, 1 onion, garlic, olive oil, vinegar, vegetable juice cocktail, water, bread, Worcestershire sauce, Tabasco sauce, salt and pepper in blender. Process until smooth. Chop remaining vegetables by hand. Chill puréed mixture and chopped vegetables for 4 hours. Pour purée into soup bowl. Top with chopped vegetables. Yield: 8 servings.

SUMMER GAZPACHO SALAD

1 1/2 tbsp. unflavored
  gelatin
1/4 c. cold water
1 1/2 c. vegetable juice
  cocktail
1 cucumber, chopped
1 green bell pepper,
  chopped
4 tomatoes, peeled,
  chopped
3/4 c. chopped celery

1/4 c. chopped green
  onions
1/2 tsp. Tabasco sauce
1 tsp. dillweed
1 1/2 tbsp. lemon juice
1 1/2 tbsp. vinegar
1 tsp. salt
Pepper to taste
2 tbsp. olive oil
1/2 c. mayonnaise
1/2 c. sour cream

Soften gelatin in cold water. Heat vegetable juice in 3-quart saucepan. Add gelatin; stir until dissolved. Cool slightly. Add chopped vegetables, Tabasco sauce, dillweed, lemon juice, vinegar, salt and pepper; mix well. Coat 6-cup mold with olive oil. Add gelatin mixture. Chill until firm. Unmold onto serving plate. Serve with a mixture of mayonnaise and sour cream. Garnish with chopped parsley. Yield: 8 servings.

Ginger

GINGER BEARS

1 c. molasses
1/2 c. sugar
1/2 c. oil
1 tsp. soda
1/3 c. hot water

4 c. all-purpose flour
1/2 tsp. cinnamon
1/4 tsp. ginger
1 tsp. salt
Silver shot

Combine molasses, sugar and oil in mixer bowl. Dissolve soda in hot water. Add soda mixture, flour, spices and salt to molasses mixture; mix well. Chill for 4 hours to overnight. Roll 1/4 inch thick on floured surface. Cut with teddy bear cookie cutter. Place on cookie sheet. Arrange silver shot for eyes, nose and buttons. Bake at 350 degrees for 10 minutes. Remove to wire rack to cool. Yield 2 1/2 dozen.

Icebox Gingerbread Muffins...batter keeps in the refrigerator for weeks.

ICEBOX GINGERBREAD MUFFINS

1 c. margarine,	*4 c. all-purpose flour*
softened	*1/8 tsp. salt*
1 c. sugar	*2 tsp. ginger*
4 eggs	*1/2 tsp. cinnamon*
1 c. molasses	*1/4 tsp. allspice*
1/2 c. raisins	*2 tsp. soda*
1/2 c. chopped pecans	*1 c. sour milk*

Cream margarine and sugar in mixer bowl until light and fluffy. Add eggs and molasses; mix well. Coat raisins and nuts with a small amount of flour. Sift remaining flour with salt and spices. Stir soda into sour milk. Add flour mixture and milk to batter alternately, mixing well after each addition. Stir in pecans and raisins. Store in refrigerator for up to 1 month. Spoon into greased muffin cups. Bake at 400 degrees for 15 minutes. Yield: 4 dozen.

GINGERY SPICE LOAF

1 14-oz. package	*6 eggs*
gingerbread mix	*1 c. water*
1 18-oz. package	*1 1/2 c. raisins*
lemon cake mix	*1 1/2 c. chopped walnuts*
1 c. water	

Combine gingerbread mix, cake mix and 1 cup water in mixer bowl. Beat at medium speed for 2 minutes or until smooth. Add eggs and 1 cup water. Beat at low speed for 1 minute. Beat at medium speed for 1 minute. Fold in raisins and walnuts. Pour into 2 greased and floured 5x9-inch loaf pans. Bake at 375 degrees for 20 to 25 minutes or until loaves test done. Cool in pans for 10 minutes. Remove to wire rack to cool completely. Yield: 2 loaves.

Goose

STUFFED ROAST GOOSE

1 7 to 9-lb. goose	*Apples, chopped*
1 pkg. long grain and	*Celery, chopped*
wild rice mix	*Thyme and basil to*
Walnuts, chopped	*taste*
Green onions, chopped	*Salt and pepper to taste*
Raisins plumped in	*Orange juice*
Garlic Cognac	*1/2 c. Cognac*

Wash goose inside and out; pat dry. Cook rice mix according to package directions. Add desired amounts of walnuts, green onions, raisins, garlic, apples, celery and seasonings; mix well. Spoon into goose cavity; truss goose. Place on rack in roasting pan. Pierce with fork all over, especially at joints. Repeat piercing every 7 to 10 minutes while baking. Bake at 500 degrees for 30 to 45 minutes or until goose is dark brown and fat is no longer draining. Cover wings with foil if necessary to prevent overbrowning. Pour off drippings. Reduce temperature to 325 to 350 degrees. Bake for 20 minutes per pound, basting frequently with mixture of orange juice and water. Add water only if pan drippings become too thick and dark. Stir Cognac into pan drippings 10 minutes before serving. Serve with goose. Yield: 8 servings.

SOUTHERN WILD GOOSE

1 wild Canadian goose	*1 pkg. brown gravy mix*
1 apple, sliced	*2 onions, chopped*
4 slices bacon	*1 tsp. garlic salt*
1 c. water	*1 tsp. orange*
1 6-oz. can frozen	*marmalade*
orange juice	*1 tsp. honey*
concentrate	

Wash goose inside and out; pat dry. Stuff with apple: truss. Arrange bacon across breast of goose. Mix water, orange juice, gravy mix, onions, garlic salt, marmalade and honey in bowl. Place goose in large oven cooking bag. Pour gravy mixture into cooking bag; secure end. Make 4 or 5 puncture holes in top of bag. Place bag in roasting pan. Bake at 350 degrees for 2 hours. Remove goose to serving platter. Use pan drippings for gravy if desired. Yield: 4 servings.

Graham

GRAHAM CRACKER TREAT

24 graham crackers	*Graham Cracker Glaze*
1/2 c. chopped pecans	

Break graham crackers into halves at perforations. Line 10x17-inch baking pan with foil. Arrange crackers in prepared pan. Sprinkle with pecans. Drizzle Graham Cracker Glaze over crackers. Bake at 375 degrees for 8 minutes or until bubbly. Break into pieces. Yield: 24 servings.

Graham Cracker Glaze

1 c. packed brown	*1 c. butter*
sugar	

Combine butter and brown sugar in saucepan. Heat until bubbly.

GRAHAM CRACKER COOKIES

26 graham crackers, finely crushed	*1 15-oz. can sweetened condensed milk*
1/2 c. chopped pecans	
1 c. butterscotch chips	*Confectioners' sugar*

Combine cracker crumbs, pecans, butterscotch chips and condensed milk in bowl; mix well. Press into greased 8x8-inch baking dish. Bake at 350 degrees for 25 minutes. Cut into squares while warm. Roll each square in confectioners' sugar to coat. Wrap each square individually in foil. Yield: 2 dozen.

Granola

CHUNKY GRANOLA

6 c. oats	*1/2 c. nonfat dry milk powder*
1/2 c. sunflower seed	
1/2 c. coconut	*1/2 c. oil*
1/2 c. wheat germ	*1/2 c. water*
1/2 c. packed brown sugar	*1 tsp. vanilla extract*

Place oats in ungreased 9x13-inch baking pan. Bake at 350 degrees for 10 minutes. Stir in sunflower seed, coconut, wheat germ, brown sugar, milk powder, oil, water and vanilla. Bake for 10 to 15 minutes longer, or until golden brown, stirring every 3 to 5 minutes. Let stand until cool. Break into chunks. May add raisins, dates or other dried fruit after breaking into chunks. Store in airtight container. Yield: 10 cups.

COCONUT GRANOLA SNACK

2²/3 c. flaked coconut	*1/4 c. chopped prunes*
1 c. quick-cooking oats	*2 tbsp. sesame seed*
1/4 c. packed light brown sugar	*1/4 c. oil*
	1/4 c. honey
1/4 c. chopped dried apricots	*1/4 c. seedless raisins*

Combine coconut, oats, brown sugar, apricots, prunes and sesame seed in large bowl; mix well. Mix oil and honey in saucepan. Bring to a boil over medium heat. Pour over fruit mixture; mix well. Spread evenly in 10x15-inch baking pan. Bake at 325 degrees for 30 minutes, stirring frequently; do not brown. Stir in raisins. Let stand until cool, stirring occasionally to break granola apart. Store in airtight container. Yield: 7 cups.

NUTTY GRANOLA

4 c. oats	*1 c. chopped pecans*
2 c. whole wheat flour	*1 tsp. vanilla extract*
1 c. coconut	*1 c. safflower oil*
1 c. packed brown sugar	*1/2 c. water*
	1 c. raisins

Combine oats, flour, coconut, brown sugar, pecans, vanilla, oil and water in bowl; mix well. Spoon into roasting pan. Bake at 200 degrees for 2 hours, stirring every 20 to 30 minutes. Stir in raisins. Bake for 30 minutes longer or until crisp and light brown. Cool. Yield: 12 servings.

Grape

GRAPE JUICE

1 c. purple grapes	*3 c. boiling water*
1/2 c. sugar	

Wash grapes; place in hot sterilized 1-quart jar. Stir in sugar and boiling water. Add boiling water to fill jar; seal with 2-piece lid. Process in boiling water bath for 20 minutes. Yield: 4 cups.

GRAPE TART

1 15-oz. package 2-crust refrigerator pie pastry	*1 c. sour cream*
	2 eggs
	1/2 c. sugar
1¹/2 lb. seedless grapes	*1/4 c. all-purpose flour*

Fit 1 pastry into 9-inch springform pan. Cut leaf shapes from remaining pastry. Chill in refrigerator. Bake shell at 400 degrees for 5 minutes. Place grapes in partially baked shell. Mix sour cream, eggs, sugar and flour in bowl. Pour over grapes. Arrange pastry leaves on top. Bake for 1 hour or until pastry is golden brown and custard is set. Cool on wire rack. Chill until serving time. Place on serving plate; remove side of pan. Yield: 8 servings.

Grapefruit

GRAPEFRUIT WINTER SALAD

2 grapefruit	*3/4 c. boiling water*
1 3-oz. package lemon gelatin	*1 tbsp. lemon juice*
	1/3 c. slivered almonds
1 tbsp. sugar	

Peel and section grapefruit, reserving juice. Add enough water to juice to measure ³/₄ cup. Dissolve gelatin and sugar in boiling water in bowl. Stir in lemon juice and grapefruit juice. Chill until thickened. Fold in grapefruit and almonds. Spoon into 6-cup mold. Chill until firm. Unmold onto lettuce-lined plate. Yield: 8 servings.

CANDIED GRAPEFRUIT PEEL

3 lg. grapefruit	*²/₃ c. water*
1 c. honey	*Granulated sugar*

Score grapefruit vertically into quarters; remove peel. Cut into ¹/₄-inch strips. Place peel in large saucepan; add cold water to cover. Bring to a boil over high heat; drain. Add cold water to cover. Repeat boiling and draining steps 3 times. Combine peel, honey and ²/₃ cup water in large skillet. Cook over low heat for 45 minutes or until syrup is reduced, stirring frequently. Cook over very low heat for 15 minutes longer or until almost dry, stirring occasionally. Pour into colander. Cool completely. Coat strips 1 at a time with sugar. Place in single layer on waxed paper. Let dry overnight. Coat strips with sugar again. Yield: 1 pound.

Grits

CHEESE GRITS SOUFFLÉ

1 c. quick-cooking grits	*4 eggs*
3 c. boiling water	*1 c. milk*
2 tbsp. margarine	*1 c. shredded sharp*
Salt and pepper	*Cheddar cheese*

Cook grits in boiling water in saucepan until very thick. Remove from heat. Stir in margarine, salt and pepper. Mix eggs and milk in small bowl. Add to grits mixture. Stir in cheese. Pour into greased 3-quart baking dish. Bake at 350 degrees for 45 minutes. Yield: 6 servings.

SOUTHERN GARLIC GRITS

1 c. white quick-	*2 eggs, beaten*
cooking grits	*1 clove of garlic,*
¹/₃ tsp. salt	*minced*
4 c. boiling water	*¹/₂ c. chopped black*
1¹/₂ c. shredded	*olives*
Cheddar cheese	*¹/₂ c. chopped*
¹/₂ c. margarine	*jalapeño peppers*
¹/₂ c. milk	

Stir grits gradually into salted boiling water in heavy saucepan. Return to a boil; reduce heat.

Cook for 2¹/₂ to 5 minutes or until thickened, stirring occasionally. Stir in cheese, margarine, milk, eggs, garlic, olives and peppers. Cook over low heat until cheese is melted. Pour into greased 2-quart casserole. Bake at 350 degrees for 1 hour. Yield: 6 servings.

Ground Beef

BEEFY DIP

1 lb. ground beef	*1 tsp. sugar*
¹/₂ c. chopped onion	*¹/₂ tsp. oregano*
1 clove of garlic,	*8 oz. cream cheese,*
minced	*chopped*
1 8-oz. can tomato	*¹/₃ c. Parmesan cheese*
sauce	*¹/₂ c. shredded*
¹/₂ c. catsup	*Cheddar cheese*

Brown ground beef with onion and garlic in saucepan, stirring until ground beef is crumbly; drain. Add tomato sauce, catsup, sugar and oregano; mix well. Simmer, covered, for 15 minutes. Add cream cheese, Parmesan cheese and Cheddar cheese. Simmer just until cheeses are melted, stirring occasionally. Serve warm from chafing dish with wheat crackers or tortilla chips. Yield: 8 servings.

STUFFED MANICOTTI

2 10-oz. packages	*2 tbsp. Parmesan*
frozen chopped	*cheese*
spinach	*Salt and pepper to taste*
2 lb. ground chuck	*2 eggs*
2 onions, chopped	*3 slices white bread,*
2 stalks celery, chopped	*crusts trimmed*
2 cloves of garlic,	*2 8-oz. packages*
chopped	*manicotti*
1 tbsp. chopped parsley	*Favorite meat sauce*
Garlic powder to taste	*¹/₄ c. Parmesan cheese*

Cook spinach according to package directions; drain and squeeze dry. Brown ground chuck with onions, celery and garlic in skillet, stirring until ground chuck is crumbly; drain. Add parsley, garlic powder, 2 tbsp. Parmesan cheese, salt and pepper. Stir in eggs and bread soaked in water. Let stand for 30 minutes. Stuff ground chuck mixture into manicotti. Cover bottom of baking pan with meat sauce. Arrange manicotti in pan. Cover with meat sauce. Sprinkle with ¹/₄ cup Parmesan cheese. Bake, covered with foil, at 350 degrees for 1 hour. Yield: 10 servings.

CHILI CORN BREAD BAKE

2 lb. ground beef	1 8-oz. can tomato
1 onion, chopped	sauce
1 green bell pepper,	1 6-oz. package
chopped	corn muffin mix
1 tsp. salt	1 c. evaporated milk
1 env. chili	1 c. shredded sharp
seasoning mix	Cheddar cheese

Brown ground beef in skillet, stirring until crumbly; drain. Add onion and green pepper. Cook for several minutes, stirring frequently. Stir in salt, seasoning mix and tomato sauce. Spoon into 9x13-inch baking dish. Combine muffin mix and evaporated milk in bowl; mix well. Spread evenly over casserole. Top with cheese. Bake at 400 degrees for 20 to 25 minutes or until golden brown. Yield: 6 to 8 servings.

LASAGNA

1 lb. ground beef	3 c. hot water
1 onion, chopped	8 oz. lasagna noodles,
2 tsp. salt	cooked
1/4 tsp. pepper	8 oz. cottage cheese
1/4 tsp. oregano	4 oz. Swiss cheese,
1 4-oz. can	sliced
mushrooms, drained	8 oz. mozzarella
2 6-oz. cans tomato	cheese, sliced
paste	

Brown ground beef with onion in skillet, stirring until beef is crumbly; drain. Stir in salt, pepper, oregano and mushrooms. Blend tomato paste with water in bowl. Add to beef mixture. Simmer for 30 minutes. Layer a small amount of sauce, half the noodles, all the cottage cheese, all the Swiss cheese and half the mozzarella cheese in 9x13-inch baking pan. Add layers of half the remaining sauce, remaining noodles, remaining sauce and remaining mozzarella cheese. Bake at 350 degrees for 30 minutes. Let stand for several minutes before serving. Yield: 6 servings.

OVEN PORCUPINES

1 lb. ground beef	1/4 tsp. garlic powder
1/2 c. uncooked	1/4 tsp. pepper
minute rice	1 15-oz. can tomato
1/2 c. water	sauce
1/2 c. chopped onion	1 c. water
1 tsp. salt	2 tsp. Worcestershire
1/2 tsp. celery salt	sauce

Combine ground beef, rice, 1/2 cup water, onion, salt, celery salt, garlic powder and pepper in bowl; mix well. Shape by rounded tablespoonfuls into balls. Place in 8x8-inch baking dish. Combine remaining ingredients over meatballs. Bake,

covered with foil, at 350 degrees for 1 hour. Bake, uncovered, for 15 minutes longer. Yield: 4 servings.

SWEET AND SOUR MEATBALLS

1 lb. ground beef	1 1/2 tbsp.
1/2 c. milk	Worcestershire
1 c. cracker crumbs	sauce
Salt and pepper to taste	1/2 c. chopped onion
1/2 c. vinegar	1/2 c. chopped green
1/2 c. catsup	bell pepper
3 tbsp. brown sugar	

Mix ground beef with milk and cracker crumbs in bowl; season with salt and pepper. Shape into 1 1/2-inch meatballs. Place in 9x9-inch baking dish. Combine vinegar, catsup, brown sugar, Worcestershire sauce, onion and green pepper in saucepan. Bring to a boil. Pour over meatballs. Bake at 350 degrees for 1 hour, stirring occasionally. Yield: 4 servings.

COMPANY MEAT LOAF

1 1/2 lb. lean ground	2 tbsp. Worcestershire
beef	sauce
2 tbsp. chopped onion	3 tbsp. vinegar
1 5-oz. can	3 tbsp. chopped onion
evaporated milk	1/2 c. water
3/4 c. oats	1 c. catsup
1/2 tsp. salt	2 tbsp. sugar
1/4 tsp. pepper	

Combine ground beef, 2 tablespoons chopped onion, evaporated milk, oats, salt and pepper in bowl; mix well. Shape into loaf. Place in 7x12-inch baking dish. Mix Worcestershire sauce with vinegar, 3 tablespoons onion, water, catsup and sugar in bowl. Pour over loaf. Bake at 350 degrees for 1 hour. Yield: 6 servings.

SALISBURY STEAK WITH ONION GRAVY

1 1/2 lb. ground beef	1 tbsp. all-purpose
1/2 c. fine dry bread	flour
crumbs	1 tbsp. Worcestershire
1 egg, slightly beaten	sauce
1/4 tsp. salt	1/4 c. catsup
Dash of pepper	1/2 tsp. prepared
1 can onion soup	mustard

Combine ground beef, bread crumbs, egg, salt, pepper and 1/3 cup soup in bowl; mix well. Shape into 6 oval patties. Brown patties in skillet; drain. Blend remaining soup with flour in small bowl. Add remaining ingredients; mix well. Pour over patties in skillet. Cook, covered, over low heat for 20 minutes. Yield: 6 servings.

MEXICAN TORTE

1 lb. ground beef	12 flour tortillas
1 med. onion, chopped	1 lb. Cheddar cheese,
3 tbsp. oil	shredded
1 16-oz. can stewed	1/4 c. chopped black
tomatoes	olives
1 8-oz. can tomato	1 c. sour cream
sauce	1 c. guacamole
1 env. dry taco	1/2 c. salsa
seasoning mix	
1/2 c. chopped black	
olives	

Brown ground beef with onion in oil in skillet, stirring until ground beef is crumbly. Add stewed tomatoes, tomato sauce and seasoning mix; mix well. Simmer for 10 to 15 minutes. Stir in 1/2 cup olives. Place 2 tortillas on baking sheet. Layer ground beef mixture, cheese and tortillas on top. Bake for 20 to 25 minutes. Top with additional 1/4 cup olives, sour cream, guacamole and salsa. Cut into wedges. Yield: 4 to 6 servings.

GROUND BEEF-VEGETABLE STEW

2 lb. ground beef	1 8-oz. can tomato
2 onions, chopped	sauce
1 green bell pepper,	1 tsp. sugar
chopped	Salt and pepper to taste
3 cans vegetable soup	1 c. rice, cooked

Brown ground beef with onion and green pepper in skillet, stirring until crumbly; drain. Add next 4 ingredients; mix well. Simmer, covered, over low heat for 15 to 20 minutes. Add rice. Heat to serving temperature. Yield: 8 servings.

TACOS

1 lb. ground beef	Cumin to taste
Garlic salt to taste	Salt and pepper to taste
1/4 tsp. chili powder	Tabasco sauce to taste
1 onion, chopped	1/4 tsp. chili powder
Liquid smoke to taste	Taco shells
1 6-oz. can tomato	Shredded lettuce
juice	Chopped tomatoes
1 8-oz. can tomato	Shredded Cheddar
sauce	cheese
1 tbsp. oil	

Brown ground beef in skillet, stirring until crumbly; drain. Mix in garlic salt, chili powder, half the onion and liquid smoke; keep warm. Combine tomato juice, tomato sauce, oil, remaining onion and seasonings in saucepan; mix well. Simmer until thickened, stirring occasionally. Pour into serving dish. Spoon ground beef into taco shells. Serve with lettuce, tomatoes, cheese and sauce. Yield: 4 servings.

TACO SALAD

1 lb. ground beef	1 8-oz. bottle of
1 env. taco seasoning	Catalina salad
mix	dressing
1 head lettuce,	1 c. shredded Cheddar
shredded	cheese
4 tomatoes, chopped	Nacho chips
1 onion, chopped	

Brown ground beef in skillet, stirring until crumbly; drain. Add taco seasoning; mix well. Combine lettuce, tomatoes and onion in salad bowl. Top with ground beef mixture. Drizzle with salad dressing. Sprinkle with cheese and nacho chips. Yield: 6 servings.

Grouper

GROUPER CREOLE

1 green bell pepper, cut	1/8 tsp. oregano
into thin strips	1/8 tsp. thyme
1 pkg. instant chicken	1 lb. grouper fillets
broth	Salt, pepper, garlic
1 c. tomato sauce	powder and paprika
1 tbsp. sliced scallions	to taste
1 bay leaf	

Combine green pepper and broth mix in saucepan. Cook over low heat until green pepper is tender, stirring frequently. Add tomato sauce, scallions, bay leaf, oregano and thyme. Simmer for 10 minutes. Discard bay leaf. Season fillets with salt, pepper, garlic powder and paprika to taste. Arrange in greased baking dish. Pour sauce over fillets. Bake at 375 degrees for 15 minutes or until fish flakes easily. Yield: 2 servings.

GROUPER SCAMPI

4 8-oz. grouper fillets	1/4 tsp. basil
1 c. water	1/4 tsp. parsley
2 c. melted margarine	1/4 tsp. paprika
2 tbsp. minced garlic	1 tsp. lemon juice
2 tbsp. garlic powder	1/4 c. bread crumbs
1/4 tsp. oregano	

Place fish fillets in baking dish. Add water. Bake at 275 degrees for 5 minutes. Combine margarine, garlic, seasonings, lemon juice and bread crumbs in bowl; mix well. Spoon over fish. Bake for 5 minutes longer or until fish flakes easily. Serve over rice. Yield: 4 servings.

Gumbo

CAJUN CRAB GUMBO

2 tbsp. margarine	1/4 tsp. thyme
2 tbsp. all-purpose	1/2 tsp. cayenne pepper
flour	1 clove of garlic,
4 sm. zucchini, sliced	minced
1 onion, chopped	1 1/2 lb. crab meat
1 19-oz. can tomatoes	2 c. boiling water
1 bay leaf	1 tsp. salt
2 tbsp. chopped parsley	3 c. cooked rice

Melt margarine in heavy saucepan. Blend in flour. Cook for several minutes, stirring constantly. Add zucchini, onion, tomatoes, bay leaf, parsley, thyme, cayenne pepper, garlic and crab meat. Simmer for 10 minutes, stirring frequently. Add water and salt. Simmer, covered, for 1 hour. Simmer, uncovered, until consistency of thick soup, stirring frequently. Remove bay leaf. Serve over rice. Yield: 6 servings.

VEGETABLE GUMBO

2 1/2 c. chopped	1 tsp salt
tomatoes	1/4 tsp. pepper
1/2 c. chopped celery	1 tbsp. vinegar
1/4 c. chopped onion	1 tbsp. sugar
1 1/2 c. cut okra	2 tbsp. margarine

Combine vegetables in saucepan. Add salt, pepper, vinegar, sugar and margarine; mix well. Simmer over low heat for 45 minutes. Yield: 6 servings.

Haddock

FISH AND VEGETABLE CHOWDER

1/2 c. chopped	1 8-oz. can whole
mushrooms	kernel corn,
1/2 c. chopped onion	drained
1/2 c. chopped red	2 tbsp. Chablis
bell pepper	8 oz. haddock fillets,
2 tbsp. margarine	cut into 1-in. pieces
1 can potato soup	2 tbsp. chopped parsley
1 c. milk	Pepper to taste

Sauté mushrooms, onion and red pepper in margarine in 2-quart saucepan over medium heat. Stir in soup, milk, corn and Chablis. Bring to a boil. Add fish, parsley and pepper. Reduce heat. Simmer, covered, for 10 minutes or until fish flakes easily. Yield: 4 servings.

HADDOCK WITH DILL BUTTER

1 shallot, chopped	1/8 tsp. salt
2 tbsp. butter	1/8 tsp. pepper
2 tbsp. lemon juice	1 lb. haddock fillets
2 tbsp. chopped dill	

Sauté shallot in butter in small saucepan for 2 minutes or until tender. Remove from heat. Stir in lemon juice, dill, salt and pepper. Arrange haddock in buttered baking dish. Pour dill sauce over top. Bake at 375 degrees for 15 minutes or until fish flakes easily. Yield: 2 servings.

MAINE CHOWDER

2 to 3 lb. haddock fillets	Salt to taste
Salt to taste	2 lg. cans evaporated
1 onion, chopped	milk
3 tbsp. margarine	3 tbsp. margarine
4 potatoes, chopped	Pepper to taste

Simmer fish fillets in salted water to cover in saucepan until fish flakes easily. Drain, reserving cooking liquid. Sauté onion in 3 tablespoons margarine in saucepan. Add potatoes, reserved cooking liquid and salt. Cook until potatoes are tender. Mash part of the potato mixture. Add flaked fish, evaporated milk, 3 tablespoons margarine and pepper. Heat to serving temperature. Yield: 6 servings.

BRITISH FISH FRY

1 12-oz. can beer	1 c. buttermilk
Juice of 1/2 lemon	1 egg
1 onion, sliced	1 to 2 c. buttermilk
4 peppercorns	baking mix
Old Bay seasoning	Oil for deep frying
to taste	Salt and pepper to taste
3 lb. haddock fillets	

Combine beer, lemon juice, onion, peppercorns and Old Bay seasoning in bowl. Cut fish into bite-sized pieces. Add to beer mixture. Marinate in refrigerator for several hours; drain. Combine buttermilk and egg in bowl. Add fish. Marinate for 15 to 30 minutes; drain. Coat fish well with baking mix. Deep-fry fish in hot oil for 2 to 5 minutes or until golden brown. Drain on paper towel. Season with salt and pepper. Yield: 8 servings.

Halibut

Ham

HERBED HALIBUT

1/4 c. bread crumbs	*6 tbsp. melted*
1/4 c. Parmesan cheese	*margarine*
1/4 c. minced green	*4 tsp. olive oil*
onion	*4 halibut steaks*
1/4 c. parsley	*Salt and pepper to taste*
1 tsp. basil	*1/2 c. white wine*
1/2 tsp. cloves	

Mix bread crumbs, Parmesan cheese, green onions, parsley, basil and cloves in bowl. Stir in melted margarine. Brush four 12-inch foil squares lightly with oil. Place 1 fish steak on each square. Drizzle with olive oil. Sprinkle with salt and pepper. Top with crumbs. Spoon wine around each steak. Seal foil securely. Place packets on baking sheet. Bake at 450 degrees for 8 minutes or until fish flakes easily. Yield: 4 servings.

OVEN-CRISPED HALIBUT

1 lb. halibut fillets	*1 1/2 tbsp. chopped*
3/4 c. cornflakes,	*parsley*
crushed	*1 tbsp. paprika*
3 tbsp. melted	*1/4 tsp. pepper*
margarine	*1/8 tsp. cayenne pepper*
2 tbsp. lemon juice	

Coat fillets with cornflake crumbs. Place on baking sheet coated with nonstick cooking spray. Combine margarine, lemon juice, parsley, paprika, pepper and cayenne pepper in small bowl. Drizzle over fillets. Bake at 375 degrees for 20 minutes or until fish flakes easily. Yield: 4 servings.

BLUE CHEESE HALIBUT

6 boneless halibut	*1/2 tsp. celery salt*
steaks	*2 c. milk*
1 onion, chopped	*1/4 c. sliced green olives*
3 tbsp. margarine	*1/2 c. crumbled blue*
1/4 c. all-purpose flour	*cheese*
1/4 tsp. salt	

Arrange fish steaks in buttered baking dish. Sauté onion in margarine in skillet. Stir in flour and seasonings. Add milk. Cook until thickened, stirring constantly; remove from heat. Stir in olives and cheese. Pour over fish. Bake at 350 degrees for 25 to 30 minutes or until fish flakes easily. Serve over rice. Yield: 4 servings.

HAM BALL

1 6-oz. can chunky	*1 tbsp. minced onion*
ham	*1/2 tsp. dry mustard*
8 oz. cream cheese,	*1/2 tsp. Tabasco sauce*
softened	*1/2 c. finely chopped*
1/4 c. mayonnaise	*pecans*
2 tbsp. parsley flakes	

Combine first 7 ingredients in bowl; mix well. Chill until almost firm. Shape into ball. Roll in pecans, coating well. Serve with crackers or assorted breads. Yield: 4 to 6 servings.

HAM CHEESECAKE

1/2 c. bread crumbs	*24 oz. cream cheese,*
1/2 c. half and half	*softened*
1 1/4 tsp. dry mustard	*8 oz. chopped cooked*
1 1/4 tsp. salt	*ham*
1/4 tsp. ground red	*2 c. shredded Swiss*
pepper	*cheese*
4 eggs	

Sprinkle bread crumbs over bottom and side of greased 9-inch springform pan. Combine half and half, seasonings, eggs and cream cheese in mixer bowl. Beat at medium speed for 5 minutes. Stir in ham and cheese. Spread in prepared pan. Bake at 325 degrees for 1 hour. Cool. Refrigerate, covered, for up to 48 hours. Let stand at room temperature for 2 hours. Place on serving plate; remove side of pan. Garnish with pimento, parsley and olives. Serve with crackers. Yield: 20 servings.

BAKED HAM WITH RASPBERRY GLAZE

1 4 to 5-lb. cooked	*4 tsp. cornstarch*
boneless smoked or	*2/3 c. seedless raspberry*
canned ham	*jam*
1/2 c. dry white wine	*2 tbsp. margarine*
1/4 c. lemon juice	

Score ham in diamond pattern. Place on rack in shallow roasting pan. Bake at 325 degrees for 1 hour and 45 minutes or to 140 degrees on meat thermometer. Combine wine, lemon juice and cornstarch in small saucepan. Stir in 1/3 cup jam. Cook over low heat until bubbly, stirring constantly. Stir in remaining 1/3 cup jam and margarine. Heat until margarine is melted, stirring frequently. Brush glaze over ham. Bake for 10 minutes longer. Place ham on serving platter. Spoon remaining glaze over ham. Yield: 12 servings.

CHEESY CREAMED HAM

1 chicken bouillon cube	1 tsp. prepared mustard
1/2 c. margarine	2 c. cubed ham
1/4 c. all-purpose flour	1 3-oz. can sliced
11/2 c. milk	black olives, drained
1 tsp. Worcestershire	2 tbsp. chopped
sauce	pimento
1 c. cubed Velveeta	2 tbsp. chopped parsley
cheese	

Melt bouillon cube and margarine in 2-quart saucepan. Whisk in flour. Add milk, whisking constantly. Cook over medium heat until thickened, whisking constantly. Add Worcestershire, cheese and mustard. Stir until cheese is melted. Add ham, olives, pimento and parsley. Cook just until heated through. Serve in patty shells or over baked potatoes. Yield: 6 servings.

DIJON HAM

1 3-lb. canned ham	1/4 c. maple syrup
1/4 c. Dijon-style	2 tbsp. cider vinegar
mustard	1 c. red wine
Whole cloves	1/3 c. cola
1/3 c. orange	
marmalade	

Place ham in shallow baking dish. Spread with mustard. Stud with cloves. Spoon marmalade over ham. Drizzle with maple syrup and mixture of cider vinegar, wine and cola. Bake at 350 degrees for 1 hour, basting every 15 minutes. Let stand for 15 minutes before slicing. Yield: 8 servings.

HAM AND BROCCOLI STRATA

1 20-oz. package	3 c. chopped cooked
frozen chopped	ham
broccoli	6 eggs, beaten
12 bread slices, crusts	31/2 c. milk
trimmed	1/2 tsp. salt
3 c. shredded Cheddar	1/4 tsp. dry mustard
cheese	Onion flakes to taste

Cook broccoli according to package directions; drain well. Layer 6 bread slices, 1 cup Cheddar cheese, remaining bread, 1 cup Cheddar cheese, broccoli, ham and remaining Cheddar cheese in greased 9x13-inch baking dish. Combine eggs, milk, salt and dry mustard in bowl; mix well. Pour over layers. Sprinkle with onion flakes. Chill, covered, if desired. Remove from refrigerator 1 hour before baking. Bake at 325 degrees for 1 hour. Let stand for 10 minutes before serving. Yield: 10 servings.

HAM AND BROCCOLI CASSEROLE

1 20-oz. package	1 soup can milk
frozen chopped	3 c. chopped cooked
broccoli	ham
1/2 c. chopped onion	2 c. minute rice
2 tbsp. margarine	1 c. shredded
1 can cream of	American cheese
mushroom soup	1 tsp. Worcestershire
1 can cream of	sauce
celery soup	

Cook broccoli according to package directions; drain. Sauté onion in margarine in saucepan. Add soups, milk, ham, rice, cheese and Worcestershire sauce. Spoon into 21/2-quart baking dish. Bake at 350 degrees for 45 to 50 minutes. Yield: 8 servings.

UPSIDE-DOWN HAM LOAF

3 tbsp. margarine	1 lb. lean ham, ground
5 tbsp. brown sugar	1/2 c. bread crumbs
9 pineapple slices	1/4 tsp. pepper
1/2 lb. lean pork,	2 eggs
ground	1/2 c. milk

Melt margarine in 8x8-inch baking pan. Stir in brown sugar. Arrange pineapple slices in prepared pan. Combine pork, ham, bread crumbs, pepper, eggs and milk in bowl; mix well. Press into baking pan. Bake at 350 degrees for 50 to 60 minutes or until cooked through. Invert onto serving plate. Garnish with red cherries. Yield: 9 servings.

DEEP-DISH HAM PIE

1/4 c. melted margarine	4 hard-cooked eggs,
1/4 c. all-purpose flour	chopped
Salt and pepper to taste	11/2 c. drained
2 c. milk	canned peas
1 tsp. chopped onion	1 recipe buttermilk
21/2 c. chopped cooked	baking mix biscuit
ham	dough

Blend margarine, flour, salt and pepper in saucepan. Stir in milk. Cook until thickened, stirring constantly. Add onion, ham, eggs and peas. Pour into 10x10-inch baking dish. Pat biscuit dough to fit baking dish. Place on top of casserole. Bake at 450 degrees for 20 minutes or until top is light brown. Yield: 4 servings.

GRILLED HAM STEAKS

1/4 c. prepared mustard	6 1/2-inch thick ham
1/2 c. packed light	steaks
brown sugar	1 20-oz. can
1/8 tsp. cloves	pineapple slices
2 tbsp. pineapple juice	

Mix mustard, brown sugar, cloves and pineapple juice in bowl. Place ham steaks on grill over hot coals. Baste with mustard mixture. Grill for 6 minutes. Turn steaks; baste with sauce. Place 2 pineapple slices on each steak. Grill for 6 minutes longer. Yield: 8 to 12 servings.

HAM AND SIX-CHEESE QUICHE

1 recipe 2-crust pie pastry	*2 c. shredded Cheddar cheese*
12 eggs, beaten	*2 c. shredded Swiss cheese*
8 oz. cream cheese, softened	*2 c. shredded American cheese*
4 c. cream	*1/4 c. melted margarine*
1 lb. ham, chopped	*1 onion, chopped*
2 c. ricotta cheese	*Salt and pepper to taste*
3 c. shredded mozzarella cheese	

Line 9x13-inch baking dish with pie pastry. Beat eggs with cream cheese and cream in bowl. Stir in ham, cheeses, margarine, onion and seasonings. Pour into prepared baking dish. Bake at 350 degrees for 35 to 40 minutes or until knife inserted in center comes out clean. Yield: 15 servings.

HAM AND POTATO CASSEROLE

1 onion, finely chopped	*4 potatoes, peeled, sliced*
3 tbsp. margarine	*1/2 c. chopped celery*
3 tbsp. all-purpose flour	*1 1/2 c. chopped cooked ham*
1/2 tsp. dry mustard	*1/2 c. chopped green bell pepper*
Salt and pepper to taste	
1 1/2 c. milk	
3/4 c. shredded Cheddar cheese	

Sauté onion in margarine in skillet. Stir in flour and dry mustard. Season with salt and pepper. Add milk gradually. Cook until thickened, stirring constantly. Stir in cheese until melted. Alternate layers of potatoes, celery, ham, green pepper and cheese sauce in 9x13-inch baking dish until all ingredients are used, ending with cheese sauce. Bake, covered, at 350 degrees for 1 hour. Bake, uncovered, for 30 minutes longer. Yield: 6 servings.

HAM AND RICE SKILLET

1 bag rice in boiling bag	*1 c. frozen peas*
1 c. chopped green onions	*1 4-oz. can chopped mushrooms*
1 c. thinly sliced celery	*1 7-oz. can chunky ham, flaked,*
2 tbsp. oil	*2 eggs, beaten*
1/4 c. sliced black olives	*1 tbsp. soy sauce*

Cook rice according to package directions; set aside. Sauté green onions and celery in oil in skillet until tender-crisp. Add olives, peas, mushrooms and ham. Stir-fry for 3 to 4 minutes; push to 1 side. Pour eggs into skillet. Cook until set, stirring to scramble. Stir in rice and soy sauce. Cook until heated through. Garnish with orange sections and celery leaves. Yield: 4 to 6 servings.

GOLDEN RISOTTO

1/2 c. chopped onion	*1 4-oz. can sliced mushrooms*
1 c. chopped cooked ham	*2 c. water*
4 oz. brown and serve sausages, sliced	*2 chicken bouillon cubes*
1 c. cooked peeled shrimp	*1/8 tsp. saffron*
1/2 c. margarine	*1 1/3 c. minute rice*
	1/4 c. Parmesan cheese

Sauté onion, ham, sausages and shrimp in margarine in skillet, stirring until sausages are cooked through. Keep warm. Drain mushrooms, reserving 1/3 cup liquid. Combine reserved liquid, water, bouillon and saffron in saucepan. Bring to a boil. Stir in rice; remove from heat. Let stand, covered, for 5 minutes. Add ham mixture and mushrooms. Spoon into serving bowl. Sprinkle with cheese. Yield: 6 servings.

Herbs

HERBED CHEESE

8 oz. cream cheese, softened	*1/2 tsp. lemon juice*
2 tbsp. margarine, softened	*1 tbsp. oregano*
1 clove of garlic, crushed	*1/8 tsp. cayenne pepper*
	1/2 tsp. salt
	2 tbsp. chopped parsley

Combine cream cheese with remaining ingredients in mixer bowl; mix well. Chill for several hours. Serve as spread with crackers. Yield: 6 servings.

HERBED PITA TOAST

2 6-in. pita bread rounds, split	*4 tsp. minced fresh parsley*
3 tbsp. margarine, softened	*1/2 tsp. dillweed*
	1/2 tsp. mixed herbs

Cut pita rounds into fourths. Combine margarine, parsley, dillweed and herbs in bowl. Spread each wedge with 1/4 teaspoon mixture. Place wedges smooth side down on baking sheet. Bake at 350 degrees for 5 minutes. Yield: 8 servings.

HERB ROLLS

1/2 c. melted margarine　*1 tbsp. Parmesan*
1 1/2 tsp. parsley flakes　　*cheese*
1/2 tsp. dillweed　　　*1　10-count can*
1 1/2 tsp. onion flakes　　　*refrigerator biscuits*

Combine first five ingredients in bowl. Spoon into baking pan. Cut each biscuit into quarters. Arrange in prepared pan. Bake at 350 degrees for 12 minutes. Invert onto serving plate.
Yield: 5 servings.

HERBED VINEGAR

3 1/4 c. (5% acidity)　　*1/4 c. chopped fresh*
*　white wine vinegar*　　*　oregano*
1/2 c. chopped parsley　*4 shallots, thinly sliced*
1/4 c. chopped fresh　　*12 peppercorns*
*　chives*　　　　　*Sprigs of fresh*
1/2 c. chopped fresh　　*　rosemary, oregano*
*　thyme*　　　　　*　and thyme*

Bring vinegar to a boil in saucepan. Place chopped herbs, shallots and peppercorns in large jar. Add boiling vinegar. Let stand, covered, at room temperature for 2 weeks. Place fresh herbs in decorative bottles. Strain vinegar into bottles. Seal with corks. Yield: Four 1/2-pint bottles.

Honey

CRANBERRY HONEY

4 c. cranberry juice　　*3 c. sugar*
*　cocktail*　　　　*1/2 tsp. orange extract*

Combine juice and sugar in saucepan. Cook over medium heat, stirring until sugar is dissolved. Cook over medium heat to 234 to 240 degrees on candy thermometer, soft-ball stage. Remove from heat. Stir in orange extract. Ladle into hot sterilized 1/2-pint jars, leaving 1/2 inch headspace. Seal with 2-piece lids. Yield: Two 1/2-pint jars.

AFRICAN HONEY BREAD

1 pkg. dry yeast　　　*1/4 tsp. cloves*
1/4 c. 110-degree water　*1 tsp. salt*
1 egg　　　　　　*1 c. lukewarm milk*
1/2 c. honey　　　　*1/4 c. melted butter*
1 tbsp. coriander　　*4 to 5 c. all-purpose*
1/2 tsp. cinnamon　　*　flour*

Dissolve yeast in lukewarm water. Let stand in warm place for 5 minutes. Combine egg, honey, coriander, cinnamon, cloves and salt in deep bowl;

mix with wire whisk. Add yeast mixture, milk and melted butter; beat until well blended. Stir in enough flour, 1/2 cup at a time, to form a soft dough. Knead on lightly floured surface for 10 minutes or until smooth and elastic. Place in greased bowl, turning to grease surface. Let rise, covered, until doubled in bulk. Spread melted butter over bottom and side of 3-quart soufflé dish. Punch dough down. Knead lightly for about 2 minutes. Shape into ball. Place in prepared dish, pressing gently to cover bottom of dish completely. Let rise, covered, until doubled in bulk. Dough rises very slowly; rising time may vary up to 2 1/2 hours. Bake at 300 degrees for 50 to 60 minutes. Yield: 1 loaf.

HONEY BARS

3/4 c. sugar　　　　*1 egg, beaten*
1/4 c. honey　　　　*1 c. chopped pecans*
3/4 c. oil　　　　　*1/2 c. confectioners'*
2 c. all-purpose flour　*　sugar*
Salt to taste　　　*1/4 tsp. vanilla extract*
1 tsp. soda　　　　*1 tbsp. mayonnaise*
1 tsp. cinnamon　　*1/2 tbsp. water*

Combine sugar, honey, oil, flour, salt, soda, cinnamon, egg and pecans in bowl in order listed, mixing well after each addition. Spread in ungreased 9x9-inch baking pan. Bake at 325 degrees for 25 to 30 minutes or until golden brown. Combine confectioners' sugar, vanilla, mayonnaise and water in bowl; mix well. Spread over warm baked layer. Cool. Cut into bars. Yield: 2 dozen.

MINTED HONEY

6 c. mild-flavored　　*6 sprigs of fresh mint*
*　honey*

Heat honey in saucepan over low heat until honey is liquified. Place 1 sprig of mint in each jar. Pour hot honey over mint sprigs. Seal with 2-piece lids. Let stand for 1 week or longer. Sample the honey. If flavor is not intense enough, remove wilted mint sprig and insert fresh one. Let stand for 1 week longer. Yield: Six 8-ounce jars.

HONEY MUFFINS

1 c. margarine,　　　*1 c. sour cream*
*　softened*　　　　*2 c. whole wheat flour*
1 c. honey　　　　*1 tsp. soda*
1 egg　　　　　　*1/2 tsp. salt*

Combine margarine and honey in bowl. Blend in egg and sour cream. Add dry ingredients; mix just until moistened. Fill greased muffin cups 2/3 full. Bake at 400 degrees for 12 to 15 minutes or until light brown. Yield: 1 1/2 dozen.

Jam

MERRY BERRY JAM

4 c. pitted cherries   4 c. raspberries
4 c. cranberries   6¹/₂ c. sugar
4 c. strawberries

Combine cherries and cranberries in large saucepan. Cook over low heat for about 10 minutes. Add strawberries and raspberries. Bring to a simmer. Simmer for 5 minutes, shaking pan occasionally; do not stir. Add sugar. Simmer for 30 minutes. Skim off foam if desired. Ladle into hot sterilized ¹/₂-pint jars, leaving ¹/₂ inch headspace. Seal with 2-piece lids. Process in boiling water bath for 10 minutes. Yield: Six to eight 6-ounce jars.

SUMMER-FRESH KIWIFRUIT JAM

1 lb. kiwifruit, peeled   1 tbsp. lemon juice
2¹/₂ c. sugar   5 tbsp. liquid pectin

Purée kiwifruit in blender container. Pour into bowl. Add sugar and lemon juice. Stir until dissolved. Let stand, covered, for 20 minutes. Add pectin. Stir for 2 minutes. Let stand, covered, for 24 hours. Pour into jars; seal with paraffin. Store in refrigerator for up to 5 weeks or in freezer for 1 year. Yield: Six to eight 6-ounce jars.

OLD-FASHIONED JAM CAKE

2 c. sugar   1 c. pear preserves
4 eggs   1 c. seedless raisins
1 tsp. allspice   1 c. chopped walnuts
1 tsp. cinnamon   1¹/₂ c. sour cream
1 tsp. nutmeg   1 tbsp. soda
1 c. blackberry jam   4 c. all-purpose flour
1 c. peach preserves   1 c. buttermilk
1 c. strawberry   Creamy Caramel Icing
  preserves

Line 5 greased 8-inch round cake pans with greased waxed paper. Combine sugar, eggs and spices in mixer bowl. Beat until light and fluffy. Add jam, preserves, raisins and walnuts. Combine sour cream and soda. Add to jam mixture alternately with flour and buttermilk, mixing well after each addition. Pour into prepared cake pans. Bake at 325 degrees for 35 to 45 minutes or until layers test done. Cover with foil to prevent overbrowning if necessary. Cool in pans for 10 minutes. Invert onto wire rack to cool completely. Spread Creamy Caramel Icing between layers and over top and side of cake. Yield: 16 to 20 servings.

Creamy Caramel Icing

2 c. butter   1 c. milk
4 c. packed light   8 c. (about) sifted
  brown sugar   confectioners' sugar

Melt butter in saucepan. Stir in brown sugar. Bring to a boil. Cook over low heat for 2 minutes, stirring constantly. Stir in milk. Bring to a boil, stirring constantly. Cool to lukewarm. Add confectioners' sugar gradually, beating constantly until of spreading consistency.

JAM SHORTBREAD

1 2-layer pkg.   1 egg
  butter recipe   1 10-oz. jar raspberry
  cake mix   jam
¹/₄ c. margarine,   ¹/₂ c. confectioners'
  softened   sugar
¹/₂ c. chopped pecans   1¹/₂ tsp. water

Combine cake mix, margarine, pecans and egg in mixer bowl. Beat at low speed until blended. Press into greased and floured 9x13-inch baking pan. Spread with jam. Bake at 350 degrees for 20 to 25 minutes or until edges are light brown. Blend confectioners' sugar and water in small bowl. Drizzle over warm shortbread. Cool completely. Cut into bars. Yield: 2 dozen.

Old-Fashioned Jam Cake...reminds you of the ones your grandmother used to make.

Jambalaya

JAMBALAYA WITH SUMMER VEGETABLES

4 slices bacon, chopped
1 lb. bulk sausage
1 lb. link sausage, sliced
1 lb. chicken pieces
3 tbsp. (about) all-purpose flour
2 stalks celery, chopped
1 onion, chopped
1 green bell pepper, chopped
4 cloves of garlic, chopped
1 bunch green onions, chopped
2 c. uncooked rice
4 c. hot water
1½ tsp. Creole seasoning
1 tsp. thyme
1 tsp. parsley
Tabasco sauce to taste

Cook bacon, sausage and chicken in skillet until cooked through. Remove to large baking pan with slotted spoon. Add enough flour to pan drippings to make roux. Add celery, onion, green pepper and garlic. Cook until tender, stirring frequently. Add green onions, rice, water and seasonings. Bring to a boil. Stir into baking pan. Bake, covered with foil, at 350 degrees for 50 minutes. Bake, uncovered, for 5 minutes longer.
Yield: 8 to 10 servings.

SHRIMP AND SAUSAGE JAMBALAYA

1 lb. smoked sausage, sliced
3 onions, chopped
2 cloves of garlic, minced
1½ c. chopped green bell pepper
2 stalks celery, chopped
1½ c. canned tomatoes
2 tbsp. tomato paste
1 bay leaf
1 tbsp. chopped parsley
½ tsp. thyme
1 c. uncooked rice
1 tsp. salt
¼ tsp. cayenne pepper
1½ c. water
2 lb. medium shrimp, peeled

Sauté sausage and onions in stockpot until onions are tender. Add garlic, green pepper and celery. Sauté until vegetables are tender. Add tomatoes, tomato paste, bay leaf, parsley, thyme and rice. Season with salt and cayenne pepper. Add water. Bring to a boil. Add shrimp. Reduce heat. Cook over very low heat for 30 to 45 minutes. Remove bay leaf. May add 1 dozen oysters, 1 pound chopped smoked ham or 1 teaspoon Creole seasoning if desired. Yield: 8 servings.

Jelly

PEPPER JELLY

½ c. finely chopped cherry peppers
6½ c. sugar
1½ c. vinegar
1 3-oz. package fruit pectin
Red food coloring

Combine cherry peppers, sugar and vinegar in saucepan. Bring to a boil over medium-high heat. Cook for 4 minutes. Stir in pectin. Bring to a boil; remove from heat. Add food coloring. Ladle into hot sterilized ½-pint jars, leaving ½ inch headspace. Seal with 2-piece lids. Store in refrigerator. Serve over cream cheese on crackers or in tiny pastry shells. Use 2 envelopes fruit pectin for firmer jelly. Yield: Three 8-ounce jars.

ZUCCHINI JELLY

3 c. shredded zucchini
3 c. sugar
3 tbsp. lemon juice
1 3-oz. package any flavor gelatin

Mix zucchini, sugar and lemon juice in saucepan. Bring to a boil over low heat. Stir in gelatin. Ladle into hot sterilized 8-ounce jars, leaving ½ inch head space. Seal with 2-piece lids.
Yield: Three to four 8-ounce jars.

Kiwifruit

KIWIFRUIT MERINGUE

3 egg whites
¼ tsp. cream of tartar
¾ c. sugar
1 c. chilled whipping cream
2 tbsp. sugar
¼ c. chopped almonds
4 kiwifruit, chilled, sliced

Beat egg whites and cream of tartar in mixer bowl until frothy. Add ¾ cup sugar gradually, beating until stiff peaks form. Spread in 9-inch round baking pan lined with baking parchment. Bake at 225 degrees for 1½ hours. Turn off oven. Let meringue stand in closed oven for 1 hour. Cool completely. Invert carefully onto serving plate. Beat whipping cream and 2 tablespoons sugar in mixer bowl until soft peaks form. Spread over sides and top of meringue. Sprinkle with almonds. Arrange kiwifruit slices on top. Yield: 6 servings.

SUMMER KIWIFRUIT TRIFLE

3 eggs, beaten	*4 kiwifruit*
2 c. milk	*1/2 c. whipping cream*
1/4 c. sugar	*1 tbsp. confectioners'*
2 tsp. vanilla extract	*sugar*
1 10-oz. pound cake	*1/4 tsp. vanilla extract*
1/2 c. raspberry	*1/4 c. sliced almonds*
preserves	

Combine eggs, milk and sugar in double boiler. Cook over hot water until mixture coats silver spoon, stirring constantly. Cool; stir occasionally. Stir in 2 teaspoons vanilla. Cut cake into 1/2-inch slices. Spread 2/3 of the slices with raspberry preserves. Place 1/2 of the slices spread with jam in bottom of 2 1/2-quart serving bowl. Spread 1/2 cup custard over cake. Repeat layers. Top with plain cake and remaining custard. Chill for 1 hour or longer. Peel and slice kiwifruit. Arrange on custard. Whip cream with confectioners' sugar and 1/4 teaspoon vanilla in mixer bowl until soft peaks form. Pipe around edge of trifle. Sprinkle almonds over top. Yield: 12 servings.

Lamb

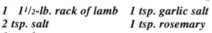

BARBECUED RACK OF LAMB

1 1 1/2-lb. rack of lamb	*1 tsp. garlic salt*
2 tsp. salt	*1 tsp. rosemary*
1 tsp. lemon pepper	

Rub lamb on all sides with mixture of seasonings 6 hours or longer before cooking. Cook at 350 degrees over indirect heat in covered barbecue for 1 hour. Yield: 4 servings.

BROILED SPRING LAMB CHOPS

2 loin lamb chops	*1/4 c. orange juice*
1/4 c. honey	

Place lamb chops on rack in broiler pan. Broil 4 inches from heat source for 5 minutes. Season with salt to taste; turn chops over. Broil for 5 minutes or to desired degree of doneness. Top with mixture of honey and orange juice. Broil for 3 minutes longer. Yield: 2 servings.

ROAST LEG OF LAMB

1 5 to 7-lb. leg of lamb	*Salt to taste*
1 clove of garlic,	*Pepper to taste*
slivered	

Make 4 or 5 slits in lamb with tip of knife; insert garlic slivers into slits. Sprinkle lamb with salt and pepper. Place lamb fat side up on rack in shallow roasting pan. Insert meat thermometer so tip is in center of thickest part of lamb and does not touch bone or rest in fat. Do not add water. Roast, uncovered, at 325 degrees for 2 1/2 hours for 5-pound roast, 3 1/2 hours for 7-pound roast or 140 degrees on meat thermometer for rare, 160 degrees for medium or 170 degrees for well done. Let stand for 15 to 20 minutes before carving for easier slicing. Lamb may be cooked to 5 degrees lower than indicated and will continue to cook while standing. Yield: 8 servings.

GREEK MEATBALLS

1 lb. ground lamb	*1/2 tsp. crushed dried*
1/2 c. dry bread crumbs	*mint*
1/4 c. milk	*1 clove of garlic,*
1 egg	*minced*
1 med. onion, finely	*1/2 tsp. crushed dried*
chopped	*oregano leaves*
1 tsp. salt	*1/4 tsp. pepper*

Combine ground lamb with bread crumbs, milk, egg, onion, salt, mint, garlic, oregano and pepper in bowl; mix well. Shape into 1-inch balls. Place in ungreased 9x13-inch baking pan. Bake at 350 degrees for 25 minutes or until light brown; drain. Yield: 36 meatballs.

Lemon

EASY CHEESY LEMON BARS

1 2-layer pkg.	*8 oz. cream cheese,*
lemon cake mix	*softened*
1/2 c. margarine,	*1 16-oz. can lemon*
softened	*frosting*
1 egg	*2 eggs*

Combine cake mix, margarine and 1 egg in bowl; mix well. Press into bottom of greased 9x13-inch baking pan. Blend softened cream cheese and frosting in bowl. Reserve 1/2 cup for frosting. Add 2 eggs to remaining mixture. Beat for 3 to 5 minutes. Spread over mixture in pan. Bake at 350 degrees for 30 to 40 minutes or until light golden brown. Cool. Frost with reserved cream cheese mixture. Cut into bars. Yield: 3 dozen.

LEMON-LIME SALAD

1 3-oz. package lemon gelatin	1 c. cottage cheese
1 3-oz. package lime gelatin	1 8-oz. can crushed pineapple
1 c. boiling water	1 tsp. prepared horseradish
1 c. mayonnaise	1/2 c. pecans
1 c. sour cream	

Dissolve gelatins in boiling water in small bowl. Combine mayonnaise and remaining ingredients in bowl; mix well. Stir in gelatin. Pour into 1 1/2-quart mold. Chill until set. Unmold onto serving plate. Yield: 6 servings.

LEMON AND COCONUT COOLER

2 tsp. grated lemon rind	1/4 c. sugar
2 c. cold milk	1/4 c. lemon juice
1/4 c. coconut	6 ice cubes

Combine all ingredients in blender container. Process until ice is completely pulverized and drink is frothy. Garnish with additional grated lemon rind. Yield: 2 servings.

LEMON CHEESECAKE

30 graham crackers, crushed	1 12-oz. can evaporated milk, chilled
1 c. melted margarine	8 oz. cream cheese, softened
1/4 c. sugar	1 c. sugar
1 3-oz. package lemon gelatin	
1 c. boiling water	

Mix crumbs, margarine and 1/4 cup sugar in bowl. Pat half the mixture into 9x13-inch baking pan. Dissolve gelatin in boiling water in bowl. Cool. Whip evaporated milk in bowl until stiff peaks form. Beat cream cheese and 1 cup sugar in bowl until creamy. Fold in whipped milk and gelatin. Pour into prepared pan. Sprinkle with remaining crumbs. Chill until firm. Yield: 15 servings.

LEMON CURD

Grated rind of 3 lemons	1/2 c. margarine
Juice of 2 lemons	2 eggs, well beaten
1 c. sugar	

Combine lemon rind, juice, sugar and margarine in double boiler pan. Cook over hot water until margarine melts and sugar dissolves, stirring frequently. Add eggs. Cook until mixture coats wooden spoon, stirring frequently. Pour into hot sterilized jars, leaving 1/2-inch headspace; seal. Store in refrigerator. Yield: Two 1/2-pint jars.

LEMON LUSH

1 c. all-purpose flour	1 8-oz. container whipped topping
1/2 c. chopped nuts	1 6-oz. package lemon instant pudding mix
1/2 c. margarine, softened	2 2/3 c. milk
1 c. confectioners' sugar	Pecans, chopped
8 oz. cream cheese, softened	

Combine flour, nuts and margarine in bowl. Press into 8x11-inch glass baking dish. Bake at 375 degrees for 15 minutes. Cool. Cream confectioners' sugar and cream cheese in bowl until light and fluffy. Fold in 1 cup whipped topping. Spread over cooled crust. Combine pudding mix and milk in bowl. Beat until thickened. Spoon over creamed mixture. Top with remaining whipped topping. Sprinkle with chopped pecans. Chill until firm. Yield: 6 to 8 servings.

FROZEN LEMON PIES

4 egg yolks, beaten	1 c. whipped cream
1 14-oz. can sweetened condensed milk	4 egg whites, stiffly beaten
1 6-oz. can frozen lemonade concentrate, thawed	2 baked 9-inch pie shells

Beat egg yolks with condensed milk and lemonade concentrate. Chill. Fold whipped cream into lemonade mixture; fold in egg whites. Spoon into pie shells; cover. Freeze for 6 hours. Serve with additional whipped cream. Yield: 12 servings.

LEMON MERINGUE PIE

1 c. plus 2 tbsp. sugar	2 tbsp. margarine
1/4 c. cornstarch	3 tbsp. lemon juice
1 c. plus 2 tbsp. hot water	1 1/8 tsp. grated lemon rind
2 egg yolks, slightly beaten	1 baked 8-in. pie shell
	1 recipe meringue

Combine sugar and cornstarch in small saucepan. Stir in hot water. Cook over medium heat until thickened, stirring constantly. Cook for 1 minute. Remove from heat. Stir a small amount of hot mixture into egg yolks; stir egg yolks into hot mixture. Cook for 1 minute, stirring constantly. Remove from heat. Add margarine, lemon juice and lemon rind. Pour into 8-inch pie shell. Spread meringue over pie, sealing to edge. Bake at 400 degrees for 5 to 8 minutes. Cool to room temperature. Yield: 6 servings.

Lettuce

IMPRESSIVE LETTUCE SALAD

1 lg. Italian red onion,   *1   10-oz. can artichoke*
  thinly sliced   *hearts, drained*
¹/₃ c. vinegar   *1   10-oz. can hearts*
¹/₂ c. oil   *of palm, drained*
Salt and pepper to taste   *1   4-oz. jar chopped*
1 head romaine   *pimento, drained*
  lettuce, torn   *¹/₂ c. Parmesan cheese*
1 head iceberg lettuce,
  torn

Place onion in bowl. Add mixture of vinegar, oil, salt and pepper. Marinate for 2 hours to overnight. Combine romaine and iceberg lettuce in salad bowl. Cut artichoke hearts into halves; chop hearts of palm. Add to lettuce with remaining ingredients and onion with marinade. Yield: 8 to 12 servings.

LAYERED LETTUCE SALAD

1 head lettuce, torn   *¹/₂ c. chopped green*
1 c. chopped celery   *bell pepper*
4 hard-boiled eggs,   *8 slices crisp-fried*
  sliced   *bacon, crumbled*
1   10-oz. package   *2 c. mayonnaise*
  frozen green peas,   *2 tbsp. sugar*
  thawed   *4 oz. Cheddar cheese,*
1 onion, chopped   *shredded*

Layer lettuce, celery, eggs, peas, onion, green pepper and bacon in large salad bowl. Mix mayonnaise with sugar and enough water to make creamy mixture. Spread over layers sealing to edge. Top with cheese. Chill, covered, for 8 to 12 hours before serving. Garnish with additional bacon and parsley. Yield: 12 servings.

STUFFED HEAD LETTUCE

8 oz. cream cheese,   *2 tbsp. chopped carrot*
  softened   *1 tbsp. chopped green*
1 tsp. onion juice   *bell pepper*
Salt and pepper to taste *2 tbsp. chopped tomato*
2 tbsp. Roquefort   *1 head lettuce*
  cheese

Blend cream cheese, onion juice, salt and pepper in bowl. Mix in Roquefort cheese and chopped vegetables. Cut lettuce in half through core; remove core. Hollow out halves, leaving 1-inch shell. Stuff lettuce with cheese mixture. Place lettuce halves together. Wrap in waxed paper; chill in refrigerator. Cut into wedges. Yield: 8 servings.

MANDARIN SALAD WITH ALMONDS

¹/₂ tsp. salt   *2 tbsp. sugar*
Dash of pepper   *1 head romaine*
2 tbsp. sugar   *1 c. chopped celery*
2 tbsp. vinegar   *4 green onions, sliced*
¹/₄ c. corn oil   *2   8-oz. cans mandarin*
Dash of Tabasco sauce   *oranges, drained*
¹/₂ c. slivered almonds

Combine first 6 ingredients in bowl; mix well and set aside. Cook almonds and sugar in skillet over medium heat until sugar melts and turns light brown. Cool. Combine lettuce, celery, onions and oranges in salad bowl. Add dressing and almonds; toss to mix. Serve immediately. Yield: 6 servings.

Lime

CREAMY KEY LIME FRAPPÉ
Photograph for this recipe is on page 105.

1 pt. lime and cream   *¹/₃ c. milk*
  sorbet and cream   *Lime slices*
2 to 3 tbsp. lime juice

Combine sorbet, lime juice and milk in blender container; blend until smooth. Pour into 4 parfait glasses. Garnish with lime slices. Yield: 4 servings.

SORBET MARGARITA
Photograph for this recipe is on page 105.

1 pt. lime and cream   *1 tbsp. Triple Sec (opt.)*
  sorbet and cream   *2 tbsp. lime juice*
3 tbsp. Tequila (opt.)   *Lime slices*

Combine sorbet, Tequila, Triple Sec and lime juice in blender container; blend until smooth. Rub rims of 4 glasses with juice from lime slices. Pour sorbet mixture into glasses. Garnish with lime slices. Yield: 4 servings.

LIME HERBED SALAD DRESSING

1 c. corn oil   *1 tsp. mixed dried*
¹/₃ c. lime juice   *tarragon, chives*
1 tbsp. sugar   *and parsley*
¹/₂ tsp. paprika   *1 clove of garlic,*
¹/₄ tsp. dry mustard   *crushed*
1 tsp. salt

Combine all ingredients in 1-pint jar; shake well. Chill in refrigerator. Discard garlic. Shake well. Serve on assorted salad greens. Yield: 1¹/₃ cups.

SUMMER KEY LIME CAKE

1¹/₃ c. sugar
2 c. all-purpose flour
²/₃ tsp. salt
1 tsp. baking powder
¹/₂ tsp. soda
1 3-oz. package
*   lime gelatin*
5 eggs
1¹/₃ c. oil

³/₄ c. orange juice
¹/₂ tsp. vanilla extract
1 tsp. lemon extract
¹/₃ c. Key lime juice
¹/₃ c. confectioners'
*   sugar*
Whipped cream
Lime slices

Combine sugar, flour, salt, baking powder, soda and lime gelatin in mixer bowl. Add eggs, oil, orange juice, vanilla and lemon extract. Beat until well blended. Pour into greased 9x13-inch cake pan. Bake at 350 degrees for 25 to 30 minutes or until cake tests done. Cool in pan for 15 minutes. Prick cake all over with fork. Drizzle with mixture of lime juice and confectioners' sugar; cover. Chill in refrigerator until serving time. Cut into squares. Top with whipped cream. Garnish with lime slices. Yield: 12 servings.

LIME SHERBET SALAD

8 3-oz. packages
*   lime gelatin*
8 c. boiling water
4 c. cold water
1 gal. lime sherbet
8 c. crushed pineapple,
*   drained*

3 16-oz. packages
*   miniature*
*   marshmallows*
2 c. finely chopped
*   pecans*

Dissolve gelatin in boiling water in large container. Add cold water and sherbet; stir until sherbet is almost melted. Add drained pineapple, marshmallows and chopped pecans. Pour into 12x18-inch pan. Chill until firm. Cut into serving portions. Yield: 50 servings.

KEY LIME PIE

¹/₂ c. Key lime juice
1 14-oz. can
*   sweetened condensed*
*   milk*
4 egg yolks

1 baked 9-inch pie
*   shell*
4 egg whites
³/₄ c. sugar

Combine lime juice, condensed milk and egg yolks in bowl; beat until mixed. Pour into 9-inch pie shell. Chill. Beat egg whites in mixer bowl at high speed until soft peaks form. Add sugar gradually, beating until stiff peaks form. Spread on pie, sealing to edge. Bake at 450 degrees until browned. Refrigerate until well chilled before serving. Yield: 6 servings.

Lobster

LOBSTER CASSEROLE

2 10-oz. cans cream
*   of mushroom soup*
1 c. mayonnaise
¹/₄ c. dry Sherry
¹/₂ c. milk
1¹/₂ lbs. lobster chunks
3 c. seasoned
*   croutons*

2 5-oz. cans sliced
*   water chestnuts,*
*   drained*
¹/₂ c. minced green
*   onions*
1 c. shredded Cheddar
*   cheese*

Mix mushroom soup, mayonnaise and Sherry in bowl. Stir in milk. Combine with remaining ingredients except cheese. Spoon into 3-quart baking dish; top with cheese. Bake at 350 degrees for 1 hour. Yield: 4 servings.

CURRIED LOBSTER

¹/₄ c. melted butter
¹/₄ c. all-purpose flour
Dash of paprika
¹/₂ tsp. curry powder

1¹/₂ c. milk
3 tbsp. catsup
¹/₄ c. cooking Sherry
1¹/₂ c. cooked lobster

Blend butter, flour, paprika and curry powder in saucepan. Add milk gradually. Cook until thickened, stirring constantly. Add catsup, Sherry and lobster. Cook until heated through. Serve over rice. Yield: 4 servings.

LOBSTER FONDUE

2 lb. lobster tails
1 recipe white sauce
3 tbsp. white wine
Dash of Worcestershire
*   sauce*

2 dashes of soy sauce
8 oz. Cheddar cheese,
*   shredded*
Herb-flavored cracker
*   crumbs*

Steam lobster tails in water in saucepan until shells turn red. Remove meat from the shells; cut into 1-inch cubes. Combine white sauce, wine, Worcestershire sauce and soy sauce in saucepan. Add cheese. Cook until cheese melts. Place lobster in 2-quart baking dish; pour sauce over top. Sprinkle with cracker crumbs. Bake at 350 degrees for 20 to 30 minutes or until brown. Yield: 6 servings.

⇨

Recipes for this photograph are on pages 86, 103 and 142.

Menu
Menu
Menu
Menu
Menu
Menu
Menu
Menu
Menu
Menu
Menu
Menu
Menu
Menu
Menu
Menu
Menu
Menu
Menu

Lazy Summer Ice Cream Party

Sorbet and Cream Fruit Salad

page 86

Summer Fruit Cup

page 86

Raspberry Floating Island

page 142

Patriotic Parfait

page 86

Creamy Key Lime Frappé

page 103

Sorbet Margarita

page 103

*Summer's special occasions — from casual barbecues
to formal gatherings — call for light, refreshing and
festive foods. A cool and easy menu is the perfect
complement for all your summer activities.*

LOBSTER NEWBURG

1 lb. lobster	*Salt and pepper to taste*
1/2 c. butter	*2 c. half and half*
1/4 c. all-purpose flour	*Sherry to taste*

Sauté lobster in butter in saucepan. Sprinkle flour over lobster. Cook until lobster is red, stirring constantly. Add salt, pepper and half and half. Cook until thickened, stirring constantly. Add Sherry to taste. Yield: 4 servings.

LOBSTER QUICHE

1 unbaked deep-dish pie shell	*1/2 tsp. salt*
8 oz. Swiss cheese, cut into 1/4-inch slices	*Pinch of pepper* *Pinch of cayenne pepper*
1 1/2 c. lobster	*1 tbsp. all-purpose flour*
1 1/2 c. light cream	
4 eggs, beaten	*2 tbsp. melted butter*
1/4 tsp. nutmeg	*2 tbsp. dry Sherry*

Line pie shell with cheese slices. Layer lobster over cheese. Combine cream, eggs, seasonings and flour in bowl; mix well. Add butter and Sherry. Pour into pie shell. Bake at 375 degrees for 40 minutes or until top is brown and center is set. Let stand for 20 minutes before serving. Yield: 6 servings.

Macadamia

KONA KRUNCH PIE

3/4 c. chopped macadamia nuts	*3 oz. cream cheese, softened*
1/2 11-oz. package pie crust mix	*1/4 c. sugar*
1/4 c. packed light brown sugar	*2 tbsp. whipping cream* *1/4 c. coffee-flavored liqueur*
1 tbsp. water	*1 1/2 c. plus 3 tbsp. whipping cream*
1 tsp. vanilla extract	
4 oz. sweet baking chocolate	*1/4 c. sifted confectioners' sugar*
3 tbsp. whipping cream	

Rub macadamia nuts in tea towel to remove excess salt; place on baking sheet. Bake at 350 degrees for 8 minutes, stirring occasionally. Cool. Increase oven temperature to 375 degrees. Combine nuts, pie crust mix, brown sugar and water in bowl; mix with fork. Press into greased 9-inch pie plate. Bake for 15 minutes. Cool. Heat vanilla, chocolate and 3 tablespoons cream in heavy saucepan over low heat until chocolate is melted. Beat cream cheese in mixer bowl. Add sugar, 2 tablespoons cream and chocolate mixture; mix well. Add liqueur gradually; set aside. Whip remaining cream in mixer bowl at high speed until soft peaks form. Add confectioners' sugar. Fold in chocolate mixture gently. Spoon into pie shell. Chill until firm. Yield: 6 servings.

MACADAMIA NUT-CHOCOLATE CHIP COOKIES

1/2 c. sugar	*2 c. unbleached flour*
1 c. packed light brown sugar	*1 tsp. soda* *1/2 tsp. salt*
1 c. margarine, softened	*12 oz. semisweet chocolate chips*
1 egg	*3/4 c. coarsely chopped macadamia nuts*
2 tsp. vanilla extract	

Cream sugar, brown sugar and margarine in mixer bowl until light and fluffy. Add egg and vanilla. Sift in flour, soda and salt; mix well. Stir in chocolate chips and macadamia nuts. Shape into balls. Place several inches apart on cookie sheet. Bake on top oven rack at 375 degrees for 12 minutes. Cool on cookie sheet. Yield: 3 dozen.

Macadamia Nut-Chocolate Chip Cookies...are a new version of an old favorite.

Macaroni

CROCK•POT MACARONI AND CHEESE

2 tbsp. shortening
1 8-oz. package macaroni
1 12-oz. can evaporated milk
1½ c. milk
2 eggs
2 c. shredded sharp Cheddar cheese

1 c. shredded medium Cheddar cheese
¼ c. melted margarine
1 tsp. salt
Pepper to taste
4 oz. Cheddar cheese, sliced
⅛ tsp. paprika

Grease Crock•Pot with 2 tablespoons shortening. Cook macaroni according to package directions; drain. Combine with evaporated milk, milk, eggs, shredded cheeses, margarine, salt and pepper in large bowl; mix well. Spoon into greased Crock•Pot. Top with cheese slices. Sprinkle with paprika. Cook, covered, on Low for 3 to 4 hours. Yield: 10 servings.

MACARONI AND CHEESE CASSEROLE

1 8-oz. package elbow macaroni
2 c. small curd cottage cheese
1 c. sour cream
1 egg, slightly beaten

¾ tsp. salt
Pepper to taste
2 c. shredded sharp American cheese
Paprika to taste

Cook macaroni according to package directions; drain. Combine Cottage cheese, sour cream, egg, salt and pepper in bowl; mix well. Add shredded cheese and macaroni; mix well. Spoon into greased baking dish. Sprinkle with paprika to taste. Bake at 350 degrees for 45 minutes. Yield: 4 servings.

MACARONI SALAD

1 8-oz. package macaroni
½ c. chopped green onions
½ c. chopped green bell pepper
1 2-oz. jar dried beef, chopped

½ c. chopped celery
1 pkg. Knorr vegetable soup mix
1 c. shredded mozzarella cheese
1½ c. mayonnaise
Pepper to taste

Cook macaroni according to package directions. Rinse with cold water; drain. Combine green onions, green pepper, dried beef, celery, soup mix and cheese in bowl. Add macaroni. Stir in mayonnaise and pepper. Chill until serving time. Yield: 8 servings.

SPRING MACARONI SALAD

8 oz. macaroni shells
2 tomatoes, chopped
1 avocado, sliced

1 c. sliced black olives
½. sliced green onions
⅔ c. Italian dressing

Cook macaroni according to package directions. Rinse with cold water; drain. Combine with tomatoes, avocado, olives, green onions and dressing in serving bowl; mix well. Chill until serving time. Yield: 6 servings.

ITALIAN MACARONI SALAD

1 lb. small shell macaroni
4 oz. provolone cheese, chopped
4 oz. salami, chopped
4 oz. pepperoni, chopped
2 small onions, chopped
1 sm. can pitted black olives, chopped

1 7-oz. jar green olives, chopped
½ c. chopped celery
½ c. chopped green bell pepper
½ c. chopped red bell pepper
Italian Salad Dressing
4 tomatoes, chopped
Fresh parsley to taste

Cook macaroni according to package directions. Rinse and drain. Combine with cheese, salami, pepperoni, onions, olives, celery, and peppers in serving bowl. Add Italian Salad Dressing to salad; mix well. Chill for 24 hours. Add tomatoes and parsley at serving time. Yield: 15 servings.

Italian Salad Dressing

¾ c. olive oil
½ c. white vinegar
3 tbsp. sugar

1 tbsp. oregano
1 tbsp. salt
1 tsp. pepper

Combine olive oil, vinegar, sugar, oregano, salt and pepper in small bowl; mix well.

SUMMER PASTA DELI SALAD

3 c. three-colored twist macaroni
1 c. broccoli flowerets
1 to 2 c. cauliflowerets
1 c. sliced fresh mushrooms
½ c. chopped green bell pepper

¼ c. chopped onion
½ c. sliced black olives
½ c. sliced pepperoni
½ c. shredded mozzarella cheese
1 16-oz. bottle of Italian salad dressing

Cook macaroni according to package directions. Rinse and drain. Combine with broccoli, cauliflower, mushrooms, green pepper, onion, olives, pepperoni, cheese and salad dressing in bowl; mix well. Chill for 6 hours or longer. Yield: 10 servings.

Maple

DOUBLE MAPLE MUFFINS

1¹/₂ c. all-purpose flour	¹/₂ c. milk
¹/₂ c. sugar	¹/₂ c. maple syrup
1 tbsp. baking powder	1 tbsp. margarine,
¹/₂ tsp. salt	softened
¹/₄ c. shortening	¹/₄ c. sifted
³/₄ c. oats	confectioners' sugar
1 egg, slightly beaten	1 tbsp. maple syrup

Combine flour, sugar, baking powder and salt in bowl. Cut in shortening until crumbly. Mix in oats. Combine egg, milk and ¹/₂ cup syrup in small bowl. Add to oats mixture; mix just until moistened. Batter will be lumpy. Fill greased or paper-lined muffin cups ²/₃ full. Bake at 400 degrees for 18 to 20 minutes or until muffins test done. Drizzle with mixture of margarine, confectioners' sugar and 1 tablespoon syrup. Yield: 1 dozen.

MAPLE SYRUP SOUFFLÉ

1 c. maple syrup	2 tsp. baking powder
4 egg whites	¹/₂ c. maple syrup
¹/₂ c. confectioners'	3 tbsp. Cognac
sugar	1 tbsp. margarine

Simmer 1 cup maple syrup in saucepan until reduced to ³/₄ cup. Remove from heat; cool slightly. Beat egg whites in mixer bowl until very stiff peaks form. Beat in confectioners' sugar and baking powder. Add reduced syrup gradually, beating constantly. Combine ¹/₂ cup maple syrup and Cognac in soufflé dish. Dot with margarine. Spoon in egg white mixture. Place in shallow pan with 2 inches water. Bake at 300 degrees for 1 hour. Yield: 6 servings.

Marinade

MEAT MARINADE FOR BARBECUE

2 cloves of garlic,	1 tsp. salt
chopped	¹/₄ tsp. pepper
¹/₂ medium onion,	¹/₂ c. white vinegar
chopped	¹/₄ c. soy sauce

Combine all ingredients in bowl; mix well. Place meat to be marinated in glass dish. Pour marinade over meat. Marinate for several hours, turning meat occasionally. Broil or grill meat to desired degree of doneness. Yield: 1 cup.

MARINADE FOR CHICKEN

¹/₂ c. Sherry	Crushed garlic to taste
¹/₄ c. oil	Oregano, rosemary or
¹/₄ tsp. dry mustard	chives to taste
Pepper to taste	

Combine all ingredients in bowl; mix well. Use to marinate chicken halves or quarters for 30 minutes. Drain, reserving marinade. Grill chicken over hot coals for 20 minutes on each side, basting frequently with reserved marinade. Yield: ³/₄ cup.

MARINADE FOR VEGETABLES

¹/₂ c. vinegar	³/₄ tsp. celery salt
¹/₂ c. water	1 clove of garlic,
¹/₂ c. sugar	minced
12 peppercorns	¹/₈ tsp. salt
4 bay leaves	

Combine all ingredients in saucepan. Bring to a simmer, stirring constantly; do not boil. Cool. Pour over vegetables such as quartered tomatoes, sliced onions or strips of green and red pepper. Let stand for 2 hours before serving. Yield: 1 cup.

Marmalade

WINTER PEAR MARMALADE

3 c. chopped pears	2 3-oz. packages
3 c. sugar	strawberry gelatin

Purée pears in blender. Add sugar and gelatin. Pour into saucepan. Bring to a boil, stirring constantly. Cook for 5 minutes. Pour into sterilized jars; seal with paraffin. Store in refrigerator. Yield: 4 cups.

ZUCCHINI MARMALADE

6 c. seeded, peeled,	¹/₂ c. lemon juice
grated zucchini	1 env. unflavored
1 c. water	gelatin
6 c. sugar	2 tbsp. cold water
1 16-oz. can crushed	2 3-oz. packages
pineapple	peach gelatin

Cook zucchini in 1 cup water in saucepan until clear; drain. Stir in sugar, pineapple and lemon juice. Soften unflavored gelatin in 2 tablespoons water. Stir into zucchini. Bring to a boil over medium heat. Cook for 20 minutes, stirring occasionally. Remove from heat. Stir in peach gelatin until dissolved. Pour into sterilized jars, leaving ¹/₂-inch head space. Seal with 2-piece lids. Yield: Six ¹/₂-pint jars.

Meringue

FORGOTTEN MERINGUES

2 egg whites	*1 c. chopped pecans*
1/8 tsp. salt	*1 c. chocolate chips*
2/3 c. sugar	

Beat egg whites and salt in mixer bowl until stiff peaks form. Add sugar gradually, beating constantly until very stiff. Fold in pecans and chocolate chips. Drop on ungreased foil-lined baking sheets. Place in 350-degree oven. Turn off oven. Let stand in closed oven overnight. Yield: 2 dozen.

MERINGUE CRUNCH SUNDAE

4 egg whites, at room	*4 c. fresh raspberries*
temperature	*1 c. sugar*
1/4 tsp. cream of tartar	*3 to 4 tbsp. Chambord*
1/4 tsp. vanilla extract	*1 qt. vanilla ice cream*
1 c. sugar	*Chopped pistachio nuts*
1/2 c. finely chopped	
blanched almonds	

Beat egg whites in mixer bowl until soft peaks form. Beat in cream of tartar, vanilla and 1 tablespoon sugar. Add remaining 1 cup sugar gradually, beating until stiff peaks form. Fold in almonds. Spread meringue evenly into two 8-inch circles on greased parchment-lined baking sheets. Bake at 250 degrees for 1 hour. Turn off oven. Let stand in closed oven for 1 hour or until dry. Cool completely. Crush coarsely. Mix raspberries, 1 cup sugar and Chambord in bowl. Chill in refrigerator. Roll ice cream scoops in meringue crumbs. Place in dessert dishes. Top with raspberry sauce and pistachio nuts. Garnish with whipped cream and additional raspberries. Yield: 6 serving.

PAVLOVA WITH STRAWBERRIES

4 egg whites	*1 tsp. vinegar*
3 tbsp. cold water	*1 20-oz. package*
1 c. sugar	*frozen strawberries,*
1 tsp. cornstarch	*thawed*
1 tsp. vanilla extract	

Beat egg whites in mixer bowl until stiff peaks form. Add cold water; beat until very stiff. Add 1 cup sugar, beating constantly. Fold in cornstarch, vanilla and vinegar. Spread in 2-inch thick circle on waxed paper-lined baking sheet. Bake at 320 degrees for 10 minutes. Turn off oven. Let stand in closed oven until oven is cold. Mash strawberries. Cut pavlova into wedges. Top with mashed strawberries. Garnish with whipped cream. Top with whole strawberry. Yield: 10 servings.

MERINGUE TORTE

8 egg whites	*1 pt. whipping cream*
1 c. sugar	*1 tbsp. confectioners'*
1 tbsp. vinegar	*sugar*
Salt to taste	*1/2 tsp. vanilla extract*
1 tsp. vanilla extract	
12 dry macaroon	
cookies	

Beat egg whites in mixer bowl until stiff peaks form. Beat in sugar gradually. Beat in vinegar, salt and 1 teaspoon vanilla. Pour into 2 greased and waxed paper-lined 8-inch cake pans. Bake at 250 degrees for 1 hour. Chill in pans overnight. Crush macaroon cookies into crumbs. Whip cream in bowl, adding confectioners' sugar and 1/2 teaspoon vanilla. Fold in cookie crumbs. Spread whipped cream mixture between layers and over top and side of torte. Chill for 2 hours. Yield: 8 servings.

Mincemeat

HOMEMADE MINCEMEAT

2 c. apple cider	*1 c. currants*
1 c. packed light brown	*8 oz. candied citron*
sugar	*8 oz. candied lemon*
1 1/2 lb. lean boneless	*rind*
beef chuck, ground	*8 oz. candied orange*
1 orange	*rind*
1 lemon	*2 tsp. cinnamon*
8 c. chopped, peeled	*1 tsp. allspice*
tart apples	*1 tsp. cloves*
2 c. raisins	*1 c. Brandy*

Combine apple cider and brown sugar in large stockpot. Bring to a boil over medium heat; stir occasionally. Stir in ground chuck. Cut unpeeled orange and lemon into quarters; discard seed. Put through food grinder until finely chopped. Add to stockpot with apples, raisins, currants and candied fruit; mix well. Bring to a boil over medium heat; cover. Cook over low heat for 1 hour, stirring frequently. Mix in spices and Brandy. Simmer, uncovered, until of desired consistency, stirring frequently. Ladle into hot sterilized 1-pint jars, leaving 1/2 inch headspace. Seal with 2-piece lids. Store in refrigerator for 3 days or longer to improve flavor. Yield: Six 1-pint jars.

MINCEMEAT NUT LOAVES

3 c. all-purpose flour	1 tsp. nutmeg
2 c. sugar	2 c. Homemade
2 tsp. soda	Mincemeat
1 tsp. salt	2/3 c. corn oil
1 tsp. baking powder	1/2 c. apple juice
1 tsp. cloves	3 eggs, beaten
1 tsp. cinnamon	2 c. chopped walnuts

Combine flour, sugar, soda, salt, baking powder and spices in large bowl; mix lightly. Add Homemade Mincemeat, oil, apple juice, eggs and walnuts; stir just until mixed. Pour into 2 greased 5x9-inch loaf pans. Bake at 375 degrees for 10 minutes. Remove to wire rack to cool completely. Wrap loaves individually. Let stand at room temperature for 24 hours or longer before slicing. Yield: 2 loaves.

MINCEMEAT AND CREAM CAKE

4 c. whipping cream, chilled	2 c. Homemade Mincemeat
1/4 c. sugar	1 tsp. Brandy extract

Beat whipping cream in chilled bowl until slightly thickened. Add sugar gradually, beating constantly until soft peaks form. Fold in Homemade Mincemeat and Brandy extract. Spoon into chilled 9-inch springform pan; smooth top. Cover with foil. Freeze for 4 hours or longer. Place on serving plate. Loosen edge with knife; remove side of pan. Store in freezer. Yield: 12 servings.

CREAMY MINCEMEAT CHEESECAKE

1/4 c. melted margarine	1 env. unflavored gelatin
1 c. graham cracker crumbs	1/4 c. lemon juice
1/4 c. sugar	1 1/3 c. mincemeat
16 oz. cream cheese, softened	1/2 c. chopped pecans
1 14-oz. can sweetened condensed milk	1 tbsp. grated lemon rind
	1 c. whipping cream, whipped

Mix margarine, crumbs and sugar in bowl. Press into 9-inch springform pan. Chill. Beat cream cheese in large mixer bowl until fluffy. Add condensed milk; beat until smooth. Soften gelatin in lemon juice in small saucepan. Heat until dissolved, stirring constantly. Add to creamed mixture with mincemeat, pecans and lemon rind; mix well. Fold in whipped cream. Pour into prepared pan. Chill for 3 hours or until set. Garnish with sour cream, additional nuts and candied cherries. Yield: 12 servings.

MINCEMEAT PIES WITH HARD SAUCE

8 c. mincemeat	1 1/2 c. sifted confectioners' sugar
2 baked 9-in. deep-dish pie shells	2 tbsp. Drambuie
1/2 c. margarine, softened	

Spoon mincemeat into pie shells. Cream margarine in mixer bowl until fluffy. Add confectioners' sugar and Drambuie gradually, beating until light and fluffy. Pipe confectioners' sugar mixture through decorating tube into circles on tops of pies. Yield: 2 pies.

MINCEMEAT TARTS

1 c. all-purpose flour	3 tbsp. cold water
1/2 tsp. salt	4 c. Homemade Mincemeat
1/3 c. shortening	

Mix flour and salt in bowl. Cut in shortening until crumbly. Sprinkle with water 1 tablespoon at a time; mix lightly with fork until mixture clings together. Roll 1/8 inch thick on lightly floured surface; cut into 5-inch rounds. Fit into muffin cups; flute edges. Prick with fork. Bake at 475 degrees for 8 minutes or until golden brown. Cool. Spoon Homemade Mincemeat into tart shells. Yield: 8 tarts.

Mint

CRÈME DE MENTHE BUNDT CAKE

1 2-layer pkg. white cake mix	1/2 c. vegetable oil
4 eggs	1/4 c. water
1 3-oz. package vanilla instant pudding mix	1/4 c. green Crème de Menthe
	1/4 tsp. vanilla extract
1/2 c. fresh orange juice	1 5-oz. can chocolate syrup

Combine cake mix, eggs, pudding mix, orange juice, oil, water, Crème de Menthe and vanilla in mixer bowl; mix well. Pour 2/3 of the batter into greased and floured bundt pan. Stir chocolate syrup into remaining batter. Pour into pan; do not stir. Bake at 350 degrees for 35 minutes or until toothpick inserted in center comes out clean. Cool in pan for 25 minutes. Invert onto cake plate. Yield: 16 servings.

FRANGO MINTS

*1 c. milk chocolate
chips
1 c. semisweet
chocolate chips
1/2 c. butter, softened
2 eggs*

*1 c. plus 2 tbsp.
confectioners' sugar
1 tsp. vanilla extract
1/2 tsp. peppermint
extract*

Melt chocolate chips in double boiler; mix well. Combine remaining ingredients in mixer bowl; beat until smooth. Add chocolate; mix well. Drop by teaspoonfuls into bonbon cups or onto waxed paper. Let stand until firm. Store in freezer. Yield: 1 1/4 pounds.

CHOCOLATE MINT PARFAIT BARS

*1 2-layer pkg.
chocolate mint
cake mix
1 egg
1/3 c. margarine,
softened
1 env. unflavored
gelatin
1/4 c. cold water
1/2 c. shortening*

*1/2 c. margarine,
softened
1/4 tsp. peppermint
extract
2 or 3 drops of green
food coloring
1 16-oz. package
confectioners' sugar
1 1/2 c. chocolate chips
3 tbsp. margarine*

Mix cake mix, egg and 1/3 cup margarine in mixer bowl until crumbly. Press into greased 10x15-inch baking pan. Bake at 350 degrees for 10 minutes. Cool. Soften gelatin in water in saucepan. Heat until dissolved. Add shortening, 1/2 cup margarine, peppermint, food coloring and half the confectioners' sugar. Beat for 1 minute. Beat in remaining confectioners' sugar. Spread over cooled layer. Melt chocolate chips and 3 tablespoons margarine in saucepan. Add enough hot water to make of spreading consistency. Spread over top. Chill until firm. Cut into bars. Yield: 3 dozen.

MINTED FRESH FRUIT COMPOTE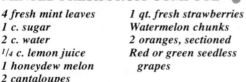

*4 fresh mint leaves
1 c. sugar
2 c. water
1/4 c. lemon juice
1 honeydew melon
2 cantaloupes*

*1 qt. fresh strawberries
Watermelon chunks
2 oranges, sectioned
Red or green seedless
grapes*

Combine mint leaves, sugar and water in saucepan. Bring to a boil. Boil rapidly for 5 minutes. Remove from heat; cool. Add lemon juice. Remove mint leaves. Cut melons into balls; slice strawberries. Combine fruit in bowl. Pour mint syrup over fruit. Let stand for 1 hour or longer, stirring occasionally. Garnish with fresh mint leaves. Yield: 10 servings.

FRENCH MINT PIE

*1/2 c. margarine,
softened
1 c. confectioners'
sugar
2 eggs
1 tsp. peppermint
extract*

*1 tsp. vanilla extract
2 1-oz. squares
unsweetened baking
chocolate
1 baked 8-in. pie shell
1 c. whipping cream,
whipped*

Cream margarine and confectioners' sugar in mixer bowl until light and fluffy. Blend in eggs and flavorings. Melt chocolate in double boiler over hot water. Add to creamed mixture; beat until fluffy. Pour into pie shell. Top with whipped cream. Chill overnight. Yield: 6 servings.

MINT ICE CREAM PIES

*1 2-layer pkg. devil's
food cake mix
3/4 c. water
1/4 c. oil*

*6 c. mint chocolate
chip ice cream,
softened
3/4 c. fudge frosting*

Combine cake mix, water and oil in large mixer bowl; beat at low speed until moistened. Beat at high speed for 2 minutes. Spread batter in 2 greased 9-inch pie plates. Bake at 350 degrees for 25 to 30 minutes. Cool completely. Stir ice cream until smooth. Spread in pie shells. Heat frosting in saucepan until softened. Spread on top of ice cream. Freeze until firm. Yield: 2 pies.

Mocha

MOCHA CAKE

*6 eggs, at room
temperature
2/3 c. sugar
1 1/2 c. all-purpose flour
1 tsp. vanilla extract*

*3 tbsp. melted
margarine
1 c. very strong coffee
1/4 c. sugar
Mocha Frosting*

Beat eggs with 2/3 cup sugar in mixer bowl for 10 minutes or until thick and lemon-colored. Fold in flour. Fold in vanilla and margarine. Pour into 2 greased and floured cake pans lined with waxed paper. Bake at 350 degrees for 30 minutes. Cool in pans for 10 minutes. Invert onto wire racks to cool completely. Split each layer into halves horizontally. Brush layers with mixture of coffee and 1/4 cup sugar. Spread Mocha Frosting between layers and over top and side of cake. Store in refrigerator. Yield: 16 servings.

Mocha Frosting

3/4 c. strong coffee	*8 egg yolks*
1/2 c. sugar	*1 c. unsalted butter*

Combine coffee and sugar in large mixer bowl, stirring to dissolve sugar. Add egg yolks. Beat for 5 minutes or until very pale and fluffy. Add butter 1 slice at a time, beating constantly at medium speed until mixture is of consistency of thick whipped cream. Do not attempt this frosting on very warm day.

MOCHA DREAM CAKE

1 baked angel food cake	*2 tbsp. sugar*
2 4-oz. packages chocolate fudge instant pudding mix	*1 c. semisweet chocolate chips*
	1/4 c. confectioners' sugar
3 c. milk	*1 tbsp. water*
2 tbsp. instant coffee powder	*Chopped pecans*

Slice 3/4-inch layer from top of cake; set aside. Scoop out center of cake, leaving 1/2 to 3/4-inch shell. Tear scooped-out cake into small pieces; set aside. Combine pudding mix and milk according to package directions, adding coffee powder and sugar. Mix in cake pieces. Spoon pudding into cake shell; replace top layer. Melt chocolate chips in double boiler. Blend in confectioners' sugar and water. Drizzle over top of cake. Chill until serving time. Garnish servings with pecans.
Yield: 12 servings.

MYSTERY MOCHA CAKE

3/4 c. sugar	*1 tsp. vanilla extract*
1 c. all-purpose flour	*1/2 c. packed light brown sugar*
2 tsp. baking powder	
1/8 tsp. salt	*1/4 c. sugar*
1 1-oz. square unsweetened baking chocolate	*1/4 c. unsweetened baking cocoa*
	1 c. cold double-strength coffee
2 tbsp. margarine	
1/2 c. milk	

Sift 3/4 cup sugar, flour, baking powder and salt into large bowl. Melt baking chocolate and margarine in double boiler over hot water. Add to flour mixture; mix well. Add milk and vanilla; mix well. Pour into greased 8x8-inch cake pan. Mix brown sugar, 1/4 cup sugar and baking cocoa in small bowl. Sprinkle mixture over batter. Pour cold coffee over top. Bake at 350 degrees for 35 to 40 minutes or until cake tests done. Serve warm.
Yield: 6 servings.

MOCHA ALMOND CHEESECAKE

1 c. sifted all-purpose flour	*1 1/2 c. sugar*
	1/4 c. all-purpose flour
1/4 c. sugar	*1/2 tsp. salt*
Grated rind of 1 lemon	*6 eggs*
1 egg yolk	*2 tbsp. instant coffee powder*
1/2 c. cold butter	
40 oz. cream cheese, softened	*1/3 c. almond liqueur*

Mix 1 cup flour, 1/4 cup sugar and lemon rind in bowl. Add egg yolk and butter; mix with fingers to form dough. Shape into ball; wrap in plastic wrap. Chill for 1 hour. Press over bottom and side of ungreased 9-inch springform pan. Beat cream cheese in large mixer bowl until light. Beat in 1 1/2 cups sugar, 1/4 cup flour and salt gradually. Add eggs 1 at a time, mixing well after each addition. Dissolve coffee powder in liqueur. Add to batter; mix well. Pour into prepared pan. Bake at 250 degrees for 1 1/2 hours or until center is set. Cool. Chill in refrigerator. Place on serving plate; remove side of pan. Yield: 12 servings.

MOCHA BRAN BROWNIES

6 oz. semisweet chocolate chips	*3/4 c. all-purpose flour*
	1/4 tsp. soda
1/2 c. margarine	*2 tbsp. instant coffee powder*
1/2 c. sugar	
2 eggs, beaten	*1/2 tsp. salt*
1 tsp. vanilla extract	*1/2 c. chopped almonds*
1/2 c. All-Bran cereal	*Special Mocha Frosting*
1/3 c. water	

Melt chocolate chips and margarine in double boiler over hot water. Stir in sugar; remove from heat. Blend in eggs and vanilla. Mix cereal and water in small bowl. Let stand for several minutes. Add to chocolate mixture; mix well. Add mixture of flour, soda, coffee powder and salt; mix well. Stir in almonds. Pour into greased 8x8-inch baking pan. Bake at 350 degrees for 30 minutes or just until set. Cool. Frost with Special Mocha Frosting. Cut into squares. Yield: 16 servings.

Special Mocha Frosting

2 1/2 tbsp. margarine	*1/2 tsp. vanilla extract*
2 tsp. unsweetened baking cocoa	*1 1/2 c. (about) confectioners' sugar*
1 tbsp. strong coffee	

Combine margarine, cocoa, coffee and vanilla in bowl; mix well. Add enough confectioners' sugar gradually to make of desired consistency.

MOCHA CHIFFON TORTE

2 tbsp. unflavored
  gelatin
1 c. water
1/2 c. sugar
1/4 c. instant coffee
  granules
2 c. water

1 tbsp. Angostura
  aromatic bitters
16 oz. whipped topping
6 oz. semisweet
  chocolate chips
1/2 c. coarsely chopped
  pecans

Soak gelatin in 1 cup water. Combine with sugar and coffee granules in saucepan. Cook over low heat until gelatin and sugar are dissolved. Add remaining 2 cups water and bitters. Chill until slightly thickened. Fold in half the whipped topping. Pour mixture into 9-inch springform pan. Chill until firm. Melt chocolate chips in double boiler over warm water. Place a piece of foil in bottom of 9-inch layer pan. Spread melted chocolate evenly over foil. Chill just until firm. Cut chocolate circle carefully into 8 wedges using a knife dipped into boiling water. Chill wedges. Place torte on serving platter; remove side. Spread remaining whipped topping over top. Push wedges of chocolate diagonally into topping. Sprinkle with pecans. Chill until serving time. Yield: 12 servings.

Mocha Chiffon Torte...a light and festive treat for any occasion.

MOCHA ICE CREAM DESSERT

24 Oreo cookies,
  crushed
1/3 c. melted margarine
1/2 gal. coffee ice
  cream, softened
3 oz. unsweetened
  baking chocolate
2 tbsp. margarine
1 c. sugar

1/8 tsp. salt
2 6-oz. cans
  evaporated milk
1/2 tsp. vanilla extract
1 1/2 c. whipping cream
2 tbsp. confectioners'
  sugar
1 1/2 oz. coffee liqueur
3/4 c. chopped pecans

Mix cookie crumbs and 1/3 cup margarine in bowl. Press into 9x13-inch dish. Chill until firm. Spread ice cream evenly over crumb layer. Freeze until firm. Melt chocolate with 2 tablespoons margarine

in double boiler. Add sugar, salt and evaporated milk. Cook until thickened, stirring constantly. Remove from heat. Stir in vanilla. Chill in refrigerator. Spread over ice cream. Freeze until firm. Whip cream with confectioners' sugar in mixer bowl until soft peaks form. Fold in liqueur. Spread over chocolate layer. Top with pecans. Freeze until serving time. Yield: 16 servings.

Molasses

MOLASSES TAFFY

1 c. molasses
1 c. sugar

1 tsp. vinegar
1 tbsp. butter

Combine all ingredients in saucepan. Cook over low heat to 270 degrees on candy thermometer, stirring constantly. Pour onto greased platter. Cool, lifting edges toward center. Shape into ball. Pull until light yellow in color. Stretch into long rope; cut into 1-inch pieces. Wrap each piece in waxed paper when cooled completely. Yield: 1 1/4 pounds.

SOFT MOLASSES COOKIES

1 c. boiling water
2/3 c. shortening
2 tsp. salt
1 1/2 c. molasses
1 c. sugar
2 eggs

5 c. sifted all-purpose
  flour
4 tsp. baking powder
1 tsp. soda
2 tsp. ginger
2 tsp. cinnamon

Pour boiling water over shortening and salt in bowl; stir until shortening is melted. Stir in molasses and sugar. Blend in eggs. Add sifted dry ingredients. Drop by spoonfuls onto greased cookie sheet. Bake at 375 degrees for 12 to 15 minutes. Cool on wire rack. Yield: 4 to 5 dozen.

MOLASSES PIE

1 3/4 c. all-purpose
  flour
1/2 c. sugar
1/4 tsp. ginger
1/3 tsp. salt
1/4 c. margarine

1 unbaked pie shell
1/2 c. molasses
1/2 c. packed brown
  sugar
1 tsp. soda
1/2 c. hot water

Mix first 4 ingredients in bowl. Cut in margarine until crumbly. Sprinkle half of crumbs in pie shell. Mix molasses and remaining ingredients in bowl. Pour into prepared pie shell. Sprinkle with remaining crumbs. Bake at 375 degrees for 40 to 45 minutes or until set. Yield: 6 servings.

Mushroom

STUFFED MUSHROOMS

24 lg. mushrooms	*1/2 tsp. pepper*
1/2 c. shredded	*1/2 tsp. Italian*
Cheddar cheese	*seasoning*
2 green onions, finely	*1/2 tsp. Worcestershire*
chopped	*sauce*
1/2 c. fine dry bread	*1/4 tsp. garlic powder*
crumbs	*Dash of hot pepper*
1/4 c. melted margarine	*sauce*
1/2 tsp. salt	*Paprika to taste*

Remove stems from mushrooms. Chop stems finely. Place in medium bowl. Add remaining ingredients. Spoon into mushroom caps, mounding slightly in center. Sprinkle with paprika. Arrange in shallow baking dish. Bake at 325 degrees for 20 minutes. Yield: 2 dozen.

SPINACH-STUFFED MUSHROOMS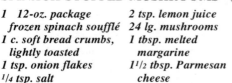

1 12-oz. package	*2 tsp. lemon juice*
frozen spinach soufflé	*24 lg. mushrooms*
1 c. soft bread crumbs,	*1 tbsp. melted*
lightly toasted	*margarine*
1 tsp. onion flakes	*1 1/2 tbsp. Parmesan*
1/4 tsp. salt	*cheese*

Remove cover from soufflé. Bake at 350 degrees for 15 minutes. Combine soufflé with bread crumbs, onion flakes, salt and lemon juice in bowl; mix well. Clean mushrooms with damp paper towel. Remove mushroom stems and reserve for another use. Place mushrooms cap side down in shallow baking dish. Brush with melted margarine. Spoon spinach mixture into caps. Sprinkle with Parmesan cheese. Bake at 350 degrees for 15 minutes. Arrange on serving plate lined with spinach leaves. Yield: 2 dozen.

MARINATED MUSHROOMS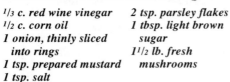

1/3 c. red wine vinegar	*2 tsp. parsley flakes*
1/2 c. corn oil	*1 tbsp. light brown*
1 onion, thinly sliced	*sugar*
into rings	*1 1/2 lb. fresh*
1 tsp. prepared mustard	*mushrooms*
1 tsp. salt	

Combine vinegar, oil, onion, mustard, salt, parsley flakes and brown sugar in saucepan. Bring to a boil. Add mushrooms. Simmer for 5 to 6 minutes. Pour into glass bowl. Chill, covered, for 2 hours or longer, stirring occasionally. Drain and serve. Yield: 8 servings.

MUSHROOM TURNOVERS

9 oz. cream cheese,	*1/4 c. sour cream*
softened	*2 tbsp. all-purpose*
1/2 c. butter, softened	*flour*
1 1/2 c. all-purpose flour	*1/2 tsp. salt*
1/2 lb. mushrooms,	*1/4 tsp. thyme*
sliced	*Freshly ground pepper*
1 onion, chopped	*to taste*
3 tbsp. margarine	

Mix cream cheese, butter and 1 1/2 cups flour in bowl. Chill, covered, in refrigerator. Sauté mushrooms and onion in margarine in skillet. Stir in sour cream, 2 tablespoons flour and seasonings; mix well. Roll chilled dough to 1/8 inch thickness on floured surface. Cut into 3-inch circles. Place 1/2 teaspoon filling on each circle. Fold circles in half; seal edges. Place on baking sheet. Bake at 350 degrees for 15 minutes. Yield: 2 dozen.

CHEESY MUSHROOM CASSEROLE

3 slices bread, cubed	*1/2 tsp. pepper*
1/2 c. chopped onion	*6 slices bread*
1/2 c. chopped celery	*1/2 c. margarine,*
1/2 c. chopped green	*softened*
bell pepper	*1/2 c. milk*
1/2 c. mayonnaise	*2 eggs*
1 lb. fresh mushrooms,	*1 can mushroom soup*
sliced	*2 c. shredded Cheddar*
Pinch of sage	*cheese*
3/4 tsp. salt	

Place cubed bread in 3-quart baking dish. Combine onion, celery, green pepper and mayonnaise in bowl. Spread over cubed bread layer. Sauté mushrooms lightly in skillet. Stir in sage, salt and pepper. Spoon over mixed vegetables. Spread sliced bread with margarine; cut into cubes. Sprinkle 1/2 the cubes over casserole. Beat milk and eggs in bowl. Pour over layers. Chill for 1 hour. Spoon soup over top. Sprinkle remaining bread cubes over top. Bake at 325 degrees for 50 minutes. Sprinkle with cheese. Bake for 10 minutes. Yield: 10 servings.

SPRING MUSHROOM SALAD

1 lb. mushrooms, sliced	*1 clove of garlic, finely*
1/4 c. lemon juice	*chopped*
1/2 c. olive oil	*3/4 tsp. salt*
2 green onions with	*1/4 tsp. freshly ground*
tops, thinly sliced	*pepper*
1/4 c. chopped parsley	

Combine mushrooms with lemon juice in large bowl. Add oil, green onions, parsley, garlic, salt and pepper; toss lightly. Chill, covered, for 3 hours or longer. Drain. Place in serving bowl. Garnish with paprika and parsley sprigs. Yield: 6 servings.

Mustard

CHAMPAGNE MUSTARD

4 eggs
3/4 c. sugar

1/2 c. cider vinegar
2/3 c. dry mustard

Beat eggs in saucepan. Add remaining ingredients; mix well. Bring to a simmer, stirring constantly. Simmer for 8 minutes, stirring constantly. Pour into hot sterilized jars, leaving 1/2 inch headspace. Seal with 2-piece lids. Store in refrigerator. Serve as dip with summer sausages or fresh vegetables or as spread on sandwiches. Yield: 2 cups.

MUSTARD RING

1 env. unflavored
gelatin
1/4 c. water
4 eggs, beaten
1 c. vinegar

3/4 c. sugar
1 tbsp. dry mustard
1 c. whipping cream,
whipped
1 tsp. horseradish

Soften gelatin in water. Combine with eggs, vinegar, sugar and dry mustard in double boiler. Cook until smooth and creamy, stirring constantly. Cool. Add whipped cream and horseradish. Grease mold with mayonnaise. Pour mustard mixture into prepared mold. Chill for 24 hours. Serve with baked ham. Yield: 12 servings.

Noodles

PINEAPPLE NOODLE PUDDING

8 oz. wide noodles
1/2 c. margarine
1 8-oz. container
creamed cottage
cheese
1 c. sour cream

2 eggs, beaten
1 c. crushed pineapple
1/2 c. sugar
1 tsp. vanilla extract
1/2 tsp. salt

Cook noodles according to package directions; drain. Add remaining ingredients; mix well. Spoon into greased 2-quart baking dish. Bake at 350 degrees for 1 hour or until pudding is set. Yield: 6 servings.

NOODLE CLUSTERS

12 oz. butterscotch
chips
3 c. chow mein noodles

1 10 1/2-oz. package
roasted peanuts

Melt butterscotch chips in saucepan over low heat; remove from heat. Stir in noodles and peanuts. Drop by teaspoonfuls onto waxed paper. Let stand until firm. Yield: 36 pieces.

POPPY SEED NOODLES

1 12-oz. package
noodles
1/4 c. margarine

1 tbsp. poppy seed
1/3 c. slivered almonds

Cook noodles according to package directions; drain. Brown margarine in skillet. Stir in poppy seed and almonds. Add noodles; toss lightly to mix. Yield: 10 servings.

SOUR CREAM NOODLES

1 c. cottage cheese
1 1/2 c. sour cream
1 lg. clove of garlic,
crushed
1 tsp. Worcestershire
sauce
3/4 c. chopped onions

1 tsp. salt
1/8 tsp. pepper
1 sm. can mushrooms
1 8-oz. package thin
noodles, cooked
1/2 c. Parmesan cheese

Combine first 8 ingredients in bowl; mix well. Add noodles; mix well. Spoon into greased casserole. Sprinkle with Parmesan cheese. Bake at 325 degrees for 30 minutes. Yield: 4 to 6 servings.

Nutmeg

NUTMEG NUT TART

2 c. mixed macadamia
nuts, hazelnuts,
walnuts, pecans,
cashews and almonds
1 unbaked 10-in. tart
shell
1/4 c. butter, softened

1/2 c. packed dark
brown sugar
1 c. dark corn syrup
3 eggs
1 tbsp. Brandy
1/2 tsp. vanilla extract
1/2 tsp. nutmeg

Toast macadamia nuts and hazelnuts together. Toast walnuts, pecans and cashews together. Toast almonds separately. Cool. Place in tart shell. Cream butter and sugar in bowl until light and fluffy. Add corn syrup and eggs; mix well. Stir in brandy, vanilla and nutmeg. Pour over nuts. Bake at 350 degrees for 5 minutes. Yield: 8 servings.

NUTMEG CUSTARD PIE

Photograph for this recipe is on page 17.

1 unbaked 9-in. pie shell	*3 eggs*
3 c. milk	*3 egg yolks*
1 bay leaf	*1/2 c. sugar*
1 3-in. cinnamon stick	*1 tsp. vanilla extract*
	3/4 tsp. nutmeg
	1/8 tsp. salt

Bake pie shell in preheated 425-degree oven for 7 minutes or until light brown. Remove pie shell. Reduce temperature to 325 degrees. Scald milk with bay leaf and cinnamon stick in saucepan. Combine eggs, egg yolks, sugar, vanilla, nutmeg and salt in bowl. Strain milk over egg mixture; mix well. Pour into pie shell. Bake for 55 minutes or until knife inserted in center comes out clean. Cool on wire rack. Serve at room temperature with whipped cream sprinkled with nutmeg.
Yield: 8 servings.

Oat Bran

OAT BRAN COOKIES

1 c. raisins	*1/2 tsp. soda*
1/2 c. boiling water	*1/2 tsp. salt*
2 c. oats	*1 c. margarine, softened*
2/3 c. oat bran	
1 c. coarsely chopped walnuts	*1 c. packed brown sugar*
1 1/3 c. all-purpose flour	*1 tsp. vanilla extract*
2 tsp. pumpkin pie spice	*2 eggs*

Combine raisins with boiling water in small bowl. Let stand for several minutes. Spread oats, oat bran and chopped walnuts on greased cookie sheets. Toast at 350 degrees until lightly browned. Cool. Combine all-purpose flour, pumpkin pie spice, soda and salt in bowl. Cream softened margarine, brown sugar and vanilla in mixer bowl until light. Blend in eggs 1 at a time. Stir in flour mixture. Drain raisins. Add raisins and oats mixture to batter. Stir just until blended. Drop by teaspoonfuls onto cookie sheet. Bake at 350 degrees for 10 to 12 minutes or until golden brown. Remove to wire rack to cool. Store in airtight container.
Yield: 5 dozen.

OAT BRAN GRANOLA

8 c. oats	*1/2 c. sliced almonds*
3/4 c. packed brown sugar	*1/2 c. coconut*
1 1/2 c. wheat germ	*3/4 c. honey*
1 1/2 c. oat bran	*1/2 c. oil*
1/2 c. chopped walnuts	*2 tsp. vanilla extract*

Combine first 7 ingredients in large bowl; mix well. Mix next 3 ingredients in saucepan. Bring to a boil, stirring frequently. Add to dry ingredients; mix well. Spread in 2 greased 10x15-inch baking pans. Bake at 325 degrees for 20 minutes. Cool to room temperature, stirring occasionally. Store in airtight container. Yield: 16 cups.

OAT BRAN MUFFINS

1 3/4 c. oat bran	*1 tsp. cinnamon*
1/4 c. all-purpose flour	*1 c. skim milk*
1/2 tsp. salt	*1 6-oz. can apple juice*
1/2 tsp. soda	
1/4 tsp. baking powder	*6 tbsp. raisins*
1/4 tsp. allspice	*2 egg whites*

Mix first 7 ingredients in bowl. Stir in next 3 ingredients. Let stand for 10 minutes. Beat egg whites in mixer bowl until soft peaks form. Fold gently into batter. Spoon into 2 1/2-inch muffin cups lined with foil baking cups. Bake at 350 degrees for 25 minutes. Yield: 1 1/2 dozen.

Oatmeal

OVERNIGHT OATMEAL BREAD

2 pkg. dry yeast	*2 tbsp. molasses*
1/4 c. sugar	*2 tsp. salt*
1/2 c. 115-degree water	*5 to 6 c. all-purpose flour*
1 3/4 c. milk, scalded, cooled	
3 tbsp. margarine	*1 c. quick-cooking oats*

Dissolve yeast and 1 teaspoon sugar in warm water in mixer bowl. Let stand until bubbly. Add remaining sugar, milk, margarine, molasses, salt and 2 cups flour. Beat at medium speed until smooth. Add oats and 1 cup flour. Beat until smooth. Mix in additional flour to form a soft dough. Knead on floured surface for 10 minutes. Cover with plastic wrap and towel. Let rest for 10 minutes. Shape into 2 loaves; place in greased loaf pans. Brush tops with oil; cover with plastic wrap. Chill for 2 hours. Let dough stand at room temperature for 10 minutes. Bake at 375 degrees for 30 to 40 minutes or until brown. Yield: 2 loaves.

OATMEAL CAKE

1¹/₂ c. boiling water	*2 eggs, beaten*
1 c. quick-cooking oats	*1¹/₃ c. all-purpose flour*
1 c. sugar	*1 tsp. soda*
1 c. packed light brown	*1 tsp. cinnamon*
sugar	*¹/₂ tsp. nutmeg*
¹/₂ c. margarine,	*¹/₂ tsp. salt*
softened	*Coconut Topping*

Combine boiling water and oats in bowl. Let stand for 20 minutes. Cream sugar, brown sugar, margarine and eggs in mixer bowl until light and fluffy. Add to oats mixture; mix well. Stir in dry ingredients; mix well. Pour into greased and floured 9x13-inch cake pan. Bake at 350 degrees for 35 to 45 minutes or until cake tests done. Pour warm Coconut Topping over warm cake. Bake for 5 minutes longer or broil until topping is golden brown. Serve warm with whipped cream. Yield: 15 servings.

Coconut Topping

1 c. packed light brown	*1 c. coconut*
sugar	*1 c. chopped pecans*
6 tbsp. margarine	*1 tsp. vanilla extract*
¹/₂ c. milk	

Combine sugar, margarine and milk in saucepan. Boil for 3 minutes. Add coconut, pecans and vanilla; mix well.

O'HENRY BARS

4 c. oats	*1 c. margarine,*
1 c. packed brown	*softened*
sugar	*1 c. chocolate chips*
¹/₂ c. white corn syrup	*³/₄ c. peanut butter*

Combine oats, brown sugar, corn syrup and margarine in bowl; mix well. Press into greased 9x13-inch baking pan. Bake at 350 degrees for 10 to 15 minutes or just until mixture begins to bubble; do not overbake. Cool. Melt chocolate chips with peanut butter in double boiler; mix well. Spread over crust. Cool. Cut into bars. Store in refrigerator. Yield: 3 dozen.

OATMEAL COOKIES

1 c. shortening	*2¹/₂ c. all-purpose flour*
1 c. sugar	*2¹/₂ c. oats*
1 c. packed brown	*1 tsp. baking powder*
sugar	*1 tsp. soda*
2 eggs	*¹/₂ tsp. salt*
1 tsp. vanilla extract	*2 c. coconut*

Cream shortening and sugars in mixer bowl until fluffy. Blend in eggs and vanilla. Mix in flour, oats, baking powder, soda, salt and coconut. Drop by spoonfuls onto cookie sheet. Bake at 350 degrees for 15 minutes. Remove to wire rack to cool. Yield: 3 dozen.

OATMEAL PIE

¹/₄ c. margarine	*1 c. oats*
³/₄ c. packed brown	*³/₄ c. coconut*
sugar	*1 tsp. vanilla extract*
³/₄ c. light corn syrup	*1 unbaked 8-in. pie*
2 eggs	*shell*

Cream margarine and brown sugar in mixer bowl until light and fluffy. Add corn syrup, eggs, oats, coconut and vanilla; mix well. Pour into pie shell. Bake at 350 degrees for 40 to 45 minutes or until brown and set. Yield: 6 servings.

Okra

OKRA AND RICE CASSEROLE

1 16-oz. package	*6 onions, chopped*
brown rice	*2 10-oz. packages*
1 lb. bacon, finely	*cut okra, thawed*
chopped	

Cook rice according to package directions; rinse in cold water. Chill in refrigerator. Fry bacon in skillet until crisp; remove with slotted spoon. Cook onions in bacon drippings until golden brown. Add okra and bacon. Cook until okra is tender. Mix with rice. Spoon into 2 greased 9x13-inch baking dishes. Bake at 350 degrees for 1¹/₂ hours. Yield: 20 servings.

SMOTHERED OKRA AND TOMATOES

2 lb. okra	*¹/₂ c. chopped green*
2 tbsp. safflower oil	*bell pepper*
1 tbsp. all-purpose	*2 stalks celery, chopped*
flour	*5 tomatoes, chopped*
1 tbsp. safflower oil	*1 tbsp. Creole*
1 onion, chopped	*seasoning*

Cut okra into 1-inch slices. Sauté in 2 tablespoons oil in skillet until tender-crisp; set aside. Blend flour with 1 tablespoon oil in saucepan. Cook until medium brown, stirring constantly. Add onion, green pepper and celery. Simmer until tender-crisp. Add tomatoes. Simmer for 5 minutes longer. Add okra and seasoning. Simmer over very low heat for 1 hour or to desired consistency and tenderness. Yield: 8 servings.

Olive

OLIVE-CHEESE PUFFS

2 c. shredded Cheddar   1 tsp. paprika
  cheese   1 c. sifted all-purpose
1/2 c. butter, softened   flour
1/2 tsp. salt   100 stuffed green olives

Blend cheese and butter in bowl. Mix salt, paprika
and flour in bowl. Add to cheese mixture; mix
well. Shape by teaspoonfuls around each olive.
Place on baking sheet. Chill for several minutes.
Bake at 400 degrees for 10 to 15 minutes or until
light brown. Yield: 100 puffs.

MARINATED OLIVES

2 5-oz. jars stuffed   6 tbsp. tarragon
  Spanish olives   vinegar
2 6-oz. cans pitted   6 tbsp. wine vinegar
  black olives   1/2 tsp. pepper
2 lg. cloves of garlic   3/4 c. olive oil
6 fresh basil leaves
  or 1 tbsp. dried basil

Drain olives. Place in bowl. Add garlic and basil.
Combine vinegars, pepper and oil in bowl; mix
well. Pour over olives. Marinate, covered, in
refrigerator for 3 days or longer. Pack into jars.
Drain olives and discard garlic before serving.
Yield: 4 cups.

OLIVE SALAD

2 6-oz. cans pitted   2 tbsp. finely chopped
  black olives, drained   onion
1 10-oz. jar pimento-   1 clove of garlic,
  stuffed green olives,   minced
  drained   1 tbsp. oregano
2 4-oz. jars button   1 tbsp. basil
  mushrooms, drained   1/3 c. vinegar
1/2 c. oil   1 jar pepperoncini

Combine olives and mushrooms in large bowl with
tight-fitting cover. Add oil. Chill overnight, invert-
ing bowl occasionally. Add remaining ingredients;
mix well. Marinate in refrigerator for 1 hour to
overnight. Yield: 8 servings.

Omelet

CAJUN OMELETS

1 lb. lean ground beef   1 tbsp. hot sauce
2 cloves of garlic,   1 c. tomato sauce
  minced   12 eggs
1 c. chopped green   4 tsp. all-purpose flour
  onions

Brown ground beef with garlic in skillet over
medium heat, stirring until ground beef is crumbly;
drain. Stir in green onions, hot sauce and tomato
sauce. Simmer, covered, over medium heat for 15
minutes, stirring occasionally. Beat 3 eggs with 1
teaspoon flour in bowl. Pour into small skillet
sprayed with nonstick cooking spray. Cook until
eggs are set. Spoon 1/2 cup ground beef mixture
over half the omelet. Fold omelet in half. Slide
onto heated plate. Repeat process with remaining
eggs and flour, spraying skillet before making each
omelet. Cut each omelet into halves to serve.
Garnish with green grapes. Yield: 6 to 8 servings.

CONFETTI OVEN OMELET

1/2 c. chopped onion   3/4 tsp. salt
1 tbsp. bacon drippings   3 tbsp. chopped
6 slices bacon, crisp-   pimento
  fried, crumbled   1 c. shredded Cheddar
8 eggs, slightly beaten   cheese
1 c. milk   1 tbsp. all-purpose
1 tbsp. chopped parsley   flour

Sauté onion in bacon drippings in skillet until
tender. Combine sautéed onion, bacon, eggs, milk,
parsley, salt and pimento in bowl; mix well. Combine cheese and flour in bowl; toss to mix. Add to
egg mixture. Pour into greased 11/2-quart casserole.
Bake at 350 degrees for 40 minutes. Serve hot.
Yield: 10 servings.

Onion

ONION PIE

11/2 c. crushed butter   11/2 c. milk
  crackers   4 eggs
21/2 c. thinly sliced   1 lb. sharp Cheddar
  onions   cheese, shredded
1/2 c. melted margarine

Place cracker crumbs in 9-inch pie plate. Sauté
onions in margarine in skillet. Spoon into prepared
plate. Heat milk in saucepan. Cool. Add eggs and
cheese; mix well. Bake at 350 degrees for 30 to
45 minutes or until custard is set. Yield: 6 servings.

FRENCH ONION SOUP

3 lb. yellow onions
1/4 c. olive oil
1/4 c. margarine
3 tbsp. all-purpose
  flour
11 beef bouillon cubes
8 c. water

10 1-in. slices Italian
  bread
2 tsp. oil
2 c. shredded Swiss
  cheese
1/4 c. Parmesan cheese

Brown onions in olive oil and margarine in stock-pot over medium heat for 20 minutes. Stir in flour. Dissolve beef bouillon cubes in water. Add to onion. Cook over low heat for 20 minutes. Place bread on baking sheet. Drizzle 1 teaspoon oil on bread slices. Turn bread; drizzle with remaining oil. Bake at 350 degrees for 20 minutes. Pour soup into heat-proof bowls. Float 1 slice bread in each serving. Top with cheeses. Bake at 350 degrees for 15 minutes or until cheese is melted.
Yield: 10 servings.

SCALLOPED ONIONS

3 onions, sliced
3 tbsp. margarine
3 tbsp. all-purpose
  flour

1/2 tsp. salt
1 c. milk
1 c. shredded
  American cheese

Cook onions in water to cover in saucepan for 8 to 10 minutes; drain. Place in ungreased 1-quart baking dish. Melt margarine in saucepan. Blend in flour and salt. Stir in milk. Cook until mixture is thickened, stirring constantly. Stir in cheese. Pour over onions. Bake at 350 degrees for 40 minutes. Yield: 4 servings.

SPINACH-STUFFED ONIONS

1 10-oz. package
  frozen chopped
  spinach
8 lg. onions, peeled
1 c. mayonnaise
1/4 c. lemon juice

1/3 c. milk
2 tbsp. mayonnaise
1 tsp. seasoned salt
2 pimentos, cut into
  strips

Cook spinach according to package directions; drain and set aside. Cook onions in boiling salted water to cover in saucepan for 20 minutes; drain. Combine 1 cup mayonnaise, lemon juice and milk in bowl; mix well. Remove centers from onions, reserving shells. Chop onion centers. Combine with spinach, 2 tablespoons mayonnaise and seasoned salt in bowl; mix well. Spoon into onion shells. Top with pimento. Place in baking dish. Pour mayonnaise mixture over top. Bake at 350 degrees for 20 minutes. Yield: 8 servings.

VIDALIA ONION CASSEROLE

5 lg. Vidalia onions
1/2 c. margarine

Parmesan cheese
Butter cracker crumbs

Peel and slice onions into thin rings. Sauté onions in margarine in skillet until tender. Place half the onions in 1 1/2-quart casserole. Cover with cheese and crumbs. Repeat layers. Bake at 325 degrees for 30 minutes or until golden brown.
Yield: 6 servings.

Orange

ORANGE SOUR CREAM DIP

1 6-oz. can frozen
  orange juice
  concentrate, thawed
1 3-oz. package vanilla
  instant pudding mix

1 1/2 c. milk
1/8 tsp. cinnamon
1/8 tsp. nutmeg
1/4 c. sour cream

Combine orange juice concentrate, pudding mix and milk in mixer bowl. Beat for 2 minutes or until smooth. Stir in spices and sour cream. Chill, covered, for 2 hours. Serve with bite-sized fresh fruit. Yield: 2 1/2 cups.

ORANGE CHIFFON CAKE

2 c. all-purpose flour
1 1/2 c. sugar
1 tbsp. baking powder
1 tsp. salt
1/2 c. oil
7 egg yolks
3/4 c. cold water
3 tbsp. grated orange
  rind
1 c. egg whites

1/2 tsp. cream of tartar
3 c. confectioners'
  sugar
1 tbsp. margarine,
  softened
2 tbsp. orange juice
2 tsp. grated orange
  rind
1/8 tsp. salt

Sift flour, sugar, baking powder and salt into bowl. Make a well in center. Place oil, unbeaten egg yolks, cold water and orange rind in well. Beat with spoon until smooth. Beat egg whites in mixer bowl until foamy. Add cream of tartar. Beat until stiff peaks form. Fold gently into cake batter. Spoon into ungreased 10-inch tube pan. Bake at 325 degrees for 55 minutes. Increase oven temperature to 350 degrees. Bake for 10 minutes longer. Invert on funnel to cool. Loosen side of cake with knife. Remove to serving plate. Combine confectioners' sugar, margarine, orange juice, orange rind and salt in mixer bowl. Beat until smooth. Spread on cool cake. Yield: 12 servings.

MANDARIN ORANGE CAKE

1 2-layer pkg.	*1 20-oz. can crushed*
yellow cake mix	*pineapple*
1 c. oil	*1 4-oz. package vanilla*
1 8-oz. can mandarin	*instant pudding mix*
oranges	*8 oz. whipped topping*
4 eggs	

Combine cake mix, oil, undrained oranges and eggs in mixer bowl. Pour into greased and floured 9x13-inch cake pan. Bake at 350 degrees for 35 minutes. Cool completely. Mix pineapple, pudding mix and whipped topping in bowl. Spread over cake. Store in refrigerator. Yield: 12 servings.

ORANGE COOKIES

1 c. shortening	*1 16-oz. package*
2 c. sugar	*confectioners' sugar*
2 eggs	*1/2 c. margarine,*
4 c. all-purpose flour	*softened*
1 1/2 tsp. soda	*1 tsp. vanilla extract*
1 tsp. baking powder	*1/8 tsp. salt*
1 tsp. salt	*Grated orange rind to*
1/2 c. orange juice	*taste*
1 c. buttermilk	*3 tbsp. orange juice*

Cream shortening in mixer bowl until light and fluffy. Add sugar and eggs, beating until smooth. Sift in flour, soda, baking powder and 1 teaspoon salt; mix well. Stir in 1/2 cup orange juice and buttermilk. Drop by teaspoonfuls onto greased cookie sheet. Bake at 375 degrees for 10 minutes or until brown. Remove to wire rack to cool. Mix remaining ingredients in bowl. Spread on cookies. Yield: 9 dozen.

ORANGE STREUSEL MUFFINS

2 c. all-purpose flour	*1 tbsp. grated orange*
1/2 c. chopped pecans	*rind*
1/3 c. sugar	*1 egg, slightly beaten*
1 tbsp. baking powder	*1/4 c. sugar*
1 tsp. salt	*1 tbsp. all-purpose*
1/2 c. orange juice	*flour*
1/2 c. orange	*1/2 tsp. cinnamon*
marmalade	*1/4 tsp. nutmeg*
1/4 c. milk	*1 tbsp. margarine*
1/4 c. oil	

Combine 2 cups flour, pecans, 1/3 cup sugar, baking powder and salt in bowl. Mix orange juice, marmalade, milk, oil, orange rind and egg in bowl. Add to flour mixture; mix just until moistened. Fill paper-lined muffin cups 2/3 full. Combine 1/4 cup sugar, 1 tablespoon flour, cinnamon, nutmeg and margarine in small bowl; mix until crumbly. Sprinkle over muffins. Bake at 400 degrees for 20 minutes. Yield: 1 dozen.

ORANGE BUTTER

1/2 c. thawed frozen	*1 c. butter, softened*
orange juice	*4 c. confectioners'*
concentrate	*sugar*

Combine orange juice, butter and confectioners' sugar in small mixer bowl. Beat until fluffy. Store in covered container in refrigerator. Use as glaze on warm bread or serve as spread. Yield: 2 cups.

ORANGE FLUFF

1 8-oz. can crushed	*16 oz. container*
pineapple, drained	*large curd*
1 11-oz. can mandarin	*cottage cheese*
oranges, drained	*8 oz. whipped topping*
1 6-oz. package	
orange gelatin	

Combine pineapple, oranges, dry gelatin and cottage cheese in bowl. Fold in whipped topping. Spoon into 8x12-inch dish. Chill overnight. Serve on lettuce-lined salad plates. Yield: 6 servings.

WINTER ORANGES AND RED ONIONS

1/2 c. corn oil	*Salt and pepper to taste*
1/4 c. white wine	*2 heads Bibb lettuce*
vinegar	*2 red onions, thinly*
1/4 tsp. dry mustard	*sliced*
1/4 tsp. sweet basil	*1 cup orange sections*
1/4 tsp. sugar	

Combine oil, vinegar, dry mustard, basil, sugar, salt and pepper in small covered jar. Shake until well blended. Refrigerate for up to 2 weeks. Tear lettuce into bite-sized pieces. Place in salad bowl. Add onion rings and oranges. Pour dressing over salad; toss to coat well. Yield: 8 servings.

Orange Roughy

BAKED ORANGE ROUGHY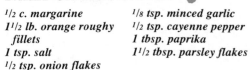

1/2 c. margarine	*1/8 tsp. minced garlic*
1 1/2 lb. orange roughy	*1/2 tsp. cayenne pepper*
fillets	*1 tbsp. paprika*
1 tsp. salt	*1 1/2 tbsp. parsley flakes*
1/2 tsp. onion flakes	

Melt margarine in 9x13-inch baking dish. Coat fillets with margarine on both sides. Sprinkle with salt, onion flakes, garlic, cayenne pepper, paprika and parsley. Bake at 375 degrees for 45 minutes. Yield: 4 servings.

BASIL ORANGE ROUGHY

3 tbsp. olive oil
1 onion, sliced
2 sm. zucchini, thinly
  sliced
1 lb. mushrooms, sliced
1/2 c. chopped fresh
  basil

1 1/2 lb. orange roughy
  fillets
Salt and pepper to taste
2 fresh tomatoes,
  peeled, sliced
1/2 c. Parmesan cheese

Heat oil in large skillet. Add onion, zucchini, mushrooms and basil. Sauté over medium heat for 4 minutes, stirring frequently. Season fillets with salt and pepper. Place over vegetables. Arrange tomato slices over fillets. Simmer, covered, for 8 minutes or until fish flakes easily. Sprinkle cheese over tomatoes. Simmer, covered, until cheese melts. Serve immediately. Yield: 4 servings.

Oysters

OYSTERS PARMESAN

1 onion, chopped
1/2 c. olive oil
5 cloves of garlic,
  chopped
1 pt. oysters, undrained

1 1/2 c. seasoned bread
  crumbs
4 slices bacon, crisp-
  fried, crumbled
1/4 c. Parmesan cheese.

Sauté onion in olive oil in skillet. Remove with slotted spoon. Add garlic to skillet. Sauté for several minutes. Add oysters and onion. Cook until edges of oysters begin to curl. Remove from heat. Add bread crumbs, bacon and cheese. Spoon into baking dish. Bake at 350 degrees for 30 minutes. Yield: 4 servings.

OYSTER PIE

1 recipe 2-crust pie
  pastry
1 onion, finely chopped
1 stalk celery, chopped
2 tbsp. margarine
2 tbsp. all-purpose
  flour
1/2 tsp. mace

1/2 tsp. nutmeg
1/2 tsp. salt
1/2 tsp. pepper
Several drops of hot
  sauce
1 qt. medium oysters
1 c. light cream

Roll half the pastry to fit 9-inch pie plate. Prick with fork. Roll remaining pastry to fit top of pie. Place top pastry on baking sheet. Bake pie shell and top at 400 degrees until light brown and crisp. Sauté onion and celery in margarine in saucepan. Combine with flour, seasonings and hot sauce in double boiler. Drain oysters, reserving liquid. Stir reserved liquid into flour mixture. Simmer over hot water for several minutes, stirring constantly;

do not boil. Add oysters. Heat until edges of oysters curl. Pour into pie shell. Place top pastry on pie. Serve immediately. Yield: 6 servings.

OYSTER STUFFING

3/4 c. chopped onion
1/2 c. margarine
1 pt. oysters
1 1/2 c. (about) milk
1 24-oz. loaf bread,
  torn

4 eggs, beaten
2 tsp. salt
1/2 tsp. pepper
1 tsp. sage

Sauté onion in margarine in skillet; set aside. Drain oysters, reserving liquid. Add enough milk to reserved liquid to measure 2 cups. Combine with bread in bowl, mashing bread to mix well. Add enough additional milk to make very moist. Add onion; mix well. Add oysters, eggs and seasonings; mix well. Use as stuffing for turkey or other poultry. Yield: 10 servings.

Pancakes

FLUFFY PANCAKES

3 egg yolks
1 2/3 c. buttermilk
1 tsp. soda
1 1/2 c. all-purpose flour
1 tbsp. sugar

1 tsp. baking powder
3 tbsp. margarine,
  softened
3 egg whites

Beat egg yolks in mixer bowl. Beat in buttermilk and soda. Add flour, sugar and baking powder; mix well. Add margarine; beat until smooth. Beat egg whites in mixer bowl until stiff peaks form. Fold gently into batter. Bake on lightly greased 400-degree griddle until golden brown on both sides. Yield: 16 pancakes.

⇨
Recipe for this photograph is on
page 128.

Menu
Menu
Menu
Menu
Menu
Menu
Menu
Menu
Menu
Menu
Menu
Menu
Menu
Menu
Menu
Menu
Menu
Menu
Menu

Super Summer Brunch

Grape Juice

page 90

Red Bell Pepper Dip

page 130

Pineapple and Sausage Omelet or

page 152

Summer Vegetable Frittata

page 81

Pear-Chocolate Chip Muffins

page 128

Café au Lait

page 67

*Summer is a perfect time to combine efforts
and serve one great brunch to late risers and
early lunchers alike. Unusual treats get
everyone ready for fun in the sun.*

OVEN-BAKED PANCAKE AND SAUSAGE

3 eggs
1¹/₂ c. milk
3 tbsp. melted
  shortening
1³/₄ c. sifted
  all-purpose flour

4 tsp. baking powder
1¹/₂ tbsp. sugar
1 tsp. salt
2 12-oz. packages
  brown and serve
  sausages

Beat eggs in mixer bowl until light. Beat in milk and shortening. Sift flour, baking powder, sugar and salt together. Add to egg mixture gradually, beating until smooth. Pour into greased 10x15-inch baking pan. Arrange sausage over batter. Bake at 450 degrees for 10 minutes or until cooked through. Yield: 8 servings.

Pasta

RED PEPPER PASTA

2 tbsp. boiling water
2 tsp. dried hot pepper
  flakes
1 c. semolina flour
1 c. all-purpose
  flour

¹/₂ tsp. salt
1 tbsp. corn oil
1 tbsp. tomato paste
2 eggs, slightly beaten
1 tbsp. olive oil

Combine boiling water and pepper flakes in small bowl. Let steep for 15 minutes. Combine semolina flour, flour and salt in food processor container. Add pepper flakes, corn oil, tomato paste and eggs, processing constantly until mixture forms ball. Let rest, wrapped in plastic wrap, for 20 minutes. Roll dough on lightly floured surface. Cut into strips by hand or with pasta machine. Place in boiling water in saucepan to which 1 tablespoon olive oil has been added. Cook for 2 minutes; drain. Yield: 4 servings.

FETTUCINI ALFREDO

1 lb. pasta
8 oz. whipping
  cream

¹/₄ c. butter
8 oz. Parmesan
  cheese

Cook pasta according to package directions. Drain. Combine cream and butter in saucepan. Cook over medium-low heat until butter is melted. Add to hot pasta alternately with Parmesan cheese, tossing to mix well. Serve hot. May add sautéed scallops, shrimp or sliced mushrooms and season with Sherry and freshly ground black pepper. Yield: 3 to 4 servings.

MARINATED TORTELINI SALAD

1 lb. tortelini
¹/₄ c. vinegar
1 tsp. Dijon mustard
¹/₂ to ³/₄ c. olive oil
Salt and pepper to taste
2 cloves of garlic,
  chopped
1 green bell pepper,
  julienned

1 bunch scallions,
  chopped
2 tomatoes, peeled,
  seeded, chopped
¹/₄ c. chopped fresh
  parsley
¹/₂ c. julienne strips
  ham
¹/₄ c. Parmesan cheese

Cook tortelini al dente according to package directions. Rinse and drain. Whisk vinegar and mustard in large bowl until blended. Add olive oil, salt, pepper and garlic; whisk until blended. Add vegetables and ham; mix well. Add tortelini and cheese; toss lightly to mix. Chill, covered, for several hours to overnight. Yield: 8 servings.

STUFFED SHELLS FLORENTINE

1 16-oz. package
  jumbo pasta shells
5 qt. water
1 10-oz. package
  frozen chopped
  spinach
2 lb. ricotta cheese
1 egg

2 tbsp. Parmesan
  cheese
1 32-oz. jar spaghetti
  sauce
1 c. shredded
  mozzarella cheese
Parmesan cheese

Cook pasta in boiling salted water in saucepan for 9 minutes. Drain immediately. Cook spinach according to package directions; drain. Add ricotta cheese, egg and 2 tablespoons Parmesan cheese to spinach; mix well. Spoon into shells. Spread half the spaghetti sauce in two 2-quart baking dishes. Arrange filled shells in prepared dishes. Pour remaining sauce on shells. Sprinkle with shredded mozzarella cheese and additional Parmesan cheese. Bake at 350 degrees for 15 to 20 minutes. Yield: 6 servings.

Stuffed Shells Florentine...can be prepared ahead for an easy and festive dinner.

PASTA PRIMER

NAME	MEANS	DESCRIPTION
Anelli	rings	Small ring-shaped pasta often used in soups and salads
Bucatini	small cave	Long macaroni with a small hole in the middle
Capellini d'Angelo	angel's hair	Delicate long thin threads of pasta
Cannelloni	big pipes	Large tubes of pasta for stuffing
Capelletti	little hats	Dumplings usually filled with minced chicken or meat
Conchiglie	shells	Shell-shaped pasta that comes in various sizes; small ones for soups and salads, large ones for stuffing
Ditalini	little thimbles	Small tubular macaroni cut very short and often used in soup
Farfalle	butterflies	Pasta shaped like bows or butterflies with fluted edges
Fettuccini	small ribbons	Pasta shaped like ribbons
Fusilli	twisted spaghetti	Long strands of spiraled spaghetti
Gemelli	twins	Two short pieces of spaghetti twisted together
Lasagna	Latin for 'pot'	A flat, broad pasta with ruffled edges
Linguine	small tongues	Narrow flat strands of pasta
Macaroni	dumpling	Short tubes of pasta that are slightly curved
Manicotti	small muffs	Large, long tubes which are usually stuffed
Mostaccioli	small mustaches	Large macaroni with ridged or plain surfaces; ends are cut diagonally
Orzo	barley	Resembles rice and is often used as a rice substitute
Pastina	little pasta	Tiny pasta shapes used in soups
Penne	quill	Hollow pasta cut on a diagonal like a quill pen
Rigatoni	large, grooved	Grooved macaroni that is slightly curved and often used for stuffing
Rotelle, Rotini	spirals	Spiraled pasta about $1\frac{1}{2}$ inches long
Ruote	wagon wheels	Die-cut shapes that resemble wheels
Spaghetti	a length of string	Long thin solid strands of pasta
Stellini	little stars	Tiny star-shaped pasta, often used in soups
Tagliatelle	to cut	Similar to fettuccini, but broader
Tripolini	little bows	Named in honor of the conquest of Tripoli
Vermicelli	little worms	Thin strands of spaghetti
Ziti	bridegrooms	Tube-shaped pasta that resembles macaroni

SEAFOOD PASTA

1/2 c. margarine
4 cloves of garlic,
  minced
2 shallots, finely
  chopped
8 lg. shrimp, peeled,
  butterflied
8 oz. grouper, cut into
  1x1-inch pieces
8 oz. scallops
1 tbsp. thyme
Salt to taste
1/2 tsp. pepper

1 yellow bell pepper,
  cut into julienne
  strips
4 oz. mushrooms, sliced
4 scallions, finely
  chopped
1 4-oz. jar chopped
  pimento
Juice of 1 lemon
1/2 c. white wine
1 lb. linguine
1 bunch parsley, finely
  chopped

Heat margarine in skillet over medium heat until foamy. Add garlic and shallots. Sauté for 1 minute. Add seafood, thyme, salt and pepper. Cook until grouper is almost white, stirring frequently. Add vegetables. Sauté for several minutes. Add lemon juice and wine. Simmer for 5 minutes. Cook linguine *al dente* according to package directions. Place in serving dish. Spoon sauce over top. Sprinkle with parsley. Yield: 4 servings.

Peach

PEACH BUTTER

6 lb. fresh peaches
1/4 c. fresh lemon juice

1 tsp. cinnamon
3 1/4 c. sugar

Peel peaches; cut into fourths. Purée in blender container. Combine 11 cups purée, lemon juice and cinnamon in large saucepan. Cook, uncovered, over medium heat for 2 hours, stirring frequently. Add sugar. Cook mixture, uncovered, until of desired consistency, stirring frequently. Ladle into hot sterilized jars, leaving 1/2 inch headspace. Seal with 2-piece lids. Process in boiling water bath for 10 minutes. Yield: Six 8-ounce jars.

PEACHES AND CREAM SALAD

1 3-oz. package
  lemon gelatin
1 c. boiling water
3 oz. cream cheese
1 c. orange juice
8 oz. whipped topping

1 3-oz. package
  lemon gelatin
1 c. boiling water
1 22-oz. can peach
  pie filling
1/2 c. chopped pecans

Dissolve 1 package gelatin in 1 cup boiling water in bowl. Add cream cheese; beat with wire whisk until blended. Mix in orange juice and whipped topping. Pour into 9x13-inch dish. Chill until firm. Dissolve 1 package gelatin in 1 cup boiling water

in bowl. Add pie filling and pecans. Cool. Pour over congealed layer. Chill. Yield: 12 servings.

PEACH MOUSSE

1/3 c. sugar
2 env. unflavored
  gelatin
4 eggs
3 egg yolks

1 29-oz. can sliced
  peaches, drained
1/4 c. Amaretto
2 c. whipping cream,
  whipped

Mix sugar and gelatin in 2-quart saucepan. Beat eggs and egg yolks in bowl until thick and lemon-colored. Stir into gelatin mixture. Cook over medium heat just until mixture comes to a boil, stirring constantly. Remove from heat. Purée peaches in blender container. Add peaches and Amaretto to cooked mixture. Chill until partially set. Fold in whipped cream gently. Pour into 8-cup mold. Refrigerate until firm. Unmold onto serving plate. Yield: 6 servings.

SUMMER PEACH CREAM PIE

1/2 c. margarine
1 1/2 c. all-purpose flour
1/2 tsp. salt
4 c. sliced peaches
1/4 c. sugar
2 tbsp. all-purpose
  flour
3/4 c. sugar

1 egg
1/2 tsp. salt
1/2 tsp. vanilla extract
1 c. sour cream
1/3 c. sugar
1/3 c. all-purpose flour
1/4 c. margarine
1 tsp. cinnamon

Cut 1/2 cup margarine into mixture of 1 1/2 cups flour and 1/2 teaspoon salt in bowl. Press into 9-inch pie plate. Mix peaches with 1/4 cup sugar in bowl. Let stand for several minutes. Combine 2 tablespoons flour, 3/4 cup sugar, egg, 1/2 teaspoon salt and vanilla in bowl; mix well. Fold in sour cream. Stir into peaches. Pour into pie shell. Bake at 400 degrees for 15 minutes. Reduce temperature to 350 degrees. Bake for 20 minutes longer. Mix remaining ingredients in bowl until crumbly. Sprinkle over pie. Increase temperature to 400 degrees. Bake for 10 minutes. Yield: 6 servings.

UPSIDE-DOWN PEACH PIE

Margarine, softened
Sugar
Fresh peaches, sliced

1 recipe 1-crust pie
  pastry
Whipped cream

Layer 1/2 inch softened margarine, 1/4 inch sugar and peach slices in 9-inch pie plate. Sprinkle with additional sugar. Top with slices of additional margarine. Cover layers with pastry; trim to fit. Bake at 375 degrees for 30 minutes. Loosen edges of crust with knife; invert onto serving plate. Serve warm with whipped cream. Yield: 6 servings.

Peanut

PEANUT BUTTER-OATMEAL BREAD

1¹/2 c. sifted	*¹/2 c. chunky peanut*
all-purpose flour	*butter*
1 c. sugar	*1 c. oats*
1 tbsp. baking powder	*1 egg, beaten*
¹/2 tsp. salt	*1 c. milk*

Sift flour, sugar, baking powder and salt into bowl. Cut in peanut butter until crumbly. Add oats, egg and milk; stir just until moistened. Pour into greased 5x9-inch loaf pan. Bake at 350 degrees for 1 hour or until loaf tests done. Cool on wire rack. Yield: 12 servings.

LOW-CHOLESTEROL MUFFINS

¹/2 c. corn oil	*2 tsp. baking powder*
1 c. honey	*¹/2 tsp. cloves*
³/4 c. peanut butter	*1 tsp. cinnamon*
Egg Beaters to equal	*¹/2 c. oats*
2 eggs	*¹/2 c. raisins*
¹/3 c. skim milk	*³/4 c. whole wheat flour*

Blend oil and honey in bowl. Add remaining ingredients in order listed, mixing well after each addition. Spoon into greased muffin cups. Bake at 350 degrees for 15 to 20 minutes or until light brown. May bake in tube or loaf pan if preferred. Yield: 10 to 12 muffins.

HEAVENLY PEANUT BUTTER FUDGE

1 c. evaporated milk	*¹/2 c. packed brown*
2 c. sugar	*sugar*
1 tsp. salt	*¹/2 c. corn syrup*
¹/4 c. margarine	*2 c. confectioners'*
2 c. peanut butter chips	*sugar*
6 tbsp. margarine	*1 c. chopped walnuts*

Combine evaporated milk, sugar, salt and ¹/4 cup margarine in heavy saucepan. Bring to a boil over medium heat. Boil for 8 minutes, stirring constantly. Remove from heat. Add peanut butter chips. Stir until smooth. Spread in foil-lined 9x9-inch pan. Chill for 30 minutes. Combine 6 tablespoons margarine, brown sugar and corn syrup in heavy saucepan; stir until smooth. Bring to a boil; remove from heat. Add confectioners' sugar and walnuts; mix well. Spread over peanut butter layer. Chill until firm. Lift from pan; cut into 1-inch squares. Yield: 4 pounds.

PEANUT BUTTER CUP BARS

1 c. margarine	*2¹/2 c. confectioners'*
2¹/2 c. graham cracker	*sugar*
crumbs	*2 c. chocolate chips,*
1 c. peanut butter	*melted*

Melt margarine in saucepan. Add crumbs, peanut butter and confectioners' sugar; mix well. Spread evenly in greased 9x13-inch pan. Spread melted chocolate over top. Chill until firm. Cut into bars. Yield: 2 dozen.

PEANUT PUDDING PIES

¹/2 c. margarine,	*1 c. peanut butter*
softened	*1 c. whipped topping*
1 c. all-purpose flour	*2 pkg. chocolate*
¹/2 c. chopped roasted	*instant pudding mix*
peanuts	*3 c. milk*
1 c. confectioners'	*2 c. whipped topping*
sugar	*¹/4 c. chopped roasted*
8 oz. cream cheese,	*peanuts*
softened	

Cut margarine into flour in bowl. Mix in ¹/2 cup peanuts. Press into two 8-inch pie plates. Bake at 350 degrees for 20 minutes or until light brown. Cool. Cream confectioners' sugar, cream cheese and peanut butter in mixer bowl until fluffy. Mix in 1 cup whipped topping. Spread in prepared crusts. Prepare pudding mix with milk in mixer bowl. Spread over peanut butter layer. Top with 2 cups whipped topping and ¹/4 cup peanuts. Chill. Yield: 2 pies.

Pear

PEAR-CHOCOLATE CHIP MUFFINS
Photograph for this recipe is on page 123.

1³/4 c. flour	*1 tsp. vanilla extract*
1 c. sugar	*1¹/2 c. chopped pears*
2 tsp. baking powder	*1 c. miniature*
¹/4 tsp. salt	*chocolate chips*
2 eggs, slightly beaten	*¹/4 c. chopped walnuts*
1 c. sour cream	*¹/4 c. sugar*
¹/4 c. melted butter	*2 tbsp. butter, softened*

Combine flour, 1 cup sugar, baking powder and salt in mixing bowl. Add mixture of eggs, sour cream, ¹/4 cup butter, vanilla, pear chunks and chocolate chips; mix just until moistened. Fill 12 greased muffin cups ³/4 full. Mix ¹/4 cup walnuts, ¹/4 cup sugar and 2 tablespoons butter in bowl until crumbly. Sprinkle over muffins. Bake at 400 degrees for 18 to 20 minutes or until muffins test done. Yield: 12 muffins.

FRESH PEAR CAKE

1 tsp. instant coffee powder	*3 c. finely chopped unpeeled pears*
3/4 c. hot water	*1/2 c. packed light brown sugar*
3/4 c. margarine, softened	*3 tbsp. flour*
1 1/2 c. sugar	*1 tsp. cinnamon*
2 eggs	*2 tbsp. butter*
2 1/4 c. all-purpose flour	*1/2 c. finely chopped pecans or walnuts*
1 tsp. soda	
1/2 tsp. salt	

Dissolve coffee powder in hot water; cool. Cream 3/4 cup margarine and sugar in mixer bowl until light and fluffy. Blend in eggs. Add mixture of 2 1/4 cups flour, soda and salt alternately with coffee mixture, mixing well after each addition. Fold in pears. Spoon into greased and floured 9x13-inch pan. Mix brown sugar, 3 tablespoons flour and cinnamon in bowl. Cut in 2 tablespoons margarine with pastry cutter. Stir in pecans. Sprinkle over cake batter. Bake at 350 degrees for 45 to 50 minutes or until cake tests done. Serve warm with whipped cream. Yield: 12 to 14 servings.

Peas

STUFFED SNOW PEAS

3 oz. cream cheese, softened	*1 1/2 tbsp. chopped pimento*
1 1/2 tbsp. catsup	*1/3 c. finely chopped pecans*
3 tbsp. chopped green bell pepper	*1/4 tsp. salt*
2 tbsp. finely chopped onion	*1/4 tsp. pepper*
	30 tender snow peas

Combine first 8 ingredients in bowl; mix well. Chill for 1 hour or longer. String snow peas. Blanch in boiling water in saucepan for 30 seconds. Plunge into cold water; drain. Slit the straight side of each snow pea to open. Spread with 1 1/2 teaspoons filling. Yield: 2 1/2 dozen.

GREEN PEA AND RICE SALAD

1 10-oz. package frozen peas	*1/2 c. chopped dill pickle*
1/2 tsp. salt	*4 green onions, chopped*
1 1/2 c. water	*1 c. shredded Swiss cheese*
1 1/3 c. minute rice	*3/4 c. mayonnaise*
1 c. chopped ham	

Bring peas, salt and 1 1/2 cups water to a boil in saucepan. Stir in rice. Let stand, covered, for 13 minutes. Uncover; fluff with fork. Let stand until cooled to room temperature. Combine with remaining ingredients in large bowl. Chill until serving time. Yield: 12 servings.

PEANUTTY PEA-POPPY SEED SALAD

2 20-oz. packages frozen green peas	*1 12-oz. bottle of ranch salad dressing*
1 1/2 lb. dry roasted salted peanuts	*1/2 2-oz. bottle of poppy seed*
2 or 3 green onions, sliced	

Place frozen peas in bowl; break apart. Add peanuts, green onions, dressing and poppy seed; mix well. Let stand for 3 1/2 to 4 hours before serving. Yield: 25 servings.

PEA AND POTATO SAUTÉ

6 potatoes	*2 tbsp. chopped parsley*
1/4 c. olive oil	*1 10-oz. package frozen peas, cooked*
8 oz. fresh mushrooms	*2 tbsp. lemon juice*
1/4 c. margarine	*1 tbsp. basil*
1 clove of garlic, minced	*1/4 tsp. nutmeg*

Peel potatoes and cut into cubes. Cook in water to cover in saucepan for 4 to 5 minutes; drain. Sauté potatoes in olive oil in heavy skillet until evenly browned. Slice mushrooms. Sauté in margarine in skillet. Add garlic and parsley. Cook for 30 seconds. Combine potatoes, peas, mushrooms, lemon juice, basil and nutmeg in serving bowl; toss lightly to mix well. Serve immediately. Yield: 8 servings.

Pecan

FROSTED PECANS

1 egg white	*1 c. sugar*
1 tsp. cold water	*1 tsp. cinnamon*
1 lb. large pecan halves	*1 tsp. salt*

Beat egg white with water in mixer bowl until frothy. Stir in pecans. Mix remaining ingredients in small bowl. Add to pecans; mix well. Spread on baking sheet. Bake at 225 degrees for 1 hour, stirring occasionally. Cool. Place in decorative airtight containers. Yield: 1 pound.

PECAN CRESCENTS

1 c. margarine, softened	1/2 tsp. salt
6 tbsp. confectioners' sugar	1 c. finely chopped pecans
1 tsp. vanilla extract	1 c. confectioners' sugar
2 c. all-purpose flour	

Cream margarine in mixer bowl until light. Add 6 tablespoons confectioners' sugar and vanilla, beating until fluffy. Add flour and salt gradually; mix well. Fold in pecans. Chill for 2 hours. Shape into small rolls. Shape into crescents on cookie sheet. Bake at 350 degrees for 10 to 15 minutes or until very light brown. Roll in 1 cup confectioners' sugar while warm. Cool on wire rack. Yield: 30 cookies.

PECAN SQUARES

2 c. all-purpose flour	1/2 c. sugar
1/2 c. sugar	1/2 c. packed light brown sugar
1 c. margarine, softened	4 egg whites
2 egg yolks	4 c. chopped pecans
1 tbsp. water	1 1/2 tsp. cinnamon

Combine flour, 1/2 cup sugar, margarine, egg yolks and water in bowl; mix well. Press into baking pan. Bake at 350 degrees for 15 minutes. Combine remaining ingredients in saucepan. Heat until sugars are dissolved, stirring to mix well. Spread over crust. Bake for 25 minutes or until light brown. Cool. Cut into squares. Yield: 24 squares.

MYSTERY PECAN PIE

8 oz. cream cheese, softened	1 unbaked 9-in. pie shell
1/3 c. sugar	1 c. pecans
1/4 tsp. salt	1/4 c. sugar
1 tsp. vanilla extract	1 tsp. vanilla extract
4 eggs	1 c. light corn syrup

Combine cream cheese, 1/3 cup sugar, salt, vanilla and 1 egg in bowl. Beat until well blended; pour into pie shell. Sprinkle with pecans. Combine remaining 3 eggs, 1/4 cup sugar, 1 teaspoon vanilla and corn syrup in bowl; blend well. Pour over pecans. Bake at 350 degrees for 35 to 40 minutes or until center is firm. Yield: 8 servings.

Peppermint

PEPPERMINT PATTIES

1 tbsp. melted margarine	1 1/2 tsp. peppermint extract
2 c. confectioners' sugar	3/4 c. semisweet chocolate chips
3 tbsp. (about) evaporated milk	

Combine margarine, confectioners' sugar, evaporated milk and flavoring in large bowl; mix well with fork. Knead until smooth. Roll 1/8 inch thick on waxed paper. Melt chocolate in double boiler over hot water. Spread over peppermint layer. Cut into small circles. Garnish with decorative candies if desired. Chill until serving time. Yield: 24 servings.

PEPPERMINT ICE CREAM ROLL

4 egg yolks	1 tsp. baking powder
1/4 c. sugar	1/4 tsp. salt
1/2 tsp. vanilla extract	Confectioners' sugar
4 egg whites	1 quart peppermint ice cream, softened
1/2 c. sugar	
2/3 c. sifted cake flour	1 c. whipped topping
1/4 c. unsweetened baking cocoa	1/4 c. crushed peppermint candy

Beat egg yolks in small mixer bowl until thick. Beat in 1/4 cup sugar gradually. Add vanilla. Beat egg whites in large mixer bowl until soft peaks form. Add 1/2 cup sugar gradually, beating until stiff peaks form. Fold egg yolk mixture into egg whites gently. Fold in sifted dry ingredients gently. Spread batter evenly in greased and floured 10x15-inch cake pan. Bake at 375 degrees for 10 minutes. Loosen from side of pan; invert onto towel sprinkled with sifted confectioners' sugar. Roll in towel as for jelly roll. Cool. Unroll. Spread with ice cream; reroll. Freeze until firm. Frost with mixture of whipped topping and candy. Yield: 10 servings.

Peppers

RED BELL PEPPER DIP

6 very lg. red bell peppers, finely chopped	3/4 c. apple cider vinegar
1 1/2 c. sugar	1 tsp. salt
	1 tbsp. cornstarch

Combine all ingredients in saucepan. Bring to a boil; reduce heat. Simmer for 5 to 6 minutes. Store in refrigerator. Serve over cream cheese with wheat crackers. Yield: 3 cups.

HOT PEPPERS

8 qt. hot peppers,
cut into rings
4 stalks celery,
chopped
4 c. vinegar
3 c. water

2 c. oil
3/4 c. salt
3 lg. cloves of garlic,
finely chopped
1/4 c. oregano

Combine peppers, celery, vinegar, water, oil, salt, garlic and oregano in large bowl; mix well. Let stand, covered, at room temperature for 8 hours. Spoon into jars. Store in refrigerator. Yield: 6 cups.

PEPPERONATA

2 green bell peppers
2 red bell peppers
2 yellow bell peppers
3 onions, sliced
2 tbsp. oil
1 c. chopped fresh basil

Salt and pepper to taste
2 16-oz. cans stewed
tomatoes
1 6-oz. can tomato
paste

Cut peppers into strips. Sauté onions in oil in saucepan. Add seasonings, tomatoes, tomato paste and peppers; mix well. Simmer mixture for 1 hour. Serve as soup or over spaghetti. Yield: 4 cups.

Perch

FRIED PERCH

2 lb. fresh perch fillets
1/3 c. chopped green
onions
1/3 c. olive oil
3 tbsp. lemon juice
1/2 tsp. salt
1/8 tsp. pepper

1/4 c. all-purpose flour
1 egg
1 tbsp. milk
1 c. dry bread crumbs
3 tbsp. margarine
3 tbsp. vegetable oil

Place fillets in shallow dish. Combine onions, olive oil and lemon juice. Pour over fillets. Marinate for 1 hour. Remove from marinade; pat dry with paper towel. Sprinkle fillets with salt and pepper. Coat with flour. Beat egg and milk in bowl. Dip floured fillets in egg, then in bread crumbs. Fry in mixture of margarine and oil in skillet until golden brown. Serve immediately. Yield: 8 servings.

PARMESAN BAKED FISH

1 egg
1/4 c. milk
1 c. cracker crumbs
1/3 c. Parmesan cheese

1/8 tsp. pepper
1 lb. ocean perch fillets
1/3 c. melted butter
Lemon Sauce

Beat egg and milk in bowl. Combine crumbs, cheese and pepper in bowl. Coat fillets with crumb mixture, then with egg mixture and then with crumbs again. Place in melted butter in baking dish, turning to coat both sides. Bake at 425 degrees for 15 minutes or until fish flakes easily. Serve Lemon Sauce over fish. Yield: 4 servings.

Lemon Sauce

1 tbsp. lemon juice
1 tsp. grated lemon rind

1/3 c. margarine

Combine lemon juice, lemon rind and 1/3 cup margarine in saucepan. Heat until margarine is completely melted.

Persimmon

HARVEST PERSIMMON BARS

1 c. persimmon pulp
1 1/2 tsp. lemon juice
1 tsp. soda
1 egg
1 c. sugar
1/2 c. oil
1 3/4 c. all-purpose flour
1 tsp. soda
1 tsp. salt

1 tsp. cinnamon
1 tsp. nutmeg
1/2 tsp. cloves
1 c. chopped walnuts
1 8-oz. package dates,
chopped
1 c. confectioners'
sugar
2 tbsp. lemon juice

Combine persimmon pulp, 1 1/2 teaspoons lemon juice and soda in small bowl; set aside. Beat egg in bowl. Add sugar and oil; mix well. Add mixture of dry ingredients alternately with persimmon, mixing well after each addition. Stir in walnuts and dates. Spread mixture in greased and floured 9x13-inch cake pan. Bake at 350 degrees for 25 minutes or until golden. Blend confectioners' sugar and 2 tablespoons lemon juice in small bowl. Spoon over baked layer. Cool. Cut into 1 1/2x3-inch bars. Yield: 2 dozen.

BLUE RIBBON PERSIMMON ROLL

1 1-lb. package
graham crackers,
finely crushed
1 1/2 c. persimmon pulp
1 1/2 c. sugar

20 marshmallows,
chopped
1 c. chopped pecans
1 1/2 tsp. vanilla extract

Reserve 1/2 cup crumbs. Combine remaining crumbs and ingredients in bowl; mix well. Shape into roll. Roll in reserved crumbs. Chill, wrapped, overnight. Cut into slices. Serve with whipped topping, sauce or ice cream. Yield: 8 servings.

Pickle

PICKLED SPRING ASPARAGUS

2 lb. fresh asparagus	2¹/₂ c. white wine
4 sprigs of fresh	vinegar
dillweed	¹/₄ c. salt
¹/₂ tsp. cayenne pepper	2¹/₂ c. water
2 cloves of garlic	¹/₂ c. light corn syrup

Wash asparagus; drain. Trim asparagus spears to fit glass jars, removing tough portions of stalks. Pack asparagus spears vertically into hot sterilized jars, leaving 1-inch headspace. Place 2 sprigs of fresh dillweed between asparagus and side of jar. Add ¹/₄ teaspoon cayenne pepper and 1 clove of garlic to each jar. Combine wine vinegar, salt, water and corn syrup in saucepan. Bring to a boil. Pour into jars, leaving ¹/₂-inch headspace; seal. Refrigerate for several weeks. Rinse before serving. Yield: Two 1-quart jars.

RED CINNAMON PICKLES

2 gal. large cucumbers	2 c. vinegar
2 c. pickling lime	10 c. sugar
8¹/₂ qt. water	3 c. water
1 c. vinegar	8 cinnamon sticks
1 1-oz. bottle of red	1 8-oz. package red
food coloring	hot cinnamon
1 tbsp. alum	candies

Peel and seed cucumbers; cut into sticks. Combine with lime and 8¹/₂ quarts water in large bowl. Let stand for 24 hours, stirring occasionally. Drain and rinse well. Cover with fresh water. Let stand for 3 hours. Drain. Combine cucumbers, 1 cup vinegar, food coloring and alum in saucepan. Add water to cover. Simmer for 2 hours. Drain. Combine 2 cups vinegar, sugar, 3 cups water, cinnamon sticks and candy in saucepan. Cook until candies dissolve. Pour over cucumbers. Let stand overnight. Drain into saucepan. Reheat syrup and repeat process 3 times. Pack into hot sterilized jars, leaving ¹/₂-inch headspace; seal with 2-piece lids. Process in boiling water bath for 10 minutes. Yield: 6 quarts.

SWEET AND SOUR PINEAPPLE PICKLES

2 med. fresh pineapples	2 c. water
2 c. packed light	1 3-in. cinnamon stick
brown sugar	2 tbsp. whole cloves
1 c. cider vinegar	

Peel pineapple. Cut into spears, discarding core. Combine brown sugar, cider vinegar and water in large saucepan. Tie cinnamon stick and cloves in cheesecloth. Add to vinegar mixture. Bring to a boil. Cook for 5 minutes. Add pineapple. Simmer, covered, for 5 minutes. Remove spice bag. Pack pineapple into hot sterilized jars, leaving ¹/₂-inch headspace; seal with 2-piece lids. Process in boiling water bath for 15 minutes. Yield: 3 pints.

ZUCCHINI PICKLES

24 med. zucchini	3 c. vinegar
¹/₄ c. pickling salt	¹/₃ c. mustard seed
3 c. sugar	4 tsp. celery seed

Cut zucchini into quarters. Cut quarters into 3-inch sticks. Place in large nonmetallic bowl. Sprinkle with pickling salt. Add enough cold water to cover. Let stand for 3 hours. Drain; rinse well. Combine sugar, vinegar, mustard seed and celery seed in large saucepan. Bring to a boil over medium heat. Add zucchini; reduce heat. Cook over low heat for 5 minutes; do not bring to a boil. Pack zucchini into hot sterilized 1-pint jars; leave ¹/₂-inch headspace. Pour in hot liquid, leaving ¹/₂-inch headspace. Seal with 2-piece lids. Process in boiling water bath for 10 minutes. Yield: 9 pints.

Pineapple

PIÑA COLADA CAKE

1 14-oz. can crushed	1 4-oz. can coconut
pineapple	1 16-oz. can cream of
1 2-layer pkg. yellow	coconut
or white cake mix	1 8-oz. container
1¹/₂ c. water	whipped topping
2 eggs, beaten	

Drain pineapple, reserving juice. Combine cake mix, water and eggs in bowl. Mix in pineapple and half the coconut. Pour into 9x13-inch cake pan. Bake at 350 degrees for 30 minutes. Punch holes in top of hot cake. Pour mixture of cream of coconut and reserved pineapple juice over cake. Cool. Spread with whipped topping; sprinkle remaining coconut on top. Yield: 12 servings.

PINEAPPLE COOKIES

³/₄ c. shortening	¹/₂ tsp. soda
1¹/₄ c. packed brown	¹/₄ tsp. salt
sugar	1 tsp. vanilla extract
1 egg	³/₄ c. drained crushed
2 c. all-purpose flour	pineapple
1 tsp. baking powder	1 c. broken walnuts

Cream shortening and brown sugar in mixer bowl until light and fluffy. Blend in egg. Sift dry ingredients 2 times. Stir into creamed mixture with wooden spoon. Add vanilla, pineapple and walnuts; mix well. Drop by teaspoonfuls onto cookie sheet. Bake at 350 degrees for 10 to 15 minutes or until light brown. Cool on wire rack.
Yield: 36 cookies.

SCALLOPED PINEAPPLE

1 c. margarine, softened	1 29-oz. can crushed pineapple
2 c. sugar	4 c. fresh bread cubes
3 eggs, beaten	

Cream margarine in bowl until light. Add sugar, beating until fluffy. Blend in eggs. Add pineapple and bread cubes. Spoon into 9x11-inch baking dish. Bake at 325 degrees for 1 hour.
Yield: 12 servings.

SUPER PINEAPPLE SPLIT

1/4 c. margarine, softened	8 oz. cream cheese, softened
2 c. confectioners' sugar	1/4 c. margarine, softened
1/2 c. semisweet chocolate chips	1 20-oz. can crushed pineapple, drained
11/2 c. evaporated milk	2 lg. bananas
1 12-oz. package vanilla wafers, crushed	2 tbsp. lemon juice
	1/2 c. chopped pecans
1/2 c. margarine softened	16 oz. whipped topping
	1 3-oz. jar maraschino cherries, drained

Combine first 4 ingredients in saucepan. Cook until thick and smooth, stirring constantly. Cool. Mix vanilla wafer crumbs and 1/2 cup margarine in bowl. Press over bottom of 9x13-inch baking dish. Beat cream cheese and 1/4 cup margarine in bowl; blend well. Add 2/3 cup pineapple; mix well. Spread over crust. Slice bananas 1/2-inch thick. Drizzle with lemon juice; drain well. Arrange over cream cheese layer. Top with chocolate sauce. Sprinkle pecans over sauce. Spread whipped topping over all. Sprinkle with remaining pineapple and cherries. Chill for several hours. Yield: 12 servings.

Pistachio

PISTACHIO ICE CREAM CAKE

1 15-oz. package Oreo cookies, crushed	11/2 c. milk
6 tbsp. melted butter	1 12-oz. container whipped topping
2 sm. package pistachio instant pudding mix	1 qt. vanilla ice cream, softened

Reserve 1/2 cup cookie crumbs. Mix remaining crumbs with butter in bowl. Press over bottom of 9x13-inch dish. Combine pudding mix and milk in mixer bowl; mix until thick and smooth. Combine whipped topping and ice cream in mixer bowl; beat until smooth. Stir into pudding mixture. Spoon over crust. Sprinkle with reserved crumbs. Freeze until firm. Yield: 12 servings.

PISTACHIO CAKE

1 2-layer pkg. white cake mix	1 3-oz. package pistachio instant pudding mix
3 eggs	
1 c. vegetable oil	Pistachio Frosting
1 c. club soda	

Beat first 5 ingredients in mixer bowl for 4 minutes. Pour into greased and floured bundt pan. Bake at 350 degrees for 45 minutes. Cool. Spread Pistachio Frosting over top. Chill. Yield: 8 servings.

Pistachio Frosting

1 env. whipped topping mix	1 3-oz. package pistachio instant pudding mix
1 4-oz. container whipped topping	1 c. cold milk

Combine whipped topping mix, whipped topping, pudding mix, and milk in mixer bowl. Beat until well blended.

Pistachio Cake...a glamorous dessert that starts with packaged convenience foods.

Pizza

QUICK BREAKFAST PIZZA

1 lb. sausage	*¹/2 tsp. salt*
1¹/2 8-count pkg. refrigerator crescent rolls	*¹/8 tsp. pepper*
	1 c. shredded sharp Cheddar cheese
1 c. frozen hashed brown potatoes, thawed	*1 c. shredded mozzarella cheese*
5 eggs, beaten	*2 tbsp. Parmesan cheese*
¹/4 c. milk	

Cook sausage in skillet until brown and crumbly; drain. Fit crescent roll dough into pizza pan, forming crust and sealing perforations. Layer sausage and potatoes over roll dough. Mix eggs, milk, salt and pepper. Pour over potatoes. Sprinkle with cheeses. Bake at 375 degrees for 25 to 30 minutes. Yield: 10 to 12 servings.

MEXICAN PIZZA

1 lb. ground beef	*1 16-oz. can refried beans with green chilies*
1 med. onion, chopped	
2 cloves of garlic, minced	*2 c. shredded Cheddar cheese*
1 8-oz. jar picante sauce	*2 c. shredded Monterey Jack cheese*
6 flour tortillas	*1 avocado, sliced*
2 tbsp. melted margarine	

Brown ground beef with onion in skillet, stirring until crumbly; drain. Add garlic and picante sauce. Brush tortillas on both sides with margarine. Place in 12-inch pizza pan, overlapping to cover bottom. Broil until lightly browned and crisp. Spread with beans; top with ground beef and cheeses. Reduce temperature to 450 degrees. Bake for 10 minutes. Garnish with avocado slices. Serve with sour cream, guacamole or taco sauce. Yield: 8 servings.

PIZZA ROLLS

1¹/2 lb. ground chuck	*¹/4 tsp. dried parsley*
¹/2 c. chopped onion	*¹/2 c. tomato sauce*
¹/2 c. chopped celery	*1 pkg. pepperoni, chopped*
1 2-oz. can mushroom pieces, drained, chopped	*1 pkg. shredded mozzarella cheese*
¹/2 tsp. sugar	*1 tbsp. all-purpose flour*
¹/2 tsp. salt	
¹/8 tsp. pepper	*1 16-oz. package won ton skins*
¹/4 tsp. oregano	
¹/4 tsp. basil	*Oil for deep frying*

Sauté ground chuck, onion and celery in large skillet; drain. Stir in mushrooms, sugar, salt, pepper, oregano, basil, dried parsley, tomato sauce and pepperoni. Simmer, uncovered, for 10 minutes. Stir in Mozzarella cheese. Blend flour with a small amount of water to make paste. Brush all 4 corners of 1 won ton skin with paste. Place 1 tablespoon ground chuck mixture in center of skin. Fold corners to center alternately; press to seal. Repeat with remaining won ton skins and ground chuck mixture. Deep-fry for 1 to 2 minutes or until light brown; drain on paper towels. Yield: 3 dozen.

UPSIDE-DOWN PIZZA

1¹/2 lb. ground beef	*12 oz. mozzarella cheese, shredded*
1 med. onion, chopped	
1 16-oz. can spaghetti sauce with mushrooms	*8 oz. Colby cheese shredded*
2 4-oz. jars mushroom stems and pieces, drained	*2 eggs*
	1 c. milk
	1 c. all-purpose flour
1 lg. green bell pepper, chopped	*¹/2 tsp. salt*
	1 tbsp. oil
1 c. chopped green olives	*¹/2 c. Parmesan cheese*

Brown ground beef with onion in skillet, stirring until crumbly; drain. Stir in spaghetti sauce, mushrooms, green pepper and green olives. Spread in greased 9x13-inch baking dish. Sprinkle mozzarella cheese and Colby cheese over top. Set aside. Beat eggs with milk, flour, salt, oil and Parmesan cheese in bowl. Pour over ground beef mixture. Bake at 400 degrees for 40 to 45 minutes or until golden brown. Cut into squares. Serve upside-down or right side up. Yield: 4 servings.

Plum

DAMSON PIE

2 tbsp. margarine	*1 tsp. vanilla extract*
2 tbsp. all-purpose flour	*¹/4 c. damson plum preserves*
1 c. packed brown sugar	*2 egg whites*
2 c. milk	*1 unbaked 9-inch pie shell*
2 egg yolks	

Combine margarine, all-purpose flour and brown sugar in mixer bowl. Mix in milk, egg yolks and vanilla. Stir in preserves. Beat egg whites in mixer bowl until stiff peaks form. Fold into preserve mixture. Pour into pie shell. Bake at 350 degrees for 25 to 30 minutes. Yield: 6 servings.

PLUM CAKE

2 c. self-rising flour	1 tsp. cinnamon
2 c. sugar	1 tsp. cloves
1 c. oil	1 16-oz. package
3 eggs	confectioners' sugar
2 sm. jars plum	1/4 c. milk
baby food	1 tbsp. lemon juice

Combine first 7 ingredients in mixer bowl; mix for 3 minutes. Pour into 2 greased and floured loaf pans or 1 tube pan. Bake at 325 degrees for 1 hour. Mix confectioners' sugar, milk and lemon juice in bowl. Drizzle over warm cake. Yield: 16 servings.

Popcorn

CARAMEL POPCORN

2 qt. popped popcorn	1/4 tsp. salt
1/2 c. margarine	2 tsp. vanilla extract
3/4 c. packed light	1/4 tsp. soda
brown sugar	1 c. peanuts
1/4 c. light corn syrup	

Place popcorn in large heatproof bowl in oven. Melt margarine in large heavy saucepan. Add sugar, corn syrup and salt. Bring to a boil, stirring constantly. Boil over medium heat for 5 minutes; do not stir. Remove from heat. Stir in vanilla and soda quickly. Pour over popcorn, stirring until coated. Mix in peanuts. Pour into greased 10x15-inch baking pan. Bake at 250 degrees for 1 hour, stirring every 15 minutes. Cool. Break into pieces. Store in airtight container. Yield: 8 cups.

PEPPY POPCORN

8 c. popped popcorn	1/2 c. Parmesan cheese
11/2 c. canned	1/4 c. margarine
shoestring potatoes	1/2 tsp. onion powder
7 oz. roasted salted	1/2 tsp. chili powder
peanuts	1/2 tsp. garlic salt

Combine popcorn, potatoes, peanuts and Parmesan cheese in large bowl. Melt margarine in saucepan. Add seasonings; mix well. Pour over popcorn mixture, tossing to mix well. Yield: 10 cups.

PERKY POPCORN

6 c. popped popcorn	1/3 c. sugar
2 c. pretzel sticks,	1/4 c. honey
broken	1/4 c. light corn syrup
2 c. peanut "M&M's"	1/3 c. peanut butter
Chocolate Candies	1/2 tsp. vanilla extract

Mix popcorn, pretzels and "M&M's" in large bowl. Combine sugar, honey and corn syrup in 1-quart saucepan. Bring to a full boil, stirring constantly. Boil for 2 minutes, stirring constantly; remove from heat. Stir in peanut butter and vanilla until smooth. Pour over popcorn mixture; toss to coat well. Spread on baking sheet. Bake at 250 degrees for 30 minutes, stirring after 15 minutes. Cool. Break into pieces. Yield: 10 cups.

POPPYCOCK

1 c. melted margarine	1/2 tsp. soda
2 c. sugar	5 qt. popped popcorn
1/2 c. light corn syrup	1 c. almonds
1 tsp. salt	1 c. pecan halves
1 tsp. vanilla extract	

Bring margarine, sugar, corn syrup and salt to a boil in saucepan, stirring constantly. Cook for 5 minutes; do not stir. Remove from heat. Stir in vanilla and soda. Pour over popcorn and nuts in large bowl. Spread in two 9x13-inch baking pans. Bake for 1 to 11/2 hours, stirring every 20 minutes. Store in airtight containers. Yield: 12 cups.

Poppy Seed

FOOD PROCESSOR POPPY SEED CAKE

1 2-layer pkg.	1 tsp. almond extract
yellow cake mix	1/4 c. poppy seed
1 sm. package vanilla	1/2 c. confectioners'
instant pudding mix	sugar
1/2 c. oil	1 tbsp. margarine,
3/4 c. water	softened
4 eggs	Lemon juice

Process first 7 ingredients in food processor until smooth. Pour into greased bundt pan. Bake at 350 degrees for 45 minutes. Cool in pan for 5 minutes. Invert onto cake plate to cool. Glaze with mixture of remaining ingredients. Yield: 16 servings.

POPPY SEED DRESSING

3/4 c. sugar	1 sm. onion, chopped
2 tsp. dry mustard	2 c. safflower oil
2 tsp. salt	2 to 3 tbsp. poppy seed
2/3 c. vinegar	

Combine first 6 ingredients in blender container. Process for 1 minute. Add poppy seed. Process several seconds. Store in refrigerator. Yield: 31/2 cups.

Pork

ROAST PORK WITH ORANGE GLAZE

1 4 to 5-lb. boneless
   double loin roast,
   rolled and tied
1 clove of garlic
1 c. sweet orange
   marmalade
1/2 tsp. ground ginger

Place roast lean side down on rack in open roasting pan. Insert meat thermometer. Bake at 325 degrees for 2 to 3 hours or to 170 degrees on meat thermometer. Combine garlic, marmalade and ginger in saucepan. Cook over low heat until mixture bubbles, stirring constantly. Remove garlic. Brush glaze over roast 2 or 3 times during the last 30 minutes of roasting. Place roast on platter. Serve with remaining glaze. Yield: 8 to 10 servings.

BAKED STUFFED PORK CHOPS

4 1-in. rib pork
   chops with pockets
1/2 c. chopped celery
2 tbsp. minced onion
1 tbsp. margarine
1 c. chopped
   unpeeled apple
1/4 c. raisins
1 c. dry bread crumbs
Dash of pepper
1/4 tsp. sage
1 tsp. salt
1/2 c. apple juice
Salt and pepper to taste

Wipe chops with moist paper towels; set aside. Sauté celery and onion in margarine in skillet for 8 minutes; remove from heat. Add apple, raisins bread crumbs and seasonings; toss with fork until mixed. Spoon into pockets in chops. Brown chops on both sides in skillet; place in 2-quart baking dish. Sprinkle with apple juice and salt and pepper. Bake, covered, at 350 degrees for 1 1/4 hours or until tender. Yield: 4 servings.

EASY ITALIAN PORK DINNER

4 lg. pork loin chops
1/4 c. Italian salad
   dressing
2 tbsp. oil
4 med. potatoes,
   peeled, thinly sliced
1 sm. onion, sliced
2 tbsp. margarine
2 tbsp. Italian salad
   dressing
1/4 c. shredded
   mozzarella cheese

Marinate pork chops in 1/4 cup Italian salad dressing for 3 hours, turning occasionally. Remove chops from marinade. Brown chops on both sides in oil in skillet over medium heat. Sprinkle with salt and pepper. Return browned chops to marinade in baking dish. Layer potatoes and onion over chops. Dot with butter. Drizzle with remaining 2 tablespoons Italian salad dressing. Sprinkle mozzarella cheese over top. Cover with foil. Bake at

375 degrees for 1 hour and 15 minutes or until chops and potatoes are tender. Yield: 4 servings.

PIZZA PORK CHOPS

8 thick chops with
   pocket
8 1-in. cubes
   mozzarella cheese
Seasoned salt to taste
2 tbsp. corn oil
2 env. spaghetti
   sauce mix
1 16-oz. can stewed
   tomatoes
1 6-oz. can tomato
   paste
1 med. onion, chopped
8 oz. Cheddar cheese,
   shredded

Place mozzarella cubes in pork chop pockets; fasten with toothpick. Rub with seasoned salt. Brown in oil in skillet; place in baking pan. Bring next 4 ingredients to a boil in saucepan. Pour over chops. Bake at 350 degrees for 30 minutes. Top with Cheddar cheese. Bake for 30 minutes longer. Yield: 8 servings.

SAUERKRAUT AND SPARERIBS

2 to 3 lb. spareribs
1/2 c. hot water
1 onion, sliced
1/4 c. packed brown
   sugar
1 27-oz. can
   sauerkraut, drained
2 apples, peeled, sliced
2 tbsp. vinegar
2 lb. small potatoes,
   peeled
2 tbsp. mustard
2 tbsp. brown sugar

Brown spareribs in skillet. Simmer, covered, in hot water for 2 hours or until tender; drain. Combine next 5 ingredients in shallow baking dish. Arrange potatoes around edges. Bake, covered, at 350 degrees for 1 1/2 hours or until potatoes are tender. Arrange ribs over sauerkraut. Brush with mixture of remaining ingredients. Bake for 10 minutes or until glazed. Yield: 4 servings.

PORK TENDERLOIN WITH OLIVES AND MUSHROOMS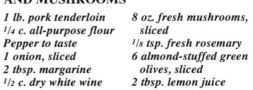

1 lb. pork tenderloin
1/4 c. all-purpose flour
Pepper to taste
1 onion, sliced
2 tbsp. margarine
1/2 c. dry white wine
8 oz. fresh mushrooms,
   sliced
1/8 tsp. fresh rosemary
6 almond-stuffed green
   olives, sliced
2 tbsp. lemon juice

Cut tenderloin into 1-inch slices. Coat with mixture of flour and pepper. Sauté with onion in margarine in skillet. Bring wine to a boil. Pour over tenderloin. Add mushrooms and rosemary. Simmer, covered, for 30 minutes. Add olives and lemon juice. Cook until heated through. Garnish with parsley. Yield: 4 servings.

TENDERLOIN MANDARIN SALAD 🍎

1¹/₂ lb. pork tenderloin, sliced ¹/₄ inch thick
¹/₂ c. teriyaki sauce
2 tbsp. brown sugar
2 tbsp. Bourbon (opt.)
1 lb. fresh spinach, torn
1 red apple, cubed
11 oz. mandarin oranges, drained
¹/₂ c. chopped scallions
¹/₄ c. oil
2 tbsp. red wine vinegar
1¹/₂ tbsp. sugar
1 tbsp. sesame seed
¹/₄ tsp. salt
¹/₄ tsp. dry mustard
¹/₄ tsp. paprika
¹/₈ tsp. Tabasco sauce

Marinate tenderloin in mixture of teriyaki sauce, brown sugar and Bourbon in refrigerator for 2 hours. Stir-fry in skillet. Combine spinach, apple, oranges, scallions and pork in salad bowl. Mix oil, red wine vinegar, sugar, sesame seed, salt, dry mustard, paprika and Tabasco sauce in small saucepan. Heat until warm. Pour over salad. Yield: 6 servings.

GREEN CHILI STEW

1¹/₂ lb. pork steak, chopped
¹/₄ c. corn oil
¹/₄ c. all-purpose flour
Garlic salt to taste
Pepper to taste
1 onion, chopped
1 tsp. cilantro
2 c. water
2 16-oz. cans stewed tomatoes
2 4-oz. cans green chilies
1 16-oz. can tomato juice

Cook pork in oil in skillet until brown, stirring frequently. Sprinkle with flour. Pour into Crock•Pot. Add remaining ingredients; mix well. Cook on Low for 4 hours or longer. Serve with flour tortillas filled with melted cheese. Yield: 6 to 8 servings.

Potato

BAKED POTATOES AND ONIONS

6 med. onions
6 med. potatoes
¹/₂ c. melted margarine
¹/₈ tsp. garlic powder
³/₄ tsp. salt
¹/₄ tsp. pepper
¹/₂ tsp. parsley flakes

Slice onions and unpeeled potatoes. Arrange in 3 rows in 9x13-inch baking dish, alternating potato and onion slices and overlapping slightly. Mix remaining ingredients in bowl. Drizzle over potatoes and onions. Bake, covered, at 400 degrees for 40 minutes. Bake, uncovered, for 20 minutes longer. Yield: 8 servings.

CHANTILLY POTATOES

3 c. mashed cooked potatoes
¹/₂ c. heavy cream
¹/₂ c. shredded Swiss cheese
Salt and pepper to taste

Spread potatoes in baking dish. Whip cream in mixer bowl until soft peaks form. Fold in cheese. Add seasonings. Spread over potatoes. Bake at 350 degrees for 30 minutes. Yield: 4 servings.

CROCK•POT POTATOES

10 med. potatoes
1 med. onion, chopped
1 8-oz. container sour cream
2 10-oz. cans Cheddar cheese soup
¹/₂ c. melted margarine

Place potatoes and onion in Crock•Pot. Blend sour cream, soup and margarine in bowl. Add to potatoes. Cook on High for 3 or 4 hours. May prepare with cooked potatoes. Cook on Low for 1 hour. Yield: 15 servings.

FRENCH-FRIED POTATO CASSEROLE

³/₄ c. chopped green bell pepper
³/₄ c. chopped celery
¹/₃ c. margarine
¹/₃ c. all-purpose flour
¹/₂ tsp. salt
¹/₈ tsp. pepper
3 c. milk
³/₄ c. coarsely shredded carrots
¹/₃ c. chopped pimento
³/₄ c. shredded American cheese
1 32-oz. package frozen French-fried potatoes

Sauté green pepper and celery in margarine in large saucepan until tender but not brown. Stir in flour, salt and pepper. Add milk all at once. Cook until bubbly, stirring constantly. Cook for 1 minute longer, stirring constantly. Add carrots, pimento and half the cheese, stirring until cheese is melted. Combine potatoes and cheese sauce in 9x13-inch baking dish. Bake at 375 degrees for 30 minutes. Sprinkle remaining cheese on top. Bake for 5 minutes longer. Garnish with additional chopped green pepper. Yield: 12 servings.

HOMEMADE POTATO SOUP

6 lg. potatoes
2 med. onions, chopped
4 chicken bouillon cubes
1 tbsp. parsley flakes
1 tbsp. salt
5 to 6 c. water
¹/₂ c. margarine
¹/₄ tsp. pepper
1 12-oz. can evaporated milk
¹/₂ c. all-purpose flour

Peel and chop potatoes. Combine with onions, bouillon, parsley, salt, water, margarine, pepper, evaporated milk and flour in Crock•Pot; mix well. Cook on Low for 10 to 12 hours. Yield: 6 servings.

MASHED POTATO CASSEROLE

8 to 10 med. potatoes,
  peeled, chopped
Salt and pepper to taste
8 oz. cream cheese,
  softened
2 tbsp. all-purpose
  flour

2 eggs, slightly beaten
3 tbsp. minced fresh
  parsley
2 tbsp. minced chives
1 3-oz. can French-
  fried onions

Cook potatoes in water to cover in saucepan until tender; drain. Combine with salt and pepper in mixer bowl; beat until smooth. Add cream cheese; beat until smooth. Beat in flour, eggs, parsley and chives. Spoon into greased 8x12-inch baking dish. Crush onions lightly; sprinkle over top. Bake at 325 degrees for 30 minutes or until puffed and golden brown. Yield: 8 servings.

NEW SPRING POTATOES

6 green onions,
  coarsely chopped
2 tbsp. margarine
4 thick slices bacon,
  chopped
1 c. beef broth

1 c. chopped peeled
  tomatoes
24 sm. new potatoes
Salt and pepper to taste
Chopped parsley

Sauté green onions in margarine in 6-quart saucepan until light brown. Add bacon. Cook for 5 minutes. Add beef broth and tomatoes. Bring to a boil. Cook for 2 minutes. Add potatoes and salt and pepper. Simmer, covered, for 15 minutes or until potatoes are tender. Spoon into serving bowl; sprinkle with parsley. Yield: 4 servings.

SICILIAN POTATOES

8 med. potatoes
3/4 c. olive oil
2 tbsp. garlic powder
1 tbsp. salt

1 tsp. pepper
2 tbsp. oregano
1 c. Parmesan cheese
2 tbsp. paprika

Cut potatoes into halves lengthwise. Coat well with olive oil. Place cut side up on greased baking sheet. Sprinkle with mixture of garlic powder, salt and pepper. Top with oregano, cheese and paprika. Bake at 350 degrees for 1 hour or until tender, turning potatoes over if topping becomes too brown. Yield: 8 servings.

GREEK POTATO SALAD

1 1/2 lb. new potatoes
1/4 c. fresh lemon juice
1/2 c. drained pimento
1/2 c. pitted black olives
3 scallions, minced

3/4 tsp. dried oregano
1/4 c. olive oil
1/2 c. feta cheese,
  crumbled
Salt and pepper to taste

Cut unpeeled potatoes into bite-sized pieces. Steam in steamer for 8 to 10 minutes or until tender; drain. Place in large bowl. Add 2 teaspoons lemon juice; toss gently. Cool. Add pimento, black olives and scallions. Combine remaining lemon juice, oregano and olive oil in small bowl; whisk until blended. Pour over potato mixture. Add cheese and seasonings; toss gently. Yield: 6 servings.

Pound Cake

BROWN SUGAR POUND CAKE

1 lb. light brown sugar
1 c. sugar
1 1/2 c. shortening
5 eggs
3 c. all-purpose flour

1 tsp. baking powder
1/2 tsp. salt
1 c. milk
1 tsp. vanilla extract

Cream sugars and shortening in mixer bowl. Add eggs 1 at a time, beating well after each addition. Sift flour, baking powder and salt 3 times. Add to creamed mixture alternately with milk, mixing well after each addition. Mix in vanilla. Pour into greased bundt pan. Bake at 375 degrees for 1 hour. Cool. Invert onto serving plate. Yield: 12 servings.

APRICOT POUND CAKE

1 3/4 c. sugar
1 c. vegetable oil
3 eggs
1 7 3/4-oz. jar apricots
  with tapioca baby
  food

2 c. all-purpose flour
1 tsp. salt
2 tsp. baking powder
Confectioners' sugar
  glaze

Mix sugar and oil in bowl. Add eggs and baby food; mix well. Add dry ingredients; mix well. Pour into bundt pan sprayed with nonstick cooking spray. Bake at 350 degrees for 40 minutes. Cool. Invert onto serving plate. Garnish with thin confectioners' sugar glaze. Yield: 12 servings.

Praline

PRALINE CREME DESSERT

2 eggs
3 c. packed light
  brown sugar
3/4 c. all-purpose flour

1 tsp. soda
1 c. chopped pecans
2 c. whipping cream
Sugar to taste

Beat eggs in mixer bowl until frothy. Blend in brown sugar. Add flour, soda and pecans; mix well. Spread in greased 9x13-inch baking pan. Bake for 35 to 40 minutes or until golden brown. This usually rises during baking but will fall. Cool completely. Cut or break into 1/4 to 1/2-inch pieces. Whip cream in mixer bowl; sweeten with sugar to taste. Fold in crumbs. Spread in 9x13-inch pan. Freeze for 24 hours or longer. Cut into squares. Yield: 12 servings.

STRAWBERRY AND CREAM PRALINES

*1/2 c. packed brown
  sugar*
1/4 c. butter
1/4 c. light corn syrup
Dash of salt

1/8 c. ground pecans
1/4 c. all-purpose flour
Whipped cream
Strawberries

Combine brown sugar, butter, corn syrup and salt in saucepan. Bring to a boil, stirring constantly to prevent burning. Add pecans and flour; mix well. Remove from heat. Drop by teaspoonfuls 3 inches apart onto foil-lined cookie sheet. Bake at 350 degrees for 8 minutes. Cool on wire rack. Place praline on serving plate. Spread circle of whipped cream on top. Arrange strawberries in circle; dot strawberries with whipped cream. Repeat layers 2 times. Garnish with rosette of whipped cream and whole strawberry. Yield: 9 servings.

Prune

PRUNE CAKE

3/4 c. butter, softened
1 1/2 c. sugar
3 eggs
3 tbsp. sour cream
2 c. all-purpose flour
1 tsp. soda
1 tsp. cinnamon
1 tsp. allspice
1/4 tsp. salt

*1 c. chopped cooked
  prunes*
1 c. chopped walnuts
*1 16-oz. package
  confectioners' sugar*
1/4 c. milk
*1 tbsp. lemon or
  orange juice*

Cream butter and sugar in mixer bowl until light and fluffy. Blend in eggs. Add sour cream alternately with flour, soda, cinnamon, allspice and salt, mixing well after each addition. Stir in prunes and walnuts. Spoon into greased and floured 10-inch tube pan. Bake at 325 degrees for 25 minutes or until cake tests done. Combine confectioners' sugar, milk and lemon juice in mixer bowl; mix well. Drizzle glaze over warm cake. Remove to wire rack to cool. Yield: 16 servings.

PRUNE-BRAN MUFFINS

1 1/3 c. All-Bran cereal
1 c. all-purpose flour
2 tsp. baking powder
1/2 tsp. soda
1/4 tsp. salt
*16 whole moist
  pitted prunes*
1/2 c. sugar

3/4 c. buttermilk
1/4 c. oil
2 eggs
1 tsp. vanilla extract
*1 c. finely chopped
  pecans, walnuts
  or almonds*
Cinnamon-sugar

Process All-Bran cereal in food processor container fitted with metal blade for 30 seconds or until finely chopped. Add flour, baking powder, soda, salt, prunes, sugar, buttermilk, oil, eggs and vanilla. Process for 3 seconds. Scrape down side of bowl. Process for 2 seconds. Stir in pecans. Fill 12 greased muffin cups 2/3 full. Bake in center of 375-degree oven for 25 minutes or until muffins are firm to the touch and tops are golden brown. Sprinkle with cinnamon-sugar. Cool in muffin cups for 8 minutes. Remove to wire rack. Serve warm. Yield: 12 servings.

Pudding

UPDATED STEAMED PUDDING

1 c. boiling water
1 c. Grape Nuts cereal
1/2 c. butter
1 c. sugar
2 eggs
1 tsp. vanilla extract

1 1/4 c. all-purpose flour
1 tsp. baking powder
1 tsp. soda
1 tsp. cinnamon
1/2 tsp. salt

Pour boiling water over Grape Nuts and butter in bowl. Let stand for 5 minutes or until softened. Add sugar, eggs and vanilla; mix well. Add sifted flour, baking powder, soda, cinnamon and salt; mix well. Pour into greased 8x8-inch baking pan. Bake at 350 degrees for 35 minutes or until pudding springs back when touched lightly. Cut into squares. Spoon warm Vanilla Sauce over pudding. Yield: 6 servings.

Vanilla Sauce

1 1/2 c. sugar
1 tbsp. cornstarch
Dash of salt

1/2 c. water
1/4 c. butter
1 tsp. vanilla extract

Mix sugar, cornstarch and salt in saucepan. Stir in water gradually. Cook over medium heat until sugar dissolves completely, stirring constantly. Bring to a boil; do not stir. Boil for several minutes; remove from heat. Sauce will be thin. Stir in butter until melted. Add vanilla. Yield: 2 cups.

BREAD PUDDING WITH AMARETTO

1 loaf stale French bread	2 tbsp. cinnamon
1 qt. milk	2 tsp. vanilla extract
4 jumbo eggs	3/4 c. sugar
2 c. sugar	1/2 c. butter
1 c. raisins	1 egg, slightly beaten
	1/2 c. Amaretto

Soak bread in milk in bowl for 1 hour. Mix in 4 eggs, 2 cups sugar, raisins, cinnamon and vanilla. Pour into 9x13-inch baking pan. Bake at 350 degrees for 1 hour. Blend 3/4 cup sugar and butter in saucepan over medium heat, stirring constantly. Stir in 1 egg. Cook for 1 minute, stirring constantly; remove from heat. Add Amaretto. Spoon over warm bread pudding. Yield: 12 servings.

Pumpkin

PUMPKIN RAISIN BREAD

3 1/2 c. all-purpose flour	4 eggs
3 c. sugar	2 c. pumpkin
2 tsp. soda	3/4 c. water
1 tbsp. cinnamon	1 c. raisins
1 1/2 tsp. salt	1 c. chopped pecans
1 c. oil	

Sift dry ingredients into bowl. Add oil, eggs, pumpkin and water, mixing well. Stir in raisins and pecans. Spoon into two greased and floured 5x9-inch pans. Bake at 350 degrees for 65 minutes. Remove to wire rack to cool. Yield: 24 slices.

PUMPKIN CHEESECAKE

1 c. sifted all-purpose flour	2 1/2 c. sugar
1/4 c. sugar	1 tsp. ginger
1 tsp. grated lemon rind	1 tsp. cinnamon
1/4 tsp. ginger	1/2 tsp. cloves
1 egg yolk	1 1/2 tsp. allspice
1/4 c. butter	1 1/2 tsp. vanilla extract
40 oz. cream cheese, softened	5 eggs
3 tbsp. all-purpose flour	2 egg yolks
	1/4 c. whipping cream
	1 c. puréed pumpkin

Combine first 6 ingredients in bowl. Remove bottom of springform pan. Roll pastry onto bottom; trim to fit. Roll and cut strips to fit side of pan. Reassemble pan. Bake at 400 degrees for 7 minutes. Cool. Combine cream cheese, flour, 2 1/2 cups sugar, spices and vanilla in bowl. Add eggs and egg yolks 1 at a time, beating well after each addition. Add cream and pumpkin. Pour into prepared pan. Bake at 325 degrees for 1 1/2 hours. Cool on wire rack. Chill for 3 hours. Remove side of pan. Yield: 20 servings.

PUMPKIN PECAN PIE

4 eggs, slightly beaten	1/4 tsp. salt
3/4 c. sugar	1 unbaked 9-in. pie shell
1 tsp. cinnamon	1 c. pecan halves
1 16-oz. can pumpkin	
1/2 c. dark corn syrup	

Combine first 6 ingredients in bowl. Pour into pie shell. Arrange pecan halves on top. Bake at 350 degrees for 45 to 50 minutes. Cool on wire rack. Yield: 8 servings.

PUMPKIN PIE SQUARES

1 18-oz. package yellow cake mix	2 eggs
1/2 c. melted margarine	2 1/2 tsp. pumpkin pie spice
1 egg	2/3 c. milk
1 16-oz. can pumpkin	1 tsp. cinnamon
1/2 c. packed brown sugar	1/2 c. chopped walnuts
	1/4 c. margarine

Reserve 1 cup cake mix. Combine remaining cake mix, melted margarine and 1 egg in bowl. Press over bottom of 9x13-inch baking pan. Combine pumpkin, brown sugar, 2 eggs, pie spice and milk in bowl; beat until smooth. Pour into prepared pan. Mix reserved cake mix, cinnamon, walnuts and margarine in small bowl; sprinkle over pumpkin layer. Bake at 350 degrees for 45 minutes. Cool. Serve with whipped cream. Yield: 16 servings.

Quiche

QUICHE

6 slices crisp-fried bacon, crumbled	1 tbsp. all-purpose flour
12 thin slices Swiss cheese, crumbled	Cayenne pepper, nutmeg and pepper to taste
1 unbaked 9-inch pie shell	2 c. half and half
4 eggs	

Sprinkle bacon and cheese into pie shell. Combine remaining ingredients in blender container; process until well mixed. Pour into pie shell. Bake at 400 degrees for 15 minutes. Reduce temperature to 325 degrees. Bake for 30 minutes. All ingredients should be at room temperature. Yield: 8 servings.

PIZZA-STYLE QUICHE

1 unbaked 9-in. deep-dish pie shell	3 eggs
1/3 c. chopped pepperoni	1 1/3 c. milk
1/2 c. chopped onion	3 tbsp. all-purpose flour
1/3 c. chopped green bell pepper	1/2 tsp. garlic salt
3/4 c. shredded Cheddar cheese	1/8 tsp. pepper
	1 c. pizza sauce
	1 tbsp. Parmesan cheese

Bake pie shell at 425 for 6 minutes. Reduce temperature to 350 degrees. Sauté pepperoni, onion and green pepper in skillet; spoon into pie shell. Add shredded cheese. Process eggs, milk, flour and seasonings in blender container until smooth. Pour over cheese. Top with pizza sauce and Parmesan cheese. Bake for 25 to 30 minutes or until knife inserted near center comes out clean. Yield: 6 servings.

FRESH SPINACH QUICHE

1 Whole Wheat Pie Shell	1/2 c. shredded provolone cheese
6 oz. mushrooms	2 eggs, beaten
1 med. onion, chopped	1 c. milk
1/2 tsp. oregano	1/2 c. cottage cheese
2 tbsp. oil	1/2 tsp. salt
4 c. chopped spinach, drained	Nutmeg to taste

Prick bottom of pie shell with fork. Bake at 375 degrees for 5 minutes. Reduce temperature to 350 degrees. Sauté chopped mushrooms, onion and oregano in oil in skillet. Spoon into pie shell. Layer spinach and provolone cheese over top. Pour mixture of eggs, milk, cottage cheese and salt over top. Sprinkle with nutmeg. Bake for 40 to 50 minutes. Let stand for 10 minutes before serving. Yield: 6 servings.

Whole Wheat Pie Shell

1/2 c. shortening	1 1/4 c. whole wheat flour
1/2 tsp. salt	

Cut shortening into salt and flour in bowl. Add enough cold water to make dough; mix well. Roll 1/8 inch thick on floured surface. Fit into plate.

Raisin

RAISIN AND APPLE CAKE

Photograph for this recipe is on page 53.

1 1/2 c. oil	1/2 tsp. salt
2 c. sugar	1/4 tsp. nutmeg
3 eggs	2 c. finely chopped, peeled apples
1 tsp. vanilla extract	1 c. raisins
2 c. all-purpose flour	3/4 c. finely chopped walnuts
1 c. whole wheat flour	
1 tsp. soda	
1 tsp. cinnamon	

Beat oil and sugar in mixer bowl until thick. Add eggs 1 at a time, beating well after each addition. Blend in vanilla. Sift in flour, whole wheat flour, soda, cinnamon, salt and nutmeg. Stir in apples, raisins and walnuts. Pour into greased and floured 10-inch cake pan. Bake at 325 degrees for 1 hour and 5 minutes. Cool in pan on wire rack for 15 minutes. Remove to cake plate to cool completely. Store, wrapped in foil, before slicing. Yield: 10 servings.

RAISIN-FILLED COOKIES

1/2 c. sugar	1 c. shortening
2 tbsp. all-purpose flour	2 c. packed brown sugar
1/8 tsp. salt	3 eggs
1 c. water	3 1/2 c. all-purpose flour
1 tsp. vanilla extract	1 tbsp. vanilla extract
1 15-oz. package raisins	1/8 tsp. salt
	1 tsp. (heaping) soda

Combine sugar, 2 tablespoons flour and 1/8 teaspoon salt in saucepan. Blend in water and 1 teaspoon vanilla. Add raisins. Cook until thickened, stirring constantly. Cool. Cream shortening and brown sugar in mixer bowl. Blend in eggs. Add 3 1/2 cups flour, 1 tablespoon vanilla, 1/8 teaspoon salt and soda; mix well. Chill dough. Roll dough on floured surface. Cut into 3-inch circles. Spoon raisin filling onto half the cookies. Top with remaining cookies. Do not seal edges. Place on cookie sheet. Bake at 350 degrees for 8 minutes. Cool on wire rack. Yield: 36 cookies.

Raspberry

RASPBERRY BARS

2¹/2 c. all-purpose flour
1 c. margarine
1 c. sugar
1 egg
1 c. chopped pecans
1 10-oz. jar raspberry
  preserves

Combine flour, margarine, sugar, egg and pecans in mixer bowl. Beat at low speed until crumbly. Reserve 1¹/2 cups mixture. Press remaining mixture into greased 9x13-inch baking pan. Spread preserves to within ¹/2 inch of edge. Top with reserved crumbs. Bake at 350 degrees for 40 to 45 minutes. Cool completely. Cut into bars. Yield: 24 bars.

APPLE RASPBERRY CRUMBLE

3 Granny Smith
  apples, peeled, sliced
Juice of 1 lemon
1 10-oz. package
  frozen raspberries
1 c. all-purpose flour
¹/2 c. sugar
¹/2 c. unsalted butter
¹/4 tsp. nutmeg

Arrange apples in buttered 8x8-inch baking dish. Sprinkle with lemon juice. Drain raspberries. Sprinkle over apples. Mix flour and sugar in bowl. Cut in butter until crumbly. Add nutmeg. Sprinkle over fruit. Bake at 375 degrees for 25 minutes. Serve with whipped cream. Yield: 4 servings.

RED RASPBERRY AMBER PIE

1 c. sugar
¹/4 tsp. salt
1 c. sour cream
¹/4 c. all-purpose flour
2 c. red raspberries
  with juice
1 baked 9-in. pie shell

Combine sugar, salt, sour cream, flour and raspberries in saucepan; mix well. Bring to a boil, stirring until thickened. Pour into cooled pie shell. Yield: 6 servings.

RASPBERRY FLOATING ISLAND

Photograph for this recipe is on page 105.

¹/3 c. apricot nectar
1 tbsp. Amaretto
  (opt.)
1¹/2 lb. fresh apricots
1 pound cake
1 pt. raspberry and
  cream sorbet and
  cream
1 pt. raspberries
Mint leaves

Combine nectar and Amaretto in bowl; mix well. Combine apricots and ¹/4 cup of nectar mixture in blender container; purée until smooth. Spoon ¹/4 cup onto 4 serving plates. Trim crust from cake;

slice into 12 slices. Cut each slice into a diamond. Arrange 3 diamonds on each plate. Brush with remaining nectar mixture. Place 1 scoop sorbet on top. Garnish with raspberries and mint leaves. Yield: 4 servings.

RASPBERRY CREAM PIE

8 oz. cream cheese
1 tsp. milk
¹/3 c. sugar
1 c. sour cream
1 tbsp. grated orange
  rind
1 tsp. vanilla extract
2 c. whipped topping
1 baked 9-in. graham
  cracker pie shell
1 c. orange sections
¹/4 cup raspberry jam

Soften cream cheese. Combine with milk and sugar in mixer bowl. Beat until light and fluffy. Add sour cream, orange rind and vanilla; mix well. Fold in whipped topping. Spoon into pie shell. Chill for 4 hours or longer. Arrange orange sections over chilled filling. Strain raspberry jam. Spoon over oranges. Yield: 6 to 8 servings.

RASPBERRY RIBBON PIE

1 3-oz. package
  raspberry gelatin
¹/4 c. sugar
1¹/4 c. boiling water
1 10-oz. package
  frozen red
  raspberries
1 tbsp. lemon juice
1 tsp. vanilla extract
3 oz. cream cheese,
  softened
¹/3 c. confectioners'
  sugar
¹/4 tsp. salt
1 c. whipping cream,
  whipped
1 baked 9-in. pie shell

Dissolve gelatin and sugar in boiling water in bowl. Add raspberries and lemon juice. Stir until raspberries thaw. Chill until partially set. Beat vanilla extract, cream cheese, confectioners' sugar and salt in bowl until smooth. Fold in ¹/4 of the whipped cream. Fold in remaining whipped cream. Layer half the cream cheese mixture, all the raspberry mixture and remaining cream cheese mixture in pie shell. Chill for several hours. Yield: 6 servings.

TWO-BERRY PARFAITS

1 10-oz. package
  frozen raspberries
¹/4 c. sugar
2 tbsp. cornstarch
2 c. sliced strawberries
2 tsp. lemon juice
1 qt. vanilla ice cream
1 c. sour cream

Drain raspberries, reserving juice. Add enough water to reserved juice to measure 1 cup. Stir into mixture of sugar and cornstarch in saucepan. Add strawberries. Bring to a boil over medium-high heat, stirring constantly. Stir in raspberries and lemon juice. Chill. Layer ice cream, berry sauce, sour cream and berry sauce in parfait glasses. Repeat layers. Yield: 8 servings.

Relish

EASY CRANBERRY RELISH

1/4 c. orange juice
2 tsp. lemon juice
1 12-oz. package
cranberries
1 1/2 c. sugar

2 1-in. strips orange
rind
1/2 c. chopped pecans
1 lemon slice

Combine first 5 ingredients in saucepan. Simmer for 15 minutes or until cranberries burst, stirring frequently. Remove orange rind. Stir in pecans. Pour relish into serving dish. Garnish with lemon twist. Serve warm or chilled. Yield: 2 cups.

APPLE AND BEET RELISH

6 c. chopped cooked
beets
6 c. chopped peeled
apples
2 lg. onions, cut into
quarters

1 1/2 c. sugar
1 1/2 c. vinegar
2 2-in. cinnamon
sticks
1/2 c. water

Shred first 3 ingredients in food processor container. Combine remaining ingredients in large saucepan. Simmer, covered, for 20 to 25 minutes, stirring frequently. Remove cinnamon sticks. Ladle into hot sterilized 1/2-pint jars, leaving 1/2-inch headspace; seal with 2-piece lids. Process in boiling water bath for 15 minutes. Yield: 5 1/2 pints.

ZUCCHINI RELISH

12 c. peeled grated
zucchini
4 c. chopped onions
2 lg. green bell
peppers, chopped
5 tbsp. canning salt
2 1/4 c. white vinegar
2 1/2 c. sugar

1 tsp. celery seed
1 tbsp. cornstarch
1 tsp. nutmeg
1 tsp. dry mustard
1 tsp. turmeric
1 4-oz. jar chopped
pimento

Marinate zucchini, onions and peppers in salt in covered container in refrigerator overnight. Drain. Rinse with cold water; drain well. Combine with remaining ingredients in saucepan. Cook for 30 minutes. Pack hot relish in hot sterilized jars; seal. Yield: 4 quarts.

Rhubarb

YOGURT RHUBARB CAKE

1/2 c. margarine,
softened
1 c. packed brown
sugar
2 eggs
1 tsp. vanilla extract
8 oz. cherry yogurt
3 tbsp. milk
1 c. whole wheat flour
1 c. all-purpose flour
1 1/2 tsp. baking powder

1/2 tsp. soda
1 tsp. cinnamon
1/2 tsp. salt
2 1/2 c. chopped rhubarb
2 tbsp. melted
margarine
1/2 c. packed brown
sugar
1/4 c. all-purpose flour
1 tsp. cinnamon
1/2 c. chopped pecans

Cream 1/2 cup margarine and 1 cup brown sugar in mixer bowl until light and fluffy. Beat in eggs and vanilla. Add yogurt and milk; mix well. Stir in whole wheat flour, 1 cup all-purpose flour, baking powder, soda, 1 teaspoon cinnamon and salt. Fold in rhubarb. Spoon into 9x13-inch cake pan. Combine remaining ingredients in bowl. Sprinkle over cake. Bake at 350 degrees for 45 minutes or until cake tests done. Yield: 15 servings.

RHUBARB DESSERT SALAD

3 c. sliced rhubarb
3/4 c. sugar
1/4 c. water
1 6-oz. package
raspberry gelatin
2 c. pineapple juice

1/2 c. lemon juice
1 apple, chopped
1 13-oz. can crushed
pineapple, drained
1 c. chopped pecans

Bring rhubarb, sugar and 1/4 cup water to a boil in saucepan. Simmer for 5 minutes. Add gelatin; stir until thickened. Stir in next five ingredients. Spoon into serving dish. Chill. Yield: 12 servings.

Zucchini Relish and Apple and Beet Relish...preserve summer's bounty all year.

RHUBARB MERINGUE TORTE

1 c. melted margarine, cooled	2¹/₂ c. sugar
2 c. all-purpose flour	4 egg yolks
2 egg yolks	¹/₄ c. all-purpose flour
¹/₈ tsp. salt	6 egg whites
5 c. finely chopped rhubarb	1 c. sugar

Combine margarine, 2 cups flour, 2 egg yolks and salt in bowl; mix well. Pat mixture into 9x13-inch baking pan. Bake at 350 degrees for 10 minutes or until light brown. Combine rhubarb, 2¹/₂ cups sugar, 4 egg yolks and ¹/₄ cup flour. Pour over baked crust. Bake for 35 minutes. Beat egg whites in bowl until stiff peaks form. Add 1 cup sugar, beating until stiff and glossy. Spread over rhubarb. Bake until brown. Yield: 15 servings.

Rice

ALMOND PILAF

¹/₂ c. rice	¹/₈ tsp. pepper
1 med. onion, chopped	1 tbsp. instant chicken bouillon
¹/₄ c. margarine	3 c. hot water
¹/₂ tsp. salt	¹/₄ c. slivered blanched almonds
¹/₂ tsp. allspice	
¹/₂ tsp. turmeric	
¹/₄ tsp. curry powder	

Sauté rice and onion in margarine in skillet until onion is tender. Stir in salt, allspice, turmeric, curry powder and pepper. Pour into 2-quart baking dish. Stir in instant bouillon and water. Sprinkle with almonds. Bake, covered, at 325 degrees for 40 minutes or until rice is tender. Yield: 6 servings.

GREEN RICE

1 lg. onion, chopped	1 c. cooked rice
2 stalks celery, chopped	1 10-oz. package chopped broccoli, cooked
2 tbsp. oil	
1 can cream of mushroom soup	1 8-oz. jar Cheez Whiz
1 can cream of celery soup	

Sauté onion and celery in oil in skillet until clear. Stir in soups, rice, broccoli and cheese. Spoon into greased medium casserole. Bake at 325 degrees for 25 minutes or until rice is tender. Yield: 4 servings.

RICE JARDIN

³/₄ c. chopped onion	1 16-oz. can whole kernel corn, drained
1¹/₂ lb. zucchini, thinly sliced	1¹/₂ tsp. salt
3 tbsp. margarine	¹/₄ tsp. pepper
3 c. cooked rice	¹/₂ tsp. oregano
1 16-oz. can tomatoes	

Sauté onion and zucchini in margarine in skillet until tender. Add remaining ingredients. Simmer, covered, for 15 minutes. Yield: 8 servings.

PUNJABI RICE PILAF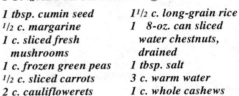

1 tbsp. cumin seed	1¹/₂ c. long-grain rice
¹/₂ c. margarine	1 8-oz. can sliced water chestnuts, drained
1 c. sliced fresh mushrooms	
1 c. frozen green peas	1 tbsp. salt
¹/₂ c. sliced carrots	3 c. warm water
2 c. cauliflowerets	1 c. whole cashews

Sauté cumin seed in margarine in 12-inch skillet for 2 minutes. Add vegetables. Sauté for 5 minutes. Stir in rice, water chestnuts, salt and water; cover. Bring to a boil over medium heat. Stir in cashews; reduce heat. Simmer for 30 minutes. Let stand, covered, for 15 minutes. Yield: 12 servings.

RICE PUDDING

2¹/₂ c. milk	1 tsp. almond extract
¹/₄ tsp. salt	¹/₃ c. sugar
¹/₂ c. rice	¹/₂ c. whipping cream, whipped
1 tsp. vanilla extract	

Heat milk and salt to the boiling point in medium saucepan. Stir in rice; reduce heat. Simmer for 5 minutes, stirring constantly. Cook, covered, until milk is almost absorbed and rice is creamy, stirring occasionally. Stir in vanilla, almond extract and sugar. Pour into large bowl. Chill, covered, for 2 hours. Fold in whipped cream gently. Chill, covered, in refrigerator. Yield: 4 servings.

GOLDEN GARDEN RICE SALAD

Photograph for this recipe is on page 53.

¹/₄ c. olive oil	1¹/₂ c. sliced mushrooms
3 tbsp. white wine vinegar	4 c. cooked rice
2 tsp. Dijon-style mustard	³/₄ c. golden raisins
2 c. broccoli flowerets, blanched	¹/₄ c. sliced green onions
	¹/₄ c. chopped cilantro

Combine olive oil, vinegar and mustard in bowl; blend with wire whisk. Add remaining ingredients; toss to coat. Yield: 6 servings.

SKILLET SPANISH RICE

2 med. onions,
  chopped
1 med. green bell
  pepper, chopped
2 c. rice
1/2 c. corn oil

3 1/2 c. hot water
4 8-oz. cans tomato
  sauce
2 tsp. prepared mustard
Dash of pepper

Sauté onions, green pepper, and rice in oil in skillet over high heat until lightly browned, stirring constantly. Add hot water and remaining ingredients; mix well. Bring to a boil; cover tightly. Simmer for 25 minutes. Yield: 4 to 6 servings.

HARVEST RICE

1 lb. sausage
3 c. cooked rice
1 tart red apple,
  chopped
1/2 c. chopped onion
1/2 c. chopped celery

1/2 c. raisins
1 tbsp. brown sugar
1/2 tsp. salt
1/4 tsp. allspice
1/4 tsp. cinnamon
1/8 tsp. pepper

Preheat oven to 350 degrees. Cook sausage in skillet until brown and crumbly; drain well. Combine with rice, apple, onion, celery, raisins, brown sugar and seasonings in bowl; mix well. Spoon into well-buttered 2-quart baking dish. Bake for 25 minutes. Yield: 8 servings.

EPICUREAN WILD RICE

1/4 c. chopped parsley
1/4 c. chopped green
  onions
1 c. sliced celery
1/3 c. oil
1 1/4 c. wild rice

1/2 c. rice
1 1/2 c. boiling water
1 can consommé
1/2 tsp. marjoram
1/2 tsp. thyme
1/2 c. Sherry

Sauté parsley, green onions and celery in oil in skillet for 10 minutes; do not brown. Add next 6 ingredients. Cook, tightly covered, over low heat for 45 minutes. Stir in Sherry. Cook, uncovered, for 3 minutes longer. Yield: 6 servings.

Rolls

COTTAGE CHEESE DINNER ROLLS

2 pkg. dry yeast
1/2 c. lukewarm water
2 c. small curd
  cottage cheese
1/4 c. sugar

2 eggs, slightly beaten
1/2 tsp. soda
2 tsp. salt
4 c. (or more)
  all-purpose flour

Dissolve yeast in lukewarm water. Heat cottage cheese to lukewarm in saucepan. Combine cottage cheese, yeast, sugar, eggs, soda and salt in bowl. Stir in enough flour to make a soft dough. Place in greased bowl, turning to grease surface. Let rise, covered, in warm place for 1 1/2 hours or until doubled in bulk. Punch dough down. Divide into 2 portions. Shape each portion into 12 rolls. Roll in additional flour. Place in 2 greased 8-inch baking pans. Let rise in warm place until doubled in bulk. Bake at 350 degrees for 20 minutes. Yield: 24 rolls.

CROISSANTS

1 env. dry yeast
1 c. warm water
3/4 c. evaporated milk
1 1/2 tsp. salt
1/3 c. sugar
1 egg

1 c. all-purpose flour
1/2 c. melted margarine
1 c. cold margarine
4 c. all-purpose flour
1 egg
1 tbsp. water

Dissolve yeast in warm water. Add next 5 ingredients. Beat until smooth. Add melted margarine. Cut cold margarine into 4 cups flour in bowl with pastry blender until crumbly. Pour yeast mixture over dry mixture; blend until moistened. Chill, covered, for 4 hours to 4 days. Knead 6 times on floured surface. Divide dough into 4 portions. Chill 3 portions. Roll remaining portion into 17-inch circle. Cut circle into 8 wedges. Roll up from wide end; shape into crescent. Place on foil-lined baking sheet; cover with towel. Let rise in warm place until doubled in bulk. Brush with mixture of egg and water. Bake at 325 degrees for 25 minutes. Yield: 32 croissants.

ENGLISH MUFFIN ROLLS

1 1/4 c. all-purpose flour
1 pkg. dry yeast
1 tbsp. sugar
1 tsp. salt
1 1/4 c. warm water

2 tbsp. shortening
1 1/2 to 2 c. all-purpose
  flour
2 tbsp. cornmeal

Combine 1 1/4 cups flour, yeast, sugar and salt in mixer bowl. Add warm water and shortening. Blend at low speed until moistened. Beat for 3 minutes. Stir in enough remaining 1 1/2 to 2 cups flour to make firm dough. Knead for 5 minutes. Place in greased bowl, turning to grease surface. Let rise, covered, for 45 minutes or until doubled in bulk. Roll on floured surface to 1/4-inch thickness. Cut into 3-inch circles. Place on baking sheet sprinkled with cornmeal. Let rise, covered, for 30 minutes. Bake on lightly oiled griddle for 8 minutes on each side. Yield: 18 rolls.

FABULOUS OVERNIGHT ROLLS

1 c. milk
3/4 c. margarine
1/4 c. sugar
1/2 tsp. salt
1/4 c. water

1 pkg. dry yeast
2 c. unbleached flour
2 eggs
2 c. unbleached flour

Combine milk, margarine, sugar, salt and water in saucepan. Heat to 185 degrees. Combine yeast and 2 cups flour in mixer bowl. Add milk mixture. Beat until smooth. Add eggs; beat well. Add remaining 2 cups flour; beat well. Chill, covered, overnight. Punch dough down. Let rest for 10 minutes. Shape into rolls. Place in greased 10x15-inch baking pan. Let rise until doubled in bulk. Bake at 350 degrees for 12 minutes. Yield: 32 rolls.

PINEAPPLE WHOLE WHEAT ROLLS

1/3 c. pineapple juice
1/3 c. milk
3 tbsp. oil
3 tbsp. brown sugar
1/4 tsp. salt
1 c. all-purpose flour
1 pkg. dry yeast

1 8-oz. can juice-pack crushed pineapple, drained
2 to 2 1/4 c. whole wheat flour
1/4 c. honey
1/4 c. margarine, melted

Heat first 5 ingredients in saucepan to 120 degrees. Combine with all-purpose flour and yeast in mixer bowl. Beat at low speed for 30 seconds. Beat at high speed for 3 minutes. Stir in pineapple and enough whole wheat flour to make medium dough. Knead in remaining whole wheat flour on floured surface. Place in greased bowl, turning to grease surface. Let rise, covered, for 1 hour or until doubled in bulk. Punch dough down. Let rest for 10 minutes. Shape into 45 balls. Place 3 balls in each of 15 greased muffin cups. Let rise, covered, for 20 minutes. Bake at 350 degrees for 15 minutes. Brush with mixture of honey and margarine. Yield: 15 rolls.

Romaine

MANDARIN ROMAINE SALAD

1/2 c. slivered almonds
1/2 c. corn oil
1/4 c. rice vinegar
1 1/2 tbsp. orange juice
1 1/2 tbsp. honey
1 lg. bunch romaine

1 8-oz. can mandarin oranges, drained
4 green onions, chopped
Salt and pepper to taste

Bake slivered almonds in baking pan at 350 degrees for 5 minutes or until toasted and golden brown. Cool. Combine oil and next 3 ingredients

in jar; shake well. Toss romaine, mandarin oranges and green onions in salad bowl. Add dressing, toasted almonds and salt and pepper; toss lightly. Yield: 6 servings.

ROMAINE SALAD

1 head romaine lettuce, torn
5 green onions, chopped
1/4 c. chopped marinated artichoke hearts
1 1/2 tsp. lemon pepper

1 1/2 tsp. toasted sesame seed
1 avocado
Juice of 1 lemon
2 tbsp. Italian salad dressing
2 tbsp. Parmesan cheese

Combine first 5 ingredients in salad bowl. Chop avocado. Toss with lemon juice in small bowl. Add avocado, salad dressing and Parmesan cheese to salad. Toss to mix well. Yield: 6 to 8 servings.

Salad Dressing

FRENCH SALAD DRESSING

1 c. sugar
2 tbsp. dry mustard
1 tsp. salt
2 tsp. celery seed
1/2 tsp. pepper
1 c. oil
1 1/2 c. catsup

1 1/2 c. apple cider vinegar
1/4 c. Worcestershire sauce
6 drops (about) of garlic juice

Mix dry ingredients in small bowl. Combine oil, catsup, vinegar and Worcestershire sauce in quart bottle. Add dry ingredients. Add garlic juice; shake well until no lumps remain. Yield: 5 cups.

HONEY DRESSING

6 tbsp. honey
1/2 c. plus 2 tsp. yellow mustard
1 1/2 c. mayonnaise

3/4 c. chopped onion
9 tbsp. oil
2 c. chopped fresh parsley

Place all ingredients in blender container. Process for 30 seconds or until creamy. May be stored in refrigerator indefinitely. Yield: 4 cups.

GREEN GODDESS DRESSING

1 clove of garlic,	*3 tbsp. tarragon wine*
mashed	*vinegar*
5 tbsp. anchovy paste	*1/3 c. sour cream*
1 med. onion, chopped	*1 c. mayonnaise*
1 tbsp. lemon juice	*1/2 c. minced parsley*

Combine garlic, anchovy paste, onion, lemon juice and vinegar in blender container. Process until smooth. Combine with sour cream, mayonnaise and parsley in bowl; mix well. Refrigerate, tightly covered, several hours before using. Delicious on green salads or pasta. Yield: 2 cups.

SOUTH OF THE BORDER DRESSING

1 c. corn oil	*2 tsp. sugar*
1/3 c. white vinegar	*1 1/2 tsp. salt*
1/4 c. orange juice	*1 tsp. cumin*
1 tbsp. minced onion	*1 tsp. oregano*
1 sm. clove of garlic,	*1/4 tsp. crushed red*
crushed	*pepper flakes*

Combine all ingredients in 1-pint jar; shake well. Chill in refrigerator. Discard garlic. Shake well. Serve on assorted salad greens. Yield: 1 1/2 cups.

SUMMER SALAD DRESSING

1 c. corn oil	*2 tsp. dillweed*
1/2 c. lime juice	*1/2 tsp. celery seed*
1 1/2 tsp. salt	*1 sm. clove of garlic,*
1 tsp. sugar	*crushed*
1 tsp. minced onion	

Combine all ingredients in 1-pint jar; shake well. Chill in refrigerator. Discard garlic. Shake well. Serve on assorted salad greens. Yield: 1 1/2 cups.

Salmon

GRILLED SALMON

1/4 c. butter	*2 dashes dillweed*
2 c. packed brown	*Dash of cayenne*
sugar	*pepper*
2 tbsp. lemon juice	*6 1-in. salmon steaks*

Combine butter, brown sugar, lemon juice, dillweed and cayenne pepper in saucepan. Heat until sugar is dissolved. Grill salmon over hot coals for 5 to 7 minutes. Brush with sauce. Grill for 5 minutes longer or until salmon flakes easily. Yield: 6 servings.

SALMON CROISSANTS

4 croissants	*3 oz. cream cheese,*
2 c. red salmon,	*softened*
drained	*1 1/2 tsp. dried dillweed*
3 tbsp. lemon juice	*1 cucumber*

Split croissants; set aside. Combine next 4 ingredients in bowl; toss gently. Score cucumber with fork; slice thinly. Fill croissants with salmon mixture and cucumber slices. Garnish with fresh dill sprigs or parsley. Yield: 4 servings.

SALMON STUFFED WITH CRAB

1 1/2 lb. crab meat	*2 c. bread cubes*
1/2 c. melted butter	*1/2 c. finely chopped*
1/4 c. parsley flakes	*onion*
1/2 c. chicken stock	*Juice of 2 lemons*
1 c. finely chopped	*1 8-lb. salmon*
celery	

Combine first 8 ingredients in bowl; mix well. Stuff salmon, tie salmon together. Wrap in foil. Bake at 350 degrees for 1 hour and 45 minutes. Uncover. Bake for 15 to 20 minutes or until salmon is browned. Serve with melted butter, lemon and caper sauce. Yield: 10 to 12 servings.

DELICIOUS SALMON LOAF

2 tbsp. minced onion	*1/2 can cream of celery*
1/2 c. chopped celery	*soup*
1 tbsp. butter	*1/2 c. milk*
2 eggs, beaten	*1 16-oz. can salmon,*
1/2 tsp. salt	*boned, flaked*
1/4 tsp. pepper	*1 c. cooked rice*
2 tbsp. mayonnaise	*Olive-Celery Sauce*

Sauté onion and celery in butter in skillet until soft. Combine with eggs, salt, pepper, mayonnaise, celery soup, milk, salmon and rice in bowl; mix well. Spoon into greased glass loaf pan. Bake at 350 degrees for 55 minutes. Invert onto platter. Slice and serve with Olive-Celery Sauce. Yield: 8 servings.

Olive-Celery Sauce

1/2 can cream of celery	*2 tbsp. mayonnaise*
soup	*1/4 c. sliced black olives*
1/2 c. milk	*1 tsp. olive liquid*

Combine all ingredients in saucepan. Heat to serving temperature. Yield: 1 cup.

SPRING SALMON FLORENTINE

2 c. cooked or canned salmon	1/4 tsp. salt
1 1/4 c. milk	1/2 tsp. Tabasco sauce
1/4 c. butter	1 1/2 c. shredded cheese
1/4 c. all-purpose flour	2 c. cooked spinach, drained
1/2 tsp. dry mustard	1/2 c. shredded cheese

Drain and flake salmon, reserving liquid. Add enough milk to salmon liquid to measure 1 1/2 cups. Melt butter in saucepan. Add flour; stir with wire whisk until blended. Bring milk mixture to a boil in saucepan. Add flour-butter mixture. Cook until sauce is thickened and smooth, whisking constantly. Season with mustard, salt and Tabasco sauce. Stir in 1 cup cheese. Place spinach in 1-quart casserole. Top with salmon and sauce. Sprinkle with remaining cheese. Bake at 425 degrees for 15 minutes. Yield: 4 servings.

SALMON LOG

1 16-oz. can salmon, drained	2 tsp. grated onion
8 oz. cream cheese, softened	1 tsp. horseradish
1 tbsp. lemon juice	1/4 tsp. salt
	1/4 tsp. liquid smoke
	1 c. chopped pecans

Flake salmon, discarding skin and bones. Mix with cream cheese, lemon juice, grated onion, horseradish, salt and liquid smoke in bowl. Shape into log. Wrap with plastic wrap. Chill in refrigerator. Roll in pecans. Store, tightly covered, in refrigerator. Serve with assorted crackers. Yield: 12 servings.

Sandwiches

CB SANDWICH

1 12-oz. can corned beef, crumbled	1/4 c. chopped onion
1 c. shredded Cheddar cheese	2 tbsp. Worcestershire sauce
1/2 c. catsup	4 to 6 hamburger buns

Combine corned beef, Cheddar cheese, catsup, chopped onion and Worcestershire sauce in large bowl; mix well. Spread mixture between hamburger buns. Wrap each sandwich in 12-inch foil square. Place on a cookie sheet. Bake at 350 degrees for 15 minutes. Yield: 4 servings.

HOT ITALIAN ROAST BEEF SANDWICHES

1 5 to 6-lb. sirloin or round roast	1 tbsp. parsley
3 tbsp. oil	1 onion, chopped
2 stalks celery, chopped	1 8-oz. can tomato sauce
5 or 6 bay leaves	Salt and pepper to taste
1 to 2 tsp. rosemary	1 c. water
1 to 2 tsp. oregano	20 hard rolls

Brown roast in oil in Dutch oven. Add celery, bay leaves, rosemary, oregano, parsley, onion, tomato sauce and salt and pepper. Bake at 350 degrees for 3 to 4 hours or until very tender. Remove bay leaves. Shred roast with fork. Add additional water if mixture seems dry. Serve on hard rolls. Yield: 20 sandwiches.

PIZZA BURGERS

1 lb. ground beef	2 c. spaghetti sauce
1 sm. onion, chopped	1 tsp. parsley flakes
1/2 lb. bologna	1 1/2 tsp. oregano
1/2 lb. mozzarella cheese	1/2 tsp. salt
	16 hamburger buns

Brown ground beef and onion in skillet, stirring frequently. Grind bologna and mozzarella cheese. Stir into browned ground beef. Add spaghetti sauce, parsley, oregano and salt; mix well. Split buns. Spoon ground beef mixture onto each bun. Place on baking sheet. Bake at 450 degrees for 10 to 12 minutes or until cheese is melted. Yield: 16 sandwiches.

SANDWICH STROGANOFF

1 tsp. salt	1/4 c. chili sauce
1 lb. ground beef	3/4 c. sour cream
1/4 c. chopped onion	1/2 loaf French bread, sliced lengthwise
1/4 tsp. garlic juice	4 3/4-oz. slices American cheese
1/4 tsp. pepper	4 tomato slices
1/2 tsp. Worcestershire sauce	4 green bell pepper rings
2 tbsp. all-purpose flour	

Sprinkle salt into preheated skillet. Add ground beef and onion. Cook until brown and crumbly, stirring frequently; drain. Add garlic juice, pepper and Worcestershire sauce; mix well. Sprinkle with flour. Stir in chili sauce; reduce heat. Add sour cream; mix well. Heat to serving temperature. Spoon onto bread. Add cheese slices, tomato slices and pepper rings. Broil until cheese melts. Serve immediately. Yield: 4 servings.

RIBBON SANDWICHES

¹/₂ 16-oz. loaf unsliced white bread	2 tbsp. chopped green bell pepper
¹/₂ 16-oz. loaf unsliced whole wheat bread	1 tbsp. chopped onion
³/₄ c. cottage cheese	2 tbsp. chopped pimento
³/₄ c. margarine, softened	¹/₈ tsp. thyme
	¹/₈ tsp. celery salt

Trim crusts from bread loaves; set aside. Beat cottage cheese in mixer bowl until creamy. Add margarine, green pepper, onion, pimento and seasonings; beat until well mixed. Spread top of each loaf with cottage cheese mixture. Cut thin lengthwise slice from top of each. Repeat process as many times as desired. Assemble loaf alternating slices of white and whole wheat bread beginning and ending with white slices. Press together lightly. Chill, wrapped in waxed paper until serving time. Slice through layers carefully. Yield: 24 servings.

BUFFET SANDWICH TRAY

16 oz. cream cheese, softened	1 7-oz. can chunk ham, drained
¹/₃ c. mayonnaise	1 tomato, peeled, chopped
1¹/₂ tsp. mustard	
Salt and pepper to taste	1 7-oz. can chunk chicken breast
1 sm. can sliced black olives, drained	4 green onions, sliced
2 hard-cooked eggs	White and whole wheat bread slices

Cream first 3 ingredients in bowl. Add salt and pepper. Spread ¹/₂ inch thick in center of large platter. Arrange the following ingredients in strips on cream cheese mixture; olives, sieved egg whites topped with sieved egg yolks, ham, drained tomato, chicken and green onions. Chill until serving time. Arrange bread around edge of platter just before serving. Yield: 10 to 12 servings.

Sauces

BIG BATCH TOMATO SAUCE

3 med. onions, sliced	1¹/₂ tsp. basil
3 lg. carrots, thinly sliced	2 tbsp. salt
2 med. green bell peppers, chopped	¹/₂ tsp. pepper
	12 lb. tomatoes, peeled, chopped
2 cloves of garlic, minced	1 12-oz. can tomato paste
¹/₄ c. oil	¹/₄ c. packed brown sugar
2 tsp. oregano	

Sauté onions, carrots, green peppers and garlic in oil in heavy stockpot over medium heat until tender. Add remaining ingredients; mix well. Bring to a boil; reduce heat. Simmer, loosely covered, for 2 hours, stirring occasionally. Pour into hot sterilized 1-pint jars leaving ¹/₂-inch headspace. Seal with 2-piece lids. Process in boiling water bath for 15 minutes. Serve over spaghetti or use with Swiss steak or pizza. Yield: 9 pints.

TEXAS-STYLE SUMMER PICANTE

4 to 8 fresh jalapeño peppers	¹/₂ tsp. pepper
4 cloves of garlic	1 tbsp. salt
1 sm. can tomato paste	4 c. finely chopped fresh tomatoes
¹/₂ c. sugar	1 c. finely chopped onion
1 c. vinegar	
¹/₄ tsp. alum	1 green bell pepper, finely chopped
¹/₂ tsp. cumin	

Combine jalapeño peppers, garlic, tomato paste, sugar, vinegar, alum and spices in blender container. Process until smooth. Combine with chopped vegetables in large saucepan. Bring to a boil; reduce heat. Simmer for 45 minutes. Pour into hot sterilized 1-pint jars, leaving ¹/₂-inch headspace. Seal with 2-piece lids. Process in boiling water bath for 15 minutes. Yield: 3 pints.

ALL-PURPOSE PASTA SAUCE

1 lb. ground beef	¹/₄ tsp. garlic salt
¹/₂ c. chopped onion	¹/₈ tsp. pepper
1 8-oz. can tomato sauce	¹/₂ tsp. sugar
2 c. tomato juice	1 tbsp. chopped parsley
¹/₄ tsp. salt	¹/₄ tsp. oregano
	1 bay leaf

Cook ground beef with onion in skillet, stirring until crumbly; drain. Add remaining ingredients. Simmer for 30 minutes, stirring occasionally. Discard bay leaf. Yield: 4 servings.

BAR-B-QUE SAUCE

1 c. melted margarine	1 11-oz. bottle of catsup
4 c. tomato juice	
¹/₂ c. vinegar	1¹/₂ tsp. dry mustard
1 oz. garlic salt	4 bay leaves
1 oz. onion salt	2 c. packed brown sugar
1 oz. celery salt	
1 oz. Worcestershire sauce	2 tsp. lemon juice
	1¹/₂ oz. liquid smoke
1 oz. hot sauce	

Bring margarine and tomato juice to a boil in large saucepan. Add remaining ingredients. Simmer for 30 minutes. Discard bay leaves. Yield: 1¹/₂ quarts.

MORNAY SAUCE

1 c. butter	1/2 tsp. white pepper
3/4 c. all-purpose flour	Pinch of cayenne
4 c. milk, scalded	pepper
1 lb. Swiss Gruyère	3 oz. grated Parmesan
cheese, shredded	cheese
1 tsp. salt	

Melt butter in saucepan. Blend in flour; remove from heat. Pour in milk. Stir vigorously with wire whisk until roux is completely dissolved. Place over high heat; stir constantly. Add Swiss cheese, salt, pepper, cayenne pepper and grated Parmesan cheese. Allow sauce to come to a boil momentarily, stirring constantly. Taste and adjust seasonings if necessary. Remove from heat immediately; pour into bowl. Yield: 6 to 7 cups.

SWEET AND SOUR SAUCE

1/2 c. packed brown	1 tbsp. soy sauce
sugar	1/4 tsp. garlic powder
1 tbsp. cornstarch	1/4 tsp. ginger
1/3 c. red wine vinegar	1/4 c. chopped green
1/3 c. chicken broth	bell pepper

Combine brown sugar and cornstarch in saucepan. Stir in vinegar, broth, soy sauce, garlic powder and ginger. Add green pepper. Cook until sauce is thick and bubbly, stirring constantly. Yield: 5 servings.

ZIPPY MUSTARD SAUCE

1 c. dry mustard	3 eggs
1 c. malt vinegar	1 c. sugar

Blend mustard and vinegar in nonaluminum double boiler. Let stand, covered, overnight. Beat eggs and sugar in mixer bowl until thick and lemon-colored. Stir into mustard mixture. Cook over boiling water for 20 minutes or until thickened, stirring constantly. Cool. Refrigerate, covered, for 3 days before servings. Spoon into airtight containers. Store in refrigerator for up to 1 month. Yield: 3 cups.

JEZEBEL SAUCE

1 10-oz. jar apple jelly	1 6-oz. jar cream-style
1 10-oz. jar apricot	horseradish
preserves	1/2 1 1/2-oz. can dry
1 tsp. pepper	mustard

Combine apple jelly, apricot preserves, pepper, horseradish and dry mustard in saucepan. Bring to a boil, stirring constantly. Cool. Pour mixture into decorative jars; seal. Store jars in refrigerator. Serve over cream cheese as spread or as relish for ham or pork. Yield: 3 cups.

HOT FUDGE SAUCE

2/3 c. semisweet	1 14-oz. can sweetened
chocolate chips	condensed milk
2 tbsp. margarine	1 tsp. vanilla extract
1/8 tsp. salt	

Melt chocolate and butter in heavy saucepan over low heat, stirring constantly. Stir in salt and sweetened condensed milk. Cook for 5 minutes or until slightly thickened, stirring constantly. Blend in vanilla. Serve warm or cold over ice cream. Yield: 1 1/2 cups.

CHERRY SAUCE

1 12-oz. jar whole	1/2 tsp. cinnamon
cherry preserves	1/4 tsp. nutmeg
2 tbsp. light corn syrup	1/4 tsp. cloves
1/4 c. wine vinegar	

Combine preserves, corn syrup, vinegar and spices in saucepan; mix well. Bring to a boil over medium heat, stirring frequently. Simmer for 5 minutes, stirring frequently. Pour into serving dish. Serve warm as sauce for goose. Yield: 2 cups.

CRANBERRY-ORANGE SAUCE

3/4 c. sugar	1/4 c. water
1/4 c. ginger Brandy	2 c. fresh cranberries
3 tbsp. orange juice	1 tsp. cornstarch
concentrate	1 tbsp. water

Mix first 5 ingredients in saucepan. Cook over medium heat until cranberries burst, stirring occasionally. Stir in cornstarch dissolved in water. Cook for 3 minutes or until thickened and bubbly, stirring constantly. Yield: 3 cups.

Sauerkraut

CHOCOLATE SAUERKRAUT CAKE

2/3 c. margarine,	2 1/4 c. sifted flour
softened	1 tsp. baking powder
1 1/2 c. sugar	1 tsp. soda
3 eggs	1/4 tsp. salt
1 tsp. vanilla extract	1 c. water
1/2 c. unsweetened	2/3 c. chopped
baking cocoa	sauerkraut

Cream margarine and sugar in bowl. Beat in eggs and vanilla. Add sifted dry ingredients alternately with water, mixing well after each addition. Rinse and drain sauerkraut; stir into batter. Pour into 2 greased and floured 8 or 9-inch cake pans. Bake at 350 degrees for 30 minutes. Remove from pans to wire rack to cool. Frost cake with coffee-flavored frosting. Store in refrigerator after cutting. Yield: 12 servings.

MARINATED SAUERKRAUT SALAD

1 c. chopped onion	*1 31-oz. can*
1 c. chopped celery	*sauerkraut*
1 c. chopped green bell	*1 c. sugar*
pepper	*1/2 c. vinegar*
1 c. shredded carrots	*1/2 c. corn oil*

Mix vegetables in bowl. Bring sugar, vinegar and oil to a boil in saucepan. Pour over vegetables; mix well. Marinate for up to 3 days. Yield: 16 to 20 servings.

SAUERKRAUT BALLS

8 oz. sausage	*2 tbsp. prepared*
1/4 c. finely chopped	*mustard*
onion	*1/8 tsp. garlic salt*
1 14-oz. can	*1/8 tsp. pepper*
sauerkraut, drained	*3 tbsp. milk*
2 tbsp. dry bread	*1 egg*
crumbs	*1/3 c. all-purpose flour*
3 oz. cream cheese,	*1 1/4 c. dry bread crumbs*
softened	*Oil for deep frying*

Brown sausage with chopped onion in skillet, stirring frequently; drain. Squeeze sauerkraut dry between paper towels. Add to sausage with next 5 ingredients; mix well. Chill until firm. Shape into balls. Beat milk and egg in bowl. Coat sauerkraut balls with flour. Dip into egg mixture and then roll in 1 1/4 cups bread crumbs. Deep-fry at 400 degrees until golden brown. Drain. Yield: 8 servings.

REUBEN CASSEROLE

1 27-oz. can	*12 oz. Swiss cheese,*
sauerkraut	*sliced*
1 cup Thousand	*1 loaf party rye bread*
Island salad dressing	*Margarine, softened*
1 12-oz. can corned	
beef	

Wash and drain sauerkraut. Mix with salad dressing. Place in 9x13-inch baking dish. Layer corned beef and Swiss cheese over sauerkraut. Spread both sides of rye bread slices with margarine. Arrange on casserole, overlapping edges. Bake at 350 degrees for 35 to 45 minutes or until brown and bubbly. Yield: 8 servings.

Sausage

ONION-POTATO CHOWDER WITH ITALIAN SAUSAGE

3 tbsp. margarine	*12 to 16 oz. mild*
3 c. chopped onions	*Italian sausage*
4 c. chopped potatoes	*2 c. milk*
4 c. beef broth	*1/2 tsp. basil*

Melt margarine in stockpot. Add onions. Sauté for 2 minutes. Stir in potatoes and broth. Bring to a boil; cover. Reduce heat. Simmer for 15 minutes. Brown sausage in skillet, stirring until crumbly; drain. Add to soup with milk and basil. Season with salt and pepper to taste. Yield: 6 servings.

SAUSAGE SWIRLS

4 c. sifted all-purpose	*1/4 c. cornmeal*
flour	*2/3 c. oil*
1/4 c. sugar	*2/3 to 1 c. milk*
1 tsp. salt	*2 lb. hot sausage, at*
2 tbsp. baking powder	*room temperature*

Sift dry ingredients into bowl. Stir in oil and enough milk to make soft dough. Divide dough into 2 portions. Roll each into 10x18-inch rectangle on floured surface. Spread sausage on rectangles. Roll as for jelly roll from long edge. Seal edges. Chill in refrigerator or store, tightly wrapped, in freezer. Cut into 1/2-inch slices. Place on baking sheet. Bake at 350 degrees for 15 to 20 minutes or until light brown. Yield: 36 swirls.

SAUCISSON EN CROUTE

1 lb. pork sausage	*Salt to taste*
1 bunch green onions	*1/2 c. fresh bread*
with tops, chopped	*crumbs*
8 oz. mushrooms,	*1 tbsp. whole mustard*
chopped	*seed*
3 to 4 cloves of garlic,	*1 16-oz. package*
chopped	*frozen puff pastry*
2 eggs, slightly beaten	*dough*
1/2 tsp. red pepper	*1/4 c. melted butter*

Brown sausage in skillet, stirring until crumbly; drain. Combine with next 8 ingredients in bowl: mix well. Roll out each sheet of pastry 1/8 inch thick and 12 inches long on floured surface. Spread sausage filling over 1/3 of long edge. Roll as for jelly roll to enclose filling, turning ends under. Repeat with remaining pastry and filling. Place on baking sheet. Brush with butter. Bake at 425 degrees for 45 minutes, brushing occasionally with butter. Slice to serve. Yield: 8 servings.

STUFFED FRENCH TOAST

1/2 c. chopped onion	*1/2 tsp. pepper*
8 oz. hot sausage	*4 oz. bacon, crisp-*
2 tbsp. margarine	*fried, crumbled*
4 oz. cream cheese,	*1 loaf unsliced bread*
softened	*6 eggs, beaten*
1/4 tsp. salt	*1/2 c. (about) milk*

Sauté onion and sausage in margarine in skillet, stirring until sausage is brown and crumbly; drain. Combine with cream cheese, salt, pepper and bacon in bowl; mix well. Cut bread into slices, making every other cut to but not through bottom to form pockets. Spoon 2 1/2 tablespoons sausage mixture into each pocket. Dip filled slices into mixture of eggs and milk as for French toast. Cook in a small amount of oil on grill until brown on both sides. Yield: 6 to 8 servings.

PINEAPPLE AND SAUSAGE OMELET

1 15-oz. can juice-	*1 tbsp. margarine*
pack pineapple slices	*12 oz. pork sausage*
4 eggs, separated	*links*
1 tsp. baking powder	*1/2 c. packed light*
1/2 tsp. salt	*brown sugar*
1/8 tsp. white pepper	

Drain pineapple, reserving juice. Beat egg yolks, 1/4 cup reserved juice, baking powder, salt and pepper in small bowl. Beat egg whites in large mixer bowl until stiff but not dry. Stir 1/4 of the egg whites into yolks; fold yolk mixture into whites. Heat margarine in medium ovenproof skillet until bubbly; pour in egg mixture. Cook over low heat for 5 minutes or until bottom of omelet is golden. Bake at 350 degrees for 15 minutes or until set. Cook sausages in medium skillet over low heat until cooked through; drain. Add 1/2 cup reserved pineapple juice and brown sugar to skillet. Bring to a boil; reduce heat. Simmer for 10 to 12 minutes or until thickened. Add pineapple slices. Cook for 2 to 3 minutes or until heated through. Slide omelet onto large platter; surround with glazed sausages and pineapple. Yield: 4 servings.

SAUSAGE CALZONE

2 1-lb. loaves frozen	*1/2 c. shredded*
bread dough	*mozzarella cheese*
8 oz. sweet Italian	*1/2 c. cottage cheese*
sausage	*2 tbsp. Parmesan*
1/2 c. chopped onion	*cheese*
2 cloves of garlic,	*1 egg, slightly beaten*
minced	*2 egg whites, slightly*
1 8-oz. can tomato	*beaten*
sauce	*2 egg yolks*
1/2 tsp. basil	*1 tbsp. milk*
1 tsp. oregano	

Thaw bread dough, loosely wrapped in plastic wrap, in refrigerator overnight. Let stand at room temperature for 1 hour. Cook sausage in skillet until brown and crumbly; drain. Add onion and garlic. Cook until tender. Stir in tomato sauce, basil and oregano. Simmer for 5 minutes. Cool. Stir in cheeses and whole egg. Divide dough into 8 portions. Roll each into 6-inch circle on lightly floured surface. Place 1/3 cup filling on each. Brush edge of circle with beaten egg whites; fold over and press to seal. Place on baking sheet. Brush with egg yolks beaten with milk. Bake at 425 degrees for 12 to 15 minutes. Yield: 8 servings.

HOT ITALIAN SAUSAGE SANDWICHES

3 lb. hot Italian	*1 lg. jar spaghetti sauce*
sausage, cut into	*1 sm. green bell*
4-in. lengths	*pepper, chopped*
2 tbsp. oil	*1 tsp. sugar*
1 6-oz. can tomato	*1 sm. onion, chopped*
paste	*1 tsp. garlic powder*
2 to 3 stalks celery,	*Cayenne pepper to*
chopped	*taste*

Brown sausage in oil in skillet. Place in slow cooker. Add remaining ingredients. Cook on High until tender. Simmer until of desired flavor and consistency. Yield: 10 sandwiches.

Scallops

BAKED SCALLOPS WITH MUSHROOMS

1/4 c. butter	*1/8 tsp. pepper*
1/4 c. all-purpose flour	*1/4 c. chopped parsley*
1/2 c. light cream	*8 oz. mushrooms, sliced*
1 c. milk	*1/4 c. butter*
2 tbsp. white wine	*2 lb. scallops*
1/4 tsp. cayenne pepper	*1/2 c. shredded Swiss*
1/8 tsp. thyme	*cheese*
1/4 tsp. salt	

Melt 1/4 cup butter in saucepan; stir in flour to thicken. Add cream and milk gradually. Cook until thickened, stirring constantly. Add wine, cayenne pepper, thyme and salt and pepper to taste. Cook for 1 minute longer. Stir in parsley. Sauté mushrooms in remaining 1/4 cup butter in skillet. Place half the scallops in buttered 2 to 3-quart baking dish. Add half the mushrooms. Cover with 1 cup cream sauce. Repeat layers. Sprinkle with cheese. Bake at 400 degrees for 20 minutes or until hot and bubbly. Yield: 6 servings.

PASTA ALLA MARINARA

1 lb. scallops	*1 lb. cooked shrimp,*
1/2 c. water	*steamed*
1/2 c. white wine	*1/4 c. chopped parsley*
1 16-oz. can peeled	*1/2 tsp. oregano*
tomatoes	*1 tsp. brown sugar*
2 tbsp. olive oil	*Splash of white wine*
2 cloves of garlic,	*8 oz. spinach noodles,*
crushed	*cooked*
1 tbsp. tomato paste	

Cut scallops into halves. Cook in mixture of water and 1/2 cup wine in saucepan for 2 minutes. Drain. Chop tomatoes in blender container. Heat olive oil in large skillet. Add tomatoes, garlic and tomato paste; mix well. Cook for 2 minutes. Add seafood. Cook for 1 minute. Add parsley, oregano, brown sugar, salt and pepper to taste. Add splash of white wine. Stir pasta sauce into hot spinach noodles in deep serving dish. Serve immediately. Yield: 4 servings.

Sesame

CHEESE SESAME ROLLS

1 package dry	*1 egg*
yeast	*1 1/2 tsp. baking*
1/4 c. warm water	*powder*
3/4 c. milk	*1/2 c. butter, softened*
2 tbsp. sugar	*1/2 c. Parmesan*
1/3 c. shortening	*cheese*
1 tsp. salt	*1 egg white, beaten*
2 1/2 c. all-purpose	*1/4 c. sesame seed*
flour	

Dissolve yeast in water. Scald milk in saucepan. Mix with sugar, shortening and salt in bowl. Cool. Add 1 cup flour; beat until smooth. Add egg, yeast mixture and 1/2 cup flour; mix well. Stir in baking powder and 1/2 cup flour; mix well. Stir in enough remaining flour to make dough easy to handle. Let rest for 15 minutes. Knead on lightly floured surface for 5 minutes or until smooth and elastic. Place in greased bowl, turning to grease surface. Let rise in a warm place until doubled in bulk. Punch dough down; divide into 3 portions. Let rest for 5 minutes. Roll each portion into circle on floured surface. Cut into 8 wedges. Spread each wedge with 1 teaspoon butter. Sprinkle with cheese. Roll wedges from wide ends. Shape into crescents on greased baking sheet. Brush with egg white. Sprinkle with sesame seed. Let rise in a warm place until doubled in bulk. Bake at 400 degrees for 12 minutes or until golden brown. Yield: 24 rolls.

PEANUT BUTTER SESAME BALLS

3/4 c. peanut butter	*1 tsp. vanilla extract*
1/4 c. toasted sesame	*1/2 to 3/4 c. nonfat dry*
seed	*milk powder*
1/2 c. honey	*Sesame seed*

Combine peanut butter, 1/4 cup sesame seed, honey and vanilla in bowl; mix well. Add dry milk powder, mixing with hands when mixture becomes very stiff. Shape into small balls; roll in additional sesame seed, coating well. Chill in refrigerator. Yield: 2 dozen.

Shortbread

GLORIFIED SHORTBREAD

1 c. butter	*1 c. sifted*
2 c. all-purpose	*confectioners'*
flour	*sugar*
1/2 c. confectioners'	*2 tbsp. orange juice*
sugar	*1/2 tsp. grated orange*
1 1/2 tsp. cornstarch	*rind*
Pinch of salt	*12 walnuts*

Cut butter into mixture of next 4 ingredients until crumbly. Press into 9-inch baking pan. Bake at 350 degrees for 30 minutes. Combine confectioners' sugar, orange juice and orange rind in bowl. Spread on shortbread. Cut into 12 wedges. Top each wedge with 1 walnut half. Yield: 2 dozen.

Glorified Shortbread...dresses up an all-time favorite for special occasions.

SHORTBREAD

1 c. butter, softened	*3/4 c. cornstarch*
3/4 c. confectioners'	*1 1/2 c. all-purpose*
sugar	*flour*

Cream butter in mixer bowl until light. Add confectioners' sugar gradually, beating until fluffy. Add cornstarch gradually, beating constantly. Blend in flour gradually with wooden spoon. Press evenly into ungreased 9-inch round pan. Bake at 300 degrees for 45 minutes or until very light brown. Cut into wedges while warm. Sprinkle with tinted sugar before baking if desired.
Yield: 12 servings.

Shrimp

SHRIMP MOUSSE WREATH

1 c. sour cream	*1/3 c. cold water*
1 c. mayonnaise	*2 tsp. instant vegetable*
2 lb. cooked shrimp,	*bouillon*
ground	*1 c. boiling water*
2/3 c. chopped onion	*8 oz. cream cheese,*
1 c. chopped celery	*softened*
2 tsp. Worcestershire	*3 tbsp. sour cream*
sauce	*1 bunch parsley,*
2 tsp. salt	*chopped*
1/8 tsp. pepper	*Pimento Bow*
2 env. unflavored	*1 pint cherry*
gelatin	*tomatoes*

Blend 1 cup sour cream and mayonnaise in large bowl. Add shrimp, onion, celery, Worcestershire sauce, salt and pepper; mix well. Soften gelatin in cold water. Dissolve bouillon in boiling water. Add softened gelatin. Stir until gelatin is dissolved. Stir into shrimp mixture. Pour into shallow 8-cup ring mold. Chill for 8 hours or until firm. Unmold onto serving plate. Combine cream cheese and 3 tablespoons sour cream in bowl; mix well. Spread over mold. Sprinkle parsley around mold to resemble wreath. Chill for 30 minutes. Decorate with Pimento Bow. Fill center of mold with whole cherry tomatoes. Serve with crackers.
Yield: 20 servings.

Pimento Bow

Pat 3 whole pimento halves dry. Place 2 pimento halves, narrow ends together, at top of wreath. Open and flatten wide ends carefully; trim. Cut remaining pimento in half lengthwise. Trim outer edges to resemble ribbon. Place on wreath to complete bow.

SHRIMP CACCIATORE

1/2 c. chopped onion	*1 8-oz. can tomato*
1 med. green bell	*sauce*
pepper, cut into strips	*1/2 tsp. oregano*
1 clove of garlic,	*1/2 tsp. dried basil*
minced	*1 1/2 c. rice*
2 tbsp. margarine	*1 lb. shrimp,*
1 28-oz. can whole	*cooked*
tomatoes	

Sauté onion, green pepper and garlic in margarine in saucepan. Add tomatoes, tomato sauce and seasonings. Bring to a boil. Simmer for 30 to 45 minutes. Prepare rice according to package directions. Add shrimp to sauce. Serve over rice.
Yield: 4 servings.

NEW ORLEANS SHRIMP
Photograph for this recipe is on page 157.

1 c. chopped onion	*1/2 tsp. basil*
1 c. chopped green bell	*1/8 tsp. cayenne pepper*
pepper	*1 16-oz. can whole*
1 c. coarsely chopped	*tomatoes, drained*
celery	*1 15-oz. can tomato*
2 cloves of garlic,	*sauce*
minced	*1 3/4 c. sliced okra*
3 tbsp. butter	*1 lb. shrimp, peeled*
1 bay leaf	*and deveined*
1 tsp. salt	*8 oz. egg noodles*
1 tsp. thyme	

Sauté onion, green pepper, celery and garlic in butter in large skillet until almost tender. Stir in bay leaf, salt, thyme, basil and cayenne pepper. Chop tomatoes; add to skillet. Cook for 5 minutes, stirring frequently. Add tomato sauce and okra. Simmer, covered, for 10 minutes. Remove bay leaf; add shrimp. Bring to a boil. Simmer for 5 minutes or just until shrimp turn pink. Cook noodles using package directions; drain. Serve sauce over noodles. Yield: 4 to 6 servings.

GRILLED SWEET AND SOUR SHRIMP

1 20-oz. can pineapple	*2 tsp. salt*
chunks	*1/4 tsp. garlic salt*
1/2 c. sugar	*2 tbsp. cornstarch*
1/2 c. white vinegar	*2 tbsp. water*
1/4 c. butter	*60 to 70 jumbo shrimp,*
2 tbsp. soy sauce	*peeled*

Drain pineapple, reserving juice. Mix juice with enough water to measure 1 cup. Combine with next 6 ingredients in saucepan. Bring to a boil. Stir in mixture of cornstarch and water. Cook until liquid is thickened, stirring constantly. Cool. Combine with pineapple and shrimp in bowl. Marinate, covered, in refrigerator for 2 to 6 hours, stirring several times. Thread shrimp and pineapple alternately on skewers; reserve marinade. Grill shrimp over hot coals for 5 to 6 minutes on each side, basting with reserved marinade. Yield: 6 servings.

ORIENTAL SHRIMP AND PASTA STIR-FRY

1 to 1¹/₂ lb. shrimp,	*2 to 3 oz. snow peas*
cleaned	*2 oz. bean sprouts*
1 2-oz. can water	*2 oz. bamboo shoots*
chestnuts	*4 tbsp. sesame seed oil*
2 stalks of celery,	*1 lb. cooked linguine*
sliced diagonally	*1 oz. soy sauce*
1 carrot, sliced	*Salt and pepper to*
1 head Napa cabbage,	*taste*
sliced	

Sauté shrimp and vegetables in 2 tablespoons sesame oil in skillet until shrimp turn pink. Sauté linguine in remaining 2 tablespoons sesame oil in skillet. Add soy sauce, salt and pepper. Add shrimp mixture. Mix well and serve immediately. Yield: 4 to 6 servings.

RAGIN' CAJUN SHRIMP

4 lb. shrimp, peeled	*1 tsp. pepper*
1 c. corn oil	*¹/₂ tsp. dried red pepper*
¹/₂ c. chopped green	*flakes*
onions	*¹/₂ tsp. dried thyme*
2 cloves of garlic,	*¹/₂ tsp. dried rosemary*
minced	*¹/₄ tsp. dried oregano*
1 tsp. cayenne pepper	*Bamboo skewers*

Combine shrimp with next 9 ingredients in large bowl, stirring to coat shrimp. Refrigerate, covered, for 2 hours, stirring occasionally. Soak bamboo skewers in ice water for 2 hours. Drain shrimp, reserving marinade. Thread shrimp on skewers. Grill just until pink, basting with marinade. Serve immediately. Yield: 8 servings.

SHERMAN'S SHRIMP CASSEROLE

1 5-oz. package	*¹/₂ tsp. Worcestershire*
saffron rice mix	*sauce*
1 10-oz. can cream	*1 tsp. prepared mustard*
of mushroom soup	*1 16-oz. package*
3 tbsp. melted	*frozen uncooked*
margarine	*shrimp*
2 tbsp. chopped green	*Salt and pepper to taste*
bell pepper	*¹/₂ c. shredded*
2 tbsp. chopped onion	*Cheddar cheese*

Cook saffron rice according to package directions. Add remaining ingredients, reserving a small amount of cheese. Spoon into 2-quart casserole sprayed with nonstick cooking spray. Sprinkle reserved cheese over top. Bake at 350 degrees for 30 minutes. Yield: 4 to 6 servings.

SPICY SHRIMP

2 c. broccoli flowerets	*¹/₃ c. picante sauce*
1 c. snow pea halves	*¹/₃ c. Italian salad*
2 lb. cooked peeled	*dressing*
shrimp	*2 tsp. shredded fresh*
1 med. red bell pepper,	*ginger*
cut into thin strips	*1 cucumber*
2 tsp. soy sauce	

Cook broccoli and snow peas in a small amount of water in separate saucepans over medium heat until tender-crisp; drain. Combine broccoli, snow peas, shrimp and red pepper in large bowl. Mix soy sauce, picante sauce, Italian dressing and ginger in bowl; mix well. Pour over shrimp mixture. Chill for 4 hours, tossing several times. Peel and seed cucumber. Cut into strips. Add to shrimp mixture, tossing lightly. Yield: 12 servings.

WINTER SHRIMP-BROCCOLI SALAD

1 c. bulgur	*2 tsp. lemon juice*
2 c. water	*1 c. shrimp, cooked*
2 tbsp. margarine	*1¹/₂ c. broccoli*
1 tsp. seasoned salt	*flowerets*
¹/₂ c. mayonnaise	*1 c. sliced celery*
¹/₂ c. whole milk	*6 cherry tomatoes*
yogurt	

Mix first 4 ingredients in medium saucepan. Bring to a boil, covered; reduce heat. Simmer for 15 minutes. Cool. Combine bulgur mixture with mayonnaise, yogurt and lemon juice in bowl. Add shrimp, broccoli and celery; toss lightly. Chill, covered, until serving time. Spoon onto salad plates. Add cherry tomatoes. Yield: 6 servings.

Soup

CREAM OF VEGETABLE SOUP

3 potatoes, chopped	*¹/₂ c. c. peas*
¹/₃ c. sliced onions	*3 c. skim milk*
¹/₂ c. sliced carrots	*2 tbsp. margarine*
¹/₂ c. chopped celery	*Salt and pepper to taste*
¹/₂ c. cut green beans	

Cook potatoes in water in saucepan until tender. Mash potatoes in saucepan. Stir in remaining vegetables. Simmer until tender. Add milk, butter, salt and pepper. Heat to serving temperature. Yield: 4 servings.

HARVEST SOUP

3 c. cubed peeled potatoes	*1 chicken bouillon cube*
1/2 c. sliced carrots	*2 tbsp. all-purpose flour*
1/2 c. sliced celery	*1 1/2 to 2 1/2 c. milk*
1/2 c. chopped onion	*2 tsp. parsley*
1 c. water	*8 oz. Velveeta cheese*

Combine first 6 ingredients in saucepan. Cook for 15 to 20 minutes or until vegetables are tender. Blend flour and milk in bowl. Add to soup. Cook until thickened, stirring constantly. Stir in parsley and cheese. Season with salt and pepper to taste. Cook until cheese is melted. Yield: 6 servings.

Sour Cream

SOUR CREAM CAKE

1 c. butter, softened	*3 c. sifted all-purpose flour*
3 c. sugar	
6 eggs, separated	*1 c. sour cream*
1/4 tsp. soda	

Cream butter and sugar in mixer bowl until light and fluffy. Blend in egg yolks, 1 at a time. Add sifted mixture of soda and flour alternately with sour cream, mixing well after each addition. Beat egg whites in mixer bowl until stiff peaks form. Fold gently into batter. Spoon into greased and waxed paper-lined 10-inch tube pan. Bake at 300 degrees for 1 1/2 hours. Cool on rack.
Yield: 16 servings.

SOUR CREAM MUFFINS

1/4 c. butter, softened	*1/2 c. buttermilk baking mix or self-rising flour*
1/4 c. sour cream	

Combine butter and sour cream in bowl; mix well. Stir in baking mix. Spoon into greased miniature muffin cups. Bake at 425 degrees for 12 minutes or until golden brown. Serve hot. Yield: 1 dozen.

SOUR CREAM TWISTS

1 c. margarine	*1 pkg. dry yeast*
3 1/2 c. all-purpose flour	*1 tsp. nutmeg*
1 egg	*1 tsp. salt*
2 egg yolks	*1 c. sugar*
1 c. sour cream	

Cut margarine into flour in bowl until crumbly. Add whole egg, egg yolks and half the sour cream. Mix yeast with remaining sour cream, nutmeg and salt in bowl. Add to flour mixture; mix well. Dough will be stiff. Chill, covered, in refrigerator for 2 hours or longer. Sprinkle work surface with sugar; coat rolling pin with sugar. Roll dough 1/4 inch thick on prepared surface. Cut into strips; twist. Place on ungreased baking sheet. Let rise at room temperature for 20 minutes. Bake at 350 degrees for 15 to 20 minutes. Cool on rack. Yield: 40 twists.

Spaghetti

CHICKEN SPAGHETTI

1 med. onion, chopped	*1 10-oz. can cream of chicken soup*
1 stalk celery, chopped	
3 tbsp. margarine	*2 1/2 c. chicken broth*
2 c. chopped cooked chicken	*1/4 tsp. salt*
	1/2 tsp. pepper
1 6-oz. package spaghetti	*1 c. sliced mushrooms*
	1/2 c. Parmesan cheese

Sauté onion and celery in margarine in skillet until clear. Layer chicken and uncooked spaghetti over vegetables. Add mixture of soup, broth, salt and pepper. Top with layers of mushrooms and Parmesan cheese. Bring to a boil; reduce heat. Simmer, covered, for 30 minutes, stirring occasionally. Yield: 6 servings.

SPAGHETTI BOLOGNESE

1 lb. lean ground beef	*1/2 c. finely chopped parsley*
1 c. finely chopped red onion	
	2 14-oz. cans whole peeled tomatoes, cut into chunks
2 med. green bell peppers, cut into strips	
2 med. red bell peppers, cut into strips	*2 8-oz. cans tomato sauce*
2 cloves of garlic, minced	*1/2 tsp. salt*
	1/4 tsp. pepper
2/3 c. finely chopped fresh basil	*16 oz. spaghetti, linguine or fettucini*

Cook ground beef in skillet until partially cooked. Add onion. Cook until tender. Add peppers. Cook for 3 minutes. Add garlic. Sauté for 30 seconds. Add next 6 ingredients. Bring to a boil; reduce heat. Simmer for 20 minutes or until thickened. Cook spaghetti according to package directions; drain. Serve sauce over spaghetti. Yield: 8 servings.

⇨
Recipe for this photograph is on page 154.

Autumn Seafood Buffet

Crab Puffs and Clam Canapés

pages 74 and 65

One-Pot French Fish Chowder

page 173

New Orleans Shrimp and Noodles

page 154

Baked Scallops with Mushrooms

page 152

Fruit and Nut Tropical Slaw

page 40

Cornmeal Crisps

page 70

Lemon Lush

page 102

*Fall is a great time for seafood, and a buffet featuring
everyone's favorites is sure to be a hit. Set up indoors
if the weather is chilly or enjoy the lingering
crisp, sunny days with an outdoor spread.*

SPICE AND HERB CHART

Allspice	Pungent aromatic spice, whole or in powdered form. It is excellent in marinades, particularly in game marinade, or in curries.
Basil	Can be chopped and added to cold poultry salads. If the recipe calls for tomatoes or tomato sauce, add a touch of basil to bring out a rich flavor.
Bay leaf	The basis of many French seasonings. It is added to soups, stews, marinades and stuffings.
Bouquet garni	A must in many Creole cuisine recipes. It is a bundle of herbs, spices and bay leaf tied together. It can be added to soups, stews or sauces.
Celery seed	From wild cherry rather than domestic celery. It adds pleasant flavor to bouillon or a stock base.
Chervil	One of the traditional *fines herbes* used in French-derived cooking. (The others are tarragon, parsley and chives.) It is good in omelets or soups.
Chives	Available fresh, dried or frozen, it can be substituted for raw onion or shallot in any poultry recipe.
Cinnamon	Ground from the bark of the cinnamon tree, it is important in desserts as well as savory dishes.
Coriander	Adds an unusual flavor to soups, stews, chili dishes, curries and some desserts.
Cumin	A staple spice in Mexican cooking. To use, rub seeds together and let them fall into the dish just before serving. Cumin also comes in powdered form.
Garlic	One of the oldest herbs in the world, it must be carefully handled. For best results, press or crush garlic clove.
Marjoram	An aromatic herb of the mint family, it is good in soups, sauces, stuffings and stews.
Mustard (dry)	Brings a sharp bite to sauces. Sprinkle just a touch over roast chicken for a delightful flavor treat.
Oregano	A staple herb in Italian, Spanish and Mexican cuisines. It is very good in dishes with a tomato foundation; it adds an excellent savory taste.

Paprika	A mild pepper that adds color to many dishes. The very best paprika is imported from Hungary.
Rosemary	A tasty herb important in seasoning stuffing for duck, partridge, capon and other poultry.
Sage	A perennial favorite with all kinds of poultry and stuffings. It is particularly good with goose.
Tarragon	One of the *fines herbes*. Goes well with all poultry dishes.
Thyme	Used in combination with bay leaf in soups and stews.

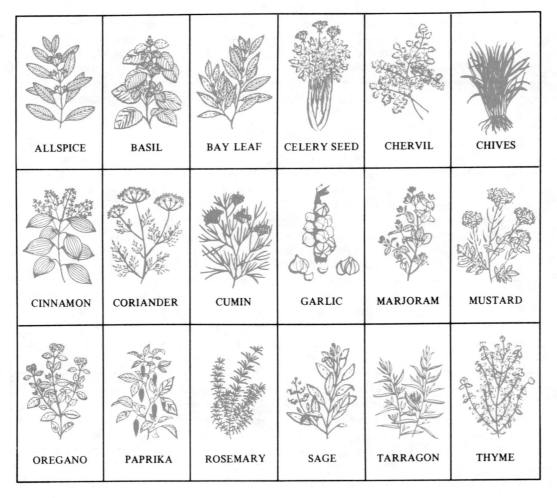

Spinach

SPINACH BALLS

2 10-oz. packages frozen spinach	1/2 c. melted margarine
3 c. herb-seasoned stuffing mix	1/2 c. Parmesan cheese
1 onion, chopped	1 tbsp. pepper
6 eggs, well-beaten	1 1/2 tsp. garlic salt
	1/2 tsp. thyme

Cook spinach according to package directions; drain. Combine spinach with remaining ingredients in bowl; mix well. Shape into 1-inch balls. Place on greased baking sheet. Bake at 350 degrees for 15 to 20 minutes or until golden brown. Yield: 36 appetizers.

SPINACH AND CHEESE PUFF BALLS

1 10-oz. package frozen spinach	1/2 c. Parmesan cheese
1/2 c. chopped onion	2 tbsp. margarine, melted
2 eggs, slightly beaten	1/8 tsp. garlic powder
1/3 c. blue cheese salad dressing	Dijon-style mustard to taste
1/2 c. shredded Cheddar cheese	1 8 1/2-oz. package corn muffin mix

Cook chopped spinach according to package directions, adding onion; drain well and press dry. Combine eggs, salad dressing, cheeses, margarine, garlic powder and mustard in bowl; mix well. Stir in spinach and muffin mix. Chill, covered, for 1 hour or until easy to handle. Shape into 1-inch balls; arrange on baking sheet. Chill, covered, until 20 minutes before serving. Bake at 350 degrees for 10 to 15 minutes or until light brown. Serve warm with mustard. Yield: 50 puff balls.

PHYLLO SPINACH TRIANGLES

3/4 c. chopped onion	8 oz. mozzarella cheese, shredded
1/2 c. butter	8 oz. Parmesan cheese
2 10-oz. packages frozen chopped spinach, thawed	3 oz. blue cheese, crumbled
8 oz. Monterey Jack cheese, shredded	1/4 tsp. Tabasco sauce
	1 pkg. phyllo dough

Sauté onion in butter in skillet until clear. Add spinach. Cook for 5 minutes. Remove from heat. Add cheeses and Tabasco sauce; mix well. Set aside. Follow directions on phyllo package for handling dough. Cut sheets into strips. Place 1 rounded teaspoonful spinach mixture on each strip and fold like a flag. Bake at 400 degrees for 15 to 20 minutes or until golden brown. Yield: 6 to 8 dozen.

CHEESY SPINACH PIE

1 1/2 c. frozen spinach, thawed	1/2 c. Parmesan cheese
1/4 c. butter	1/2 c. whipping cream
1 8-oz. container ricotta cheese	1/2 tsp. nutmeg
3 eggs, slightly beaten	1 unbaked 9-inch pie shell

Cook spinach according to package directions, adding butter; drain well. Add ricotta cheese, eggs, Parmesan cheese, cream and nutmeg; mix well. Pour into pie shell. Bake at 375 degrees for 30 minutes or until crust is brown and filling is set. Yield: 6 servings.

SPINACH AND ARTICHOKE CASSEROLE

4 10-oz. packages frozen spinach	1 can artichoke hearts, drained
8 oz. mushrooms, sliced	1/2 c. Parmesan cheese
1/2 c. margarine	3 tomatoes, sliced
1/2 mayonnaise	1/2 c. bread crumbs
1/2 c. sour cream	

Cook chopped spinach according to package directions; drain. Place in 2 1/2-quart baking dish. Sauté mushrooms in margarine in skillet; remove from heat. Add mayonnaise, sour cream, artichokes and cheese; mix well. Pour over spinach; mix gently. Top with tomatoes and bread crumbs. Bake at 325 degrees for 20 to 30 minutes or until bubbly. Yield: 12 servings.

SPINACH LASAGNA

1 16-oz. container sm. curd cottage cheese	3/4 tsp. oregano
1 c. shredded mozzarella cheese	1/8 tsp. pepper
2 eggs	2 15 1/2-oz. jars spaghetti sauce
1 10-oz. package frozen chopped spinach, thawed	8 oz. lasagna noodles
1 tsp. salt	1/2 c. shredded mozzarella cheese
	1 c. water

Mix first 7 ingredients in bowl. Layer 1/2 cup sauce, 1/3 of the noodles and half the cheese mixture in greased 9x13-inch baking dish. Repeat layers. Top with remaining noodles and sauce. Sprinkle with remaining cheese. Pour water around edges. Bake, covered, for 1 1/4 hours. Let stand for 15 minutes. Yield: 8 servings.

TOMATOES STUFFED WITH 🍎 SPINACH

6 med. tomatoes
1 10-oz. package
   frozen spinach
4 oz. fresh shelled
   shrimp
2 cloves of garlic,
   crushed

1 sm. onion, finely
   chopped
2 tbsp. margarine
1 tsp. Dijon mustard
3 tbsp. sour cream
Salt and pepper to taste

Cut tops from tomatoes; scoop out pulp. Squeeze thawed spinach dry. Cook shrimp as desired; do not overcook. Sauté garlic and onion in margarine in skillet until onion is transparent. Combine with spinach, shrimp, mustard and sour cream in bowl. Add salt and pepper; mix gently. Spoon into tomatoes; place in greased baking dish. Bake at 325 degrees for 15 minutes. Yield: 6 servings.

SPRING SPINACH SALAD FLAMBÉ

1 bunch fresh spinach,
   torn
1 sm. head Bibb or
   Boston lettuce, torn
8 oz. fresh mushrooms,
   sliced
6 slices bacon cut into
   1-inch pieces

1/4 c. freshly squeezed
   lemon juice
3 tbsp. sugar
2 tbsp. Worcestershire
   sauce
3 tbsp. Brandy

Combine spinach, lettuce and mushrooms in large bowl. Cook bacon in skillet until crisp; do not drain. Add lemon juice, sugar and Worcestershire sauce; bring to a boil. Pour over salad mixture, leaving bacon in skillet. Toss salad well. Divide salad mixture among 8 salad plates. Add Brandy to bacon in skillet; heat and ignite. Spoon over salads. Serve immediately. Yield: 8 servings.

FRESH SPINACH SALAD

1 lb. fresh spinach, torn
1 20-oz. can bean
   sprouts, rinsed,
   drained
1 8-oz. can sliced
   water chestnuts
4 hard-cooked eggs,
   sliced
1 med. onion, thinly
   sliced

8 oz. bacon, crisp-
   fried, crumbled
3/4 c. sugar
1/4 c. oil
2 tsp. salt
3/4 c. vinegar
1/3 c. catsup
1 tsp. Worcestershire
   sauce

Place chilled spinach in large salad bowl. Add chilled bean sprouts, drained water chestnuts, eggs, onion and bacon. Mix sugar, oil, salt, vinegar, catsup and Worcestershire sauce in small bowl; mix well. Pour over spinach mixture; toss to mix well. Serve immediately. Yield: 8 servings.

FLORENTINE SALAD

1 3-oz. package
   lemon or lime gelatin
1 c. boiling water
1 10-oz. package
   frozen chopped
   spinach, thawed, well
   drained

1 c. mayonnaise
1 c. large-curd cottage
   cheese
1/4 tsp. wine vinegar
1/2 c. chopped parsley
1 tbsp. chopped onion

Dissolve gelatin in boiling water in bowl. Stir in spinach, mayonnaise, cottage cheese, wine vinegar, parsley and chopped onion in order listed. Pour into lightly greased 9x9-inch pan. Chill until firm. Yield: 6 servings.

PORTUGUESE GREEN SOUP 🍎

2 med. onions,
   coarsely chopped
2 cloves of garlic,
   minced
1 tablespoon olive oil
2 lg. potatoes, peeled,
   sliced

6 c. chicken broth
2 10-oz. packages
   frozen chopped
   spinach, thawed
1 tsp. salt
1/4 tsp. freshly ground
   pepper

Sauté onions and garlic in oil in large saucepan until tender. Add potatoes and broth. Simmer, covered, for 45 minutes. Mash potatoes slightly with masher. Stir in spinach, salt and pepper. Bring to a boil; reduce heat. Simmer, covered, for 20 minutes longer or until spinach is tender. Yield: 6 to 8 servings.

Squash

CALABACITA CASSEROLE

1 1/2 lb. calabacita,
   chopped
1 med. onion, chopped
2 tbsp. margarine
1 4-oz. can chopped
   green chili peppers
2 tbsp. all-purpose
   flour

1 tsp. salt
1/4 tsp. pepper
1 1/2 c. shredded
   Monterey Jack cheese
1 egg, beaten
1 c. cottage cheese
2 tbsp. chopped parsley
1/2 c. Parmesan cheese

Sauté calabacita and onion in margarine in skillet until tender-crisp; drain well. Add green chilies, flour, salt and pepper; mix well. Pour into greased 2-quart baking dish. Sprinkle with shredded cheese. Combine egg, cottage cheese and parsley in bowl; mix well. Pour over casserole. Sprinkle with Parmesan cheese. Bake at 400 degrees for 45 minutes. Yield: 4 to 6 servings.

BAKED ACORN SQUASH

4 med. acorn squash
1 c. boiling water
3/4 c. apple jelly
2 tbsp. bacon drippings

4 tart red cooking
  apples, chopped
4 slices crisp-cooked
  bacon, crumbled

Cut squash in half lengthwise; discard seed. Place cut side up in large baking pan. Pour boiling water around squash. Bake, covered with foil, at 325 degrees for 1 hour. Melt jelly with drippings in saucepan. Remove from heat; stir in apples. Fill squash with apple mixture. Bake for 15 minutes longer or until squash is tender. Sprinkle with bacon. Yield: 8 servings.

BUTTERNUT SQUASH SOUFFLÉ

2 c. mashed cooked
  butternut squash
1 tsp. salt
1/4 c. maple syrup
2 tbsp. brown sugar
3 tbsp. cornstarch

3 egg yolks
1 1/4 c. whipping cream
1/2 c. melted butter
3 egg whites, stiffly
  beaten
1/2 c. slivered almonds

Combine squash, salt, syrup, brown sugar and cornstarch in mixer bowl; beat until fluffy. Add egg yolks, cream and butter; beat well. Fold in stiffly beaten egg whites gently. Pour into greased 1 1/2-quart casserole. Sprinkle with almonds. Bake at 350 degrees for 1 hour. Serve soufflé immediately. Yield: 8 servings.

STUFFED SQUASH

3 to 4 lb. yellow
  squash
1 sm. onion, chopped
3 tbsp. melted
  margarine
1/2 tsp. Worcestershire
  sauce

Cracker crumbs
Milk
8 oz. Cheddar cheese,
  cut into thin strips
Paprika

Cook squash in boiling water to cover in saucepan just until tender; drain. Cut squash into halves lengthwise. Scoop out pulp, reserving shells. Mix pulp with onion, margarine, Worcestershire sauce and 2 tablespoons cracker crumbs for each squash in bowl. Add enough milk to moisten. Spoon into reserved shells. Place on baking sheet. Top with additional cracker crumbs. Dot with additional margarine and cheese. Sprinkle with paprika. Bake at 375 degrees for 30 minutes. Yield: 6 servings.

Strawberry

STRAWBERRY AND CHEESE RING

12 oz. sharp Cheddar
  cheese, shredded
12 oz. medium
  Cheddar cheese,
  shredded
1 sm. onion, chopped
1 c. chopped pecans

1 c. mayonnaise
1 tsp. red pepper
1 16-oz. jar
  strawberry jam
1 15-oz. package
  Triscuits

Combine first 6 ingredients in food processor container. Process until smooth. Press into 6-cup mold. Chill for 4 hours. Unmold onto serving plate. Spoon jam into center. Serve with Triscuits. Yield: 50 servings.

SPRING STRAWBERRY SOUP

3 c. sliced strawberries
1 c. sugar
1/2 c. water
1 tbsp. cornstarch

1 tbsp. water
3/4 c. Rosé wine
1 c. fresh orange juice
1 1/4 c. sour cream

Combine strawberries, sugar and water in saucepan. Bring to a boil. Simmer for 5 minutes. Stir in cornstarch dissolved in water, wine and juice. Bring to a boil, stirring constantly. Cool for 15 minutes. Purée in blender or food processor container. Stir in sour cream. Chill. Garnish with additional sliced strawberries and mint leaves. Yield: 6 to 8 servings.

STRAWBERRY BLITZ TORTE

1 c. sifted cake flour
1 tsp. baking powder
1/4 tsp. salt
1/2 c. shortening
1/2 c. sugar
4 egg yolks
3 tbsp. milk
1 tsp. vanilla extract
4 egg whites

1/2 tsp. salt
1/2 tsp. cream of tartar
1 c. sugar
1/2 tsp. vanilla extract
1/2 c. whipping cream
2 tbsp. confectioners'
  sugar
1 1/2 c. sliced
  strawberries

Sift flour, baking powder and 1/4 teaspoon salt 3 times. Cream shortening in bowl. Add sugar gradually, creaming until light and fluffy. Beat egg yolks until thick. Add to creamed mixture. Stir in milk and vanilla. Add dry ingredients. Beat until smooth. Spread into 2 greased 8-inch cake pans. Beat egg whites, 1/2 teaspoon salt and cream of tartar until soft peaks form. Add sugar 2 tablespoons at a time, beating until stiff peaks form. Add vanilla. Mound half the meringue mixture over batter in each pan. Bake at 350 degrees for 35 minutes. Loosen from sides of pans. Remove to wire rack, keeping meringue side up. Cool. Whip cream with confectioners' sugar. Fold in strawberries. Spread strawberry mixture between layers. Yield: 12 servings.

STRAWBERRY BREAD

2 10-oz. packages	*2 c. sugar*
frozen strawberries,	*1 tbsp. cinnamon*
thawed	*1 tsp. soda*
4 eggs	*1 tsp. salt*
1 1/4 c. oil	*1 c. chopped pecans*
3 c. all-purpose flour	

Mix strawberries, eggs and oil in medium bowl. Combine flour, sugar, cinnamon, soda, salt and pecans in large bowl. Add strawberry mixture to dry ingredients; stir just until mixed. Pour into 2 greased and floured 5x9-inch loaf pans. Bake at 350 degrees for 1 hour or until toothpick inserted in center comes out clean. Yield: 24 slices.

FRESH STRAWBERRY MUFFINS

1 c. chopped	*1/4 c. vegetable oil*
strawberries	*1/2 c. milk*
1 tbsp. sugar	*1 tsp. grated orange*
2 c. all-purpose flour	*rind*
3/4 c. sugar	*8 oz. cream cheese*
2 tsp. baking powder	*1/4 c. crushed*
1 tsp. salt	*strawberries*
3 eggs	

Sprinkle chopped strawberries with 1 tablespoon sugar; set aside. Sift dry ingredients into large bowl. Beat eggs in small bowl until light. Blend in oil, milk and orange rind. Add to flour mixture; stir for 10 to 15 strokes until mixed. Drain chopped berries; fold into batter. Fill paper-lined muffin cups 2/3 full. Bake at 400 degrees for 15 minutes. Serve warm with cream cheese mixed with crushed strawberries. Yield: 1 dozen.

STRAWBERRIES CHANTILLY

1/3 c. whipping cream	*1 pt. fresh strawberries*
2 tsp. sugar	*1/4 c. Melba Sauce*
1/4 tsp. vanilla extract	*Kirsch to taste*
Dash of salt	*Whipped cream*

Combine cream with sugar, vanilla and salt in chilled mixer bowl. Beat with chilled beaters until doubled in bulk. Rinse, drain and hull strawberries; drain on paper towels. Mix whole strawberries with 1/4 cup Melba Sauce and Kirsch in bowl. Spoon into clear dessert dishes. Top with whipped cream. Yield: 4 servings.

Melba Sauce

1 10-oz. package	*1 tbsp. lemon juice*
frozen raspberries	*1/4 tsp. grated lemon*
1/2 c. red currant jelly	*rind*
1/4 c. sugar	*Dash of salt*

Thaw raspberries. Simmer, covered, in saucepan for 15 minutes. Press through fine strainer into 1 cup measure. Add enough water to measure 2/3 cup. Combine with remaining ingredients in saucepan. Simmer until smooth, stirring constantly. Store in airtight container in refrigerator. For thicker sauce, use additional jelly or reduce water. Yield: 1 1/4 cups.

CHAMPAGNE DESSERT SALAD

8 oz. cream cheese,	*2 or 3 bananas, sliced*
softened	*1 20-oz. can pineapple*
3/4 c. sugar	*tidbits, drained*
1 10-oz. package	*1/2 c. chopped walnuts*
frozen strawberries,	*1 8-oz. container*
thawed	*whipped topping*

Blend cream cheese and sugar in large bowl. Combine undrained strawberries, bananas, pineapple, walnuts and whipped topping in bowl; mix well. Add to cream cheese mixture; mix gently. Spoon into loaf pan. Freeze until firm. Slice and serve. Yield: 18 servings.

STRAWBERRY SHORTCAKE DESSERT

1 10-in. angel food or	*8 oz. cream cheese,*
sponge cake without	*softened*
hole in center	*3/4 c. sugar*
1 1/2 qt. fresh	*1 env. unflavored*
strawberries	*gelatin*
1/4 c. sugar	*1 1/2 c. whipping cream*
1 tsp. vanilla extract	*1/4 c. sugar*

Slice cake into 3 layers. Purée 2 cups strawberries with 1/4 cup sugar in blender container. Place 1 cake layer on serving plate. Top with strawberry purée and second cake layer. Beat next 3 ingredients in mixer bowl until thickened. Spread over cake. Slice 3 cups strawberries. Arrange over cream cheese. Top with remaining layer. Chill for 6 hours. Soften gelatin in whipping cream for 5 minutes. Whip until soft peaks form. Add 1/4 cup sugar gradually. Whip until mixture holds shape. Frost top and sides of cake. Cut remaining 1 cup strawberries into halves. Arrange stem ends toward center on top of cake. Yield: 12 servings.

STRAWBERRY GLACÉ PIE

1/3 c. butter	*8 oz. cream cheese,*
3 tbsp. sugar	*softened*
1 egg yolk	*1 qt. strawberries*
1 c. all-purpose flour	*1 c. sugar*
1 c. flaked coconut	*3 tbsp. cornstarch*
1/2 c. sugar	*1 c. whipped cream*
1 tsp. lemon juice	

Cream butter and 3 tablespoons sugar in mixer bowl until light and fluffy. Blend in egg yolk. Stir in flour and coconut. Press over bottom and side of 9-inch pie plate; flute edge. Prick with fork. Bake at 325 degrees for 25 minutes or until light brown. Cool on wire rack. Cream 1/2 cup sugar, lemon juice and cream cheese in bowl until light and fluffy. Spread in cooled pie shell. Arrange whole strawberries stem side down over filling. Chill for 1 hour. Mash and strain remaining strawberries. Add enough water to strawberry juice to measure 1 1/2 cups. Bring juice to a boil in saucepan. Add mixture of 1 cup sugar and cornstarch gradually, stirring constantly. Cook for 1 minute, stirring constantly. Cool. Spoon glaze over strawberries. Chill for several hours. Top with whipped cream. Yield: 6 servings.

WINTER STRAWBERRY CHIFFON PIE

1 env. unflavored gelatin	*1/8 tsp. salt*
2 tbsp. cold water	*3 egg whites, stiffly beaten*
1 1/2 c. strawberry preserves	*1 c. whipping cream, whipped*
3 tbsp. lemon juice	*1 baked 10-in. pie shell*

Soften gelatin in cold water in saucepan. Heat until dissolved, stirring frequently. Remove from heat. Stir in preserves, lemon juice and salt. Chill for 30 minutes. Fold into egg whites gently. Fold into whipped cream gently. Chill for 15 minutes. Spoon into pie shell. Chill until firm. Garnish with whipped cream and mint. Yield: 8 servings.

Sweet Bread

CHERRY ROSE ROLLS

3/4 c. milk	*3 to 4 c. flour*
1 pkg. dry yeast	*1 21-oz. can cherry pie filling*
1/2 c. warm water	
1 c. sourdough starter	*1 c. confectioners' sugar*
1/2 c. melted butter	
1/2 c. sugar	*1 tsp. vanilla extract*
1 1/2 tsp. salt	*1 tbsp. milk*

Bring 3/4 cup milk just to the simmering point in saucepan. Cool for 10 minutes. Dissolve yeast in warm water. Combine milk, yeast, sourdough starter, butter, sugar and salt in bowl. Add enough flour to form a soft dough. Knead on floured surface for 5 minutes or until smooth and elastic. Place in greased bowl, turning to grease surface. Chill, covered, for 2 hours to overnight. Punch dough down. Divide into 24 portions. Roll each

to 15-inch rope on floured surface. Coil ropes 2 inches apart on greased baking sheet, tucking ends under. Let rise, covered, in a warm place for 2 hours or until doubled in bulk. Make 1-inch wide indentation in tops of rolls. Fill with pie filling. Bake at 400 degrees for 15 to 20 minutes or until golden. Cool. Combine confectioners' sugar, vanilla and 1 tablespoon milk in bowl; mix until smooth. Pipe onto rolls. Yield: 24 rolls.

BUBBLE BREAD

1/2 c. chopped pecans	*1/2 c. packed brown sugar*
1 3-oz. package butterscotch pudding and pie filling mix	*1/2 c. margarine*
	18 frozen rolls

Sprinkle pecans in greased bundt pan. Combine pudding mix, brown sugar and margarine in saucepan. Bring to a boil. Cool slightly. Place frozen rolls in prepared pan. Pour brown sugar mixture over rolls. Let rise, covered, overnight. Bake at 350 degrees for 30 minutes. Invert onto serving plate. Yield: 8 servings.

CINNAMON TWIST ROLLS

1 3/4 c. all-purpose flour	*2 eggs, at room temperature*
3/4 c. sugar	*3/4 c. raisins*
1 tsp. salt	*3 3/4 to 4 3/4 c. all-purpose flour*
2 pkg. dry yeast	
1 c. milk	*Margarine, softened*
2/3 c. water	*3/4 c. sugar*
1/4 c. margarine	*2 tsp. cinnamon*
1/2 c. all-purpose flour	

Combine first 4 ingredients in large mixer bowl; set aside. Heat milk, water and margarine in saucepan until very warm, 120 to 130 degrees. Add to flour mixture. Beat at medium speed for 2 minutes. Add 1/2 cup flour and eggs. Beat at high speed for 2 minutes. Stir in raisins. Add enough remaining flour to make stiff dough. Knead on floured surface for 8 to 10 minutes or until smooth and elastic. Cover with plastic wrap and towel. Let rest for 20 minutes. Divide into 2 portions. Roll each portion to 1/4-inch thickness. Brush center with softened margarine. Sprinkle with mixture of 3/4 cup sugar and cinnamon. Fold left side over center to cover filling; fold right side over top. Seal edges. Cut crosswise into 1-inch strips. Twist and place in greased baking pan. Cover with oiled waxed paper. Chill for 2 to 24 hours. Let stand for 15 minutes. Bake at 375 degrees for 25 to 30 minutes. Yield: 2 dozen.

MONKEY BREAD

3 10-ct. cans	*²/₃ c. packed brown*
refrigerator biscuits	*sugar*
²/₃ c. sugar	*3 oz. pecans, coarsely*
1 tbsp. cinnamon	*chopped*
6 tbsp. margarine	

Cut biscuits into fourths. Coat with mixture of sugar and cinnamon. Layer biscuits in well-greased bundt pan. Combine melted margarine and brown sugar in bowl; mix well. Drizzle over biscuits. Sprinkle with pecans. Place in cold oven. Set temperature at 350 degrees. Bake for 30 minutes. Let stand for 10 minutes. Invert onto serving plate. Yield: 30 servings.

SWIRLED CHOCOLATE SWEET ROLLS

1 pkg. hot roll mix	*2 tbsp. margarine*
1 tbsp. sugar	*2 tbsp. sugar*
¹/₄ c. unsweetened	*¹/₂ c. miniature*
baking cocoa	*chocolate chips*
1¹/₄ c. (120-degree)	*Confectioners' sugar*
water	*¹/₄ c. miniature*
2 tbsp. margarine	*chocolate chips*
1 egg	*1 tsp. shortening*

Combine yeast and flour from roll mix, 1 tablespoon sugar and cocoa in bowl. Stir in water, 2 tablespoons margarine and egg until dough pulls from side of bowl. Knead on floured surface until smooth. Cover with large bowl. Let rest for 5 minutes. Roll into 12x15-inch rectangle; spread with 2 tablespoons margarine. Sprinkle with 2 tablespoons sugar and ¹/₂ cup chocolate chips. Roll up from short end; press edges to seal. Cut into 12 slices. Arrange in greased 9x13-inch pan. Let rise, covered, for 30 minutes on wire rack over hot water. Bake at 375 degrees for 15 to 20 minutes. Sprinkle with confectioners' sugar. Melt remaining ingredients in saucepan over low heat. Drizzle over rolls. Yield: 1 dozen.

Sweet Potato

HARVEST SWEET POTATO BISCUITS

1 egg, slightly beaten	*2 tbsp. margarine,*
1 c. mashed cooked	*softened*
sweet potatoes	*2 c. (about) self-rising*
¹/₄ to ¹/₂ c. sugar	*flour*
3 tbsp. shortening	

Combine egg, sweet potatoes, sugar, shortening and margarine in bowl; mix well. Stir in enough flour to make soft dough. Knead lightly several times on floured surface. Roll to ¹/₄-inch thickness; cut with 2-inch biscuit cutter. Place on greased baking sheet. Bake at 350 degrees for 15 minutes. Yield: 17 biscuits.

SWEET POTATO NUT BREAD

2¹/₂ c. sugar	*3¹/₃ c. all-purpose flour*
²/₃ c. oil	*2 tsp. soda*
4 eggs	*¹/₂ tsp. baking powder*
1 16-oz. can sweet	*1 tsp. cinnamon*
potatoes, drained	*1¹/₂ tsp. salt*
²/₃ c. water	*1 c. chopped pecans*

Combine sugar, oil, eggs, sweet potatoes and water in large mixer bowl. Beat until smooth. Stir in remaining ingredients. Grease bottoms of two 5x9-inch pans. Pour in batter. Bake at 350 degrees for 1 hour and 10 minutes or until toothpick inserted in center comes out clean. Cool slightly in pans. Remove to wire rack to cool completely. Store, wrapped in plastic wrap, in refrigerator for up to 10 days. Yield: 24 slices.

SWEET POTATO BALLS IN WALNUTS 🍎

2¹/₂ c. mashed cooked	*¹/₂ tsp. salt*
sweet potatoes	*Pinch of pepper*
2 tbsp. melted	*¹/₃ c. honey*
margarine	*1 c. chopped walnuts*

Combine sweet potatoes, margarine, salt and pepper in bowl; mix well. Chill until easy to handle. Shape into 2-inch balls. Heat honey in small heavy skillet over medium heat. Place potatoes 1 at a time in honey, turning carefully with 2 forks to coat well. Roll in walnuts, coating well. Place in greased shallow baking dish with sides not touching. Bake at 350 degrees for 20 to 25 minutes or until heated through. Yield: 10 servings.

SPECIAL SWEET POTATO CASSEROLE

2 c. mashed cooked	*¹/₂ c. flaked coconut*
sweet potatoes	*1¹/₂ c. miniature*
²/₃ c. evaporated milk	*marshmallows*
Juice and grated rind	*1¹/₂ c. sugar*
of 1 med. orange	*¹/₂ c. melted margarine*
¹/₂ c. chopped pecans	*3 eggs*

Combine sweet potatoes with remaining ingredients in bowl in order listed, mixing well after each addition. Spoon into 3-quart baking dish. Bake at 350 degrees for 45 minutes. Yield: 12 servings.

SWEET POTATO-PINEAPPLE BAKE

2   1-lb. cans sweet   1 tsp. vanilla extract
    potatoes   1 c. miniature
1 tbsp. margarine   marshmallows
1   8-oz. can crushed   ¹/₂ c. broken walnuts
    pineapple, drained

Heat sweet potatoes in saucepan; drain. Mash with margarine. Add pineapple and vanilla. Spread in 8x8-inch baking dish. Top with marshmallows and walnuts. Bake at 350 degrees for 35 minutes or until marshmallows are golden brown.
Yield: 6 to 8 servings.

HOLIDAY SWEET POTATO PIES

3¹/₂ c. mashed cooked   ¹/₂ tsp. salt
    sweet potatoes   2 tsp. lemon extract
¹/₂ c. margarine,   1   13-oz. can
    softened   evaporated milk
2 c. sugar   2 unbaked 9-in. pie
4 eggs   shells
¹/₂ tsp. nutmeg

Combine sweet potatoes, margarine and sugar in mixer bowl; beat until smooth. Add eggs 1 at a time, mixing well after each addition. Stir in nutmeg, salt, lemon extract and evaporated milk. Pour into pie shells. Bake at 425 degrees for 20 minutes. Reduce temperature to 325 degrees. Bake for 30 to 45 minutes longer or until set. Yield: 2 pies.

Tomato

SUMMER SALSA

3 lg. tomatoes, peeled,   1 med. onion, finely
    chopped   chopped
1 chili pepper, seeded,   Dash of cayenne
    finely chopped   pepper
3 jalapeño peppers,   1 tbsp. finely chopped
    seeded, finely   parsley
    chopped   ¹/₂ tsp. cumin
3 cloves of garlic,   ¹/₂ tsp. salt
    pressed   1 tsp. sugar
Pinch of black pepper

Combine all ingredients in bowl; mix well. Adjust seasonings to taste. Refrigerate for several hours.

Serve with tortilla chips or with Mexican dishes.
Yield: 2¹/₂ cups.

TOMATO AND COTTAGE CHEESE SALAD

1   4-oz. package lemon   2 tbsp. chopped green
    gelatin   bell pepper
1¹/₂ c. hot tomato juice   ¹/₂ c. finely diced celery
1 tbsp. vinegar   2 c. shredded cabbage
2 tbsp. cold water   ¹/₃ c. mayonnaise
1¹/₄ c. cottage cheese   1 tsp. (scant) salt

Dissolve gelatin in hot tomato juice in saucepan. Stir in vinegar. Combine ¹/₂ cup tomato mixture with cold water in ring mold. Chill until firm. Chill remaining gelatin until thickened. Fold in remaining ingredients. Pour over congealed layer. Chill until firm. Yield: 6 servings.

TOMATO AND MOZZARELLA SALAD

6 tbsp. extra virgin   6 oz. fresh mozzarella
    olive oil   cheese, thinly sliced
2 tbsp. balsamic   8 thin slices red onion
    vinegar   Salt and pepper to
8 lg. Roma tomatoes,   taste
    sliced

Combine olive oil and vinegar in jar. Chill in refrigerator. Arrange slices of tomato, cheese and onion on salad plates. Mix oil and vinegar well; drizzle over salad. Season to taste.
Yield: 4 servings.

HEARTY TOMATO SOUP

1 onion, chopped   1   28-oz. can tomatoes,
1 stalk celery, chopped   chopped
1 carrot, chopped   1 tbsp. sugar
1 clove of garlic,   1 tsp. oregano
    minced   1 tsp. basil
2 tbsp. oil   2 tsp. salt
2 tbsp. whole wheat   4 white peppercorns
    flour   3 c. hot milk
1¹/₂ c. cooked rice   1 tbsp. margarine

Sauté onion, celery, carrot and garlic in oil in 4-quart saucepan until onion is golden. Add flour and rice. Sauté until rice is golden. Stir in tomatoes, sugar and seasonings. Simmer for 15 minutes or longer. Purée in blender container if desired. Add milk and margarine. Heat just to serving temperature; do not boil. Yield: 6 servings.

CHEESY ITALIAN TOMATO CASSEROLE

4 tomatoes, sliced	*1/2 c. crumbled crisp-*
8 c. bread, cubed	*fried bacon*
1/2 c. chopped onion	*1/2 tsp. garlic salt*
1/2 c. chopped celery	*1/2 tsp. oregano*
2 eggs, well beaten	*3 c. shredded*
1/2 c. melted margarine	*mozzarella cheese*

Line greased 2 1/2-quart baking dish with tomato slices. Combine bread crumbs, onion, celery, eggs, margarine, bacon, seasonings and 2 cups cheese in bowl; mix well. Pour into prepared baking dish. Top with remaining tomato slices and 1 cup cheese. Bake at 350 degrees for 20 minutes. Yield: 8 servings.

SCALLOPED HERB TOMATOES

6 c. canned tomatoes,	*1/2 tsp. oregano*
chopped	*1/4 tsp. rosemary*
2 c. herb-seasoned	*1/4 tsp. pepper*
poultry stuffing	*1/3 c. herb-seasoned*
1 onion, chopped	*poultry stuffing*
2 tbsp. sugar	*2 tbsp. margarine*
1 tbsp. salt	

Combine tomatoes, herb-seasoned poultry stuffing, onion, sugar, salt, oregano, rosemary and pepper in bowl; mix well. Spoon into greased casserole. Top with 1/3 cup stuffing mix. Dot with butter. Bake at 375 degrees for 45 minutes. Yield: 10 servings.

SUMMER'S EVE STUFFED TOMATOES

4 tomatoes	*1 tsp. basil*
1 clove of garlic,	*1 tsp. salt*
crushed	*1/8 tsp. pepper*
1/4 c. oil	*1/4 c. Parmesan cheese*
4 c. fresh bread crumbs	*1 tbsp. oil*
1/4 c. chopped parsley	

Cut off tops of tomatoes. Remove and chop pulp, leaving shells. Invert shells on paper towel to drain. Sauté chopped tomato and garlic in 1/4 cup oil in skillet for 2 minutes. Stir in bread crumbs, parsley, basil, salt, pepper and 2 tablespoons cheese. Spoon into tomato shells. Place in 8x8-inch baking dish. Sprinkle with remaining 2 tablespoons cheese. Brush with 1 tablespoon oil. Bake at 400 degrees for 5 minutes. Yield: 4 servings.

Tuna

TUNA BALL

1 6 1/2-oz. can tuna	*2 tbsp. bacon bits*
8 oz. cream cheese,	*1 tbsp. Worcestershire*
softened	*sauce*
1 sm. onion, finely	*2 tsp. seasoned salt*
chopped	*Parsley flakes*

Drain and flake tuna in bowl. Add cream cheese; mix well. Add onion, bacon bits and seasonings; mix well. Shape into ball; roll in parsley flakes. Serve with club crackers. Yield: 8 servings.

TUNA ESCABECHE

2 6 1/2-oz. cans	*1/4 c. minced celery*
tuna, drained	*1 tsp. red pepper*
2 sm. onions	*flakes, crumbled*
1/4 c. olive oil	*1/2 c. white wine*
1 clove of garlic,	*vinegar*
minced	*Salt and pepper to taste*
1/2 c. minced carrot	*1 or 2 seedless*
1/4 c. minced red bell	*hothouse cucumbers,*
pepper	*sliced 1/4 in. thick*

Break tuna into large flakes; arrange in single layer in shallow dish. Cut onions into halves lengthwise; slice thinly crosswise. Sauté onions in skillet over moderately low heat until tender. Add garlic. Sauté for 1 minute. Add carrot, bell pepper, celery, red pepper flakes and vinegar. Bring to a boil. Simmer for 5 minutes, stirring occasionally. Add salt and pepper. Pour over tuna. Marinate, covered, overnight or up to 2 days. Top cucumber slice with tuna mixture; arrange on serving tray. Use oil-pack chunk light tuna. Yield: 40 hors d'oeuvres.

BROILED TUNA MELT

2 tbsp. mayonnaise	*2 tbsp. chopped sweet*
1 tsp. lemon juice	*pickle*
Several drops red	*2 English muffins,*
pepper sauce	*split, toasted*
1 6 1/2-oz. can tuna	*1/2 avocado, sliced*
1/4 c. finely chopped	*1/2 c. alfalfa sprouts*
onion	*2 slices Cheddar*
3 tbsp. chopped	*cheese*
cucumber	

Blend first 3 ingredients in bowl. Add tuna, onion, cucumber and pickle; toss gently. Place English muffins on cookie sheet, overlapping sides slightly. Place avocado slices and alfalfa sprouts over each pair, dividing evenly. Spoon tuna mixture over top. Arrange cheese triangles over top. Broil for 2 minutes or until cheese melts. Serve immediately. Use water-pack tuna. Yield: 2 servings.

TUNA NUGGETS

2 6¹/₂-oz. cans tuna	2 tsp. horseradish
6 oz. cream cheese, softened	¹/₄ tsp. hot pepper sauce
1 tbsp. lemon juice	1 c. chopped parsley

Drain and flake tuna. Combine cream cheese, lemon juice, horseradish, hot pepper sauce, parsley and tuna in bowl; mix well. Shape by teaspoonfuls into balls. Roll in parsley. Chill until firm. Yield: 48 appetizers.

TUNA CASSEROLE DELIGHT

1 8-oz. package noodles	1 tbsp. vinegar
1 6¹/₂-oz. can tuna	1 soup can milk
1 can cream of mushroom soup	1 c. shredded Cheddar cheese
¹/₂ c. grated onion	¹/₄ c. Parmesan cheese

Cook noodles according to package directions; drain. Combine tuna, soup, onion, vinegar, milk and Cheddar cheese in bowl; mix well. Stir in noodles. Spoon into 2-quart baking dish. Sprinkle with Parmesan cheese. Bake at 350 degrees for 1 hour. Yield: 8 servings.

TUNA AND VEGETABLE CASSEROLE

2 13-oz. cans tuna, drained, flaked	¹/₂ c. chopped onion
2 10-oz. packages frozen Chinese pea pods	1 c. bean sprouts
	¹/₂ c. chopped green bell pepper
2 10-oz. packages frozen green beans	¹/₂ c. chopped red bell pepper
1 c. sliced fresh mushrooms	2 tsp. garlic salt
1 c. chopped celery	2 c. milk
	Crushed cheese crackers

Combine all ingredients except cracker crumbs in bowl; mix well. Spoon into 8x12-inch baking dish. Sprinkle with cracker crumbs. Bake at 350 degrees for 15 minutes. Serve with rice or noodles. Yield: 6 servings.

TUNA AND RICE MUFFINETTES

2 c. cooked brown rice	1 tsp. seasoned salt
1 6¹/₂-oz. can tuna, drained	¹/₈ tsp. pepper
1 c. shredded Cheddar cheese	2 eggs, slightly beaten
	2 tbsp. milk
¹/₂ c. sliced pitted black olives	1 tbsp. capers
	¹/₄ c. melted margarine
2 tbsp. minced onion	Parsley sprigs
2 tbsp. minced parsley	Lemon wedges

Combine first 10 ingredients in bowl; mix well. Pack into 12 well-greased muffin cups. Bake at 375 degrees for 15 minutes or until brown. Let stand for 5 minutes; remove from pans. Invert onto hot platter. Add capers to melted margarine. Pour butter over muffinetts. Garnish with parsley and lemon wedges. Use water-pack chunk light tuna. Yield: 4 servings.

TUNA RING

1 egg, slightly beaten	¹/₂ c. chopped parsley
2 6¹/₂-oz. cans tuna, drained	1 tsp. celery salt
	¹/₄ tsp. pepper
¹/₂ c. shredded sharp Cheddar cheese	1 recipe biscuit dough
¹/₄ c. chopped onion	1 recipe cheese sauce

Reserve about 2 tablespoons egg. Mix remaining egg with tuna, cheese, onion, parsley, celery salt and pepper. Roll biscuit dough into large rectangle. Spread with tuna mixture. Roll as for jelly roll from long edge. Shape into circle on greased baking sheet. Cut 12 slices ³/₄ inch through roll. Fan each slice back and to side. Brush with reserved egg. Bake at 375 degrees for 25 minutes. Serve with hot cheese sauce. Yield: 6 servings.

TUNA THERMIDOR

¹/₃ c. chopped green bell pepper	¹/₂ c. milk
¹/₄ c. chopped onion	¹/₂ c. shredded Cheddar cheese
2 tbsp. margarine	1 6¹/₂-oz. can tuna
1 can cream of potato soup	1 3-oz. can tuna
	1 tbsp. dry Sherry

Sauté green pepper and onion in margarine in saucepan. Add soup and milk. Cook until heated through, stirring constantly. Add cheese. Cook until cheese melts, stirring constantly. Add tuna and Sherry. Cook until heated through. Serve over rice. May substitute crab meat or shrimp for tuna. Yield: 4 servings.

TUNA AND SHELLS

4 c. shell macaroni	¹/₃ c. chopped onion
1 6¹/₂-oz. can tuna	¹/₃ c. chopped carrot
1 c. sliced celery	1 c. mayonnaise
¹/₂ c. sliced sweet pickles	1 tbsp. sweet pickle juice

Cook macaroni according to package directions; drain well. Combine with remaining ingredients in bowl; mix well. Chill until serving time. Garnish with parsley and paprika. Yield: 6 servings.

TUNA OVEN SANDWICHES

1 6¹/₂-oz. can tuna,
   drained
¹/₄ c. chopped onion
¹/₃ c. chopped celery
¹/₂ c. shredded
   mozzarella cheese
¹/₂ tsp. parsley flakes

¹/₈ tsp. salt
Dash of pepper
2 tbsp. mayonnaise
3 hamburger buns
1 tbsp. margarine,
   softened

Combine tuna, onion, celery, mozzarella cheese, parsley flakes, salt, pepper and mayonnaise in bowl; mix well. Separate hamburger buns; spread cut sides with margarine. Spread with tuna mixture; place on baking sheet. Broil until golden.
Yield: 3 servings.

Turkey

PUMPKIN-TURKEY FALL STEW

8 to 10-in. (diameter)
   pumpkin
2 tbsp. all-purpose
   flour
1 tsp. salt
¹/₈ tsp. ginger
¹/₂ tsp. pumpkin pie
   spice

2 lb. turkey, cubed
2 tbsp. oil
1 med. onion, chopped
2 or 3 carrots, peeled,
   sliced
³/₄ c. green beans
1 c. beef bouillon

Slice top off pumpkin; reserve. Scoop out, leaving 1-inch shell. Reserve 1 cup pumpkin pieces. Combine flour, salt, ginger and pumpkin spice in bowl. Add turkey; toss to coat. Brown turkey in oil in skillet. Add pumpkin and remaining ingredients. Bring to a boil. Simmer for 10 minutes, stirring constantly. Spoon turkey mixture into pumpkin shell. Replace top. Pour 1-inch boiling water into cake pan. Place pumpkin in water. Bake at 350 degrees for 1¹/₄ hours. Cover pumpkin with foil. Bake for 1¹/₂ hours. Serve with apple butter, mashed potatoes and salad. Yield: 6 servings.

TURKEY-WILD RICE CASSEROLE

1 lg. onion, chopped
¹/₂ c. chopped celery
¹/₂ c. margarine
²/₃ c. all-purpose flour
2 tsp. salt
Pepper to taste
3 c. turkey broth
2 cans cream of
   mushroom soup
1 pkg. long grain and
   wild rice mix, prepared

5 cups chopped cooked
   turkey
1 2-oz. can chopped
   pimento
¹/₂ c. coarsely chopped
   green bell pepper
1 4-oz. package
   slivered almonds
¹/₂ c. Parmesan
   cheese

Sauté onion and celery in margarine in skillet. Stir in flour and seasonings. Stir in turkey broth and soup gradually. Cook until mixture thickens, stirring constantly. Add rice, turkey, pimento, green pepper and almonds to soup mixture; mix well. Spoon into greased 9x13-inch baking dish. Sprinkle with Parmesan cheese. Bake at 425 degrees for 30 to 45 minutes or until bubbly.
Yield: 12 servings.

PETITE TURKEY LOAF

1 egg yolk, beaten
3 tbsp. soft whole
   wheat bread crumbs
1 tbsp. sliced green
   onion
1 tbsp. water
1 tsp. snipped parsley

¹/₈ tsp. salt
Dash of ground sage
4 oz. ground fresh
   turkey
1 tbsp. cranberry-
   orange relish

Combine egg yolk, bread crumbs, green onion, water, parsley, salt, sage and ground turkey in bowl; mix well. Shape into 1x4¹/₂-inch loaf; place in small shallow baking dish. Bake, uncovered, at 350 degrees for 25 to 30 minutes; drain. Spoon relish on top. Bake for 2 to 3 minutes longer. Serve with baked sweet potato and fresh garden salad.
Yield: 1 serving.

STUFFED TURKEY ROLL

1 pkg. chicken-
   flavored stuffing
   mix
1 egg

2 1-lb. rolls frozen
   ground turkey,
   thawed
³/₄ c. dry bread crumbs

Prepare stuffing mix according to package directions decreasing water by ¹/₂ cup. Combine egg, turkey, bread crumbs and salt and pepper to taste in bowl; mix well. Spread turkey mixture into 10x15-inch rectangle on waxed paper. Spread stuffing mixture on top to within ¹/₂ inch of edges. Roll as for jelly roll from short side. Place in greased 4x8-inch loaf pan. Bake at 350 degrees for 1 hour. Let stand for 10 to 15 minutes before slicing. Yield: 6 servings.

EASY TURKEY PIE

¹/₂ c. chopped onion
¹/₃ c. margarine
¹/₃ c. all-purpose
   flour
1¹/₂ tsp. salt
3 c. turkey broth
4 c. chopped cooked
   turkey
1 c. cooked peas

1 c. chopped cooked
   carrots
1 c. chopped cooked
   potatoes
1 6-oz. can mushrooms
1 c. buttermilk baking
   mix
²/₃ c. milk

Sauté onion in margarine in skillet until tender. Stir in flour and salt. Add broth gradually, stirring constantly. Cook until thickened, stirring constantly. Add turkey and vegetables. Pour into 9x13-inch baking dish. Combine baking mix and milk in bowl; mix well. Drop by spoonfuls over turkey. Bake at 450 degrees for 10 to 12 minutes or until golden brown. Yield: 6 servings.

Veal

VEAL BAGNA MARIA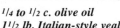

1/4 to 1/2 c. olive oil	*1/4 c. parsley*
1 1/2 lb. Italian-style veal cutlets	*Parmesan cheese*
1 lg. clove of garlic	*Salt and pepper to taste*
	1/4 c. white wine

Pour 2 inches water in bottom of double boiler. Cover bottom of top pan with olive oil. Place layer of veal cutlets in pan. Sprinkle minced garlic, parsley, cheese, salt and pepper over veal. Repeat layers with remaining ingredients. Add wine. Cook, covered, over hot water for 35 minutes. Veal should be slightly pink. Yield: 6 servings.

VEAL CUTLETS WITH MUSTARD SAUCE

8 2-oz. veal cutlets	*1 tbsp. all-purpose flour*
1/3 c. all-purpose flour	*1 tbsp. Dijon-style mustard*
2 eggs, slightly beaten	*1/2 tsp. sugar*
3/4 c. dry bread crumbs	*1/2 tsp. salt*
2 tbsp. margarine	*1/4 tsp. pepper*
2 tbsp. corn oil	*1 c. light cream*
1 sm. onion, sliced	
1/3 c. beef broth	

Flatten cutlets to 1/4 inch between 2 sheets of waxed paper. Coat cutlets 1 at a time with 1/3 cup flour. Dip into eggs and coat with crumbs. Brown several at a time on both sides in mixture of margarine and oil in skillet. Remove to serving platter; cover. Keep warm. Sauté onion in remaining margarine and oil in skillet for 5 minutes or until tender. Stir in mixture of broth and 1 tablespoon flour and next 4 ingredients. Cook until thickened, stirring constantly. Stir in cream. Heat for 1 minute, stirring constantly. Pour over cutlets. Yield: 4 servings.

FAVORITE VEAL MEAT LOAF

4 sm. onions, chopped	*Salt and pepper to taste*
1 clove of garlic, minced	*2 eggs*
	1 or 2 c. boiling water
4 1/2 lb. ground veal	*8 oz. flavored bread crumbs*
Catsup to taste	

Sauté onions in skillet. Add garlic. Sauté for 1 minute longer. Combine with next 4 ingredients in bowl. Mix by hand. Add eggs, water and bread crumbs; mix well by hand. Shape into loaves. Place in 2 loaf pans. Bake at 350 degrees for 30 to 40 minutes. Yield: 10 servings.

Vegetable

FRESH VEGETABLE STEW

1 1/2 c. chopped onions	*2 tsp. salt*
1 c. sliced celery	*12 c. bite-sized mixed fresh green beans, red and green bell peppers, zucchini, eggplant, potatoes, summer squash, mushrooms and kale*
2 cloves of garlic, crushed	
2 tbsp. olive oil	
1 19-oz. can cannellini	
1 19-oz. can chick peas	
3 c. chopped fresh tomatoes	*4 c. steamed brown rice*
1 tbsp. Italian seasoning	*Parmesan cheese*

Sauté onions, celery and garlic in olive oil in large saucepan for 5 minutes or until tender. Drain cannellini and chick peas, reserving liquid. Add enough water to reserved liquid to measure 2 1/2 cups. Add to sauce pan with tomatoes, Italian seasoning and salt. Bring to a boil; reduce heat. Simmer, covered, for 15 minutes. Add fresh vegetables. Simmer, covered, for 8 minutes or until almost tender, stirring occasionally. Stir in cannellini and chick peas. Heat to serving temperature. Serve over steamed brown rice. Garnish with Parmesan cheese. Yield: 8 servings.

WINTER POT ROAST VEGETABLES

6 c. sliced onions	*4 turnips, peeled, cubed*
2 tbsp. oil	*1 c. sliced celery*
4 carrots, peeled, sliced	*1 c. beef broth*

Sauté onions in oil in saucepan. Add vegetables and broth. Simmer, covered, for 30 minutes or until tender. Serve with favorite pot roast. Yield: 8 servings.

Walnut

WALNUT YULE BREAD

2 c. all-purpose flour	*1 egg, beaten*
1 pkg. RapidRise	*1 c. finely chopped*
yeast	*walnuts*
1/3 c. sugar	*1 c. all-purpose flour*
1 tbsp. ground	*1 egg, beaten*
cardamom	*Walnut halves*
1 tsp. salt	*3 tbsp. coarsely*
1/4 c. margarine	*crushed sugar cubes*
3/4 c. half and half	

Combine 2 cups flour, yeast, sugar, cardamom and salt in large bowl. Heat margarine and half and half in saucepan over medium heat to 125 to 135 degrees. Stir into flour mixture. Add 1 egg, chopped walnuts and enough remaining 1 cup flour to make soft dough, mixing well after each addition. Knead on lightly floured surface for 8 minutes or until smooth and elastic. Let rest, covered, for 10 minutes. Shape into 36-inch rope. Place 1 end of rope in center of lightly greased baking sheet. Coil rope into round loaf; seal end to loaf. Brush with remaining egg; garnish with walnut halves and sprinkle with crushed sugar. Cut loaf at 1-inch intervals around edge with scissors or sharp knife. Let rise, covered, in warm place for 40 minutes or until almost doubled in bulk. Place in lower third of oven. Bake for 25 to 30 minutes or until loaf is brown and tests done. Cover with foil during last few minutes of baking if necessary to prevent overbrowning. Cool on wire rack. Yield: 1 loaf.

FRENCH WALNUT TORTE

1 1/2 c. sugar	*2 tbsp. sugar*
3 eggs	*1/2 c. margarine,*
1 tbsp. vanilla extract	*softened*
1 3/4 c. all-purpose	*8 oz. cream cheese,*
flour	*softened*
2 tsp. baking powder	*4 c. confectioners'*
1 c. ground walnuts	*sugar*
1 1/2 c. whipping cream,	*1 tsp. vanilla extract*
whipped	*1 c. ground walnuts*
1 c. peach preserves	

Beat 1 1/2 c. sugar, eggs and 1 tablespoon vanilla in mixer bowl at high speed for 5 minutes. Mix flour, baking powder and 1 cup walnuts in bowl. Add walnut mixture and whipped cream alternately to sugar mixture, beginning and ending with walnut mixture and mixing well after each addition. Pour into 2 greased and floured 9-inch cake pans. Bake at 350 degrees for 25 to 30 minutes or until toothpick inserted in center comes out clean. Cool in pans for 15 minutes. Heat preserves and 2 tablespoons sugar in saucepan until sugar is dissolved. Reserve 1/2 cup preserve mixture. Brush remaining glaze over warm layers. Chill layers and reserved preserve mixture for 30 minutes. Combine margarine, cream cheese, confectioners' sugar and 1 teaspoon vanilla in mixer bowl. Beat at medium speed for 2 minutes. Spread between layers and over top of cake. Sprinkle with 1/2 cup walnuts. Chill for 30 minutes. Spread reserved glaze over side of torte. Press remaining 1/2 cup walnuts into glaze. Store in refrigerator. Yield: 16 servings.

BLACK WALNUT CAKE

1 c. butter, softened	*1/2 tsp. baking powder*
1/2 c. margarine,	*1/2 tsp. salt*
softened	*1 c. milk*
3 c. sugar	*1/2 tsp. vanilla extract*
5 eggs	*1 c. crushed black*
3 c. all-purpose	*walnuts*
flour	

Cream butter, margarine and sugar in mixer bowl until light and fluffy. Add eggs 1 at a time, mixing well after each addition. Add sifted dry ingredients alternately with milk, mixing well after each addition. Stir in vanilla and walnuts. Pour into greased 10-inch tube pan. Place in cold oven. Set oven temperature at 300 degrees. Bake for 2 hours. Remove to wire rack to cool. Yield: 16 servings.

HONEY AND WALNUT DRESSING

1 1/2 c. chopped onions	*1/2 tsp. pepper*
1 1/2 c. chopped celery	*1/2 tsp. salt*
2 tbsp. margarine	*1/2 tsp. cinnamon*
6 c. cooked rice	*1/4 c. honey*
1 c. raisins	*2 tbsp. lemon juice*
2/3 c. chopped walnuts	*1/4 c. snipped parsley*

Sauté onions and celery in margarine in skillet until tender-crisp. Add rice, raisins, walnuts, pepper, salt, cinnamon, honey and lemon juice; toss lightly to mix well. Spoon into greased 2 1/2-quart baking dish. Bake, covered, at 350 degrees, for 35 minutes. Sprinkle with parsley. Yield: 12 servings.

Whitefish

WHITE FISH CHOWDER

*1/2 c. chopped
 mushrooms*
1/2 c. chopped onion
*1/2 c. chopped red bell
 pepper*
2 tbsp. margarine
*1 can condensed
 potato soup*
1 c. milk

*1 8-oz. can whole
 kernel corn, drained*
2 tbsp. Chablis
*8 oz. white fish fillets,
 cut into 1-in. pieces*
*2 tbsp. fresh chopped
 parsley*
Dash of pepper

Sauté mushrooms, onion and red pepper in margarine in 2-quart saucepan over medium heat until tender. Stir in soup, milk, corn and Chablis. Bring to a boil. Add fish, parsley and pepper. Reduce heat. Simmer, covered, for 10 minutes or until fish flakes easily. Yield: 4 cups.

ONE-POT FRENCH FISH CHOWDER

1 med. onion, chopped
3/4 c. chopped celery
3 or 4 tbsp. parsley
1 29-oz. can tomatoes
1 c. dry white wine
1 can chicken broth

1 tsp. thyme
1/2 tsp. sage
*1/8 tsp. turmeric
 (optional)*
*1 lb. firm white fish,
 chopped*

Sauté onion, celery and parsley in stockpot for 10 minutes. Add tomatoes, wine, broth, thyme, sage, and turmeric. Simmer for 20 minutes. Cool. Add fish. Simmer for 5 minutes. Serve hot with French bread. Yield: 4 servings.

Yogurt

ORANGE YOGURT COFFEE CAKE

1 egg, beaten
1 c. orange yogurt
*1 1-layer pkg. yellow
 cake mix*

1/2 c. raisins
3 tbsp. sugar
1/2 tsp. cinnamon

Mix egg and orange yogurt in medium bowl. Add cake mix; mix well. Stir in raisins. Pour into greased 8x8-inch baking pan. Sprinkle with mixture of sugar and cinnamon. Bake at 350 degrees for 30 minutes. Cool. Yield: 12 servings.

YOGURT SUPREME PIE

*2 6-oz. containers
 vanilla yogurt*
3 1/2 c. whipped topping

1/2 c. chopped fruit
*1 graham cracker pie
 shell*

Combine first 2 ingredients. Add fruit; mix gently. Spoon into pie shell. Freeze for 4 hours. Refrigerate 45 minutes before serving. Yield: 6 servings.

YOGURT POPSICLES

*1 6-oz. can frozen
 orange juice
 concentrate, thawed*

2 c. unflavored yogurt
1 tsp. vanilla extract

Combine all ingredients in blender container. Process until smooth. Pour into popsicle molds. Freeze until firm. Unmold onto serving plates. Yield: 6 servings.

Zucchini

ZUCCHINI CRESCENT SUMMER PIE

*4 c. thinly sliced
 unpeeled zucchini*
1 c. chopped onion
1/2 c. margarine
1/2 c. chopped parsley
1/2 tsp. salt
1/2 tsp. pepper
1/4 tsp. garlic powder
1/4 tsp. basil leaves

1/4 tsp. oregano leaves
2 eggs, well beaten
*2 c. shredded Muenster
 cheese*
*1 8-ct. package
 refrigerator crescent
 rolls*
*2 tbsp. Dijon-style
 mustard*

Sauté zucchini and onion in margarine in 10-inch skillet for 10 minutes. Stir in parsley and seasonings. Beat eggs with cheese in bowl. Stir in vegetable mixture. Separate dough into 8 triangles. Press over bottom and side of ungreased 10-inch pie plate to form crust. Spread with mustard. Pour in vegetable mixture. Bake at 375 degrees for 18 to 20 minutes. Let stand for 10 minutes.
Yield: 6 servings.

ZUCCHINI SQUARES

3 c. thinly sliced zucchini	2 tbsp. chopped parsley
1 c. buttermilk baking mix	1/2 tsp. seasoned salt
1/2 c. chopped onion	1/2 tsp. oregano
1/2 c. Parmesan cheese	Dash of pepper
4 eggs, beaten	1 clove of garlic, chopped
	1/2 c. oil

Combine all ingredients in bowl; mix well. Spread in greased 9x13-inch baking pan. Bake at 350 degrees for 25 minutes. Cut into squares. Yield: 48 appetizers.

ZUCCHINI CAKE

3 c. grated zucchini	3 c. self-rising flour
1 1/4 c. oil	2 tsp. cinnamon
3 c. sugar	1 1/2 c. chopped pecans
4 eggs, slightly beaten	

Combine ingredients in order listed in mixer bowl, mixing well after each addition. Pour into greased and floured 10-inch tube pan. Bake at 350 degrees for 1 hour. Cool on wire rack. Frost with cream cheese frosting if desired. Yield: 12 servings.

ZUCCHINI BOATS

4 med. zucchini	Dash of pepper
1/3 c. onion, chopped	1 c. shredded sharp Cheddar cheese
1 tbsp. margarine	
3/4 c. chopped tomatoes	4 strips bacon, crisp-fried, crumbled
1/4 tsp. salt	

Cook zucchini in boiling salted water in saucepan for 5 to 8 minutes or until tender-crisp; drain. Cut into halves lengthwise. Scoop out and chop pulp, reserving shells. Sauté onion in margarine in skillet. Stir in zucchini pulp, tomatoes, salt, pepper, cheese and bacon; mix well. Spoon into zucchini shells. Place in 7x11-inch baking dish. Bake at 350 degrees for 25 to 30 minutes or until mixture is heated through. Yield: 4 to 8 servings.

ZUCCHINI AND RICE CASSEROLE

1 c. chopped onion	2 1/2 c. half and half
3 tbsp. melted margarine	1/2 c. uncooked long grain white rice
2 tsp. minced garlic	3/4 c. Parmesan cheese
5 c. shredded zucchini	Salt and pepper to taste
1 tbsp. all-purpose flour	1/4 c. Parmesan cheese

Sauté onion in margarine in skillet until tender. Add garlic and zucchini. Stir-fry for 5 minutes. Sprinkle with flour. Stir-fry for 1 minute longer. Add half and half, rice, 3/4 cup Parmesan cheese and salt and pepper; mix well. Pour into greased 9x13-inch baking dish. Sprinkle with 1/4 cup Parmesan cheese. Bake at 425 degrees for 30 minutes or until golden and rice is tender. Let stand for 10 minutes before servings. Yield: 12 servings.

ZUCCHINI SOUP

4 sm. zucchini, sliced	3 1/2 c. chicken broth
3 tbsp. margarine	2 tbsp. chopped fresh parsley
2 onions, chopped	
1 clove of garlic, crushed	1 tsp. lemon juice
	1/3 c. heavy cream

Place zucchini in colander; sprinkle with salt to taste. Let stand for 30 minutes. Melt margarine in heavy saucepan. Add onion and garlic. Cook over low heat for 5 minutes or until translucent. Rinse and dry zucchini. Add to cooked onion. Cook for 5 minutes. Add broth. Simmer for 15 minutes. Purée in blender container. Return to saucepan. Add parsley, lemon juice and cream; whisk until well blended. Add pepper and salt to taste. Reheat. May serve hot or cold. Yield: 4 servings.

GARDEN TOMATO-ZUCCHINI BAKE

2 tomatoes, sliced	2 zucchini, thinly sliced
2 baking potatoes, thinly sliced	1/3 c. olive oil
	10 leaves fresh basil

Layer tomato, potato slices and zucchini alternately in lightly oiled casserole. Coat with olive oil. Bake at 400 degrees for 30 to 40 minutes or until potatoes are tender. Sprinkle basil over vegetables. Add salt and pepper to taste. Yield: 4 servings.

ZUCCHINI QUICHE

3 c. sliced zucchini	1/2 tsp. seasoned salt
1 c. buttermilk baking mix	1/2 tsp. salt
	1/2 tsp. oregano
1/2 c. chopped onion	Dash of pepper
1/2 c. Parmesan cheese	1/8 tsp. garlic salt
1 1/2 tbsp. parsley	1/4 c. Parmesan cheese

Combine zucchini, baking mix, onion, 1/2 cup cheese, parsley, seasoned salt, salt, oregano, pepper and garlic salt in bowl; mix well. Spread in greased 9x13-inch baking pan. Sprinkle with 1/4 cup cheese. Bake at 350 degrees for 25 minutes. Cut into squares. Yield: 12 servings.

⇨
Recipe for this photograph is on page 181.

Bewitching Halloween Supper

Beefy Reuben Dip

page 181

Hot Broccoli Vinaigrette

page 182

Barley-Cheese Soup

page 181

Parmesan and Bacon Sticks

page 21

Apple Crunch over Ice Cream or

page 180

Blender Chocolate Mousse

page 63

Cranberry Chill

page 75

With goblin goings-on or just busy fall days,
make an extra easy supper with microwave
magic to fill up greedy ghosts or to treat
the hungries — whoever they are.

Microwave Basics

While it's the most radical contribution the hi-tech revolution has made to the kitchen, in the few short years since it became available for home use, the microwave oven has already become standard equipment in most American kitchens. Even those of us who only use them for reheating leftovers, thawing frozen food or heating baby bottles find it hard to imagine getting along without them, so basic a part of our lives have they become.

Microwave ovens offer that most valuable of commodities to current-day American cooks: time. In years gone by, when dinner was what you started cooking right after the lunch dishes were cleared, microwaves might have fared less well. But in an era when dinner is what you whip up (or pick up) between work and the kids' soccer game or your neighborhood board meeting, the microwave oven became an instant classic.

Most of us probably underuse our microwaves. But if properly employed, with a little planning you can easily prepare entire meals in the microwave, from appetizers to bread and desserts.

What Are Microwaves?

How do these modern miracles work? Microwaves act as a sort of magnetic force on the ions of food molecules. The force of the waves changes directions so rapidly (2.5 billion times per second) that food molecules vibrate, causing friction, which produces heat that cooks food.

Microwaves penetrate food from all sides, generating heat in the areas they touch, which is in turn spread by conduction through the food. Some food molecules, such as those of fats and sugar, especially attract microwaves, and so will cook faster than the foods around them. Use caution, for example on sugar-frosted coffeecakes or filled desserts.

Microwave Power Levels

The most important factor in preparing recipes is determining the power level and time for your particular microwave oven. The recipes in this chapter have been formulated for a microwave which operates on 650 to 700 watts power on High. Many of the smaller microwaves operate on as little as 450 to 500 watts on High.

If you have a less powerful microwave, you must add additional time to the recipes. For example, if your microwave operates on 500 watts on High, multiply the amount of cooking time by 1.3 in order to estimate your actual time. A casserole that requires 10 minutes in a 700-watt microwave may need 13 minutes in a 500-watt oven. Daily changes in line voltage may also cause changes in the length of cooking time from day to day. If you are unsure about your microwave's power, bake a 7-ounce potato on High. It will take 5 minutes at 700 watts power and 6$1/2$ minutes at 500 watts.

Time Considerations in Microwaving

Several factors besides power level also affect the length of time it takes to cook your food. The greater the volume of food, for example, the longer it takes to cook. Similarly, dense food like roasts take longer to cook than more porous foods like cakes. Food that is high in moisture like vegetables will cook faster than drier foods such as rice. Food that is cold when it begins cooking will take longer than room temperature food.

Microwave Cooking Techniques

Successful microwaving requires only a few special techniques. In general, foods will be cooked covered to keep moisture in and speed cooking. Depending on whether you have a turntable in your oven, food will need to be rotated periodically according to the recipe to insure even cooking.

Many foods, especially large items like roasts, will need to be arranged and rearranged during cooking. Other foods will require stirring on occasion during cooking. Some foods, such as turkey breast, require shielding, according to the particular oven directions.

Be thoughtful about the containers in which you cook. Use only glass, unglazed china or pottery, dishwasher-safe plastics and, for short cooking, paper. Avoid metal, plastic bags with wire twist ties and wood.

Microwave Menu Planning

Though it may seem a little more complicated than ordinary menu planning, cooking whole meals in the microwave oven is actually quite simple.

Look at each of the dishes you plan to cook, and pay special attention to the holding time and standing time called for in each recipe. Holding time is the length of time a food will stay hot if it is wrapped up or covered. You can lengthen holding time by cooking food in its serving dish. Fish, vegetables and casseroles hold better if tightly covered. An ear of corn, for example, will hold for 10 to 12 minutes if left wrapped in its husk. Wrapped in plastic, though, it will hold for 40 minutes. Meats, on the contrary, should be loosely covered to avoid taking on a steamed taste.

Standing time is the out-of-oven time a food needs to finish cooking utilizing the heat generated while in the oven. A baked potato will need 3 to 5 minutes in the oven, and another 5 to 10 minutes afterward to finish cooking. When calculating holding time in your menu planning, begin counting at the end of the dish's standing time.

Plan to first prepare any food that will be served cold or that can be reheated. Next will come large, dense foods with long standing times, and foods with long holding times (during which they will retain heat). These will be prepared and put aside to wait.

Third in line are foods that cook quickly, like vegetables, or that need to be reheated. At last, while those foods are having a short standing time, heat foods like bread and rolls that take just seconds. If you follow this plan, everything should come to the table at just the right temperature, with the freshly cooked flavor the microwave preserves so well.

Whether you're preparing one dish or an entire meal, our recipes and charts will help you microwave like a pro.

A

FIRESIDE APPLE BROWN BETTY

4 c. sliced peeled apples *1 tsp. cinnamon*
2 tbsp. sugar *1 tsp. nutmeg*
2 tbsp. lemon juice *1/3 c. butter*
1/2 c. oats *1/2 c. pecans*
2/3 c. brown sugar

Arrange apples in greased 9x12-inch glass dish. Sprinkle with sugar and lemon juice. Combine next 4 ingredients in bowl. Cut in butter until crumbly. Mix in pecans. Sprinkle mixture over apples. Microwave on Medium for 8 minutes or until apples are tender. Yield: 8 servings.

APPLE CRUNCH OVER ICE CREAM

1   21-oz. can apple pie *3 tbsp. margarine*
filling *1/3 c. packed light*
1   9-oz. package white *brown sugar*
cake mix *Vanilla ice cream*

Pour apple pie filling into 8x8-inch baking dish. Sprinkle cake mix over filling; dot with margarine. Sprinkle brown sugar over top. Microwave on High for 12 minutes. Let stand for 5 minutes. Serve warm over ice cream. Yield: 4 servings.

APRICOT CHEWIES

1 c. margarine, melted *2 c. finely chopped*
1 1/3 c. packed dark *dried apricots*
brown sugar *1 c. shredded coconut*
2/3 c. honey *1 c. chopped almonds*
3 c. quick-cooking oats *1 c. wheat germ*

Blend margarine, brown sugar and honey in large bowl. Add remaining ingredients gradually, stirring until coated. Spread in greased baking dish. Microwave on High for 6 minutes or until firm but moist, stirring once; cool slightly. Shape into bite-sized balls and store in tightly covered container. Yield: 8 dozen.

ARTICHOKE NIBBLES

2   6-oz. jars marinated *2 tbsp. chopped parsley*
artichoke hearts *1/8 tsp. Tabasco sauce*
1/2 c. chopped onion *1/8 tsp. oregano*
2 cloves of garlic, *1/8 tsp. red pepper*
minced *1/4 tsp. salt*
4 eggs *8 oz. Cheddar cheese,*
1/4 c. seasoned bread *grated*
crumbs

Drain and chop artichoke hearts, reserving liquid from 1 jar. Combine reserved liquid, onion and garlic in glass bowl. Microwave on High for 2 to 3 minutes. Beat eggs in bowl. Add bread crumbs, parsley, Tabasco sauce, oregano, red pepper and salt; mix well. Stir in cheese, artichokes and onion mixture. Spoon into greased 7x11-inch glass baking dish. Microwave on High for 7 to 8 minutes, turning dish twice. Let stand for 5 minutes. Cut into squares. Arrange on serving plate; serve hot or cold. Yield: 5 dozen.

FRESH ASPARAGUS WITH THREE CHEESE SAUCE

2 lb. fresh asparagus *Salt to taste*
spears *1 tbsp. Parmesan*
1/2 c. evaporated milk *cheese*
1   3-oz. package *1/2 c. shredded*
cream cheese, *Cheddar cheese*
softened

Microwave asparagus in 2-quart covered casserole on High for 4 minutes or until tender-crisp. Process evaporated milk and cream cheese in blender container until smooth. Microwave in measuring cup on High for 2 minutes, stirring twice. Stir in salt and Parmesan cheese. Pour over hot asparagus. Garnish with shredded Cheddar cheese.
Yield: 6 to 8 servings.

B

BANANA BREAD

2 tbsp. sugar *10 tbsp. melted*
1/4 c. chopped pecans *margarine*
1/2 tsp. cinnamon *1 egg, beaten*
1 1/2 c. flour *2 med. bananas,*
3/4 c. sugar *mashed*
1/2 tsp. salt *1/4 c. chopped pecans*
1/3 c. milk

Grease small glass bundt pan. Sprinkle with mixture of 2 tablespoons sugar, 1/4 cup pecans and cinnamon. Combine remaining dry ingredients in bowl. Add milk, margarine, egg and bananas; mix well. Fold in remaining 1/4 cup pecans. Spoon into prepared pan. Microwave on Medium for 9 minutes. Microwave on High for 3 to 5 minutes or until bread tests done. Let stand for several minutes. Remove to wire rack to cool.
Yield: 12 slices.

BEAN BURRITO CASSEROLE

1 15-oz. can refried beans with jalapeño peppers	12 7-in. flour tortillas
	2 15-oz. cans chili with beans
3 c. shredded Cheddar cheese	1 c. shredded Cheddar cheese

Spoon refried beans and 3 cups Cheddar cheese into centers of tortillas; roll tortillas to enclose filling. Place seam side down in 3-quart rectangular glass dish. Top with chili. Microwave on High for 14 to 16 minutes or until heated through, turning dish once. Sprinkle with remaining 1 cup cheese. Let stand for 5 minutes. Yield: 12 servings.

MINI BEAN TOSTADAS

1 8-oz. can refried beans	1/2 c. shredded Cheddar cheese
24 round tortilla chips	24 cherry tomato slices
1/4 c. taco sauce	

Spread 1 heaping teaspoon beans on each tortilla chip. Top each with 1/2 teaspoon taco sauce and 1 teaspoon cheese. Arrange 6 at a time on paper towel-lined plate. Microwave on Medium for 1 minute. Turn plate 1/4 turn. Microwave for 1 minute longer, turning every 30 seconds. Top each with tomato slice. Yield: 2 dozen.

BARLEY-CHEESE SOUP

Photograph for this recipe is on page 175.

2 c. water	1 clove of garlic, minced
1 c. chopped broccoli	
1 can chicken broth	1/8 tsp. pepper
1 c. sliced carrots	1 1/2 c. milk
1/2 c. chopped onion	1/3 c. all-purpose flour
1/2 c. barley	1 1/2 c. diced Swiss cheese
1 tsp. salt	

Combine first 9 ingredients in 4-quart glass bowl. Cover with waxed paper. Microwave on High for 18 minutes or until barley is tender, stirring once. Combine 1/2 cup milk and flour; mix well. Add to soup gradually with remaining 1 cup milk. Microwave, covered, on High for about 5 minutes or until thickened, stirring once. Stir in cheese. Let stand, covered, for 3 minutes. Yields: 6 servings.

BEEFY REUBEN DIP

1 c. sauerkraut, drained	4 oz. cream cheese, cubed
1 tbsp. margarine	
2 green onions, sliced	2 tsp. Dijon mustard
2 tbsp. catsup	1/4 tsp. pepper
1 1/2 c. shredded Muenster cheese	8 oz. corned beef, coarsely chopped

Place sauerkraut in 1-quart glass dish. Microwave margarine in glass bowl on High for 20 seconds. Add onions. Microwave, covered, on High for 1 minute. Add next 5 ingredients. Microwave, covered, on Medium-High for 2 1/2 minutes, stirring once. Stir in corned beef. Spoon over sauerkraut. Microwave, covered, on Medium-High for 4 minutes. Serve with rye bread. Yield: 6 servings.

BREAD PUDDING

4 c. dry bread crumbs	1 tsp. vanilla extract
3 eggs	2 tsp. cinnamon
1/2 c. packed brown sugar	2 c. milk
	2 tbsp. margarine

Crumble bread into ungreased round 2-quart dish. Beat eggs, brown sugar, vanilla, and cinnamon in mixer bowl until smooth. Microwave milk and margarine in 4-cup glass measure on High for 4 1/2 to 5 minutes or until steaming hot. Stir a small amount of hot mixture into egg mixture; stir egg mixture into hot mixture. Pour over bread. Microwave, covered, on Medium for 12 to 14 minutes or until center is almost set. Let stand for 2 minutes. Serve warm or chilled. Yield: 6 servings.

HOT BROCCOLI DIP

1 10-oz. package frozen chopped broccoli	2 tbsp. margarine
	1 6-oz. roll garlic cheese
1 onion, chopped	1/2 c. mushroom soup
1 4-oz. can sliced mushrooms	1 tsp. Tabasco sauce
	1/4 tsp. salt

Cook broccoli according to package directions; drain. Sauté onion and mushrooms in margarine in skillet. Place broccoli, mushrooms and onion in microwave dish. Add remaining ingredients and pepper to taste. Microwave on High for 30 seconds or until cheese is melted, stirring frequently. Serve hot with corn chips. Yield: 10 servings.

BROCCOLI AND RICE CASSEROLE

1 10-oz. package frozen broccoli	Salt and pepper to taste
	1 c. rice, cooked
1 lb. fresh mushrooms	1 can cream of celery soup
1/4 c. margarine	
Garlic powder to taste	4 oz. Cheez Whiz

Microwave broccoli according to package directions. Sauté mushrooms in margarine in saucepan. Stir in seasonings. Add rice and broccoli. Combine soup and Cheez Whiz in small bowl. Add to broccoli mixture; mix well. Spoon into 2-quart glass baking dish. Microwave on High for 10 minutes. Yield: 4 servings.

HOT BROCCOLI VINAIGRETTE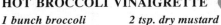

1 bunch broccoli	*2 tsp. dry mustard*
1/3 c. water	*2 tsp. sugar*
2 tbsp. cider vinegar	*3/4 tsp. salt*
3 tbsp. olive oil	*2 tbsp. cider vinegar*

Cut broccoli into spears. Arrange in 8x12-inch glass baking dish with flowerets toward center. Add water and 2 tablespoons vinegar. Microwave, covered with plastic wrap, turning back edge to vent, on High for 8 to 10 minutes or until tender-crisp, turning dish once. Combine remaining ingredients in 2-cup measure. Microwave on High for 1 minute. Pour over drained broccoli on serving plate. Yield: 4 to 6 servings.

CREAM OF BROCCOLI AND CHEESE SOUP

1 10-oz. package	*1 c. cottage cheese*
frozen chopped	*2 c. milk*
broccoli	*1 can cream of chicken*
2 c. chopped celery	*soup*
1 c. finely chopped	*1/2 tsp. salt*
onion	*1/8 tsp. white pepper*

Mix broccoli, celery and onion in 2½-quart glass dish. Microwave, covered, on High for 6 minutes, stirring after 3 minutes. Place cottage cheese in blender container; process until smooth. Add milk gradually, processing until smooth. Add chicken soup; blend well. Stir into broccoli mixture. Microwave on High for 3 minutes or just until heated through; do not allow to boil. Add salt and pepper. Yield: 6 servings.

BROWNIES À LA MODE

3/4 c. all-purpose flour	*2/3 c. margarine,*
1 c. sugar	*softened*
7 tbsp. baking cocoa	*1 tbsp. corn syrup*
1/2 tsp. baking powder	*2 eggs*
3/4 tsp. salt	*1 tsp. vanilla extract*

Sift flour, sugar, cocoa, baking powder and salt in mixer bowl. Add remaining ingredients; beat until smooth. Pour into greased 8x8-inch glass dish. Microwave on Medium-High for 8 minutes or until brownies test done. Serve warm with vanilla ice cream. Yield: 8 servings.

C

HONEY GLAZED SPRING CARROTS

1 lb. carrots	*Dash of cinnamon*
1/4 c. water	*1 tbsp. honey*
1 tbsp. margarine	*2 tbsp. chopped pecans*

Wash and peel carrots; slice ½ inch thick. Microwave carrots and water in covered 1-quart glass casserole on High for 10 to 15 minutes or until tender, stirring once. Let stand for 2 minutes; drain. Return to casserole. Stir in margarine and cinnamon. Drizzle with honey; mix gently. Microwave on High for 30 seconds. Sprinkle with pecans. Yield: 4 servings.

CAULIFLOWER

1 head cauliflower	*1/2 to 1 tsp. dry mustard*
1/2 c. mayonnaise	*1 c. shredded*
1 tsp. prepared mustard	*American cheese*

Wash cauliflower. Place undrained cauliflower in 2-quart glass baking dish. Microwave, tightly covered, on High for 7 to 8 minutes. Combine mayonnaise, prepared mustard and dry mustard in bowl; mix well. Spread over cauliflower. Sprinkle with cheese. Microwave on High for 1 minute or just until cheese is melted. Yield: 4 servings.

FRESH CHERRY SOUP

1 lb. dark sweet	*1 stick cinnamon*
cherries, pitted	*3 tbsp. sugar*
1 c. dry red wine	*2 tbsp. cornstarch*
1 lemon, sliced, seeded	*2 tbsp. lemon juice*

Combine cherries, wine, lemon and cinnamon stick in 2½-quart glass bowl. Cover tightly with plastic wrap, turning back edge to vent. Microwave on High for 17 minutes, stirring after 7 minutes. Cool slightly. Pour half the mixture into blender container. Blend until smooth. Transfer to bowl. Repeat with remaining cherry mixture. Mix sugar and cornstarch. Stir into cherry mixture. Cover tightly with plastic wrap, turning back edge to vent. Microwave on High for 8 minutes or until mixture boils, stirring 2 or 3 times. Add lemon juice. Chill in refrigerator. Garnish each serving with lemon slice and dollop of sour cream. Yield: 6 servings.

APRICOT CHICKEN

1 2½ to 3-lb. broiler,	*1 tbsp. chili sauce*
cut up	*1/2 tsp. ginger*
2 tbsp. soy sauce	*1/8 tsp. cayenne pepper*
2 tbsp. honey	*1 c. juice-pack apricot*
1 tbsp. oil	*halves, drained*

Skin chicken pieces. Arrange in 7x12-inch glass dish with thickest parts toward outside edges. Mix next 6 ingredients in bowl. Brush on chicken to coat; cover tightly. Microwave on High for 10 minutes. Brush with honey mixture. Turn dish. Microwave, covered, for 6 to 10 minutes. Arrange apricots around chicken. Brush chicken and apricots with honey mixture. Microwave, uncovered, for 1 minute. Yield: 7 servings.

BARBECUED CHICKEN

4 chicken leg quarters, skinned	*1 tbsp. Worcestershire sauce*
1 c. catsup	*1/2 tsp. liquid smoke*
1/4 c. packed brown sugar	*1/4 tsp. garlic powder*
1/2 tsp. chili powder	*1/4 tsp. hot pepper sauce*

Place chicken quarters in 7x11-inch glass baking dish. Combine remaining ingredients in bowl. Pour over chicken. Microwave on High for 20 to 25 minutes, rotating dish once. Yield: 4 servings.

CASHEW CHICKEN

1 5-oz. can chow mein noodles	*1/2 c. chopped green onions*
2 c. chopped cooked chicken	*1 c. unsalted cashews*
1 8-oz. can sliced water chestnuts, drained	*1 can cream of mushroom soup*
3/4 c. chopped celery	*1 can chicken broth*

Reserve 1/2 cup noodles. Combine remaining noodles with remaining ingredients in bowl; mix well. Spoon into greased 2-quart glass dish. Microwave, covered, on High for 8 minutes. Sprinkle with reserved noodles. Microwave for 2 minutes longer. Yield: 6 to 8 servings.

CHICKEN CORDON BLEU

4 chicken breast filets	*1 tsp. herb-seasoned salt*
4 thin slices ham	
4 1-oz. Swiss cheese cubes	*1/2 c. shredded Swiss cheese*
1/4 c. melted butter	

Pound chicken breasts with meat mallet to flatten. Top each chicken breast with ham slice and cheese cube. Fold chicken breast to enclose ham and cheese; secure with toothpick. Place in mixture of butter and salt in 8-inch glass baking dish; spoon butter over chicken. Microwave, covered with waxed paper, on High for 2 minutes. Baste with butter. Microwave, covered, on Medium for 7 to 8 minutes. Sprinkle with shredded cheese. Microwave on Medium for 2 minutes or until cheese melts. Let stand, covered, for 3 to 5 minutes before serving. Yield: 4 servings.

CHICKEN AND DUMPLINGS

1 med. onion, sliced	*1/2 c. milk*
1/4 c. chopped green bell pepper	*1 10-oz. package frozen green peas*
3 tbsp. margarine	*1 8-ct. can refrigerator biscuits*
1 can mushroom soup	*Parsley flakes*
1 1/2 c. chopped cooked chicken	

Combine first 3 ingredients in 2-quart glass dish. Microwave on High for 2 minutes. Stir in soup, chicken and milk. Microwave, covered, for 5 to 6 minutes, stirring once. Add peas. Microwave for 5 to 6 minutes, stirring once. Arrange biscuits around dish; sprinkle with parsley. Microwave for 3 to 4 minutes or until biscuits are cooked, turning dish once. Yield: 6 servings.

HAWAIIAN CHICKEN

1/4 c. chopped onion	*1 1/2 tbsp. soy sauce*
1/2 c. chopped green bell pepper	*1/4 tsp. salt*
1 tbsp. margarine	*1/8 tsp. minced garlic*
1/3 c. water	*3 c. chopped cooked chicken*
1/2 c. packed dark brown sugar	*1 16-oz. can pineapple chunks*
1/4 c. apple cider vinegar	*1 7-oz. package frozen pea pods*
2 tbsp. cornstarch	

Combine first 3 ingredients in 1 1/2-quart baking dish. Microwave on High for 2 to 3 minutes. Stir in water and next 6 ingredients. Microwave on High for 4 to 5 minutes or until thickened, stirring once. Add chicken, pineapple and pea pods. Microwave, covered, on High for 4 to 6 minutes or until pea pods are almost tender. Serve over rice with additional soy sauce. Yield: 4 servings.

EASY CHICKEN PARMESAN

6 pieces chicken	*1/2 tsp. garlic salt*
1/2 c. margarine	*1/4 tsp. pepper*
1 c. dry bread crumbs	*1 tbsp. parsley flakes*
1/2 c. Parmesan cheese	*Paprika to taste*

Wash chicken; pat dry. Microwave margarine in glass dish for 1 minute or until melted. Combine the next 5 ingredients in plastic bag. Coat chicken with margarine; shake in bag to coat evenly. Arrange in shallow glass baking dish with thicker pieces toward the outside of dish. Sprinkle remaining crumbs and margarine over top of chicken. Sprinkle with paprika to taste. Microwave on High for 17 to 20 minutes, turning twice. Let stand for 5 minutes before serving. Yield: 6 servings.

CHILI CON CARNE

1 c. chopped onion	1 16-oz. can chili
1/2 c. chopped green	beans
bell pepper	1/2 tsp. chili powder
1 lb. ground beef	Dash of cayenne
1 16-oz. can tomatoes	pepper
1 8-oz. can tomato	1/4 tsp. oregano
sauce	1 tsp. salt
1/3 c. catsup	

Microwave onion, green pepper and ground beef in 3-quart glass baking dish, covered, on High for 12 minutes or until vegetables are tender and ground beef is no longer pink, stirring once; drain. Add remaining ingredients; mix well. Microwave on Medium-High for 16 to 20 minutes or until heated through. Yield: 4 servings.

MOIST CHOCOLATE CAKE

1/4 c. margarine,	2 c. miniature
softened	marshmallows
1/2 c. sugar	1/4 c. margarine
2 eggs	1 c. sugar
1/2 c. all-purpose flour	1/4 c. evaporated milk
1/2 tsp. baking powder	1/2 c. chocolate chips
1/2 tsp. vanilla extract	1 tsp. vanilla extract
1 c. chocolate syrup	

Cream 1/4 cup margarine and 1/2 cup sugar in mixer bowl until light and fluffy. Blend in eggs. Add sifted flour and baking powder, 1/2 teaspoon vanilla and chocolate syrup; beat mixture until smooth. Spoon into 8-inch glass dish. Microwave, covered, on High for 7 minutes or until cake tests done. Sprinkle with marshmallows. Microwave 1/4 cup margarine in glass bowl on High for 30 seconds. Mix in 1 cup sugar and evaporated milk. Microwave for 2 minutes, stirring twice. Stir in chocolate chips and 1 teaspoon vanilla. Pour over cake; swirl through melted marshmallows. Yield: 9 servings.

FILLED CHOCOLATE CUPCAKES

1 2-layer pkg.	1/4 c. sugar
chocolate cake mix	1 egg
8 oz. cream cheese,	1 c. chocolate chips
softened	

Prepare cake mix according to package directions. Place paper liners in miniature glass muffin cups. Spoon 2 tablespoons cake batter into each muffin cup. Combine remaining ingredients in bowl; mix well. Spoon 1 scant tablespoon mixture into each muffin cup. Microwave 6 cupcakes at a time on High for 2 1/2 to 2 3/4 minutes. Cool on wire rack. Yield: 30 cupcakes.

ROCKY ROAD CANDY

1 c. semisweet	1 c. flaked coconut
chocolate chips	2 eggs, beaten
1 tbsp. margarine	1 1/4 c. confectioners'
1 1/2 c. chopped pecans	sugar
2 c. miniature	1/2 tsp. vanilla extract
marshmallows	

Place chocolate chips and margarine in large glass dish. Microwave on High for 3 minutes or until melted. Stir in pecans, marshmallows and coconut. Blend eggs, confectioners' sugar and vanilla in bowl. Add to chocolate mixture; mix well. Drop by teaspoonfuls onto waxed paper. Chill until firm. May microwave mixture on High for 30 seconds if candy becomes too stiff to drop. Yield: 24 pieces.

COFFEE RING

1 c. milk	2 tbsp. margarine,
1 pkg. dry yeast	softened
1/4 c. sugar	1/3 c. packed brown
1 tsp. salt	sugar
1 egg, beaten	1/3 c. chopped pecans
1/4 c. oil	2 tsp. cinnamon
3 to 3 1/2 c. all-purpose	
flour	

Microwave milk on Medium in glass bowl for 1 1/2 minutes. Dissolve yeast, sugar and salt in milk. Stir in egg and oil. Add enough flour to make medium stiff dough. Knead on floured surface for 5 minutes. Roll into rectangle. Spread with margarine. Sprinkle with brown sugar, pecans and cinnamon. Roll from wide side to enclose filling; seal edge. Shape into circle on glass plate. Make 12 cuts 2/3 through dough with scissors. Turn sections on side, overlapping slightly. Let rise in microwave on Low for 10 to 15 minutes or until doubled in bulk. Microwave on Medium-High for 5 to 6 minutes or until ring tests done. Frost with confectioners' sugar frosting. Yield: 8 servings.

CARAMEL-NUT COFFEE CAKE

1/3 c. chopped walnuts	3 tbsp. margarine
1 tsp. cinnamon	1 tbsp. water
1 10-ct. can	1/4 c. confectioners'
refrigerator biscuits	sugar
1/3 c. packed brown	1 tsp. milk
sugar	Vanilla extract to taste

Grease 8 1/2-inch glass ring mold or 6-oz. custard cup inverted in 9-inch glass bowl. Sprinkle with walnuts and cinnamon. Cut each biscuit into 4 pieces. Combine brown sugar, margarine and water in 1-cup glass measure. Microwave on High for 1 minute. Stir until margarine melts. Coat biscuits with brown sugar mixture. Arrange in prepared dish. Microwave on High for 2½ to 3 minutes or until top springs back when touched. Let stand for 2 minutes. Blend confectioners' sugar, milk and vanilla in bowl. Drizzle over coffee cake. Serve warm. Yield: 6 to 8 servings.

CRAB-STUFFED CHERRY TOMATOES

1 pt. cherry tomatoes
1 can crab meat
2 green onions, finely chopped
½ tsp. parsley flakes

1 tsp. white wine vinegar
2 tbsp. dry bread crumbs
¼ tsp. dillweed

Slice stem end from tomatoes; scoop out pulp. Combine crab meat, green onions, parsley flakes, vinegar, bread crumbs and dillweed in bowl; mix well. Stuff tomatoes with crab meat mixture. Arrange on paper towel-lined plate. Microwave on High for 2 to 4 minutes or until heated through, turning plate once or twice. Garnish with paprika. Yield: 5 servings.

HOT CRAB PUFFS

1 lb. white crab meat
2 c. mayonnaise
Juice of 1 sm. lemon
¼ tsp. salt
¼ tsp. red pepper

3 egg whites, stiffly beaten
Triscuits or melba rounds

Combine first 2 ingredients in bowl. Add lemon juice, salt and pepper. Fold in egg whites. Place heaping teaspoonful on each Triscuit. Arrange 12 puffs on 1 microwave-safe dish. Microwave on High for 1 minute. Yield: 100 crab puffs.

D

DATE CRISP COOKIES

1 egg
6 tbsp. sugar
¾ c. chopped pitted dates

½ tsp. vanilla extract
1½ c. crisp rice cereal
¾ c. (about) flaked coconut

Beat egg slightly in 1½-quart bowl. Stir in sugar and dates. Microwave, uncovered, on High for 2 to 3 minutes or until dates are soft, stirring once or twice. Stir mixture until it forms a paste (date skins will make it lumpy). Mix in vanilla and cereal. Mold mixture into 1-inch balls, using 2 spoons to form balls. Place coconut on plate or wax paper. Roll cookies in coconut, coating well. Let stand in cool place for 20 minutes or until firm. Yield: 2 dozen.

LEMON DATE PUDDING

1 c. water
1 c. chopped pitted dates
1 tsp. soda
1¼ c. all-purpose flour
1 c. chopped walnuts or pecans
¼ tsp. baking powder
¼ tsp. salt

¼ c. margarine
1 c. sugar
1 egg
1 tsp. grated lemon rind
1 tbsp. lemon juice
2 tbsp. sugar
1 tsp. ground cinnamon
½ c. slivered almonds

Microwave water in bowl on High for 2½ minutes. Add dates and soda to water. Combine flour, nuts, baking powder and salt in bowl. Cream margarine and 1 cup sugar in bowl until light and fluffy. Beat in egg, lemon rind, and lemon juice. Beat in flour mixture slowly. Add date mixture; mix well. Spoon batter into 8-inch baking dish. Combine 2 tablespoons sugar and cinnamon; sprinkle over batter. Sprinkle with almonds. Microwave, uncovered, on High for 10 minutes, turning dish 4 or 5 times. Cool in dish. Serve with whipped cream or ice cream. Yield: 8 servings.

Lemon Date Pudding...a quick dessert for a busy day.

DIVINITY

2½ c. sugar
½ c. light corn syrup
½ c. water
⅛ tsp. salt

2 egg whites
1 tsp. vanilla extract
½ to 1 c. chopped pecans

Combine first 4 ingredients in 3-quart glass casserole. Microwave on High for 5 minutes. Microwave for 8 to 12 minutes or to 260 degrees on candy thermometer, hardball stage. Beat egg whites in mixer bowl until stiff peaks form. Pour syrup over egg whites gradually, beating constantly at high speed. Add vanilla. Beat for 4 to 5 minutes or until mixture holds its shape and starts to lose its gloss. Fold in pecans. Drop by spoonfuls onto waxed paper. Yield: 20 ounces.

F

SAUCY FISH

4 frozen fish fillets,
thawed
3 tbsp. mayonnaise
2 tbsp. chopped onion
1 tsp. chopped parsley

2 tbsp. melted
margarine
1/2 tsp. mustard
1/2 tsp. dillweed

Place fish in 8x8-inch glass baking dish. Combine remaining ingredients in small bowl. Pour over fish. Cover with plastic wrap. Microwave on Medium-High for 12 minutes or until fish flakes easily, turning dish once. Yield: 4 servings.

QUICK FUDGE

1   16-oz. package
confectioners' sugar
1/2 c. unsweetened
baking cocoa

1/4 c. milk
1/2 c. margarine
1 tsp. vanilla extract
1/2 c. chopped pecans

Mix confectioners' sugar and cocoa in 8x8-inch glass baking dish. Pour in milk. Dot with margarine. Microwave, covered, on High for 2 minutes. Stir in vanilla and pecans. Freeze until firm. Cut into squares. Yield: 16 servings.

G

GRANOLA

1/2 c. sunflower oil
1/2 c. honey
1 c. packed light brown
sugar
2 tsp. cinnamon
2 tsp. vanilla extract
6 c. oats
1 c. coconut
1/2 c. wheat germ
1/2 c. sunflower seed
1/2 c. dry milk powder

1 c. blanched chopped
almonds
2/3 c. raisins
2/3 c. dried apples,
chopped
2/3 c. dried apricots,
chopped
2/3 c. dates, chopped
2/3 c. dried pineapple,
chopped

Combine first 5 ingredients in glass dish. Microwave on High for 4 to 5 minutes, stirring once. Add oats, coconut, wheat germ, sunflower seed, milk powder and almonds; mix well. Divide into 2 portions. Microwave each portion for 12 minutes or until mixture begins to appear dry, stirring several times. Stir in remaining ingredients. Spread on waxed paper to cool. Package in airtight container. Yield: 5 cups.

STUFFED GARDEN GREEN PEPPERS

6 med. green bell
peppers
1 tsp. salt
1/8 tsp. pepper
1 tbsp. Worcestershire
sauce

1/3 c. minute rice
1 egg, beaten
1 can tomato soup
1/4 c. finely chopped
onion
1 1/2 lb. ground chuck

Cut tops from peppers. Remove seed and membrane. Combine salt, pepper, Worcestershire sauce, rice, egg, 3/4 cup soup, onion and ground beef in bowl; stir lightly. Pack each pepper with approximately 1/2 cup mixture. Place filled peppers in round microwave casserole; peppers should fit tightly in casserole. Pour remaining soup over filled peppers. Cover with plastic wrap. Microwave on High for 15 to 18 minutes. Let stand for 2 to 3 minutes before serving. Yield: 6 servings.

EASY GROUND BEEF LASAGNA

3/4 lb. ground beef
1   32-oz. jar spaghetti
sauce
1 1/2 c. water
1 tsp. Italian seasoning
1 tsp. salt
1/4 tsp. pepper

2 c. cottage cheese
3 c. shredded
mozzarella cheese
2 eggs
1 c. Parmesan cheese
8 oz. lasagna noodles

Brown ground beef in saucepan, stirring until crumbly; drain. Add spaghetti sauce, water and seasonings; mix well. Simmer for 10 minutes. Mix cottage cheese, mozzarella cheese, eggs and half the Parmesan cheese in bowl. Layer 1 cup sauce, 3 uncooked noodles, 1 1/2 cups sauce and half the cheese mixture in 9x13-inch glass baking dish. Repeat layers. Top with remaining sauce and 1/2 cup Parmesan cheese. Cover with plastic wrap, turning back edge to vent. Microwave on High for 25 minutes, turning once. Let stand for 10 minutes. Yield: 8 to 10 servings.

MICROWAVE LASAGNA ROLLS

4 oz. ground beef
1 tbsp. chopped onion
1/2 c. tomato juice
2 tbsp. tomato paste
1/8 tsp. basil
1/4 tsp. oregano
1 tsp. sugar
1/4 tsp. salt
1/8 tsp. pepper

1/4 c. cottage cheese
2 tbsp. Parmesan
cheese
1/8 tsp. garlic powder
1/8 tsp. basil
1/4 c. shredded
mozzarella cheese
2 lasagna noodles,
cooked

Microwave ground beef and onion in 1-quart casserole on High for 3 minutes or until no longer pink, stirring once. Add tomato juice, tomato paste and next 5 seasonings. Microwave for 4 to 7 minutes or until thickened, stirring twice. Reserve

¼ cup mixture. Mix cottage cheese, next 3 ingredients and half the mozzarella cheese in small bowl. Layer remaining ground beef mixture and half the cheese mixture down centers of noodles; roll each as for jelly roll. Place seam side down in 14-ounce oval casserole. Top with reserved ground beef mixture and remaining mozzarella cheese. Microwave, covered, on Medium for 4 minutes or until cheese melts, turning casserole once. Yield: 1 serving.

SWEET AND SOUR MEATBALLS

1 lb. ground beef	*¹/₂ c. packed brown*
¹/₂ c. bread crumbs	*sugar*
¹/₄ c. milk	*¹/₄ c. vinegar*
¹/₄ c. finely chopped	*1 tbsp. cornstarch*
onion	*1 13¹/₄-oz. can*
1 egg	*pineapple tidbits*
1 tsp. Worcestershire	*1 tbsp. soy sauce*
sauce	*1 sm. green bell*
³/₄ tsp. salt	*pepper, cut into*
¹/₈ tsp. pepper	*¹/₂-in. pieces*

Combine first 8 ingredients in bowl; mix well. Shape into 1¹/₂-inch meatballs. Place in glass 7x12-inch baking dish. Microwave, loosely covered, on High for 3 minutes. Rearrange meatballs. Microwave for 5 to 7 minutes longer or until cooked through. Let stand for 3 minutes; drain. Blend brown sugar, vinegar and cornstarch in baking dish. Stir in undrained pineapple and soy sauce. Microwave on High for 2 minutes. Stir mixture. Microwave for 3 to 4 minutes or until thickened. Stir in meatballs and green pepper. Microwave for 3 to 4 minutes or until green pepper is tender-crisp. Yield: 4 servings.

LAYERED MEAT LOAF

2 lb. ground beef	*2 tbsp. margarine*
2 eggs, slightly beaten	*8 oz. fresh mushrooms,*
1¹/₂ c. cracker crumbs	*chopped*
¹/₂ c. chopped onion	*1 med. onion, chopped*
2 tbsp. Worcestershire	*1 tsp. thyme*
sauce	*1 tsp. cumin*
1¹/₂ tsp. salt	*1 c. sour cream*
¹/₂ tsp. pepper	*1 c. bread crumbs*

Mix first 7 ingredients in bowl; set aside. Microwave margarine in glass baking dish on High until melted. Add mushrooms and onion. Microwave for 3 minutes. Add thyme, cumin, sour cream and bread crumbs; mix well. Pat ¹/₃ of the ground beef mixture into 2-quart microwave-safe bundt pan. Add layers of mushroom mixture and remaining ground beef mixture ¹/₂ at a time, ending with ground beef mixture. Microwave on High for 5 minutes. Reduce setting to Medium-High.

Microwave for 10 to 15 minutes or to internal temperature of 140 degrees, turning pan twice. Invert onto serving plate. Yield: 6 servings.

SPICY MEAT LOAF

1 beef bouillon cube	*1 egg, beaten*
¹/₂ c. water	*1 tsp. chili powder*
10 saltine crackers,	*¹/₈ tsp. thyme*
crushed	*¹/₈ tsp. oregano*
1 sm. onion, chopped	*Catsup*
1 lb. ground beef	

Dissolve bouillon cube in water in bowl. Add next 7 ingredients; mix well. Shape into roll; place in 9x13-inch baking dish. Spread catsup over meat loaf. Microwave on High for 15 to 20 minutes or until cooked through. Yield: 6 servings.

Sweet and Sour Meatballs...an up-to-date version of an old favorite.

MEXICAN PIZZA

1 lb. ground beef	*1 jar green olives,*
1 env. taco seasoning	*drained, chopped*
mix	*1 8-oz. jar salsa*
1 12-ct. package med.	*1 8-oz. jar taco sauce*
flour tortillas	*2 c. shredded Cheddar*
1 28-oz. can refried	*cheese*
beans	*2 c. shredded Monterey*
1 can black olives,	*Jack cheese*
drained, chopped	

Brown ground beef in skillet, stirring until crumbly; drain. Add taco seasoning mix according to package directions. Layer tortillas, ground beef mixture, beans, olives, salsa, taco sauce and cheeses ¹/₃ at a time in 9x13-inch glass baking dish. Microwave on High for 2 to 3 minutes or until heated through. Garnish with shredded lettuce, chopped tomato and sour cream. Yield: 4 servings.

H

HADDOCK CREOLE

2 tbsp. margarine,
  melted
1/2 c. chopped green
  onions
1/2 c. green bell pepper
1 lb. haddock fillets
2 tbsp. lemon juice

1 tsp. basil
Salt, pepper and
  cayenne pepper
  to taste
1 4-oz. can
  mushrooms, drained
1 tomato, chopped

Microwave margarine, green onions and green pepper in 8x12-inch baking dish on High for 3 minutes or until tender. Layer remaining ingredients in order given over vegetables. Microwave, covered, for 4 minutes or until fish flakes easily, turning dish once. Let stand for 5 minutes. Yield: 4 servings.

TANGY HAM LOAF

1 lb. ground ham
1/3 c. milk
1 egg, slightly beaten
1/2 c. graham cracker
  crumbs
1/4 c. finely chopped
  onion

Dash of pepper
1/2 c. packed dark
  brown sugar
1/4 c. tomato juice
1 tsp. dry mustard
1 tsp. vinegar

Mix first 6 ingredients in bowl. Pat into 5x9-inch loaf pan. Pour mixture of brown sugar, tomato juice, mustard and vinegar over ham loaf. Microwave on High for 9 minutes or until cooked through. Yield: 4 servings.

MACARONI AND HAM DISH

1/4 c. margarine, sliced
6 oz. Parmesan cheese
1 1/2-lb. ham, slivered
2 c. shredded Swiss
  cheese

5 c. cooked macaroni
3 c. shredded
  mozzarella cheese
Pepper to taste

Place margarine slices in 2-quart glass baking dish. Layer Parmesan cheese, ham, Swiss cheese, macaroni, mozzarella cheese and pepper 1/3 at a time in prepared dish. Cover with plastic wrap. Microwave on High for 20 minutes.
Yield: 8 to 10 servings.

L

TROPICAL LEMON BARS

1/3 c. margarine
1 1/2 c. shortbread
  cookie crumbs
1 tsp. grated lemon rind

1 14-oz. can
  unsweetened
  condensed milk
1/2 c. lemon juice

Place margarine in 8x8-inch glass baking dish. Microwave on High for 45 seconds to 1 minute or until margarine is melted. Stir in cookie crumbs and lemon rind. Reserve 1/4 cup mixture. Press remaining mixture evenly in glass baking dish. Beat condensed milk and lemon juice in bowl until smooth. Spread over crumb mixture. Sprinkle with reserved crumbs. Microwave on Medium-High for 10 to 12 minutes, turning dish 1/2 turn after 5 minutes. Let stand until cool. Cut into bars. Yield: 12 bars.

LEMON PUDDING

1 c. sugar
1/3 c. cornstarch
1/8 tsp. salt
2 c. cold water
2 drops of yellow food
  coloring

3 egg yolks
3 tbsp. margarine
1/3 c. lemon juice
2 tsp. grated lemon rind
3 egg whites
6 tbsp. sugar

Combine first 5 ingredients in casserole. Microwave on High for 3 minutes; stir until smooth. Microwave for 3 minutes longer; stir. Beat egg yolks in small bowl. Stir a small amount of hot mixture into egg yolks; stir egg yolks into hot mixture. Microwave for 4 minutes or until thickened, stirring once. Stir in margarine, lemon juice and rind. Beat egg whites in mixer bowl until soft peaks form. Beat in sugar, 1 tablespoon at a time, until stiff peaks form. Fold into lemon mixture. Microwave for 3 to 4 minutes longer.
Yield: 8 servings.

LOBSTER THERMIDOR

1/4 c. butter
2 green onions, sliced
1 c. sliced mushrooms
1 clove of garlic,
  minced
1 c. chopped cooked
  fresh lobster
1/4 tsp. salt

Pepper to taste
3 tbsp. all-purpose
  flour
1 c. milk
1/2 c. shredded
  Cheddar cheese
Paprika to taste

Microwave butter, green onions, mushrooms, garlic and lobster in 1 1/2-quart casserole on Medium-High for 4 minutes. Stir in mixture of seasonings, flour and milk. Microwave for 4 minutes or until thickened, stirring once. Spoon into 4 baking shells; sprinkle with cheese and paprika. Microwave for 2 minutes. Let stand for 5 minutes. Yield: 4 servings.

M

MUSHROOMS BOURGUIGNON

1/4 c. margarine
1 c. dry red wine
1 tbsp. finely chopped
  green onion
1/2 tsp. garlic salt
1/2 tsp. dillweed
1/4 tsp. salt
Pinch of pepper
1 lb. fresh mushrooms

Place margarine in 3-quart glass dish. Microwave on Medium-High for 1 1/2 minutes or until melted. Stir in wine, green onion and seasonings. Place mushrooms, cap side down, in sauce. Microwave, covered, on Medium-High for 8 to 10 minutes or until heated through. Yield: 36 appetizers.

GOURMET STUFFED MUSHROOMS

24 med. to lg.
  mushrooms
1/2 c. shredded
  Cheddar cheese
2 green onions, finely
  chopped
1/2 c. fine dry bread
  crumbs
1/4 c. melted margarine
1/2 tsp. salt
1/2 tsp. pepper
1/2 tsp. Italian
  seasoning
1/2 tsp. Worcestershire
  sauce
1/4 tsp. garlic powder
Dash of hot pepper
  sauce
Paprika

Remove stems from mushrooms; chop finely. Place in medium bowl. Add cheese, onions, bread crumbs, margarine and next 6 seasonings; mix well. Fill mushroom caps with mixture, mounding slightly in center. Sprinkle with paprika. Arrange in shallow glass baking dish. Microwave on High for 4 to 5 minutes or bake at 325 degrees for 20 to 25 minutes. Yield: 24 appetizers.

O

O'HENRY OATMEAL BARS

2 c. quick-cooking oats
1/2 c. margarine
1/2 c. packed brown
  sugar
1/4 c. light corn syrup
1/3 c. semisweet
  chocolate chips
2 tbsp. peanut butter

Combine oats and margarine in glass bowl. Microwave, uncovered, on High for 3 to 4 minutes or until heated through. Stir in brown sugar and corn syrup. Microwave for 1 1/2 to 2 1/2 minutes or until sugar is dissolved. Press into greased 6x10-inch glass baking dish. Microwave chocolate chips in 1-cup glass measure on High for 1 1/2 to 2 1/2 minutes or until glossy; stir until smooth. Blend in peanut butter. Spread over oats layer. Chill until set. Cut into squares. Yield: 24 bars.

HERBED CHEESE OMELET

3 eggs
3 tbsp. milk
1/4 tsp. basil or dillweed
1/4 tsp. salt
1/8 tsp. pepper
1 tbsp. margarine
1/2 c. shredded
  Cheddar cheese

Beat eggs with milk and seasonings. Microwave margarine in 9-inch glass pie plate on High for 1 minute. Add egg mixture. Microwave, loosely covered, on Medium-High for 3 minutes, stirring once. Top with cheese. Microwave for 30 seconds until cheese is melted. Let stand, covered, for 2 minutes. Yield: 2 servings.

P

PEANUT BRITTLE

1 1/2 c. sugar
1/2 c. corn syrup
1/2 c. water
1/8 tsp. salt
2 c. raw peanuts
1 tbsp. margarine
1 tsp. soda
1 tsp. vanilla extract

Combine sugar, syrup, water, salt and peanuts in 2-quart glass bowl. Microwave on High for 5 minutes; stir. Microwave for 13 minutes or until syrup separates into threads. Stir in margarine, soda and vanilla until light and bubbly. Pour onto greased cookie sheet; spread into thin layer. Cool and break into pieces. Yield: 1 1/2 pounds.

CARAMEL POPCORN

1 c. packed brown
  sugar
1/4 c. light corn syrup
1/2 c. margarine
1/4 tsp. salt
1 tsp. vanilla extract
1/2 tsp. soda
3 or 4 quarts popped
  popcorn
1 c. peanuts

Combine first 4 ingredients in 2-quart glass dish. Microwave on High for 2 minutes or until mixture comes to a boil, stirring down 3 times. Microwave on High for 2 minutes longer. Add vanilla and soda; stir well. Combine popcorn and peanuts in microwave-safe cooking bag; shake vigorously. Pour cooked mixture over popcorn; shake vigorously. Microwave on High for 1 1/2 minutes longer; shake again. Shake, then pour onto waxed paper, spreading out to cool. Store in covered container. Yield: 12 cups.

SPICED PEAR COMPOTE

1 16-oz. can pear
  halves
2 med. apples, peeled,
  sliced
1/2 tsp. cinnamon

1/8 tsp. each cloves,
  allspice
1/2 c. whole cranberry
  sauce

Drain pears, reserving 1 tablespoon syrup. Cut pear halves into halves lengthwise. Layer pears and apples in 1 1/2-quart glass baking dish. Combine reserved pear syrup with remaining ingredients in bowl. Spoon over fruit. Microwave, covered, on High for 2 to 3 minutes; stir. Microwave for 3 to 4 minutes longer or until apples are tender. Yield: 6 to 8 servings.

PECAN BRITTLE

1 c. sugar
1/2 c. light corn syrup
1 c. pecans

1 tbsp. margarine
1 tsp. vanilla extract
1 tsp. baking soda

Mix sugar and corn syrup in 1 1/2-quart casserole. Microwave on High for 4 minutes. Add pecans. Microwave on High for 3 minutes. Add margarine and vanilla. Microwave on High for 1 minute. Add soda; stir. Pour onto greased baking sheet. Cool for 30 minutes. Yield: 1 pound.

DILL PICKLES

24   3-in. cucumbers
1 red bell pepper, sliced
2 heads fresh dillweed
4 cloves of garlic
2 tsp. pickling spices

1/8 tsp. alum
1 c. vinegar
1/4 c. pickling salt
2 c. water

Soak cucumbers in ice water to cover for 2 hours; drain. Place cucumbers and next 5 ingredients in two 1-quart jars. Microwave vinegar, pickling salt and water in 4-cup measure on High for 10 minutes or until mixture comes to a boil. Pour into jars; cool. Store, covered, in refrigerator for 3 months or less. Yield: 2 quarts.

MICROWAVE PARTY POTATOES

8 to 10 med. potatoes,
  peeled, chopped
1/2 c. water
8 oz. cream cheese,
  softened
Dash of pepper

1 8-oz. carton French
  onion dip
1 1/2 tsp. salt
1/2 tsp. garlic salt
Butter to taste
1/2 tsp. paprika

Place potatoes in 3-quart glass casserole. Add water. Microwave, covered, on High for 15 minutes or until potatoes are tender; drain. Beat cream cheese, pepper, onion dip, salt and garlic salt in large bowl until blended. Add hot potatoes gradual-ly, beating until light and fluffy after each addition. Spoon into 2-quart casserole. Top with butter. Microwave on Medium for 5 minutes or until heated through. Sprinkle with paprika. Yield: 8 servings.

SCALLOPED POTATOES

3 tbsp. all-purpose
  flour
1 tsp. salt
4 med. potatoes,
  peeled, thinly sliced

1 c. shredded Cheddar
  cheese
1 c. hot milk
2 tbsp. margarine
Paprika to taste

Mix flour and salt in cup. Alternate layers of potatoes, flour mixture and cheese in greased 8-inch glass baking dish, ending with cheese. Pour milk over layers. Dot with margarine; sprinkle with paprika. Microwave on High for 12 to 14 minutes or until tender, turning several times. Let stand for 5 minutes. Yield: 4 servings.

R

RAISIN SAUCE

2 tbsp. brown sugar
2 tbsp. cornstarch
1/4 tsp. cloves

1/4 c. raisins
1 c. apple juice

Combine all ingredients in 2-cup glass dish. Microwave on High for 3 to 5 minutes or until thickened, stirring once. Serve with pork roast. Yield: 1 1/4 cups.

RASPBERRY JAM CAKE

1/2 c. sugar
1/4 c. margarine,
  softened
2 eggs
1 c. all-purpose flour
1/2 tsp. soda
1 tsp. cinnamon
1/4 tsp. cloves
1/2 tsp. nutmeg

1/3 c. buttermilk
1/4 c. chopped pecans
1/2 c. raspberry jam
3 tbsp. margarine
3/4 c. packed brown
  sugar
3 c. sifted
  confectioners' sugar

Cream sugar and softened margarine in bowl until light and fluffy. Add eggs; beat until smooth. Add mixture of flour, soda and spices alternately with buttermilk, mixing just until blended after each addition. Fold in pecans and jam, leaving swirls of jam. Pour into ungreased glass 8x12-inch cake pan. Microwave on High for 3 minutes. Cool on wire rack. Microwave 3 tablespoons margarine in 1 1/2-quart glass bowl on High for 30 seconds or until melted. Add brown sugar. Microwave on High for 2 minutes, stirring twice. Let stand for 5 minutes. Add confectioners' sugar; beat until smooth. Spread mixture over cooled cake. Yield: 8 servings.

CHEESY RICE

3 tbsp. margarine	1 c. rice
2 c. water	1/3 to 1/2 c. shredded
1/2 tsp. salt	cheese
1/4 tsp. pepper	

Combine margarine, water, salt and pepper in 2-quart glass bowl. Cover with plastic wrap, turning back edge to vent. Microwave on High for 5 to 6 minutes or until mixture boils. Stir in rice. Microwave, covered, on Medium for 17 minutes; do not stir. Let stand, covered, for 5 minutes. Toss with fork. Add cheese. Yield: 4 servings.

GOURMET RICE

1/2 c. margarine	1 10-oz. can beef
2 c. minute rice	consommé
1 can French onion	1 4-oz. can sliced
soup	mushrooms, drained

Microwave margarine in 2-quart glass dish on High for 1 minute. Add remaining ingredients; mix well. Microwave, covered, for 7 minutes. Let stand for 2 minutes. Fluff with fork. Yield: 6 servings.

RHUBARB-STRAWBERRY SOUFFLÉ

4 c. sliced rhubarb	1/4 c. sugar
3/4 c. sugar	1 pt. strawberries,
1 env. unflavored	coarsely chopped
gelatin	1 c. heavy cream,
1/4 c. cold water	whipped
3 egg whites	

Combine rhubarb and 3/4 cup sugar in 2-quart casserole. Microwave, tightly covered with plastic wrap, turning back edge to vent, on High for 8 to 10 minutes or until rhubarb is tender, stirring once. Chill, covered, in refrigerator. Soften gelatin in cold water. Microwave on High for 1 minute or until gelatin is dissolved, stirring once; cool to room temperature. Beat egg whites until soft peaks form. Add 1/4 cup sugar gradually, beating until stiff. Add gelatin gradually, beating constantly at medium speed. Mix strawberries with 1 cup chilled rhubarb mixture. Fold in egg whites and half the whipped cream gently. Spoon remaining rhubarb mixture into 4-cup soufflé dish with 2-inch collar. Spoon strawberry mixture over top; smooth top. Chill for 4 hours or until set. Spoon remaining whipped cream on top. Garnish with whole straw-berries. Spoon fluffy soufflé onto dessert plates; top with rhubarb sauce from bottom of soufflé dish. Yield: 6 servings.

S

CREAMY COOKED SALAD DRESSING

1 egg yolk, beaten	2 tbsp. all-purpose
3/4 c. light cream	flour
1/2 tsp. salt	2 tbsp. vinegar
1/2 tsp. dry mustard	1 tbsp. butter
1 tbsp. sugar	

Stir mixture of egg and cream gradually into dry ingredients in bowl. Microwave on Medium for 1 1/2 minutes or until thick, stirring once. Whisk in vinegar and butter. Store in refrigerator. May stir in 1/3 cup crumbled blue cheese and dash of cayenne pepper for blue cheese dressing. Yield: About 1 cup.

BARBECUE SAUCE

1 med. onion, finely	1 15-oz. can whole
chopped	tomatoes
2 tbsp. green bell	1 tbsp. Worcestershire
pepper, finely chopped	sauce
1 clove of minced garlic	2 tbsp. brown sugar
2 tbsp. margarine	1/2 tsp. salt
1/2 tsp. dry mustard	2 drops of hot sauce

Combine onion, green pepper, garlic and margarine in 4-cup glass measure. Microwave on High for 2 minutes. Add dry mustard, tomatoes, Worcester-shire sauce, brown sugar, salt and hot sauce; mix well. Microwave on High for 2 minutes. Yield: 2 cups.

HOT FUDGE SAUCE

1 c. chocolate chips	2 to 3 tbsp. water
1 tbsp. margarine	Dash of salt
1/4 c. light corn syrup	1 tsp. vanilla extract

Combine chocolate chips and margarine in 2-cup glass measure. Microwave on High for 3 to 4 minutes, stirring every minute until smooth. Blend in corn syrup, water, salt and vanilla. Microwave on High for 1 minute or until hot. Serve immedi-ately. Yield: 1 cup.

SAUSAGE AND PEPPERS

2 lb. hot Italian
sausage
2 med. onions, cut into
¹/₂-in. cubes
1 lg. green bell pepper,
cut into 2-in. chunks

1 lg. red bell pepper,
cut into 2-in. chunks
¹/₄ c. packed fresh basil
leaves
¹/₄ c. marinara sauce

Cut sausage into 2-inch lengths. Place in glass 8x11-inch baking dish. Cover with paper towel. Microwave on High for 10 minutes, stirring twice; drain. Add remaining ingredients; stir to coat. Cover tightly with plastic wrap. Microwave for 7 minutes. Add salt to taste. Serve with mashed potatoes, pasta or hoagie rolls. Yield: 4 servings.

SALMON WITH TOMATO AND BASIL

¹/₂ c. chopped peeled
seeded tomato
¹/₂ c. chopped fresh
basil
¹/₄ tsp. fresh ground
pepper

1 tbsp. margarine
1 lb. salmon steaks
Juice of ¹/₂ lemon
¹/₄ c. fine dry bread
crumbs

Combine tomato, basil, pepper and margarine in 10-inch glass pie plate. Microwave on High for 2 minutes or until margarine is softened. Arrange salmon around edge of plate with thickest portion to outside, tucking under thinnest part of fillets for more even cooking. Squeeze lemon juice over fish. Cover loosely with waxed paper. Microwave on High for 3¹/₂ to 4¹/₂ minutes or just until firm to the touch. Remove fillets to serving plate. Add half the bread crumbs to tomato mixture; mix lightly. Spoon tomato mixture on top of fillets. Sprinkle with remaining bread crumbs. Yield: 4 servings.

SHRIMP CURRY

1 c. chopped celery
¹/₂ c. chopped onion
¹/₄ c. margarine
5 tbsp. all-purpose
flour
1 tsp. curry powder
1 tsp. salt
¹/₂ tsp. sugar

¹/₈ tsp. ginger
2 chicken bouillon
cubes
2 c. hot water
1 lb. cooked shrimp,
drained
¹/₂ tsp. lemon juice
2 tbsp. Sherry

Combine celery, onion and margarine in 1¹/₂-quart casserole. Microwave on High for 6 to 7 minutes or until celery and onions are limp. Stir in flour, curry powder, salt, sugar and ginger. Microwave for 1 minute. Dissolve bouillon cubes in water. Add to flour mixture gradually, stirring until smooth. Microwave for 5 to 7 minutes or until thick and smooth, stirring occasionally. Add shrimp and lemon juice. Microwave for 2 to 3 minutes or until shrimp are heated. Stir in Sherry.

Serve over hot rice with condiments of chopped peanuts, coconut, chopped hard-boiled egg, crisp-fried crumbled bacon, chutney or raisins. Yield: 4 servings.

SHRIMP DE JONGHE

¹/₄ c. dry bread crumbs
¹/₂ c. butter, softened
1¹/₂ tbsp. minced
parsley
1 tbsp. minced onion
2 cloves of garlic,
minced
¹/₄ tsp. salt

¹/₄ tsp. pepper
¹/₄ tsp. Worcestershire
sauce
1¹/₂ lb. shrimp, peeled
¹/₄ c. white wine
¹/₄ c. dry bread crumbs
Paprika

Combine ¹/₄ cup bread crumbs and next 7 ingredients in bowl; mix well. Shape into roll 2 inches in diameter on waxed paper. Chill, wrapped, in refrigerator. Place shrimp in glass ramekins. Sprinkle with wine. Slice chilled butter mixture. Place over shrimp. Top with ¹/₄ cup bread crumbs and paprika. Microwave on High for 5 to 8 minutes or until shrimp are cooked through and butter is bubbly. Yield: 4 servings.

CREAM OF VEGETABLE SOUP

1 c. fresh or frozen
chopped mixed
vegetables
3 tbsp. water
¹/₂ tsp. salt
¹/₂ sm. onion, chopped
3 tbsp. margarine

3 tbsp. all-purpose
flour
1¹/₂ c. milk
1 c. chicken broth
¹/₂ tsp. salt
Pepper to taste

Combine mixed vegetables, water and ¹/₂ teaspoon salt in glass baking dish. Microwave, covered, on High for 7 minutes. Combine onion and margarine in glass bowl. Microwave, covered, for 3 minutes. Stir in flour. Add milk. Microwave for 2 minutes; mix well. Add broth to milk mixture. Microwave for 8 minutes or until slightly thickened. Stir in vegetables and ¹/₂ teaspoon salt and pepper. Microwave for 2 minutes or until heated through. Ladle into soup bowls. Yield: 8 servings.

SUMMER SOUP 🍎

4 c. chicken broth
1 carrot, sliced
1 onion, chopped
2 sprigs of parsley
¹/₄ tsp. oregano
1¹/₂ c. cauliflowerets
1 8-oz. can whole
kernel corn, drained

1 c. fresh green beans,
cut into 1-in. pieces
1 med. zucchini, sliced
2 tomatoes, cut into
chunks
Salt and pepper to taste
Chopped parsley

Combine chicken broth, carrot, onion, parsley and oregano in 3-quart casserole. Cover tightly with plastic wrap, turning back edge to vent. Microwave on High for 6 minutes. Add cauliflower, corn and green beans. Microwave, covered, for 10 minutes. Add zucchini and tomatoes. Microwave, covered, for 5 minutes. Season to taste with salt and pepper. Ladle into soup bowls. Garnish with chopped parsley. Yield: 6 servings.

SPINACH CASSEROLE

4 eggs, beaten	*Pinch of pepper*
1 tbsp. flour	*1 10-oz. package*
1 c. milk	*frozen chopped*
1 c. shredded Cheddar	*spinach, lightly*
cheese	*drained*
1/4 tsp. salt	

Mix all ingredients in bowl. Spoon into greased glass baking dish. Microwave on Medium for 12 minutes. Turn dish 1/4 turn. Microwave for 11 to 16 minutes or until knife inserted comes out clean. Let stand for 5 minutes. Yield: 6 servings.

STRAWBERRY PIE

1 10-oz. package	*3 tbsp. cornstarch*
frozen strawberries	*1 c. water*
1 graham cracker pie	*1 3-oz. package*
shell	*strawberry gelatin*
3/4 c. sugar	

Place strawberries in pie shell. Combine sugar, cornstarch and water in glass baking dish. Microwave on High until mixture comes to a boil; stir. Microwave until mixture thickens and becomes clear. Stir in gelatin. Pour into prepared pie shell. Cool. Serve with whipped cream. Yield: 6 to 8 servings.

GRATED SWEET POTATO PUDDING

4 c. grated uncooked	*1/2 tsp. cloves*
sweet potatoes	*1 c. raisins*
1 c. dark corn syrup	*1/2 c. chopped pecans*
1 c. sugar	*Half and half*
1 tsp. cinnamon	*1/2 c. margarine*
1 tsp. allspice	*3 eggs, beaten*

Combine first 8 ingredients in 3-quart glass dish; mix well. Add enough half and half to make of desired consistency. Microwave margarine on High in 1-cup glass measure for 30 seconds to 1 minute or until melted. Pour over sweet potato mixture; mix well. Add eggs; mix well. Microwave, covered, on High for 7 minutes; stir. Microwave, uncovered, for 9 to 10 minutes or until set. Yield: 12 servings.

T

ENGLISH TOFFEE

1 1/3 c. sugar	*1 1/2 tsp. vanilla extract*
1 c. melted butter	*1/2 c. chocolate chips*
1 tbsp. light corn syrup	*1/2 c. chopped walnuts*
2 tbsp. water	

Combine sugar, butter, corn syrup and water in 2-quart class baking dish. Microwave on High for 10 to 12 minutes or until caramel-colored, stirring twice. Stir in vanilla quickly. Pour into greased 9x12-inch dish. Sprinkle chocolate on top. Let stand until soft; spread evenly. Sprinkle with walnuts. Let stand in cool place until set. Break into pieces. Do not substitute margarine for butter. Yield: 1 1/2 pounds.

CHEESY TOMATO PUFFS

1/4 to 1/3 lb. bacon,	*1/2 tsp. minced onion*
chopped into	*1 egg yolk*
1/4-in. pieces	*1/3 c. finely chopped*
8 oz. cream cheese	*green pepper*
1 tsp. baking powder	*50 firm cherry tomatoes*

Place bacon in 2-quart glass dish. Microwave, covered, on High for 9 minutes or until crisp, stirring every 3 minutes; drain well. Add cream cheese. Microwave for 30 seconds or until soft. Add baking powder, onion and egg yolk; mix well. Stir in chopped green pepper. Cut tops from cherry tomatoes; scoop out seed. Fill with bacon mixture. Arrange 12 at a time in circle on paper towel-lined plate. Microwave on Medium for 1 to 2 minutes or until filling appears dry on surface, turning plate 1/4 turn every 30 seconds. Serve warm. Yield: 50 puffs.

TUNA AND MACARONI CASSEROLE

1 1/2 c. water	*2 tbsp. margarine*
1 pkg. macaroni and	*1 6 1/2-oz. can tuna,*
cheese dinner	*drained*
1 can cream of	*1 sm. can French-*
mushroom soup	*fried onions*

Combine water and macaroni from dinner in 1 1/2-quart glass dish. Microwave, covered, on High for 7 minutes, stirring after 3 minutes. Stir in contents of cheese packet from dinner, soup, margarine and tuna. Microwave, covered, for 2 1/2 minutes; stir. Sprinkle with French-fried onions. Microwave, uncovered, for 2 minutes. Yield: 4 to 6 servings.

TURKEY COCKTAIL MEATBALLS

1¹/₂ lb. ground turkey	*¹/₄ c. margarine*
1¹/₂ tbsp. instant chicken bouillon	*1 c. milk*
	1¹/₂ c. stuffing mix
1 tsp. poultry seasoning	*1 10-oz. chicken-mushroom soup*
¹/₂ tsp. pepper	
¹/₂ c. chopped parsley	*¹/₄ c. water*
1 c. chopped onion	*¹/₂ c. sour cream*
¹/₂ c. chopped celery	

Combine ground turkey, chicken bouillon, poultry seasoning, pepper and chopped parsley in large bowl; mix well. Sauté onion and celery in margarine in skillet. Stir in milk. Heat just until warm. Stir in stuffing mix. Add to turkey mixture; mix well. Shape into 1¹/₂-inch meatballs. Place in glass baking dish. Microwave, loosely covered, on High for 7 minutes, turning meatballs once. Blend soup, water and sour cream in large serving dish. Heat in microwave until blended. Add meatballs. Microwave on High for 4 to 6 minutes or until heated through. Yield: 2 dozen.

TURKEY TETRAZZINI

2 tbsp. melted margarine	*1¹/₂ c. chopped cooked turkey*
1 onion, finely chopped	*1 tsp. salt*
	¹/₄ tsp. pepper
1 clove of garlic, minced	*¹/₄ tsp. cayenne pepper*
1 16-oz. can tomatoes, chopped	*1 8-oz. package spaghetti, cooked*
1 can sliced mushrooms	*¹/₂ lb. Cheddar cheese, shredded*

Combine margarine, chopped onion and garlic in large casserole. Microwave, covered, on High for 4 minutes. Stir in tomatoes, mushrooms, turkey and seasonings. Microwave, covered, for 8 minutes, stirring once. Add spaghetti, mixing well. Sprinkle with Cheddar cheese. Microwave, covered, on Medium for 4 to 6 minutes or until bubbly. Yield: 8 servings.

Z

CRUNCHY ZUCCHINI CASSEROLE

¹/₃ c. melted margarine	*1 onion, chopped*
2 eggs	*1 c. sliced water chestnuts*
³/₄ c. milk	
4 c. grated unpeeled zucchini	*1 c. herb-seasoned stuffing mix*
1 c. shredded Cheddar cheese	*Salt and pepper to taste*

Combine margarine, eggs and milk in bowl. Stir in zucchini, cheese, onion, water chestnuts, stuffing mix, salt and pepper. Pour into 9x12-inch baking dish. Microwave, covered, on High for 15 minutes. Let stand for 5 minutes.
Yield: 6 to 8 servings.

ZUCCHINI AND MUSHROOM QUICHE

3 c. cooked rice	*1 c. chopped zucchini*
2 eggs	*1 tbsp. butter*
1 c. shredded mozzarella cheese	*8 oz. cream cheese, softened*
1 c. chopped onion	*¹/₄ c. milk*
1 4-oz. can sliced mushrooms, drained	*¹/₂ tsp. salt*
	1 egg

Combine rice, 2 eggs, and mozzarella cheese in small bowl; mix well. Press mixture evenly into buttered 12-inch glass dish. Microwave on High for 6 minutes, rotating dish every 2 minutes. Place 1 tablespoon butter in shallow glass dish. Microwave on High for 1 minute. Add chopped onions, sliced mushrooms and zucchini. Microwave, covered, on High for 3 minutes or until vegetables are tender-crisp. Combine cream cheese, milk, salt and 1 egg in bowl. Beat until smooth. Stir in vegetables. Pour mixture evenly over rice crust. Microwave on High for 7 to 8 minutes or until set, rotating dish ¹/₄ turn every 2 minutes. Let stand for 5 minutes. Garnish with parsley. Yield: 6 servings.

Zucchini and Mushroom Quiche...with a nutritious and tasty rice crust.

MICROWAVE CHARTS

These charts are a handy reference guide for defrosting and cooking main dish meats, poultry, seafood and vegetables. Microwave defrosting warms and thaws food without cooking it. Standing time is a very important part of the defrosting cycle.

Meat—Poultry—Seafood

When meat is removed from the microwave, it will be icy in the center. If you thaw the meat entirely in the microwave the edges begin to cook. Most items need to stand only for about the same amount of time they have been defrosted. **Let meats stand for 10 minutes or longer after cooking to complete cooking cycle**.

MEAT		DEFROSTING & STANDING TIME per pound (Medium-Low)	COOKING TIME per pound (High)
Beef	Steak	6–8 minutes	6–8 minutes
	Roast	4–8 minutes (Let stand 1 hour or more)	5–5^1/2 minutes (Rare) 6–6^1/2 minutes (Medium) 7–8 minutes (Well)
	Hamburger	5–6 minutes	5–6 minutes
Ham	Sliced, Half Whole Ham	5–6 minutes	8–10 minutes (Fresh) 5–6 minutes (Precooked)
Lamb	Chops	4–6 minutes	8–9 minutes
	Leg	5–7 minutes	9–11 minutes
	Shoulder	4–6 minutes	9–10 minutes
Pork	Chops	4–6 minutes	8–10 minutes
	Roast	4–5 minutes	8–10 minutes
	Sausage	4–6 minutes	10–12 minutes
	Spareribs	5–7 minutes	9–12 minutes
Veal	Chops	4–6 minutes	4–6 minutes
	Cutlets	4–6 minutes	4–6 minutes
	Roast	5–7 minutes	20–25 minutes
Poultry	Chicken	5–8 minutes	6–7 minutes
	Turkey	3–5 minutes	11–12 minutes
Fish	Fillets	6–8 minutes	6–7 minutes
	Steaks	5–6 minutes	5–6 minutes
	Whole Fish	3–5 minutes	10–12 minutes
Shellfish	Clams (shucked)	3–5 minutes	3–4 minutes
	Lobster (cooked)	3–5 minutes	2–3 minutes
	Lobster (tails)	5–6 minutes	4–6 minutes
	Oysters (cooked)	3–5 minutes	2–4 minutes
	Oysters (shucked)	4–6 minutes	3–5 minutes
	Scallops	5–6 minutes	5–7 minutes
	Shrimp (cooked)	3–5 minutes	4–5 minutes

Fresh Vegetables

VEGETABLE	AMOUNT	PROCEDURE FOR COOKING	TIME
Artichoke	4 medium	In a 3-quart covered casserole combine 1 cup water, 1/2 teaspoon salt and artichokes. Rotate dish 1/2 turn after 7 minutes.	14–15 minutes
Asparagus	16 (4-inch) pieces	In a 1 1/2-quart covered casserole combine 1/2 cup water, 1/2 teaspoon salt and asparagus. Stir halfway through cooking.	6–9 minutes
Beans wax	1 pound 1-inch pieces	In a 1 1/2-quart covered casserole combine 1/2 cup water, 1/2 teaspoon salt and beans. Stir halfway through cooking.	9–11 minutes
green	1 pound 1-inch pieces	Same as above except increase water to 3/4 cup.	15–20 minutes
Beans, lima	2 pounds	Same as above.	7–8 minutes
Beets	4 medium, whole	In a 1 1/2-quart covered casserole combine 1/2 cup water, 1/2 teaspoon salt and beets. Stir halfway through cooking.	15–17 minutes
Beets	4 medium, sliced or cubed	In a 1 1/2-quart covered casserole combine 1/2 cup water, 1/2 teaspoon salt and beets. Stir halfway through cooking.	7–10 minutes
Broccoli	1 medium bunch	In a 1 1/2-quart covered casserole combine 1/2 cup water, 1/2 teaspoon salt and broccoli.	8–10 minutes
Cabbage	1 medium head	In a 1 1/2-quart covered casserole combine 1/2 cup water, 1/2 teaspoon salt and cabbage.	8–10 minutes
Carrots	6–8 sticks	In a 2-quart covered casserole combine 1/4 cup water, 1/2 teaspoon salt and carrots. Stir halfway through cooking.	10–15 minutes
Cauliflower	1 medium head	In a 1 1/2-quart covered casserole add 1/2 cup water, 1/2 teaspoon salt and cauliflower.	10–12 minutes
Corn	2 ears	Wrap ears in plastic wrap and place on shelf of oven. Turn ears over halfway through cooking.	4–6 minutes
	4 ears	Same as above.	6–8 minutes
Eggplant	1 (14 to 16 oz.) whole, not pared	Wrap pierced eggplant in plastic wrap and place on oven shelf. Turn eggplant over halfway through cooking.	8–10 minutes
Onions	4 medium, quartered	Place in covered casserole to fit. Stir halfway through cooking.	11–13 minutes
Peas	2 pounds, shelled	In a 1 1/2-quart covered casserole combine 1/4 cup water, 1/4 teaspoon salt and peas. Stir halfway through cooking.	7–10 minutes

VEGETABLE	AMOUNT	PROCEDURE FOR COOKING	TIME
Spinach	1 pound	Place spinach in a 2-quart covered casserole. Stir halfway through cooking.	6–8 minutes
Squash summer	1 pound, sliced or cubed	In a 1¹/₂-quart covered casserole combine ¹/₄ cup water, ¹/₂ teaspoon salt and 2 tbsp. butter.	10–14 minutes
Zucchini	1 pound, sliced or cubed	In a 1¹/₂-quart covered casserole combine ¹/₄ cup water, ¹/₂ teaspoon salt and 2 tbsp. butter.	10–14 minutes

Frozen Vegetables

VEGETABLE	QUANTITY	UTENSIL	INSTRUCTIONS	TIME
Asparagus	10 ounces	1-qt. glass casserole	Separate after 3 minutes. Casserole should be covered.	5–6 minutes
Broccoli	10 ounces	1-qt. glass casserole	Separate after 4 minutes. Casserole should be covered.	8–9 minutes
Beans, green, cut or wax, French cut	10 ounces	1-qt. glass casserole	Add 2 teaspoons hot water; stir. Cover.	7–8 minutes
Beans, lima, fordhook	10 ounces	1-qt. glass casserole	Add ¹/₄ cup water; stir after 5 minutes. Casserole should be covered.	7–8 minutes
Cauliflower	10 ounces	1-qt. glass casserole	Add 2 tablespoons hot water; cover.	5–6 minutes
Corn, cut	10 ounces	1-qt. glass casserole	Add ¹/₄ cup water; cover.	4–5 minutes
Corn	2 ears	1-qt. glass casserole	Add ¹/₄ cup water, turn after 3 minutes. Cover.	5–6 minutes
Mixed Vegetables	10 ounces	1-qt. glass casserole	Add ¹/₄ cup water; cover.	6–7 minutes
Okra	10 ounces	1-qt. glass casserole	Add 2 tablespoons hot water; cover.	6–7 minutes
Peas, green	10 ounces	1-qt. glass casserole	Add 2 tablespoons hot water; cover.	4–5 minutes
Peas & Carrots	10 ounces	1-qt. glass casserole	Add 2 tablespoons hot water; cover. Stir after 3 minutes.	5–6 minutes
Spinach	10 ounces	1-qt. glass casserole	Use covered casserole.	4–5 minutes

Index